The Worlds the Shawnees Made

The Worlds the Shawnees Made

Migration and Violence in Early America

STEPHEN WARREN

The University of North Carolina Press Chapel Hill

85686139

This book was published with the assistance of the
Anniversary Fund of the University of North Carolina Press.

The paper in this book meets the guidelines for permanence and durability
of the Committee on Production Guidelines for Book Longevity of the Council on
Library Resources. The University of North Carolina Press has been a member
of the Green Press Initiative since 2003.

Library of Congress Cataloging-in-Publication Data
Warren, Stephen.
The worlds the Shawnees made : migration and violence in early
America / Stephen Warren.
pages cm.
Includes bibliographical references and index.
ISBN 978-1-4696-1173-0 (hardback)
ISBN 978-1-4696-1174-7 (ebook)
1. Shawnee Indians—History. 2. Shawnee Indians—Migrations.
3. Shawnee Indians—Wars. I. Title.
E99.S35W375 2013
974.004′97317—dc23
2013029967

18 17 16 15 14   5 4 3 2 1

for Kristy

Contents

Maps and Illustrations

Maps

Illustrations

Acknowledgments

Books, like people, have histories. And this book, in particular, is inextricably tied to T. Randolph Noe. A probate lawyer living in Louisville, Kentucky, Randy collected documents related to Shawnee history for more than a decade. His love of Shawnee history compelled him to travel vast distances, at his own expense, in search of everything that had ever been published about the Shawnee people. When Randy passed away in 2003, he left behind a published bibliography and a vast archive that continues to live among Shawnee people, who have used the knowledge contained within it to create maps, grant projects, and many other efforts related to the preservation of their remarkable history.

Randy and I got to know each other in 2000, when my partner, Kristy, and I were living in Berea, Kentucky. We met several times to discuss our shared love of Shawnee history. We even managed to travel to the War Dance at the North Ceremonial Ground, in Little Axe, Oklahoma. Most historians work in private, mulling over the small details of big projects for years on end. Randy helped me to realize that the closed loop that I maintained in my mind could, in fact, be shared. We talked for hours on end about Shawnee history and began to share our documents and our knowledge with members of the federally recognized Shawnee tribes. Randy became that rare person who could and would discuss the particulars of troubling documents, the hard-to-discover villages, and the seeming non sequiturs that represent the printed knowledge of Shawnee history. When cancer claimed him, we all lost a raconteur whose generosity is rare indeed.

Kristy and I then moved to Rock Island, Illinois, to teach at Augustana College. Randy's kids thus had to drive his archive from Kentucky to Illinois, and I am grateful for the trouble they went through. With twenty-four banker-boxes of material, I struggled to find room to house it all. But the real challenge lay in the fact that this treasure trove of material arrived the night before our first child, Cormac, arrived in this world. Kristy remained, as always, more composed than I was amid the shuffling of boxes and the final adjustments to our foolproof birth plan. Miraculously, we all survived the ordeal, as the singer John Prine has sung, "in spite of ourselves." By 2005, Kristy and I had published our first books. The richness of our shared life together has only been increased by the arrival of Declan in 2006 and Josie in 2009. Our children have had to share in our professional journey, quite literally, from the beginning. But they have grown to appreciate the opportunities research presents. Cormac even had the audacity to break from vegetarianism and eat his first cheeseburger in Norman, Oklahoma, while I was on a research trip.

Since that fall night a decade ago, I have shared Randy's collection with members of the three federally recognized Shawnee tribes. Working with cultural preservation officers and Augustana students, we created a national map of Shawnee locations. We unveiled the map in 2005, and Shawnee people marveled in amazement at the depth and breadth of their travels across North America. For tribes such as the Shawnees—forced from their Ohio homeland into Indian Territory, what is now Oklahoma— the map and the documents have become a kind of repatriation of cultural and historical knowledge. Contemporary Shawnees know a thing or two about resilience, and the map seemed to confirm that this trait has stayed with the Shawnee people since colonizers arrived and reordered the natural and cultural worlds to which they were accustomed. At least initially, archival research became the means by which I have been able to participate in an extended conversation with many Shawnee people, who have worked tirelessly to maintain their culture and to recover what has been lost. Randy's archive has become a never-ending gift, as more and more Shawnee people have shared in the knowledge it contains.

Books derive as much from the authors who write them as from the editors who acquire and improve them. I did not begin researching this project in earnest until 2008, when Robbie Ethridge asked me to contribute a chapter to her book, co-edited with Sheri Shuck-Hall, *Mapping the Shatter Zone: The Colonial Indian Slave Trade and Regional Instability in the American South*. Robbie saw the potential in this project well before I did, and I am very grateful to her for being such a thoughtful editor. Robbie introduced me to Mark Simpson-Vos at the University of North Carolina Press. Mark has also refused to settle for my initial attempts to make sense of violence and migration in Shawnee and colonial-era Woodland Indian histories. At the time I agonized over the rigor of Robbie and Mark. But in hindsight, I am certain that their suggestions have improved this work. Finally, my toughest editor has been my brother, Michael Warren. He line-edited parts of this book as only a news editor for the Associated Press can. Sibling rivalries aside, I will be the first to admit that he is the superior writer, and I cannot imagine where I would be without his help over the years. Time and distance have separated us, but Mike has remained a dear friend.

A curious mixture of hubris and humility is essential to writing nonfiction. It takes hubris because a fragmented primary source record confronts us at every turn, and the silences within and between the sources frustrate our attempts to unlock past worlds. And yet I have pressed on and told a story composed out of tantalizing, but incomplete, shards of evidence. In response to such an incomplete record, I have asked for a lot of help over the years. Anthropologists and archaeologists who have provided essential guidance include Jason Baird Jackson, A. Gwynn Henderson, David Pollack, Jessica Walker Blanchard, Robert Cook, and Tom Whitley. I am also grateful to Penelope Drooker, Cheryl Ann Munson, James Morton, Tracy Brown, Brice Obermeyer, Charlie Cobb, and Gregory Waselkov for their willingness to point me in the right direction through well-timed, corrective emails and comments on papers. Among historians, I have learned a lot from Colin Calloway, R. David Edmunds, Donald Fixico, Gregory Evans Dowd, Thomas Appleton Jr., Tracy Leavelle, Josh Piker, and Alan Shackelford. Experts on material culture, including David Penney, R. Scott Stephenson, Buck Woodard, Carolyn Gilman, Adriana Greci Green, and Alan Gutchess, have greatly improved my capacity to integrate material culture into my understanding of the written and ethnographic records.

I could not have written this book without the guidance of a handful of Shawnee people who did their best to educate me. I hope that this book honors what you have tried to teach me and, at the very least, demonstrates my deep appreciation for the kindness and generosity you have shown me over the years. Many people have shared their wisdom with me. George and Sue Blanchard have mentored me from the beginning, and they have taught me much more about life than this book can possibly include. Greg Pitcher has helped me to understand the diversity of Shawnee history, and the Shawnees' various perspectives on tribal identity and culture. Ben and Joel Barnes have done all they can to help, and they have shared in the excitement of research and discovery. I would also like to thank Henryetta and Leroy Ellis, Sherman Tiger, Andy Warrior, Scott Miller, Brett Barnes, and Glenna Wallace. Niyawe!

This book, far more than my first, derives from the financial support of numerous benefactors. I am grateful to my colleagues at Augustana College, including President Steven Bahls, and my first dean, Jeff Abernathy, for supporting this project with a Presidential Research Fellowship and Reassigned Time for Major Projects in 2009. As this book came into focus, Van Symons supported my research in the United Kingdom with a travel grant from the William A. Freistat Center in the summer of 2011. My colleagues at Augustana College have done what they can to sustain my own research, and I am grateful for their support.

I am very fortunate to have received a Mellon Foundation Sabbatical Fellowship from the American Philosophical Society during 2010–11. Linda Musemeci and her colleagues at the American Philosophical Society are unusual in their commitment to funding worthy projects by scholars working at teaching institutions. I am so thankful that they have chosen to support innovation in a democratic manner, across the tumultuous academic worlds so many of us inhabit. I am also grateful to Jim Horn, Buck Woodard, and their colleagues at the Colonial Williamsburg Foundation for granting me a Gilder-Lehrman Short-Term Residential Fellowship. During my stay in Williamsburg, I was able to enjoy solitary reflection on so many primary sources. This kind of focused isolation was imperative as I strove to make sense of the complex colonial worlds inhabited by Natives and newcomers alike.

More than twenty years ago, when Kristy and I decided to share our lives, we both committed to the notion that there are really only two sins in life. The first sin is to interfere in someone else's progress. The second sin is to interfere in your own progress. As any married couple can attest, Kristy and I have had countless opportunities to act selfishly and to limit each other's progress in life over the years. But, on balance, we have not taken advantage of these prospects. We have instead put our relationship first and have trusted each other when it counts most. Kristy has saved me from interfering in my own progress on countless occasions, and she has shown me, time and again, that jumping into the stream of life and sharing in the gratitude and happiness that is ours to claim is a far better alternative to anything I could have come up with.

chapter 1

Rethinking Place and Identity in American Indian Histories

Viola Dushane's decaying homesite sits on a wooded rise above the Quapaw powwow grounds, near the Spring River, in the northeastern corner of Oklahoma. Here the dense oak and hickory forests of the Ozark Mountain foothills descend to the river's eastern banks. To the west of the allotment—a small parcel of family-owned land held in trust by the federal government after it dissolved the Quapaw reservation—wide-open spaces and vast herds of cattle dominate the landscape. This is where the Eastern Woodlands end and where two of the three distinct Shawnee tribes arrived after centuries of coexistence and conflict with colonizers and other Indian tribes. Some of them were willing travelers; others were forcibly removed to the unfamiliar tablelands of the West. What these Shawnees had in common was a long history of migration and adaptation. Shawnees had been moving along and reinventing themselves for so many generations that it became part of their collective consciousness. Their ability to survive and prosper while on the move perplexed observers during the colonial period and confuses scholars even today. But their ability to retain what it means to be Shawnee while becoming "the Greatest Travellers in America" became an essential aspect of their culture and the key to surviving and prospering against all odds.[1]

I walked the land late one winter's day with several Shawnee friends of mine, including Viola's grandchildren, Joel and Ben Barnes. We were fortunate to be visiting the home place before *pahkhahquayyah*, the time of year when the forest canopy comes in and the woods become dark. The outlines of the Spring River Baptist Church, where Shawnees, Quapaws, Delawares, and other tribes worshipped a Christian God, at the site of the Quapaw Agency, were barely visible from the crumbling foundation of Viola's home. It had been fifty years since Viola and her Shawnee, Delaware, and Quapaw relatives had actively kept the forest at bay.

Powerful tree roots now break apart the foundations of the homes on this allotment. The moss-covered foundation of a roundhouse, the site of Native American Church meetings, a blend of Christianity and indigenous spirituality founded by Comanches and Delawares in the aftermath of the Indian wars, reminded me of the complex religious lives of its occupants. Sculptures of the Virgin Mary sat atop a Quapaw burial. Beside it, a steel pipe ensconced at the head of a concrete-covered grave enabled the soul of the deceased to depart for the afterworld and identified its occupant as Shawnee.[2]

Dushane made a life for herself and her family among the Quapaws, a Dhegiha Siouan-speaking tribe originally from Arkansas. She moved there in the first decade of the twentieth century, after her branch of the Shawnee tribe was removed from Kansas in the aftermath of the Civil War.[3] Looking back, Dushane's choice seems strange. Why choose to live among the Quapaws rather than among one's own kin? After all, didn't American Indians move, live, and die as members of coherent tribes? Years ago, before I learned that history can be better understood through ethnography, the scholarly method that involves working closely with people to gain a deeper understanding of their worldviews, I believed that tribes were basically coherent, homogeneous, and inward-looking groups of extended families. Generous and patient Shawnee friends have shown me otherwise. By sharing their oral histories, rituals, and worldviews, they have demonstrated that the historical, cultural, and ethnic boundaries around their tribes were constantly shifting and that their ability to adapt to these changes, generation after generation, had become an essential aspect of "being Shawnee."[4]

Historians have long used the Indian Removal Act of 1830 as the starting point for their attempts to understand the experience of Native Americans in Oklahoma.[5] Doing so feeds the idea that Andrew Jackson's zeal for ethnic cleansing broke the tribal bonds of Native peoples who were forcibly removed to "Indian Territory." This view would suggest that Dushane somehow lost her Shawnee identity when she fell in with the Quapaws. But a closer investigation of Eastern Woodland Indian histories suggests otherwise. Dushane made choices similar to those made by Shawnees generations earlier, during conflicts ranging from the Seven Years' War to the American Revolution. In fact, migration and living among members of other tribes had been a survival strategy for the Shawnees and their neighbors for generations. Since the middle of the seventeenth century, Dushane's ancestors had abandoned their homes, often two or three times in a single generation. It could not have been easy. But moving also invites opportunity. In the Shawnees' case, migration became a kind of signature. In 1755, when Edmond Atkin, the Southern Superintendent of Indian Affairs, in an official report to the king, described the Shawnees as "the Greatest Travellers in America," he spelled out common knowledge about them.[6] This book reflects my attempt to understand how the Shawnees and their allies were able to not only survive but even reinvent themselves as they moved from home to home in the Eastern Woodlands, long before settling in along the edge of the Southern Plains. Much to the confusion of those who knew them, the Shawnees managed to carry their tribal identity with them long after they left their ancestors' familiar territory. Viola Dushane may have lived among the Quapaws, but her home village was the White Oak Stomp Ground, in nearby Craig County, Oklahoma. "Stomp Ground" is the generic name Native Oklahomans use to define a "place where the cultural and religious beliefs of a tribe are practiced." Among the Shawnees, Stomp Grounds are places in which tribal members gather every April, August, and October to conduct rituals that are the ultimate expression of their tribal identity.[7] Shawnee rituals, especially the spring and fall Bread Dances, are the physical expressions of culture, and they convey deeply held tribal values regarding gender, economic relations, and community.

■ In August 2009, before the War Dance, or Men's Dance, Chief Andy Warrior, the current *hokema*, or chief, of the North Stomp Ground, tried to explain some of the challenges associated with Shawnee rituals. "We have to compete with these cars, these video games . . . air conditioning," the chief explained. "Chopping wood out in the hot sun doesn't seem like a whole lot of fun to most kids these days. But you have to do it to get ready for the dance." As he spoke, the heat and humidity seemed to punctuate his remarks. The still, hot air of central Oklahoma underscored the challenges posed by what he calls "modern conveniences."[8] Individuals must *work* to re-create Shawnee identity. For Chief Warrior, identity and culture are not fixed traits. Rather, they are beliefs and practices that must be earned through ritual performances that are witnessed and affirmed by the community. A person becomes Shawnee through self-sacrifice and effort.[9]

We have talked about Shawnee values on many occasions. However, I recall one particular conversation we had in early August 2009. We spoke together while sitting on a wood bench within Chief Warrior's campsite at the North Stomp Ground. The War Dance was about to begin, and members of the camps lining the Stomp Ground were making their

preparations. A water truck arrived to hose down the sandy dirt, which invariably forms a great cloud during the ceremony. The truck's presence was anomalous and disconcerting. Situated in what locals jokingly refer to as "North LA," the ceremonial ground is not far from the Absentee Shawnees' casino in Little Axe. On approximately ten cleared acres, eleven extended families had set up campsites made largely of hand-cut post oak timbers. Electricity is not allowed on this Stomp Ground, and those who use tin roofs for their campsites rather than tarps or willow branch arbors face criticism. It's a humble patch of ground, but the approximately 300 members of the Stomp Ground take pride in its appearance, and they converge there every year before winter sets in and closes the ritual season. To people such as Andy and those who call him *hokema*, or chief, the North Stomp Ground is akin to a church, a place where people go to be and to become Shawnee. The North Stomp Ground is, in many ways, out of step with the world surrounding it, for it is a place in which everything from photography to electricity is forbidden.[10]

Andy Warrior is a big man, just past six feet tall, and he almost always speaks in low, unassuming tones. I have to strain to hear Andy as he proceeds slowly and deliberately to answer my questions. His replies include long, contemplative pauses, making each answer seem like an odyssey into the nuances of Shawnee ritual life. Chief Warrior's quiet confidence is remarkable because he became chief in 1998, at the age of twenty-eight. Born in 1970, he was named chief based on his membership in the Kispokotha division—the clan responsible for leadership in times of war—and for his loyalty to Chief Richard Gibson, a revered man among the Shawnee people. Chief Gibson was a combat veteran of World War II and a longtime chief, and many Shawnees assumed that he "would always be there for them." The ceremonial community became lost when he died. But leaders of the ground—council members—gathered together and chose Andy. He initially resisted the offer. According to Andy, a chief must "lead by example. . . . He has to sing until his voice becomes hoarse. He has to dance through the day and night." If he shirks his responsibility, others will "model his behavior and quit their traditional ways."

The War Dance cannot be held without Kickapoo participation. Two Kickapoo elders, one a veteran of World War II and one of Vietnam, sit under the arbor and deliver the *pikegeka*, or sacred statement of war exploits, of life-taking, that is theirs alone. Their stories of death and of war can only be expressed in the sacred space underneath the Shawnee arbor. The Shawnee War Dance thus offers the means by which these particular men, and the Shawnees and the Kickapoos as a whole, can recover from the traumatic necessity of life-taking. The Shawnees call the Kickapoos their little brothers, and the familial affection between the two tribes is obvious to outside observers. Kickapoo participation in the War Dance is imperative. But without the Kispokotha Shawnee War Bundle, the event could not take place.[11]

With nightfall, as the earth cooled, the chief's helpers built a grand fire in the center of the dance ground. By midnight, a Stomp Dance had begun. Male singers and female shell-shakers walked from their family camps to the rectangular Stomp Ground and danced from midnight until dawn. Laid according to the cardinal directions, the dance ground includes an arbor made of post oaks and willow branches at the west end of the ground. Large hewn logs, complete with "doors" allowing for the singers and dancers to enter and exit, line the perimeter. Together, they circled the fire in a counterclockwise direction and leaned into the heat of the fire. The male singers waved to the fire, imploring "grandpa" to serve as a "messenger" for the people. Humble persons need intercessors on their behalf. Fire transmits the sacred desires of the Shawnee people.

Daytime ceremonies such as the spring and fall Bread Dances evoke a vision of Shawnee identity based on the cycle of hunting and agriculture. Before sunrise on the morning of the dance, the "Queen Bee" or Head Lady of the Stomp Ground asks her twelve helpers to gather together on the Stomp Ground and sweep it clean. They gather in teams of two and rotate through the ground in a counterclockwise direction. Kerosene lanterns hanging from the family camps provide a silhouette of the women at work, and the dust drifts in the light. When they are done, the women throw their willow brooms on top of the arbor, under which the songs of the Bread Dance will be sung later that day.[12]

■ Later that morning, before sunrise, male hunters announce their return from a three-day squirrel hunt. They are led by twelve hunters and any number of younger men and boys who have decided to help with the hunt. As they arrive, they whoop for joy and fire their guns into the air in a clearing on the south side of the dance ground. The women make note of their arrival and go to greet them at the woods edge. The hunters hand over the squirrels to the women, who will later prepare them for the meal after the conclusion of the Bread Dance. The men then file into the Stomp Ground in a counterclockwise direction. They dance as the chief and his singers sing for them, using a water drum to maintain the rhythm of the song. The women form a parallel line on the outside of the men's circle. Dressed in long skirts and beautiful shawls, the women contrast with the charcoal-blackened faces of the hunters in their camping gear. After twenty minutes or more, the song ends and the men form a kind of aisle or gauntlet on the southwest corner of the Stomp Ground. The women walk down this aisle, offering corn "bread," or unleavened corn cakes, to the hunters. Before they eat, a Shawnee elder prays over the food. After the hunters have their fill, the men in each of the camps eat, followed by the women and children.

After the squirrels are prepared, the women place corn cakes on a white linen cloth at the center of the Stomp Ground. Men bring the cooked squirrels and place them beside the bread. The chief's helpers then carefully wrap the linen cloth around the foods, while the twelve hunters sit and observe from the south side of the ground, across from the twelve cooks on the north side of the ground. The Bread Dance begins in the afternoon and concludes before dinner. Between the dances, a Shawnee elder prays for all of creation, from weeds and insects to birds, the sun, and the earth itself. The Bread Dance is a prayer for all creation, one that divides the year between agriculture, and the life-giving powers of women, and hunting, and the life-taking powers of men. By the conclusion of the Bread Dance, the food has been prayed and danced over for several hours. The separate, but complementary, roles of women and of men have been affirmed by days of effort. The food is then distributed to each of the family camps. Through praying and eating together, all of the members of the Stomp Ground affirm their commitment to each other.

Back in 1937, anthropologist Erminie Wheeler-Voegelin observed Shawnee Bread Dances. In her field notes, she described how the Shawnees used rituals to mark differences between themselves and everyone else. She was "fascinated with the different emphases that the different tribes lay on generally similar activities." I have had similar ethnographic experiences. After I attended a death feast, a Shawnee elder explained to me that "each tribe has a different way of communicating with God, the spirit, the Creator."[13] For example, Andy Warrior was raised by Shawnee and Yuchi relatives. His paternal uncle, Richard Gibson, taught Warrior the sacred songs of the Bread Dance and prepared him for leadership. Warrior's maternal uncle is Simon Harry, chief of the Duck Creek Ceremonial Ground of the Yuchis. Warrior thus describes becoming Shawnee as both a choice and an action, something that neither of his parents imposed on him. For Warrior, the ritual performances enacted at the North Stomp Ground define what he calls "the Shawnee way." Being Shawnee is something that must be embodied and ritually expressed in ceremonies such as the Bread Dance and the War Dance.[14]

Today, there are three federally recognized Shawnee tribes, each reflecting a particular migratory history. The Loyal Shawnees, a name that stems from their attachment to the Union during the Civil War, were the most recent arrivals to Oklahoma. They only recently emerged as a sovereign nation, because after the Civil War the United States forced the Cherokees, who had been allied with the Confederacy, to take the Loyal Shawnees into the Cherokee Nation. U.S. government authorities compelled Shawnees and their Delaware neighbors, despite their loyalty to the United States, to abandon their lands in Kansas, to endure a second removal, and to give up their sovereignty as independent nations. They remained Cherokee citizens until 2000 and 2009, when the Shawnees and Delawares, respectively, finally regained their independence as sovereign nations.[15]

In contrast, the United States forcibly removed the Eastern Shawnees from Ohio to a shared reservation with the Seneca-Cayugas—Northern Iroquoian speakers who were part of the powerful Iroquois Confederacy in what is now New York State—to northeastern Oklahoma soon after Congress approved the Indian Removal Act. Today, the Eastern Shawnees have nearly 3,000 tribal members and are the most economically prosperous of the three Shawnee tribes. A third contingent of Shawnees, now known as the Absentee Shawnee Tribe of Oklahoma, which has more than 3,000 tribal members, abandoned its homeland in present-day Ohio during the American Revolution to escape the brutal scorched-earth campaigns between Kentuckians and their Native adversaries along the Ohio River. These Shawnees migrated across the Mississippi River and, in 1840, finally settled between the forks of the Canadian River, in what is now south-central Oklahoma.[16]

Now, approximately a century and a half later, most members of the thirty-eight federally recognized tribes in Oklahoma consider the state to be their adopted homeland, rooting against Texas every football Saturday and expressing deep pride in Oklahoma's internationally known Red Earth powwow. But they do not claim the state as their native ground, which is logical for tribes that were wrenched from the places they knew and hauled to Oklahoma in railroad cars, like the Modocs of California, or in steamboats, like the Seneca-Cayugas of New York.[17] But the Shawnees have another reason: they learned how to make do without sacred places long before President Jackson declared that "their wandering ways" had made it impossible for tribes "to continue their efforts at independence within the limits of any of the states."[18]

Scholars have long associated migration with loss. Some consider removed tribes to be "coalescent" peoples, assuming that their tribal identities were largely erased by relocation.[19] They are mistaken. In Oklahoma today, there are pan-Indian practices and iconography, to be sure, but tribes retain their identities through unique ceremonies and the sharing of oral histories, language classes, and family gatherings. Such private events are arranged through networks of kin, promoted on Facebook, and supported by tribal governments. When I attend a nighttime Stomp Dance at the South Stomp Ground in Little Axe, Oklahoma, I am struck by the unique songs of the Shawnee singers. Friends from other tribes, such as the Yuchis, listen carefully to the singers, hoping to get the dance right to avoid disrespecting their hosts. To cite another example, the Green Corn Ceremony held by the Loyal Shawnees occurs at the same time of year as the Seneca-Cayuga version of the ceremony. While both celebrate the harvest, each ceremony includes unique tribal elements. These ethnographic experiences have shown me that the lines between non-Indian, Indian, and tribal worlds are complex and multifaceted.[20]

Removal might have accelerated a preexistent multiethnic mosaic, but it did not erase the bonds between members of distinct tribes. To cite one example, members of the Seneca-Cayuga Stomp Ground, the Cowskin, have deep and abiding ties to their kinsmen who still live in western New York, as well as to more recent migratory allies. In the 1960s, Seneca-Cayuga leaders mixed soil from the Loyal Shawnee Stomp Ground at White Oak, Oklahoma, as well as ritually sanctioned soil from the Quapaws and New York Seneca-Cayugas into the floor of their longhouse. The Shawnees, Quapaws, and New York Seneca-Cayugas shared their land with that of the Cowskin ceremonial community. This ritually charged sharing of sacred space offers a symbolic illustration of tribalism as well as the shared destiny of historically allied tribes. Their allies take the responsibility toward the Cowskin Stomp Ground seriously. In fact, Shawnee elders from White Oak have, when necessary, cared for masks used in the Seneca-Cayuga False Face ceremonies and have actively participated in Cowskin ceremonial life.[21] The ground beneath the feet of Cowskin singers and dancers joins the Oklahoma Seneca-Cayugas to a vast network of allied tribes.

Since at least the late seventeenth century, Seneca-Cayuga and Shawnee people have been intimately connected. First tied to each other through trade, then war, and, later, alliance, they have lived in each other's villages for centuries. In fact, one of the three federally recognized Shawnee tribes, the Eastern Shawnee Tribe of Oklahoma, twice shared reservations with the Seneca-Cayugas, at Lewistown, Ohio, and later in the northeastern corner of Oklahoma, not far from Viola Dushane's home place. Charles Diebold, the chief of the Seneca-Cayuga Stomp Ground at Cowskin, recalls that the Loyal and Eastern Shawnee tribes are "our brother tribes." According to Charles, "For as long as anyone can remember, Shawnees and Seneca-Cayugas have been helping each other prepare for each other's ceremonies." As a Seneca-Cayuga leader, Charles feels obligated to honor this shared history by supporting the Shawnees' spring and fall Bread Dances at the White Oak Stomp Ground, which is affiliated with the Loyal Shawnee and Eastern Shawnee tribes.[22]

Absentee Shawnee visitors who "help out" during White Oak's Bread Dances often comment on the differences between the three federally recognized Shawnee communities. They believe that women at White Oak play a much more pronounced role in tribal ceremonies. For example, the

Queen Bee, or Head Lady, at White Oak does not have a male *hokema*, or chief, as her counterpart. Absentee Shawnee visitors attribute the strength of women at White Oak to the influence of the Seneca-Cayuga, whose matrilineal kinship system and ceremonial life features female leaders. The hereditary leaders of Seneca-Cayuga society are women referred to as "faithkeepers," and they are responsible for everything from the naming of babies to the appointment of chiefs. Loyal and Eastern Shawnee members of the White Oak Stomp Ground disagree with the Absentee Shawnees' characterization of gender roles. They do not dispute their feeling of mutual responsibility and kinship for one another. However, members of the White Oak and Cowskin Stomp Grounds see their ceremonies as distinctive expressions of their unique identities, not as manifestations of coalescence.[23]

Loyal and Eastern Shawnees live in the same county, and many of them are members of the White Oak Stomp Ground. However, the Loyal Shawnees seem to have migrated from the Ohio Valley to the vicinity of Fort St. Louis, in the French territory of present-day Illinois, where they lived among the Kaskaskia. Like the Shawnees, the Kaskaskia were members of the Central Algonquian language family. From Fort St. Louis, these Shawnees moved to Maryland, then to Pennsylvania. By the second decade of the eighteenth century, settlers pushed them westward, until the 1870s, when they arrived in what is now Oklahoma.[24] Their journey back and forth across the continent brought them into contact with Eastern Algonquian speakers, whom the Shawnees and their Central Algonquian relatives call "grandfathers," the Lenapes, or Delawares. At the time of their encounter with Europeans, the Delawares lived in loosely affiliated villages ranging from eastern New York and New Jersey to Pennsylvania.[25] Of the 2,226 members of the Loyal Shawnee Tribe of Oklahoma, nearly 70 percent could also be counted on the tribal roll of the Delaware Tribe of Oklahoma, headquartered in Bartlesville. According to Shawnee tribal member Greg Pitcher, their alliance "goes back a lot farther than Kansas." Extensive intermarriage and ritual sharing continue to revitalize their alliance, and their long history together has made it relatively easy for members of each group to move between Delaware and Shawnee worlds.[26]

Members of the three federally recognized Shawnee tribes recognize that near-constant movement through colonial worlds has shaped their respective identities.[27] Shawnee rituals often feature long-standing bonds with other tribes. Members of Stomp Grounds such as the North Ground, White Oak, and Cowskin honor their shared histories by participating in each other's ceremonies. These sacred places provide a strong counterpoint to those scholars who claim that tribal societies have been eclipsed by a kind of generic "Indian" identity. Each of these ceremonial grounds represents historic villages, each with its own unique history. The "basic integration of the village," today manifested by the various Stomp Grounds, has been a continuous characteristic of Shawnee history. While places such as Dushane's home have been abandoned, her descendants return to White Oak semiannually, for the spring and fall Bread Dances. These rituals serve many functions, from extended family reunions to rituals that ensure the success of agriculture and hunting. Regardless of their motives, the Shawnees who attend these ceremonies affirm the distinctiveness of their culture, and by participating in what is sacred to the tribe, they can lay claim to their Shawnee identity.

It is also the case that each of these villages could not have survived into the twenty-first century without long-standing, and migratory, allies.[28] Today, places such as Cowskin, White Oak, and the North Ceremonial Ground have enabled the Shawnees and their neighbors to resist coalescence. Today's Stomp Grounds are the modern equivalent of the colonial-era villages that were at the heart of Native American responses to the onslaught of colonists, settlers, and, eventually, U.S. armed forces. In fact, these villages represent continuous Native American communities, which formed east of the Mississippi River centuries earlier and remain vibrant and cohesive today.

■ Practicing ethnography among the Shawnees and their neighbors has redefined how I read archival sources and understand American Indian history more generally. The ritual practices at the Dushane allotment and the North Ground, for example, derive from their particular histories of migration and alliance. After visiting friends in Ottawa County, I began to wonder why two nearby Shawnee tribes, the Eastern and the Loyal, functioned so differently. Similarly, anyone who travels among the Absentee Shawnees soon learns to mind the differences between the Big Jim and the White Turkey bands. Even around Little Axe, Oklahoma, the heart of the Big Jim band, I have had to navigate carefully between those who attend the North Ground, where the War Dance is practiced every August, and those with family camps at the Old Ground or South Ground, which is the oldest Stomp Ground among the Absentee Shawnees, located on the allotment of their venerated chief, Big Jim. These distinctions are creations of history, with strands reaching back to when Shawnees traveled through the precontact Ohio Valley, the embattled Francophone world of the Upper Illinois River Valley, and the headlands of the Chesapeake Bay.

And their stories shed light on some of the most important "hot spots" in colonial America. Historically, the Shawnees tended to move into borderland zones south and north of the Mason-Dixon Line.[29] Oklahoma's Shawnee communities came about through travel and self-determination, the descendants of generations of enterprising forebears who were able to continually reimagine themselves in changing circumstances, a feat required of any human society that forsakes its homeland to survive.

■ Echoes of precontact civilizations reverberate throughout the Shawnee communities of Oklahoma.[30] Their likely ancestors, members of the Fort Ancient Tradition, shared an attachment to corn agriculture and to village-based, egalitarian social systems. Fort Ancient villages ranged from modern Louisville, Kentucky, to West Virginia. Between roughly A.D. 1000 and 1680, Fort Ancient villagers lived in villages ranging between 250 and 1,000 people. The cultures within this tradition seem to have developed peacefully over time. Archaeologists have not found evidence of chaotic violence and revolutionary changes in political structure and identity. There were many Fort Ancient societies, marked by their linguistic diversity. Algonquians predominated, but, for example, archaeologists believe that Siouan speakers with kinship ties to tribes a thousand miles to the west joined their trade networks and lived within the tradition. So while they were separated by language, local customs, and diplomacy, Fort Ancient peoples shared an attachment to place: the well-watered lands surrounding the Ohio River, in the heart of the continent.[31]

During the summer months, Fort Ancient villagers returned to their summer villages along the Ohio River and its tributaries. Extended families splintered from these villages during the winter months. They took advantage of the bison and deer herds that reached into the short-grass prairies of Kentucky and Ohio. Indeed, Fort Ancient peoples used fire to encourage the kind of forest-edge environments these animals enjoyed. When combined with the Little Ice Age, which aided in the retreat of the forests, Fort Ancient people became proficient hunters. Even so, they depended on the three sisters of corn, beans, and squash for most of their caloric intake.[32]

Fort Ancient villagers, and their Shawnee descendants, forged their sense of themselves as a people as they moved through these cycles of farming and hunting. Unlike their Mississippian neighbors to the south and west, where powerful chiefs held sway, Fort Ancient society was organized through villages where leaders exercised far less coercive authority. In fact, one Fort Ancient scholar has gone so far as to argue that Fort

Ancient had no social classes and was an intensively egalitarian world. In the centuries before contact, Fort Ancient's village chiefs, or Big Men, never developed the kind of authority that enabled them to draw summer villages together under common leadership. Without centralized authority, Fort Ancient villagers made up for their small numbers by reaching out to their neighbors.[33]

Between 1630 and 1680—the space of two generations—these human societies fell apart and largely abandoned the Middle Ohio Valley. Summer villages, some that had been continuously occupied for more than 700 years, were abandoned. In just fifty years, one of the most agrarian and place-bound peoples in the world became one of the most transient and adaptive. This transformation complicates the notion that Native Americans occupied "new worlds," what historian James H. Merrell defines as "a dramatically different milieu," one that "demand[ed] basic changes" in American Indian ways of life. But when colonizers arrived, Fort Ancient roots nurtured the various branches of the Shawnee people, today manifested by the three federally recognized Shawnee tribes and the Stomp Grounds they support. Fort Ancient villagers moved toward long-distance trading partners. Migration out of the Middle Ohio Valley became essential because their homeland had become a killing ground. Even before Europeans reached their communities, disease and slaving expeditions had devastated their people. Meanwhile, the lure of trade drew Fort Ancient peoples out of the Middle Ohio Valley. These villagers often traveled to the south, southeast, and northwest of the Ohio Valley, where their old allies took them in. Even at such great distances from home, Fort Ancient descendants found themselves among refugees whom they had known in what is now Ohio.[34]

In 1674, Henry Woodward, an English doctor and slave trader, first met Shawnees at Hickauhaugau, a center of Indian slavery along the Middle Savannah River, near modern-day Augusta, Georgia. Woodward encouraged them to participate in this human traffic. The negotiations were delicate. Hickauhaugau was an otherworldly place where human scalps hung from the rafters of longhouses. Their Westo occupants used English guns and surprise attacks against "settlement Indians" allied to the English as well as the Spanish mission towns of southern Georgia and Florida with masterful precision. Those who survived the attacks described the Westo as "man eaters," and they begged the English for help against them. These Shawnees managed to avoid becoming enslaved by first allying themselves with the Westos and then betraying them at the urging of Woodward and the men in charge of colonial Carolina. After fighting a genocidal war with the Westos, these Shawnees eventually replaced their Westo allies. Between 1680 and 1707, they served as vital middlemen in the slave trade.[35]

At roughly the same time, Shawnees appeared more than a thousand miles to the northwest, at the Grand Village of the Kaskaskias. Here they allied themselves with the Illinois Confederacy, a multitribal coalition of Central Algonquian speakers whose long history on the short-grass prairies made bison hunting a central part of their seasonal round. One branch of this confederacy, the Kaskaskia, established a village along the Upper Illinois River, near modern Utica, Illinois. Across from this village, French explorers such as Henri Tonty constructed Fort St. Louis. There, in the heart of the *pays d'en haut*, or upper country, the land between the Ohio River and the Great Lakes, the Shawnees briefly coalesced into a coalition of tribes. Nominally organized by Tonty and the French empire, the more than a dozen tribes that converged on the Upper Illinois River had strong connections to the Kaskaskias. Like the Illinois peoples of the Illinois River, the Shawnees had survived Iroquois attacks against them, and they saw the Grand Village of the Kaskaskias, and Fort St. Louis, as a place that might afford some protection.[36]

Meanwhile, at the confluence of the Susquehanna River and the Chesapeake Bay, colonists noticed "Inland Indians," whom they sometimes described as "Mixt Nations" and "Naked Indians," migrating into the region. Most of these European observers never fully understood what tribes they represented. Shawnees from both the Illinois and the Savannah rivers were among these "Inland Indians." The Shawnees were drawn to the region in 1692 by the Susquehannock survivors of Bacon's Rebellion and more than half a century of warfare with the Iroquois. Susquehannocks living along the Lower Susquehanna River were devastated in 1676, when Nathaniel Bacon led a ragtag band of backcountry settlers in a series of attacks against them. Eventually, Bacon's example of Indian hating proliferated in the Tidewater region, because ordinary settlers resented the slow pace of Indian dispossession as well as the gentry's ability to expand into the best land. The Shawnees might have migrated to the Tidewater region in order to support the Susquehannock survivors of Bacon's Rebellion. But lucrative trading with the new colony of Pennsylvania contributed to their decision as well.[37]

These violent borderlands proved to be places of opportunity as small numbers of Shawnee villagers, like their Fort Ancient ancestors, recognized that survival depended on both their ability to trade with Europeans and their capacity to serve as slave hunters, English mercenaries, and defensive buffers guarding Iroquoians from southeastern tribes with whom they were at war, such as the Catawbas. As colonial forces expanded their reach during the seventeenth century and the first decades of the eighteenth century, Shawnees became opportunists. They recognized that American Indians and Europeans needed each other, and as both sides settled around centers of trade and war, the Shawnees and their neighbors traveled vast distances to take advantage of these multiethnic gathering places.

Well before the Indian Removal Act of 1830 became the official policy of the United States, colonizers' land hunger led to violence between American Indians and settlers. Revenge killings and other betrayals drove Indians and Europeans apart. And as they became separate, Indians and Europeans began to see themselves as racially different. A curious mixture of economics, race, and identity steadily forced Native peoples from their proximity to Europeans. Between the 1720s and 1754, Native peoples, including the Shawnees, broke away from French and British settlements. From Delaware "praying towns" along the Upper Ohio River to multiethnic communities such as Conestoga Manor, in present-day Pennsylvania, land-hungry colonizers and the decline of fur-bearing animals drove a wedge between these former allies. Mid-Atlantic colonies such as Maryland and Pennsylvania no longer saw Native Americans as vital to their survival. The "Covenant Chain" of allied tribes was broken.

On the eve of the Seven Years' War, the global war between France and Great Britain that resulted in British supremacy, Algonquian tribes found a degree of autonomy in the Ohio River Valley that was no longer possible along the Lower Susquehanna River. Intimate connections among the Shawnees, Delawares, and Seneca-Cayugas, in particular, shaped multiethnic borderland towns such as Logstown, Lower Shawnee Town, and Kittanning, which represented something new. Traders and colonial officials saw them as places of opportunity, as trading centers capable of exploiting the abundance of fur-bearing animals in the Ohio Valley. But non-Indians saw them also as threateningly new and innovative. The polyglot peoples who lived there were keenly interested in economic and cultural independence from colonizers. Their villages were voluntary, pluralistic, and fiercely opposed to British, or French, dominance.

By the middle of the eighteenth century, the Shawnees had lived among many different Native societies, and they had learned the peculiar tendencies of Spanish, French, and English colonizers. Their migrations and reinventions had made it possible for them to pose a real challenge to the imperial ambitions of the French and the British alike. Theirs is an impressive story of adaptation. But as they adapted to new circumstances, they maintained a commitment to village-based loyalties and to the seasonal cycle of farming and hunting.[38]

During the War of 1812, the most famous Shawnee of all, Tecumseh, confronted the essentially paradoxical nature of Shawnee and Eastern Woodland Indian identities. Tecumseh was a Kispokotha Shawnee who was born to Shawnee parents in either Kispoko Town or Chillicothe, sometime between 1764 and 1771. His parents had spent much of their lives among the Creek Indians, at a Creek town called Tukabatchee in what is now Alabama. They had returned to Ohio just before Tecumseh's birth, at a time when both the Iroquois and the British asserted their dominion over Shawnee lands in Ohio. During, and after, the American Revolution, settlers asserted their rights to Shawnee lands with even greater intensity. In response, Tecumseh and his brother, Tenskwatawa, led a revitalization movement that turned militant and nearly stopped the American advance into the Ohio Valley.[39]

Tecumseh was frustrated by fellow Shawnees who were determined to remain in autonomous towns even when their survival was threatened. And yet these same towns were diverse, voluntary, and full of individuals interested in reinvention. Tecumseh saw how migration through new colonial worlds had created an enormous range and distribution of American Indian identities by the dawn of the nineteenth century. This diversity slowed his rise to power and limited his goal of using pan-Indian racial unity to oppose American land hunger. He decried the "bad consequences" of migration and the Shawnee habit of being "scattered about in parties." Tecumseh's followers hoped that he would overcome culture and history by enabling disparate peoples to unite around a shared history of racial oppression. As he traveled through Indian villages blighted by colonialism, Tecumseh spoke of his desire to "level all distinctions" between the various tribes by destroying the "village chiefs by whom all mischief is done." Tecumseh's fusion of racial oppression to pan-Indian resistance challenged older, more continuous histories of village-based authority. For Tecumseh, the historical fragmentation of the Shawnee people offered a kind of standard story of American Indian history. The Shawnees became iconic representatives of the destruction wrought by colonizers. Tecumseh hoped that the Shawnees' neighbors, from the upper country and beyond, might see their own tribal expression of the Shawnee dilemma. Once Indian people established the correspondence between Shawnee and American Indian history, Tecumseh believed that they would unite around his vision of reform and racial unity. His most ardent opponent, William Henry Harrison, the territorial governor of Indiana, who staked his position on the aggressive seizure of Indian lands through treaties, acknowledged Tecumseh's revolutionary plan for reimagining history and identity. In a letter to the secretary of war, William Eustis, Harrison described Tecumseh as "one of those uncommon geniuses which spring up occasionally to produce revolutions and overturn the established order of things."[40]

The Mohawk leader Thayendanegea, or Joseph Brant, also believed that the upper country was the ideal place for a grand experiment in American Indian history. All of the people who lived there had migrated vast distances and had suffered terribly from Old World diseases, and all had experienced decades, if not centuries, of war. Brant thought that this common history might enable the people who lived there to overcome their differences. He described the upper country as the "dish with one spoon." In Brant's opinion, the land between the Great Lakes and the Ohio Valley belonged "to the Confederate Indians in common," and he believed that even the Iroquois had no right to claim the country as theirs alone. Descending into tribalism, dividing American Indians between Algonquian and Iroquoian speakers and between the tribes associated with them, might prove fatal to everyone. Brant argued against local expressions of identity, from a preference for village leaders to tribal autonomy, warning that they amounted to a rejection of the vast alliance created after 1701, when the wars between Central Algonquians and Iroquoians halted, albeit temporarily. Ongoing divisions would "effectually serve our enemies whose aim has been to divide us."[41]

Brant and Tecumseh believed that the upper country offered an ideal site for a new narrative of American Indian identity and politics. Even before the early eighteenth century, when French colonizers first set foot in the region, migration and dislocation had been the common lot of the people who called this region home. Like Tecumseh, Brant believed that these migrations had fostered a common purpose and identity, as Indian people, increasingly conscious of their common racial identity, found common ground through a shared history of oppression. Brant recalled that "a moon of wampum was placed in this country with four roads leading to the center." These roads allowed Indians "from different quarters to come and settle or hunt here." Despite tribal differences, Brant and Tecumseh saw the center of the continent as a kind of social laboratory, a place where Indian people might adopt a common "Indian" identity in a homeland suited to embrace it.[42]

The most ardent champions of revitalization and Indian unity came from the upper country. Two of the most famous men, Blue Jacket and

Tecumseh, were Shawnee. The Shawnees' neighbors, including the Miamis, Potawatomis, Delawares, and Ottawas, became their most ardent supporters.[43] But, ultimately, even their supporters returned to their villages, rejoining the tribes in which they were born. They preferred a kind of localism, based in villages, each of which reflected their own trajectories of tribalism and migration. Among the most creative of experiments, these social revolutions foundered because Indian peoples in the upper country preferred life in villages. As migratory communities of kin traveled across the continent, the differences between these villages increased. Tribal peoples who once shared a common culture were now divided by uncommon histories.

Central Algonquians from the upper country, including the Shawnees, Miamis, and Illinois, along with relative newcomers, including Eastern Algonquian speakers such as the Delawares and Iroquois speakers such as the Senecas and Cayugas, argued over revitalization, tribalism, and more local expressions of political identity, as the American Revolution aroused similar debates among colonizers to the east. While most settled for some version of village-based identity, all of these players in the great drama of reform and revitalization called upon their varied histories of migration and alliance as they shaped their own particular cultural and political identities. Simultaneously parochial and cosmopolitan, they rejected ever-expanding notions of identity and nationhood that were so common among their American oppressors.[44] Native peoples fought to maintain sociopolitical systems that were much narrower, and yet more sophisticated, than most scholarly models suggest.

Like Tecumseh and Brant, scholars have struggled to make sense of the parochial cosmopolitanism of the Shawnee people. One complained about their "eccentric wanderings."[45] Another simply gave up trying to explain their migrations, reasoning that "it is useless to theorize on the origin of the Shawnee," as if they did not exist as a coherent nation because their travels have been so wide-ranging.[46] The Shawnees have thus been cast as the ultimate tricksters, always sitting there at the edge of important colonial events, mocking any historian's attempt to make sense of their actions. Some scholars settle on the idea of Shawnee exceptionalism, concluding that Shawnee mobility was extraordinary.

The Worlds the Shawnees Made subscribes to this line of thinking, to a point. My time with the Shawnees has shown me that there is much more to their story—that there were meanings to their migrations and consequences that are evident in their descendants even today. However, I seek to explain the purpose and consequences of their migrations. Far from colonial-era outcasts, standing outside the mainstream of American Indian history, the Shawnees are emblematic. As migration and reinvention became essential to the survival of Native peoples in the eastern half of North America, the Shawnees led the way and made the most of the new opportunities presented by colonization.[47]

Shawnee migrations are further complicated by regional approaches to colonial history. The word "Shawnee" is derived from the Algonquian word *sawanwa*, "person of the South."[48] Some experts on the Shawnees have speculated that they were "a northern group which wandered South at a relatively late date" or a "culture" that was essentially southern as a result of living "in the south for a long period of time."[49] As Central Algonquians from the Middle Ohio Valley, the Shawnees challenge regional approaches to culture. Their linguistic relatives, the Miamis, Illinois, Sauks, Meskwakis, Kickapoos, and Potawatomis, seem to fit within French colonial and Great Lakes Indian histories. And while the Illinois frequently raided southeastern peoples, particularly the Chickasaws, they remained closely associated with the Illinois River Valley and the Upper Mississippi River Valley. Among Central Algonquians, the Shawnees are the only tribe to have had such an extensive residence in the Southeast. It is this element of their history—long-distance migrations to multiple regions across the Eastern Woodlands—that distinguishes the Shawnees from their linguistic kinsmen. Anthropologists, in particular, continue to speculate as to whether or not the Shawnees were a coherent tribe that was shattered by colonial forces or a coalescent community borne out of the despair of the early colonial period. I suggest in this study that they were both. The archaeological, historical, and ethnographic records must come together if we are to make sense of their past associations and their present-day differences.[50]

The weight of the scholarly evidence has made Shawnee history more, rather than less, confusing. Methodological differences within and between the disciplines, particularly between archaeology and history, have exacerbated the problem. Historians generally begin their histories of modern tribes such as the Shawnees in the early colonial period. For them, the rupture of colonialism, from disease to slavery, from demographic collapse to coalescent reinvention, effectively broke their link to precontact worlds.[51] Meanwhile, archaeologists have conducted important research at late prehistoric and protohistoric sites, but colonial-era sites established between 1650 and 1776 are less well known. There is no known archaeological signature for the Shawnee people. As a result, we must rely on circumstantial archaeological evidence and the archival record if we are to link the Fort Ancient Tradition to modern tribes.[52] During the colonial period, the Shawnees did not have the luxury of occupying a territory that was "discrete and exclusive." For this reason, Shawnee history cannot be viewed in isolation.[53] Their proximity to allies and enemies created a series of "alternate identities" for Shawnee migrants. As such, the Shawnees provide an example of ethnogenesis, the adoption of new economies, new ritual practices, and new allies, as a means of adapting to the contingencies of the Indian slave trade, French exploration, and English land hunger. Shawnee peoples tailored their culture and economy to meet the demands of their European and American Indian neighbors. And yet these small-scale villages maintained the distinctions between themselves and the groups with whom they competed. The differences between Shawnee peoples accelerated in these various colonial worlds, as Shawnee villagers adapted to the demands placed on them by particular colonial regimes.[54]

Too often, American Indian histories emphasize coherent tribal identities that occupy neatly defined territories.[55] The reality on the ground is much more complicated. Algonquian villages, Muskogean *talwas*, and Iroquois "castles" were intensely multiethnic. Colonialism and its attendant miseries accelerated the multiethnic character of Indian communities. As a result, American Indian histories must reach beyond homogeneous notions of identity. Rather than view Indian peoples as members of protean nations, this study is designed to capture the lived experience of people inhabiting increasingly pluralistic worlds in which migration was commonplace. Even so, tribal identities remained important. Deeply held cultural practices helped Shawnee people survive waves of migration and coalescence, even as they intermarried, migrated, and ultimately adopted some of the characteristics of their allies. "Being Shawnee" was far from monolithic. Accordingly, this book is designed to show how Shawnees reimagined themselves as they migrated from, and returned to, the Middle Ohio Valley.[56]

This study of Shawnee villages across time and space shows that tribal societies are both dynamic and contingent—that creative reinvention was driven by the forces of colonialism and the particular Atlantic worlds that non-Natives and Native people created in early America.[57] In the case of Shawnee histories, a perspective drawn from Savannah Town in 1680 is quite distinct from that of Wakatomica, on the Ohio River, in 1753, or Little Axe, Oklahoma, in 2011. American Indian migrations were so rich and varied that any attempt to describe Native peoples in ways that place limits on tribal identification or geographic range leads to essentialist notions of history and culture. Such approaches assume a degree of coherence that oversimplifies the daily rhythms as well as the peculiar uncertainties of colonial places. By the middle of the seventeenth century, small numbers of kin, numbering in the hundreds, traveled far and wide in search of old allies, via well-worn trade networks. It makes more sense to view Eastern Woodland Indians as parochial cosmopolitans whose transient villages offer the best window into their identities. Where tribal identities falter, and thus ultimately confuse Shawnee history, village-based histories can capture the contingent, and historical, nature of American Indian identities.[58]

Indian removal and the paradigm of place complicates our understanding of Native American histories east of the Mississippi River. There is no doubt that the Indian Removal Act was a "monumental tragedy" for Indian people. And it is true that many Native people maintain deep attachments to sacred places.[59] However, moving on became a survival strategy well before forced relocation became the official policy of the United States government. It must have been devastating to abandon homes and villages, but Shawnee history shows that some tribes survived without maintaining a claim to any particular spot of land that had initially sustained and nurtured their culture. In fact, their cultural survival came to depend on mobility. As Absentee Shawnee ceremonial singer Sherman Tiger reminded me in June 2006, "Grandma's everywhere." Ceremonial Chief Andy Warrior elaborated on Tiger's point, commenting that "the things we do between the day we're born and the day God calls us home— all that in between, it's the Shawnee way. . . . All that in between is how I view what it means to be Shawnee."[60] For Andy Warrior and Sherman Tiger, extended families and rituals rather than sacred places show what it means to be Shawnee.

What motivated the Shawnees to travel so far beyond their own central place, the lands along the Ohio and the Scioto rivers, and into the Southeast? Many outsiders believe Native American religions bind Native practitioners to specific places. With the Shawnees, that is not so: their narratives about their cosmogony, the origins of their universe, show no attachment to place.[61] Instead, sacred Shawnee stories emphasize transience, mobility, and alliance. Here's how Tenskwatawa, the Shawnee Prophet and brother of famed warrior Tecumseh, explained it to government officials on the eve of the Indian Removal Act, in 1824:

[The Shawnees] were then lowered in a basket with the old man carrying a pack on his back which contained all the things the Great Spirit had entrusted to him for the benefit of the Indians. They arrived on the shore of a great lake and the old man told them that his heart was "in a northern direction . . . a great distance" which was their destination. After prayer and fasting for 12 days, the water dried up and they began a journey to the island. Calakaatha led them to the opposite shore. . . . After a 12 day march, they reached their destination.[62]

Tenskwatawa's emphasis on migration then turns to conflict with southeastern Indians such as the Creek and Catawba.[63] In his account, the Shawnees destroyed the Creeks when they first met because they doubted the power of Shawnee medicine. The Shawnees then brought the Creeks back to life and "compromised with them, calling them thereafter their brothers."[64] Migration, warfare, and alliance—hallmarks of colonial America—became sacred elements of Shawnee identity.

Sacred stories also reveal a weakened sense of unity among the five Shawnee divisions, or society clans: the Thawekila, Chalagawtha, Kispokotha, Mekoche, and Pekowitha. The stories begin by describing how each division was created separately, in different locations. In the 1930s, an Absentee Shawnee named Joe Billy told an anthropologist that the Chalagawtha division was created on some different continent before the autonomous divisions came together as the Shawnee people. According to Billy, the divisions "were worshipping at the same time but in separate camps. As they were worshipping they understood the words used in the prayers and the same terms and usages prevailed." Both camps became angry, believing that the neighboring group mocked their prayers to Kokumthena, "Our Grandmother," the Shawnee female deity. Before fighting began, someone interceded between the two divisions and convinced them that they "were worshipping the same person in the same language and manner . . . and it proved that their usages and rites were the same absolutely." From that point forward, they identified each other as Shawnees.[65]

The former governor of the Absentee Shawnee tribe, an elder named George Blanchard, told me a story that supports Tenskwatawa's emphasis on both transience and alliance. According to Governor Blanchard,

While we were out hunting it'd get real cold and they'd start telling stories. They said that at one time there was a good kill . . . a lot of deer. . . . They were sitting there feastin' and they had their fill. Across the water there was another group that sounded Shawnee so the men with the good kill went over there and shared their meat with them. We became stronger that way. . . . We would pick up another band of Shawnees . . . and we got too big for our britches. The society clans were separate back in the old days. But now we're all one big group.[66]

Taken together, these narratives convey a "historical philosophy" regarding Shawnee identities.[67] While the particular details of their stories are sometimes different, the Shawnees could inhabit shattered worlds sometimes within larger Indian communities, sometimes independently, because warfare, alliances, and travel became inherent characteristics of "being Shawnee" as they migrated across various early American worlds.

Nevertheless, most American histories continue to emphasize sacred geography and the power of place. I do not argue against "the moral significance of geographic locations" for Indian people. Rather, this study challenges the notion that American Indian religions, and the identities shaped by them, emanate from the land itself.[68]

Woodland Indians, most of whom endured a series of voluntary and forced removals from successive homelands, remain on unstable ground in the thinking of many scholars.[69] As exiles permanently torn from their homelands, they occupy an unhappy place in American Indian history. The Shawnees and their Woodlands neighbors, particularly the Illinois, Miamis, Kickapoos, Delawares, and Seneca-Cayugas, stand apart from western Native Americans, with histories that challenge widely accepted assumptions. Is this perhaps because colonial-era Woodland Indian towns were so unlike many of the Indian communities west of the Mississippi, whose lands still include sacred sites dating to the period before contact?[70] Algonquian speakers living between the Ohio Valley and the Great Lakes thought of themselves as members of autonomous villages, and yet their survival depended on the constant development of alliances with members of other communities. Their clans were patrilineal and encouraged marrying outside their own villages. Small-scale but sophisticated, Shawnee people maintained vibrant connections with Siouan, Muskogean, and Iroquoian speakers long before 1539, the year in which the Spanish conquistador, Hernando de Soto, began his *entrada* through the Southeast and set in motion the events that would ultimately redefine the eastern half of North America. Exploring the links between the precontact Fort Ancient peoples and their colonial descendants remains a daunting task. Unfortunately, many of the connections have been lost to us. But at the very least, this research suggests there are multiple horizons of migration that can be traced far back in time.[71]

For the Shawnees, migration reveals less about the power of place than the ongoing re-creation of a distinctive cultural identity associated with Shawnee ceremonial life. As North Ground Ceremonial Chief Andy Warrior once stated, "What we do here [on the ceremonial ground] makes us Shawnee."[72] To his mind, the performance of ritual, rather than the places where rituals are conducted, has perpetuated Shawnee identity into the twenty-first century.

Shawnee towns were mobile and thus separated by geographic, colonial, and geopolitical context. They functioned as autonomous political units and maintained a sense of their own distinctiveness as homes of Shawnee people. Shawnees accustomed to smallness, to clan identities, and to diplomacy for survival alternately joined and resisted amalgamation into larger colonies, confederacies, and empires. But throughout these adaptations, their villages remained. The history of these people and their towns reminds us that any discussion of "tribal" identities must first be historically situated in order for it to have any analytical value and, most important, for it to provide some sense of their humanity as they traveled through rapidly changing colonial worlds.

Explaining how one of the most place-bound cultures in the world became one of the most adaptive is a central theme of this book. I show how Shawnees made movement and dispersal integral components of their culture. Indeed, their understanding of themselves is still shaped by their historic migrations. Historically, their villages were parochial and cosmopolitan, and colonial officials struggled to make sense of their migrations. Because their villages functioned independently from each other and because they made alliances as they saw fit, it was impossible to guarantee a uniform Shawnee response to colonial decisions. Village leaders preferred to maintain their distinctions. This book examines life in these villages scattered across the eastern half of North America. It attempts to show why many American Indians concluded that staying small needed to remain at the very essence of their beliefs and values. Before 1754, coalescent, national, and even tribal identities were anathema to the Shawnees and their neighbors. *The Worlds the Shawnees Made* tells the story of these people and explains why the Shawnees were able to hold onto their language and culture even as they sacrificed their homeland and migrated across the colonial world.

part 1

Continuity and Reinvention at the Dawn of Colonization

The peoples of Fort Ancient occupied the Middle Ohio River Valley from the falls of the Ohio River, near modern Louisville, to the western foothills of the Appalachian Mountains, in what is now West Virginia. For more than 700 years they lived in a series of stable, highly egalitarian villages in which corn agriculture was the predominant means of subsistence. Women and men divided the year between hunting and farming, and the gendered differences associated with these subsistence practices shaped their identities. They lived in a series of diverse worlds marked by linguistic differences. But across this vast region, these village dwellers consistently rejected hierarchies of power and coercive authority.

Fort Ancient farmers experienced profound changes in their way of life in the seventeenth century. In a fifty-year period, their homeland fell apart when European trade goods and Old World diseases reached beyond the Appalachian Mountains. Exotic trade goods and epidemics coincided with the arrival of Native slavers and Iroquois warriors, who attacked their villages. They were a practical people, accustomed to seasonal migrations spent in the company of their kin. But colonization introduced radical changes to their ways of life, and Fort Ancient people responded by adapting to these new realities. After 1680, when the last Fort Ancient villages had been abandoned, Ohio Valley villagers migrated vast distances from their homeland, and they became known for their linguistic range, diplomatic acumen, and military prowess. They became known as "the Greatest Travellers in America."

I refer to Fort Ancient peoples as parochial cosmopolitans, because even as they adjusted their way of life to suit new, colonial circumstances they maintained their attachment to their village-based way of life. In fact, their villages structured their subsequent migrations. Chapters 2 and 3 follow the movement of Shawnee peoples out of the Middle Ohio Valley, as they responded to the collapse of their societies by reinventing themselves. They moved toward peoples with whom they had been allied before the arrival of Europeans. And when they moved, they did so as villages. Their piecemeal migrations reflect the values of Fort Ancient farmers, for they were a people committed to staying small but sophisticated. Even as they abandoned their homeland, the Shawnees maintained the subsistence practices and gender roles associated with the Middle Ohio River Valley. Precontact beliefs, values, and allegiances shaped the basic choices made by Shawnee migrants in the colonial period. In the following chapters, I describe how one of the most agrarian and place-bound peoples in the world became one of the most transient and adaptive. Amid this transformation, Shawnees maintained a sense of who they were, as a distinct people, even as they traveled far from home.

chapter 2

The Parochial Cosmopolitans
of the Middle Ohio Valley

Petersburg, in Boone County, Kentucky, is the perfect spot for a river town. Even during the great flood of 1937, when the Ohio River breached its floodplain, Petersburg remained dry. It is a stable and high spot of ground with rich soils, and human societies have recognized its virtues for millennia. Before Petersburg, Kentuckians called it Tanner Station, no doubt after the abundance of deer hides that Indians and settlers hauled into the town during the latter half of the eighteenth century. Before Tanner Station, generations of Fort Ancient villagers took advantage of this protected terrace facing the river. Today, very little in this tiny hamlet of four streets suggests that Petersburg was once one of the most favored spots, for American Indians and settlers alike, across the breadth of the Ohio Valley.[1]

Archaeologists have known something of its value since 1993, when soil tests along the riverbank revealed abundant evidence of past occupants. At that time, archaeologists David Pollack and Gwynn Henderson persuaded town officials to "stop offering permits [for] any ground disturbing activity . . . or risk unearthing human remains." Folks in Petersburg listened to their advice until 2004, when a local man wanted to build a large house facing the river, on Front Street. A permit was issued, and the backhoe operator set to his task. Human remains appeared in the back-dirt piles almost immediately. Parts of skulls, femurs, and human teeth seemed to scream out of the alluvial soils, pleading with the backhoe operator to stop the work. But he kept digging until the footprint of the basement (at least sixty by forty feet) was nearly complete.[2]

Frantic phone calls followed, and town officials arrived and informed the homeowner and the backhoe operator that they had committed a felony under Kentucky state law.[3] The mayor called Pollack and Henderson, the lead archaeologists with the Kentucky Archaeological Survey, to investigate what had occurred. Pollack and Henderson have been haunted by the memories of what they found ever since. Bones, stone-lined graves, and other funerary objects protruded from the basement walls. The brutal power of the backhoe had ripped through an ancient cemetery, destroying perhaps fifteen to twenty graves. At the times of these deaths, relatives of the deceased had placed copper ornaments, beads, beavertails, copper clips, and whole pots with them. They had laid out their kin in extended poses, on their backs, and some of the graves had been framed with cuts of limestone, making a kind of rectangular stone coffin for the deceased. Grave goods interred with the dead revealed that the backhoe operator had callously unearthed a protohistoric site, a place in which European trade goods, rather than Europeans themselves, had begun to transform Native ways of life.[4]

Petersburg is downstream from where the Great Miami drains into the Ohio, at the center of a string of Fort Ancient villages that were located along the Ohio River on the eve of colonization. Pollack and Henderson did what they could to salvage, restore, and save what remained of the Fort Ancient cemetery. They concluded that the destroyed site had been built on top of previous villages dating back seven hundred to eight hundred years. The homeowner in need of a basement had built a house atop a place that had been continuously occupied for nearly a millennium. As they worked, curious onlookers craned their necks, hoping to catch a glimpse of burials that should not have been theirs to see. When Pollack and Henderson's work was done, the state declined to prosecute either the backhoe operator or the homeowner.

Across the Middle Ohio Valley, there are places just like Petersburg. Once Europeans made contact with American Indians, Native migrants and colonizers alike desired the same things that Fort Ancient villagers had wanted from the land. Native Americans and colonizers considered the risk of flooding, the opportunities for trade, and the abundance of the land. To the east of Petersburg, at the confluence of the Little Miami and Ohio rivers, modern Cincinnati sits atop the late Fort Ancient site of Madisonville. And east of Madisonville, at the confluence of the Scioto and Ohio rivers, settlers founded modern Portsmouth, Ohio, on top of generations of Shawnee and Fort Ancient towns. Colonial-era migrants, Native and non-Native alike, favored confluences because these places combined agricultural and diplomatic opportunities. In the 1720s, Algonquian and Iroquois migrants called Portsmouth Lower Shawnee Town. The richness of the floodplain soils and the opportunities for trade and diplomacy drew Natives and settlers alike to its banks. At Lower Shawnee Town, the homes they lived in and the foods they consumed mirrored those of the past occupants of the land. Fort Ancient and Shawnee residence patterns and subsistence strategies mark just two of the ways that the historic village of Lower Shawnee Town was "patterned after [the] indigenous prehistoric and protohistoric villages of the Middle Ohio Valley."[5]

Material artifacts recovered from Petersburg, Madisonville, and Lower Shawnee Town suggest that there are basic continuities between historically known tribes such as the Shawnees and the Fort Ancient villagers of the Middle Ohio Valley. Like Petersburg, the archaeological site associated with Lower Shawnee Town, and later Portsmouth, blends precontact, protohistoric, and historic artifacts. Sites such as these are treasure troves in that they reveal basic continuities in both culture and human desire. When Shawnee migrants returned to Lower Shawnee Town in the 1720s, they returned to a spot that their ancestors had known very well. Archaeologists have unearthed Fort Ancient projectile points "in direct association" with trade goods carried by Shawnee migrants when they returned to Ohio.[6] When Shawnees briefly reclaimed the Ohio Valley, they did so as a changed people. However, they had survived the rupture of colonialism, and the material culture of continuously occupied sites reveals that the Shawnees blended old and new worlds as they migrated across the continent.

Archaeologists and historians have struggled to link precontact indigenous worlds to their modern inheritors for more than a century. They have been frustrated by the fact that European colonizers entered the Middle Ohio Valley long after the decline of the Fort Ancient Tradition. By 1680, Fort Ancient peoples had migrated out of the Ohio Valley in response to trade, warfare, and disease. In the 1720s, when Native people returned to the Ohio Valley, Shawnees were at the vanguard of settlement. Did their return amount to a kind of homecoming? Archaeological evidence from sites such as Petersburg and Portsmouth indicates that eighteenth-century Shawnee migrants knew the land and its history. Long before European colonizers set foot in the Ohio Valley, Fort Ancient villagers had abandoned these places of abundance. By 1680, when the last Fort Ancient villagers departed from the Ohio Valley, Europeans encountered people calling themselves "Shawnees" at great distances from places such as Petersburg and Portsmouth. In the space of two generations, towns that had been home to people for millennia became part of a broad vacant quarter encompassing much of the Middle Ohio Valley. French and English explorers did not make it into their homeland in time to learn or to label members of the Fort Ancient Tradition with tribal names. All that

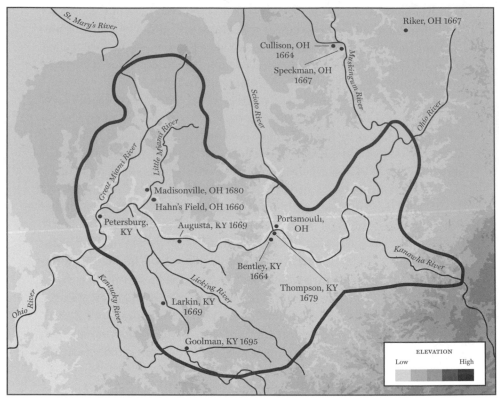

Map 1. The Boundaries of the Fort Ancient World.
With villages stretching from the falls of the Ohio to the foothills of the Appalachians,
Fort Ancient peoples lived in an abundant region that they had inhabited
continuously for more than 700 years. Map by Alex Gau.

remains is their archaeological legacy.[7] Colonial observers and the scholars who study their records have not yet succeeded in linking the protohistoric Fort Ancient to Native peoples undergoing profound changes in the colonial era.

The people buried at Fort Ancient cemeteries such as Petersburg, Madisonville, and Portsmouth would have been familiar to the Shawnee migrants who returned to the region in the eighteenth century. For more than a century, archaeologists have diligently researched precontact and protohistoric sites. Their work has been largely ignored by historians, and as a result historians generally accept the argument that American Indians endured a near-total disjuncture with their ancestors. For all intents and purposes, Native peoples became new peoples. Historians have overplayed the schism between precontact and early American worlds. As a result, the Shawnees have often been described as a kind of chaos people, whose "eccentric wanderings" across the continent seem random and ill-planned. Absent a homeland, contemporary Shawnees have sometimes been denied the right to advocate for their ancestors. By emphasizing changes wrought by colonization, scholars have profoundly impacted the lived experience of contemporary Shawnees. Because there is no definitive link between the Fort Ancient people and the Shawnees, archaeologists label human remains at sites such as Petersburg "culturally unidentifiable."[8] As such, today's Shawnees often struggle to make a case for the culturally appropriate treatment of graves unearthed at places such as Petersburg.

Similarly, English colonizers used the break between Fort Ancient villagers and Central Algonquian speakers such as the Shawnees to claim the lands west of the Appalachian Mountains. By virtue of their alliance to the Iroquois Confederacy, the English asserted their right of conquest to the Middle Ohio Valley. The rupture between the archaeological and the historical records has caused Shawnee disenfranchisement and has made it difficult for contemporary Shawnees to reclaim their sense of place, of home, from their current locations in Oklahoma. By expanding the temporal framework of American Indian history and exploring the links between the Fort Ancient peoples and the Shawnees, this chapter shows how continuities in social organization, subsistence and ritual practices, and diplomacy tie the Fort Ancient tradition, at least in part, to the Shawnees.

Exploring the Links between the Fort Ancient Tradition and the Shawnees

Scholars have casually suggested before that there might be a link between Fort Ancient peoples and the Shawnees. In Ohio, removed tribes such as the Shawnees and the Miamis remain part of local lore and history. President Andrew Jackson's brand of ethnic cleansing, legally codified by the Indian Removal Act of 1830, has not erased the knowledge that between 1748 and 1752 Miami speakers founded Pickawillany, on the Little Miami River near Cincinnati. Ohioans continue to memorialize the famous Shawnee warrior Tecumseh and his role in the epic struggle for control of the Lower Great Lakes. In 2001, Absentee Shawnee elders organized a trip to the Scioto and Ohio rivers. While the Absentee Shawnee elders were there, they attended an annual play about Tecumseh put on by the town of Chillicothe, Ohio, upstream from Portsmouth. More than forty elders fondly recall sitting in amused silence, as nervous local actors performed in front of them.[9]

In 1920, Earnest Hooton and Charles Willoughby, the first professional archaeologists to investigate the premier Late Fort Ancient site at Madisonville, speculated that the Miamis and the Shawnees might be the modern inheritors of Fort Ancient culture. Native leaders, from the Miami chief, Little Turtle, to Tecumseh, believed that the Middle Ohio Valley was their homeland. In 1795, during negotiations for the Treaty of Greenville, Little Turtle declared that "the prints of my ancestor's houses are everywhere to be seen" in what is now Ohio and Indiana. Subsequent Miami oral histories support Little Turtle's claims, to a point. Miami elders such as Gabriel Godfroy described a "coming out place" for the Miamis, near modern South Bend, Indiana, along the St. Joseph River.[10]

Since Hooton and Willoughby, archaeologists have made great strides in broadening the linguistic and cultural range of the Fort Ancient Tradition. Now even the most aggressive supporters of the Fort Ancient–Shawnee connection reject the possibility that the Shawnees represent the only modern heirs to the maize agriculturists of the Middle Ohio Valley. The stuff of life, from trade goods to housing styles, reveals subtle differences among the villagers who inhabited this vast cultural area. Even with these distinctions, Middle Ohio Valley villagers shared a common set of subsistence practices as well as an allegiance to village-based autonomy.[11]

The daily lives of Fort Ancient villagers at Hardin Village and the Bentley site, at the confluence of the Scioto and Ohio rivers, were fairly similar to those of villagers at historically known sites such as Lower Shawnee Town. From the 1720s through the Seven Years' War, returning Shawnee migrants made Lower Shawnee Town a center for diplomacy and trade. For "the day to day inhabitants" of Lower Shawnee Town, "the foods they grew and the animals they hunted . . . changed little in over seven hundred years." Peoples' daily lives followed a similar rhythm, in spite of changes brought by European traders, from new technologies to the deerskin trade.[12]

In September 1669, Jesuits living among the Senecas, keepers of the western door of the Iroquois Confederacy, described how "all the youth of the country . . . [amounting] to about 500" marched against the "Touagannha," shorthand for *Ontwaganha*, the Iroquois word for "one who utters unintelligible speech." Between 1669 and 1671, Ontwaganha became the derisive name for Shawnee captives of the Iroquois. The Iroquois captured the Ontwaganha during four successive invasions of the Middle Ohio Valley. The Jesuits witnessed people bound by slave halters, dragged by Iroquois captors from their homes on the Ohio. Once in Iroquoia, these captives were no longer called "Touagannha." They came into focus and became known by more specific tribal appellations. In interviews with the Jesuit priests, many of these captives identified themselves as Shawnees.[13]

The Senecas traded Shawnee captives to eager French explorers, and they regaled the Europeans with the "many marvels of the River Ohio." They bragged that they were "thoroughly acquainted" with the land and its peoples, including Shawnees, who occupied fifteen or twenty villages.[14] By the second half of the seventeenth century, the Iroquois and slavers from the South were trafficking in knowledge of the land and its peoples, two commodities that Europeans lacked. War, trade, and exploration created a confusing record of unparalleled violence and surprising acts of cooperation.

French explorers willingly participated in this human traffic. Captives-turned-guides had the ability to unlock the mysteries of the lands west of the Appalachian Mountains. In 1671, René-Robert Cavelier, Sieur de La Salle, a French explorer who canoed the Mississippi River and traversed the shores of the Gulf of Mexico, met a Shawnee man who had become enslaved by the Seneca. La Salle took advantage of the opportunity and bartered for his release. His Seneca captors recognized La Salle's desire for guides with knowledge of the continent's interior. La Salle's newfound Shawnee guide assured him "that in a month & a ½ of strong marching we could arrive at the principal nations which are on the Ohio River."[15] This particular expedition failed to reach the Ohio country. Nevertheless, it became the first of many in which La Salle depended on Shawnee guides.

The Iroquois made a great many claims about the Ohio Valley and the Shawnees in the colonial period. In June 1732, at a council with the governor of Pennsylvania, the Iroquois demanded that the Shawnees "Look back toward Ohioh, The place from whence you came." French imperialists resisted the Iroquois claims of dominion over Algonquians from the Ohio country. In the long run up to the Seven Years' War, the French knew that they had to curb the Iroquois to thwart British plans for the Ohio country. The Covenant Chain alliance between the Haudenosaunee, or People of the Longhouse, and the British had made both of them stronger. They asserted their right of conquest, much to the dismay of the French. Jacques-Pierre de Taffanel de la Jonquière, governor general of New France, argued that the Iroquois had "no right to the River Ohio." Rather, that right belonged to "no other Indians . . . but the Chaouanons [Shawnees]."[16]

Illinois, Odawa, and Potawatomi guides, trading partners, and their Indian slaves also linked the Middle Ohio Valley to the Shawnees. During the last decades of the seventeenth century, they told French explorers and priests about the people to the south of them. As they traveled to the north and west of the Ohio River, the French used Native accounts of the region to create base maps and reports on these unexplored lands. Father Jacques Marquette first learned of the Shawnees through an unnamed Indian slave of the Illinois. Later that year, in 1673, the year of Marquette's arrival at La Pointe, in southern Wisconsin, Marquette met Shawnees for the first time. The Shawnees carried glass beads, and they had traveled for thirty days to reach La Pointe. Marquette examined their trade goods and determined that the Shawnees had acquired the beads from the Spanish. In that same year, the Illinois told Marquette that the Shawnees "live on the banks [of the Ohio], and are so numerous that I have been informed there are thirty-eight villages of that nation." However, Marquette learned that "they are a very harmless people," who are constantly attacked and taken captive by the Iroquois "because they have no firearms."[17] Marquette grossly overestimated the number of Fort Ancient villages still in existence in 1673. By the time Europeans began to notice people calling themselves "Shawnees," their homeland had fallen apart.

French and English colonizers believed that the Shawnees originated from the Ohio Valley. English cartographer John Mitchell even described the Shawnees as the "Native proprietors" of the "River Ohio." However, Marquette's contemporaries, including a French trader with an eye for ethnography named Nicolas Perrot, believed that the Shawnees had already left the Ohio Valley by the time the French arrived. In 1673, Perrot learned that the Shawnees "inhabited the valley of the Ohio." He also claimed that "the Chaouanons [had been] driven from the shores of Lake Erie" by the Iroquois. Native intermediaries told Perrot that a people known as "Shawnee," then living in modern-day Ohio, had been "routed in several encounters" with the Iroquois. Jesuits in Iroquoia confirmed these reports. Perrot told of the Iroquois driving the Chaouanons south to Carolina. Two years earlier, in 1671, Virginia traders began closing in on the Ohio Valley. They speculated that the "Chaouanons" lived "westward and northward" of the Tidewater region of Chesapeake Bay.[18]

Colonizers first encountered Native peoples from across the eastern half of North America as the Native peoples moved toward trading opportunities, even while they fled epidemic disease and long-distance slavers. Their mobility confused European observers. Even American Indians allied to colonizers struggled to explain the transient village dwellers who appeared suddenly in their towns and trading posts. In these decades, Indian villages disappeared at a moment's notice. Native peoples became difficult to identify, and their movements were impossible to predict. To cite one example of this confusion, Marquette overestimated the number of Shawnee villages remaining in the Ohio Valley. In contrast, English traders described the Shawnees as a homeless people who were "dispersed thro' the World."[19]

The truth lies somewhere between these extremes. The trouble with all of these reports is that Middle Ohio Valley villagers were already on the move when Europeans first met them. European maps, letters, and reports describe a sea change in the land and its people. Archaeologists have confirmed these archival records. The material evidence suggests that by 1650 the Middle Ohio Valley was a region in decline, drained of its people by trade, disease, and war.[20]

The Variety of Late Fort Ancient Worlds on the Eve of Contact

The Shawnees can no longer be considered "a people without history" by those who believe that their history begins with European settlement. Fort Ancient peoples spoke a variety of languages, and they lived in multiethnic settlements. They occupied a vast territory, one that cannot be associated with a single tribe. And because such large regions do not correspond to coherent tribal identities, historians must abandon the notion that prehistoric Shawnee peoples achieved enough internal coherence to create a shared sense of Shawnee nationalism. However, Fort Ancient peoples and the modern Shawnees did share a common seasonal round, ritual life, and village-centered worldview. Conversant in multiple languages and accustomed to cultural differences, the Shawnees consistently adapted to new circumstances without losing sight of their cultural distinctiveness. Just as the spring and fall Bread Dances divide the year between summer and winter, so too did Fort Ancient villagers congregate in large villages dedicated to agricultural production every spring. Like Stomp Grounds such as White Oak, South Ground, and North Ground, Fort Ancient villagers congregated in summer villages, which became the ultimate expression of their ritual life and chiefly authority. Villagers assiduously avoided hierarchies of power and the kind of coercive authority that comes when one summer village joins itself to another.[21]

The Shawnees' devotion to their villages is vitally important to understanding Shawnee history in the colonial era. Maps of the eastern half of North America reveal Shawnee villages settled at great distances from each other. Villagers often named their towns for one of the five Shawnee divisions: the Chalagawtha, Kispokotha, Thawekila, Pekowitha, and Mekoche. These kin groups might have coalesced into summer villages during the planting season. In early America, these kin groups remained autonomous for years, if not decades, at a time. As kin groups migrated, the differences between them became more pronounced. The people they lived with and the places they called home refashioned their identities in the colonial era.[22]

Archaeologists have found "supralocal symbols" of chiefly authority, including barred copper pendants, placed in male burials at various Fort Ancient sites. Similar pendants have been found in Tennessee, Arkansas, and Iowa. These pendants are often associated with male authority, and archaeologists have speculated that they reflect centralized power. However, this argument fails to explain why copper pendants were so widespread. If they were a reflection of a complex chiefdom, then archaeologists should expect to find them concentrated at one specific Fort Ancient site. For example, if all of the pendants had been found at Madisonville, then archaeologists might have assumed that it was a summer village with wide-ranging authority over its neighbors. But Madisonville is not unique. Copper pendants are fairly widespread throughout the Fort Ancient Tradition. The absence of a centralized village with exclusive control of these symbols of authority confirms a much older, well-established paradigm in Fort Ancient studies: villagers rejected hierarchical understandings of power and authority. Chiefs depended on "personal initiative," and leadership in Fort Ancient societies was dynamic. A chief's enemies inside and outside of each summer village often undermined his power.[23]

Even highly structured Native societies such as Cahokia, the preeminent Mississippian chiefdom near modern St. Louis, failed to achieve the kind of coercive authority associated with protean nation-states. Cahokia's elite asserted only limited authority over surrounding communities. Archaeologists estimate that their range of influence was limited to about thirty kilometers from Monk's Mound, at the center of Cahokia. Even rural villages within Cahokia's grasp exercised a great deal of autonomy. Within the shadow of the largest Mississippian chiefdoms, diverse villages challenged the authority of the chiefdoms. With somewhere between 10,000 and 30,000 residents, one might guess that Cahokia's leaders established coercive authority over a wide geographic area. But, in truth, Cahokians failed to achieve anything like a pan-regional identity.[24]

Surrounded by interrelated family members, the "village acted as an independent polity," and its members placed trust in individuals who conformed to the expectations of the community. Villagers resisted placing all of their confidence in individuals with the charisma and character to lead. Town councils likely regulated village affairs, further limiting the power of village chiefs. Unlike their Mississippian neighbors to the

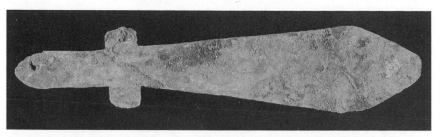

*Barred pendants associated with male leaders are distributed
fairly widely across Late Fort Ancient villages. Petersburg, Kentucky, courtesy of
Kentucky Archaeological Survey.*

south and west, where political and social influences radiated outward
from central "mother towns," such as Cahokia, to surrounding daughter
or satellite towns, Fort Ancient villages remained distinct. Villages may
have been allied, but ties between them probably did not develop into the
kind of cooperative network found among intertribal confederacies such
as the Haudenosaunee. While men of achieved status were the foremost
authorities in their villages, their authority rarely, if ever, reached beyond
the summer village.[25] Fort Ancient villagers rejected ascribed status, preferring to live in a world in which success in battle, diplomacy, and family
life determined one's ability to lead.

The Little Ice Age, Coalescence, and the
Need for Seasonal Migration in the Middle Ohio Valley

Scholars have often wondered why such an abundant land failed to create
hierarchies of power akin to those found among the Mississippians. After
1400, the Little Ice Age made the Ohio Valley colder and wetter than it
had been for hundreds of years. Corn remained the foundation of Fort
Ancient diets. But climate change meant that farming became increasingly hazardous as spring floods devastated newly planted fields. Late-
season frosts sometimes killed plants before the harvest. On average, corn
accounted for 68 percent of the overall diet. Each person required nine
bushels of corn per year. Even with a regular surplus of corn, the Little
Ice Age made cultivating the soil unpredictable. Food scarcity affected
every generation at some point. Over the seven hundred years of Fort Ancient history, families retained control of their seeds and their surplus. At
no point were chiefs able to seize food from the people they represented.
Archaeologists have shown that climate change compelled Fort Ancient
farmers to retreat to the "most productive soils" with access to "reliable

trade routes" along the Ohio River and its main tributaries. Their villages coalesced and became larger on the eve of contact.[26]

Climate change contributed to the coalescence of summer villages on the eve of colonization, and the homes they lived in reflected the increasing size of their communities. After 1450, Fort Ancient peoples turned to much larger, rectangular surface dwellings. They built homes designed to house extended families, as evidenced by the multiple hearths, storage pits, and graves that were often dug within them. Defensive palisades become more commonplace, particularly on the eastern edge of the Fort Ancient world. As summer villages increased in size, hunters ranged widely in search of game. Opportunistic hunting around summer villages became more difficult, and rival villages might have competed over increasingly scarce resources. Village life changed as well, as male hunters challenged the authority of female farmers. Fort Ancient villagers became accustomed to splitting their time between winter hunting camps and agriculturally oriented summer villages. Sheltered river valleys and the tight-knit spaces of their winter homes, or wickiups, reflected the intimacy that came with the onset of winter. No longer confined to the Ohio River, Fort Ancient hunters now traversed the hunting grounds of unrelated people.[27]

Fort Ancient peoples had a keen understanding of the world around them and the carrying capacity of the land, and they used this knowledge to determine when and where to migrate. At their winter hunting camps, Fort Ancient peoples built wickiups lined with tree bark and sometimes woven cattail maps. These were temporary structures, arranged by extended families of less than thirty people. Families traveled toward abundant hunting grounds such as those found in central Kentucky. The Goolman site in Clark County, Kentucky, offers one example of a Fort Ancient winter hunting camp. Situated along Bull Run Creek in a narrow valley surrounded by steep hills, Goolman provided extensive shelter from harsh winter winds. Only three structures have been identified, and these were small, circular buildings that were eight feet wide and sixteen feet long. Sheets of bark surrounded the base of one shelter, indicating that bark was used to cover narrow wood posts. No more than five to ten people lived in each of the bark- or mat-covered houses from November through March.[28]

Their decision to hunt and trade at greater distances from their summer villages meant that Fort Ancient peoples entered into conversations with new people. Prior to the Little Ice Age, Fort Ancient people sometimes had little awareness of similar people living downstream from them.[29] Theirs had been an agricultural world. Now hunting, gathering, and trade along the abundant streams in the Ohio Valley watershed made

Late Fort Ancient villages consolidated and became larger and
more defensive on the eve of de Soto's entrada.
Burning Spring Branch Site (46Ka142), Kanawha County, West Virginia, ca. 1500,
Courtesy of U.S. Army Corps of Engineers. Drawing by Jimmy Railey.

it possible to survive long midwestern winters more than one hundred miles from their summer villages.

During the spring, Fort Ancient hunters reunited with their extended families, to the heart of their kin groups. This kind of Miami-Potawatomi settlement pattern, in which Native peoples congregated in large summer villages during the spring and summer, only to disperse into small hunting camps in the fall and winter, was widely shared by Central Algonquians throughout the Upper and Lower Great Lakes. Algonquians divided the year between the fall and winter hunt, a time in which men are to take life, and farming in the spring and summer, a time in which women are to make life. Fort Ancient villagers, like their Algonquian descendants, associated gender roles with the logic of the natural world. The death of winter was the necessary counterpoint to the life of summer. The seasonal cycle thus affirmed the separate but complementary roles of women and men.[30]

Fort Ancient villagers adopted rituals of integration as seasonal migration became imperative. After 1400, large, permanent summer villages with upward of 500 people became commonplace along the Middle Ohio

Valley. Long-distant extended families needed a ritual means by which they could call an end to the winter hunt and reintegrate as a community. Agricultural rituals may have helped Fort Ancient villagers collectively imagine the transition from a hunting world dominated by men to a woman's world in which agriculture was the paramount concern of the community. During the colonial era, such rituals encouraged the Shawnees to coalesce, and planting ceremonies associated with the spring might have enabled Fort Ancient peoples to perform their collective identities into existence.[31]

Farmers and hunters, women and men, enjoyed a symbiotic relationship, as cycles of life and death moved from fields to forests, part of an ongoing succession of human-impacted environments. Native peoples favored land that was continually rejuvenated by spring flooding. Nutrient-rich alluvial soil was relatively easy to work with agricultural implements made of bone. Above the floodplains, Fort Ancient villages located in and around the hardwood forests had a more difficult time bending the environment to suit their needs. Fort Ancient men had to cut through the bark of large trees, girdling them near their base, a process that slowly killed the tree. Men burned dead and dying trees, along with the forest understory, as winter passed to spring. Burned lands, heavily laden with nitrogen from the fires and the forest detritus, nurtured corn, beans, squash, and sunflowers. Fort Ancient farmers chose these sites carefully. Girdling, fires, and floodplain farming enabled them to achieve an enormous amount with digging sticks and hoes. They had a more difficult time with clay soils and prairie grasses, with their dense root systems. Every five to ten years, Fort Ancient farmers started over again. They girdled the trees in small sections of forest and burned the land again, all in an effort to feed every individual nearly two pounds of corn per day throughout the year. Their abandoned forest-edge farms quickly succumbed to the wilderness. For at least the next decade, wild grapes, blackberries, and pawpaws proliferated on their old fields, luring deer, turkey, and raccoons.[32]

Fort Ancient villagers concentrated their settlements in ecotones—lands where multiple environments converged—because they are resource-rich environments suitable for both farming and hunting. With the Little Ice Age, subsistence practices became risky, and hunters and farmers left vast stretches of the Middle Ohio Valley unoccupied. With more mouths to feed, villagers competed for control of these prized areas of the Middle Ohio Valley.[33] Coalescence had the odd effect of increasing the distance between summer villages, as people sought out resource-rich environments on which to establish their villages.

Corn remained the leading crop during the Late Fort Ancient period. And with the Little Ice Age, Fort Ancient farmers turned to Eastern Eight Row corn. An early maturing corn, Eastern Eight Row lessened the anxiety that came with relying on agriculture in northern climates prone to early frosts. Archaeologists sometimes use Eastern Eight Row corn to distinguish Fort Ancient peoples from their neighbors. For example, Iroquoians seem to have preferred Northern Flint corn, while Mississippians preferred Midwestern Twelve Row. Eastern Eight Row, like its close relative, Northern Flint, was ideal in northern climates. This particular variety and method of planting corn—a domain dominated by women— became signatures of Fort Ancient culture.[34]

Fort Ancient peoples gathered nuts, fruits, and other wild plants, even as hunting and agriculture increased in importance. During the winter, hickory nuts often outranked corn in Fort Ancient cooking pots. Deer, bear, elk, and turkey were the primary sources of protein. Fish and birds, particularly ducks, never amounted to more than 10 percent of their overall diet. By 1500, the land that had supported the Fort Ancient peoples for centuries had changed dramatically. The fires they set carved farms out of the forest and attracted the animals they loved to hunt. But as they adjusted the land to their liking, the prairies of Illinois and Indiana expanded eastward, into Fort Ancient territory. Climate change furthered these changes and made Late Fort Ancient worlds basically different from those of their ancestors. These "changes in the land" enabled bison to move into the western edge of the Middle Ohio Valley. Bison took advantage of the new habitat and congregated around salt licks, where Fort Ancient hunters, accustomed to stalking deer, hunted them. By 1500, bison herds had moved to within thirty miles of Madisonville. Bison and deer were drawn to salt licks along the Ohio River. Fort Ancient hunters took advantage of the traffic and created salt pans and other drying devices that enabled them to produce salt for allies in need of the preservative.[35]

The North-South Trade Axis and the Cosmopolitan Nature of Fort Ancient Identities

From 1400 to 1539, the year in which Hernando de Soto began an expedition that forever altered the Southeast, the peoples of the Ohio Valley lived in villages ranging from 250 to 500 people. They clustered their villages within twenty kilometers of the Ohio River. The Ohio River has always been the backbone of the Midwest, joining populations along the Appalachian Mountains to peoples west of the Mississippi River. But in the centuries before contact, Fort Ancient villagers never fully enjoyed the strategic advantages offered by the Ohio. Just to their west, below the falls of the Ohio, Caborn-Welborn peoples blocked Fort Ancient traders seeking entrance into the Lower Ohio Valley. The farmers of the Middle Ohio Valley responded by developing trade networks to the north and south of them. Overland trails, rather than rivers, connected them to their allies. Two cultural groups in particular became the focus of trade, diplomacy, and the exchange of religious ideas and iconography. The Oneotas of the Northwest and the Coosa and Dallas-Phase peoples of the Southeast became their primary allies.[36]

Southeastern Mississippians, particularly those from the chiefdom at Coosa and the Koasati village of Coste in eastern Tennessee, had a profound influence on Late Fort Ancient villagers. Unlike Fort Ancient peoples, who preferred egalitarian power structures in which charisma and accomplishment determined a person's importance, Koasati peoples belonged to a simple chiefdom. Hereditary chiefs led their people from their most important town, on Bussell Island in the Little Tennessee River. Heads of families accepted the authority of chiefs. But Koasati influence did not extend far beyond Bussell Island. In the absence of tribute exacted from their less powerful neighbors, the Koasatis thrived through trade. Archaeologists associate Coste with Dallas Phase ceramics, and they have shown a close association between Coste and the larger Mississippian chiefdom of Coosa. Both Coste and Coosa carried on a long-standing trade relationship with Fort Ancient villagers. This accelerated as disease and violence became commonplace after de Soto's expeditionary force made its way through the Southeast. People from Coste migrated to what is now central Alabama, where they joined with the Alibamons, or Alabamas, who, like the Koasatis, spoke an Eastern Muskogean language.[37] Transformational migrations became a hallmark of colonial worlds, as precontact trade networks and related groups consolidated their towns, often at a distance from their homelands.

The Alabamas likely migrated from the paramount chiefdom of Tascalusa, along the border between western Alabama and eastern Mississippi. Their migration to the Coosa and Tallapoosa rivers was not complete until as late as 1720, after both the Alabamas and the Koasatis had been subject to intensive slaving, leaving both with no alternative other than to migrate and coalesce. The town they ultimately shared, Mucclassee, became one of fifty-five Creek towns in what is now Alabama and Georgia. For the Muskogee people, "the diverse experiences of individual towns and their people" reflected "a patchwork of peculiar connections."[38]

These unique histories of trade, slaving, and disease explain why colonial-era towns in Creek country often hosted migrants from outside of the Southeast.

Traders from Fort Ancient and Coosa exchanged goods and ideas long before the de Soto expedition. By 1540, both groups shared religious symbols, revealing the basic elements of a common cosmology. Artisans from Coosa traded for lightning whelk shells from the shallow bays of the Gulf Coast to communicate their religious values. They carved designs into the white interior of the shell and then used dyes to accentuate their artistry. Fort Ancient peoples sought out these "citico-style gorgets" from the people of Coosa. Their artisans incised these shells with coiled, snake-like beings and spiders. Their placement in burials suggests that these religious symbols communicated values associated with age and gender. Like the brass snakes found in the Ohio and Upper Mississippi valleys, the incised gorgets from eastern Tennessee might also reflect a common belief in a Great Horned Serpent, symbolically associated with success in hunting and in the Janus-like nature of good and evil. We may never know their precise meaning, but the distribution of this religious iconography shows that the western foothills of the Appalachians served as a corridor for trade between the peoples of Fort Ancient and the Mississippian chiefdom of Coosa.[39]

For millennia, men traded with distant people, and pipes often became the currency by which strangers became friends. In such village-based worlds, trade pipes became one of the means by which Native peoples "define[d] humanity beyond kinship." Fort Ancient villagers maintained long-standing relationships with proto-Siouan speakers associated with the Oneota Tradition of the Upper Mississippi Valley. Since at least A.D. 1000, Fort Ancient men were often buried with Oneota pipes at sites such as Madisonville. Disk pipes made of limestone, red pipestone, and, eventually, catlinite reflect amicable ties between populations separated by hundreds of miles and strong linguistic differences. Archaeologists uncovered these pipes in male burials, revealing that trade pipes became one of the ultimate measures of male achievement: the ability to trade and create alliances at long distances from home.[40]

Oneota traders believed that pipes and pipe smoking were essential to diplomacy. Over the long history of exchange, their pipes became spiritual objects, an essential part of Fort Ancient cosmology. Oneota traders brought disk pipes made from Minnesota catlinite to Fort Ancient villagers. Their wide, oval bowls and long stems were sometimes incised with thunder symbols and human figures. The presence of these disk pipes

Coosa artisans designed marine shells from the Gulf Coast with religious iconography that became an important part of Fort Ancient religious traditions. Shell maskette, Point Pleasant, West Virginia, courtesy of New York State Office of Recreation, Parks, and Historic Places.

is thought to reflect the spread of the Calumet Ceremony, revealing that Oneota traders shared their rituals with villagers from the Middle Ohio Valley. The Calumet Ceremony is the greatest example of such cross-cultural sharing. Dating to the thirteenth century, Oneota pipes and pipe ceremonies became essential to the creation of fictive kin ties between unrelated peoples. Fort Ancient villagers likely received the ritual from the Ioways or Ho-Chunks, as the Calumet Ceremony steadily diffused from west to east, into the Eastern Woodlands.[41]

Late seventeenth-century accounts of the Calumet Ceremony suggest how Native peoples used such rituals to facilitate long-distance travel and trade. When he lived among the Miamis and Mascoutins, French explorer Nicolas Perrot encountered an old man who compelled him to participate in a Calumet Ceremony before entering his village. Carrying "a calumet of red stone with a long stick at the end," the old man presented the pipe to the east and to the west and then to the sun. Perrot was impressed by the pipe, which was covered with "the heads of birds, flame-colored and had in the middle [of the pipe] a bunch of feathers colored a bright red, which resembled a great fan." Miami and Mascoutin men helped the old man conduct the ceremony. Perrot noticed that he prayed "toward the sun" for a long time, "all to assure the French man of the joy which all in the village felt at his arrival."[42]

Perrot might have been right; the old man might have felt joy at his arrival. But a closer analysis of the Calumet Ceremony shows that participants in the ritual often narrowly avoided violent conflict. Pierre Deliette, a French commander who traveled among the Illinois in the 1690s, recalled that when they approached an unrelated village the Illinois would "go in search of the man or of his wives to whom they sing the calumet." Once found, the man and his wives climb a scaffold, one commonly associated with the platform burials of the Sioux, and "sing all day long." "During all this time," Deliette wrote, "everybody comes to knock at a post" of the scaffold "to recite his exploits." After Illinois warriors have described their accomplishments in war to the leader they intend to adopt, an Illinois man "holds the calumet, which he shakes continually before the one to whom it is given." In the Illinois version of the ceremony, even close allies are made aware of the possibility of war, showing that ritually sanctified alliances can sometimes break down, leading to certain peril for fictive kinsmen. As the ultimate symbol of peace and alliance, the Calumet Ceremony made it possible for village dwellers to manage the differences between them. However, one French observer asserted that the ritual of placing chiefs on scaffolds and recalling tales of war was designed "to call the souls of those against whom war is to be waged, and by this means to kill their enemies without fail."[43] A thin line separated friends from enemies in the Eastern Woodlands. Catlinite disk pipes from Oneota traders offered a way for village dwellers to manage intraregional diversity. Yet these pipe ceremonies also obligated these ritually sanctioned allies to use violence against shared enemies.

While trade pipes and the Calumet Ceremony reveal the diplomatic initiatives of unrelated men, Fort Ancient women left behind a remarkably rich ceramic record of long-distance exchange and coalescence. Their cooking pots and the food that went into them tell multiethnic stories. How and what we eat has always reflected something of our individual and collective identities. Much of the archaeological record, including awls, beamers, digging sticks, and pottery, reflects the labor as well as the cultural imagination of the women who used them. Fort Ancient potters shared a preference for shell-tempering their pottery. Women boiled mussel shells—one of hundreds of species along the Middle Ohio River Valley—until they expanded and cracked. Once cooled, the cracked shells were mixed with local clays that helped to create cooking pots with strong, durable walls.[44] Freshwater mussels thus became an essential ingredient

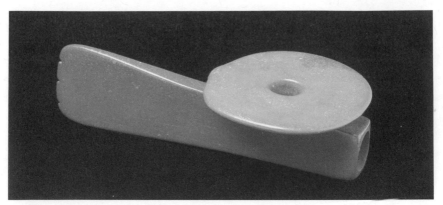

*This disk pipe came from Oneotu peoples of the Upper
Midwest and was used in the Calumet Ceremonies that were essential to intertribal
diplomacy before and after contact with colonizers. Disk pipe, Minnesota Catlinite,
courtesy of President and Fellows of Harvard College, Peabody Museum of
Archaeology and Ethnology, number 97–30–10/682.*

in the ceramic cookware used for everything from hauling water to making hominy.

Native artisans, primarily women, produced an extraordinary variety of pottery adorned with the cosmological stories of the people. Their artistry was designed to explain "the larger reality in which they understood themselves to be participants." From 1400 to 1680, potters often added animal effigies to the rims of cooking pots. Frogs and other amphibians adorned many vessels. Native peoples associated these animals with the Beneath World, the watery base that supports the Middle World occupied by humanity. Beings of extraordinary power, from the Great Horned Serpent, to animals that successfully travel through both water and land, such as snakes and frogs, are features of their pottery. On a symbolic level, cooking pots contained "the waters of the Beneath World." These effigies clearly reflect a common stock of ideas regarding agriculture and fertility, linking women from Fort Ancient societies to their Mississippian counterparts to the south. Over time Fort Ancient potters incorporated some of these motifs, along with incised guilloche designs below the rims of their jars. Strap handles evolved from two to four over time, perhaps making their pottery better suited for mobility.[45]

"An overarching religious system" enabled Eastern Woodland Indians to engage in a shared conversation. Fundamental to that system was the belief that the natural world and the cosmos were directly analogous. Among the Ojibwes, Gitchi-manitou, or master of the sky, always warred

Shawnee migrants carried late Fort Ancient vessels such as this with them across the eastern half of North America. They adjusted their styles across time and space. However, archaeologists continue to recognize Fort Ancient characteristics in these new ceramic forms. Madisonville cordmarked jar, Petersburg, Kentucky, courtesy of Kentucky Archaeological Survey.

against Matchi-manitou, or the master of the underworld. Their conflict manifested itself in violent storms, powerful currents, and other manifestations of their perpetual conflict. Survival in such a multilayered cosmos, a place in which chaos can occur at any moment, required discovering power, or *pawaka*. Peace depended on knowing who controls power and how one might gain access to it. Because power can sometimes be malevolent and destructive, Native people had to learn how to avoid being crushed by the beings and forces that journeyed through the cosmos searching for unsuspecting victims. In this shared belief system, guile was an essential characteristic.[46]

Pottery, shell gorgets, and rolled copper oriented the wearer to the location of power throughout the cosmos. Far more than being just material possessions or simple adornments, these objects helped Native peoples understand, locate, and sometimes utilize power as they journeyed from birth to death. Belief in this multilayered cosmos was widely shared. However, its religious symbols and objects were not. "Sacred knowledge" and the objects associated with it belonged "to those who procure[d] unchallengeable rights to it." So, for example, some scholars have argued that the designs of citico-style gorgets are so similar that most of them must have been manufactured in a single workshop. Prior to the arrival of Europeans, those in possession of sacred knowledge moved across the continent, spreading an "aesthetic system" that enabled intensely local people to engage in a multifaceted exchange. Trade enabled Fort Ancient peoples to understand their neighbors, friend and foe alike. A broad exchange of ideas, values, and artistic forms moved back and forth along the north-south trade axis. They were parochial cosmopolitans who remained firmly attached to their villages. At the same time, Fort Ancient villagers encountered an enormously diverse range of people—their things as well as their beliefs—across the eastern half of North America.[47]

Trade with the Iroquois

Fort Ancient villagers had deep and abiding connections to peoples living to the north and south of them. In contrast, the Haudenosaunee, or Iroquois, began trading with the "first farmers of the middle Ohio Valley" relatively late, during the middle of the sixteenth century. Iroquoian speakers, including the Haudenosaunee, the Neutrals, and the Eries, began trading with Fort Ancient villagers, particularly in villages between what is now West Virginia and central Ohio. Fort Ancient villagers had always been ethnically diverse and regionally varied, and many different ethnic groups occupied the Middle Ohio Valley. However, these distinctions accelerated between 1400 and 1650, as their villages became larger and more distinctive.[48] To the east, between the confluence of the Little Kanawha and Ohio rivers, eastern Siouans predominated. There, along the foothills of the Appalachian Mountains, a host of Algonquians, Siouans, and Iroquoian speakers converged. Iroquoian traders followed the western branches of the Potomac into the interior of the continent. By the late sixteenth century, these Massawomeck and Susquehannock traders were the first to bring European trade goods to the peoples of Fort Ancient. The abundance of deer, bison, and small game animals brought these middlemen into the Ohio Valley. Fort Ancient villagers coveted fragile blue glass beads from Dutch and English traders from the mid-Atlantic, and archaeologists have traced their spread from Iroquoia to the

Ohio Valley.[49] But they did not abandon traditional ritual objects overnight. Rattlesnake gorgets and other marine-shell ornaments from the Southeast remained important.

Trade goods, smoking pipes, and other signs of cross-cultural collaboration are widespread at Fort Ancient sites. Iroquoian speakers manufactured their pipes from clay, creating small, hand-held pipes with sharp, 90- to 135-degree angled bowls. Iroquois traders used pipes to relax and to stave off hunger on their long-distance journeys. They were practical tools for men on the move. Commonly associated with the Haudenosaunee, as well as with their Iroquoian-speaking neighbors, the Neutrals and the Eries, the widespread presence of Iroquoian pipes as far west as Madisonville suggests that trade amounted to much more than the simple exchange of goods. Archaeologists have unearthed trade pipes in trash heaps or randomly distributed in homesites. As the flotsam of travelers, these pipes were often strewn about precontact and protohistoric Fort Ancient villages. Trade delegations often stayed in Fort Ancient villages for months at a time. Close bonds between widely separated villages must have resulted from such long-term interaction. Traders would have been woven into the fabric of everyday life along the Ohio Valley. Basic differences between the treatment and use of Oneota and Iroquoian trade pipes might also stem from the long-standing relationship between the peoples of the Upper Mississippi Valley and the peoples of the Middle Ohio Valley. Ties between the Iroquoians and the Fort Ancient Tradition were much shorter, perhaps revealing that a common understanding of religious symbols had yet to be established before colonial forces upset the growing understanding between them.[50]

While trade pipes and other evidence associated with men links Madisonville to sites to the south and west, ceramic evidence associated with women ties Madisonville most strongly to northern Ohio, particularly to the Indian Hills, Sandusky, and Whittlesey traditions. Ceramic evidence suggests that people from northern Ohio intermarried with Fort Ancient farmers along the confluence of the Little Miami and Ohio rivers.[51] Historically known tribes that have been associated with these traditions include Algonquians such as the Illinois, Miamis, Mascoutins, Potawatomis, and Kickapoos, as well as Iroquoian speakers such as the Eries and the Neutrals.

Among the Fort Ancient, marriage stitched together disparate peoples. New ceramic styles, burial practices, and foodways probably resulted from marriages between men and women from different ethnic groups and language families. Fort Ancient society was relatively peaceful, lacking signs of a sudden transition brought on by outside invaders. Rather, change came about as young people sought socially acceptable marriage partners, a consequence of clan exogamy. Intermarriage and alliance did not yield ever-expanding fields of interethnic concord. The peoples of Fort Ancient did not overcome the play of village loyalty, linguistic difference, and regionalism. Rather, small-scale meritocracies, built on town councils, reinforced Fort Ancient peoples' commitment to their villages.

Haudenosaunee trade pipes and blue glass beads became an important part of Fort Ancient life. But Iroquoians to the southwest of them, in northeastern Ohio, established stronger relations with Fort Ancient villagers. Multiethnic unions between these groups had become common before 1654 and 1656, when the Iroquois attacked these Neutral and Erie villagers. Those Erie and Neutrals who survived the Iroquois wars are thought to have briefly coalesced with Fort Ancient villagers before moving farther to the south, first to the falls of the James River, where they slaved on behalf of the Virginians, and then onto the fall line of the Savannah River, where they slaved for the Charles Town traders. These heavily armed survivors of the Iroquois wars traded Indian captives for English guns in order to survive. As foreigners to the Southeast, the violence necessary for survival further estranged them from their neighbors. Between 1669 and 1672, when the Iroquois attacked villagers in the Middle Ohio Valley, Shawnees began appearing at the fall line of the Savannah River, where they temporarily renewed ties with these descendants of the Whittlesey Tradition.[52]

Villages stretching from the Upper Mississippi Valley to the Southeast eventually drew whole populations out of the Middle Ohio Valley. When Fort Ancient villagers first encountered European material culture, sometime between 1539 and 1543, these trade goods became the latest installment in a long-standing trade network. Archaeologists have unearthed a Clarksdale bell from the de Soto expedition that had been traded to the Fort Ancient at Madisonville. It was likely traded from the Coosa chiefdom of eastern Tennessee. Fort Ancient peoples initially imbued European trade goods with enormous spiritual power. Their traders carried European copper, glass beads, bells, and the occasional steel dagger into Fort Ancient settlements nearly two centuries before Europeans became familiar with their homeland. Before they first encountered Europeans, villagers tore old cooking pots apart and then rolled the various pieces into figurines of serpents and other supernatural beings. They transformed utilitarian items into objects of great spiritual, ornamental, and decorative power. Native artisans made the strange familiar by reconfiguring European objects into traditional designs. Down-the-line trading increased over time, but European trade goods remained scarce until Fort Ancient peoples and Europeans engaged in direct trade.[53]

Once made familiar, European trade goods were often buried with highly esteemed people or their children. Survivors placed reworked European trade goods, everything from blue glass beads to serpent pendants made from rolled copper, in the graves of infants and small children. Archaeologists wonder why small children were sometimes buried with the highest percentage of European and indigenous trade goods, while adolescents were the least likely to be buried with items of spiritual power.[54] It could be that the general absence of trade goods associated with adolescent burials reflects the values of the Fort Ancient world. This was a meritocratic society. It is likely that adolescents and teenagers had not earned the respect that came with exploits in hunting, war, and, for women, the planting of crops and the raising of children.[55]

Rituals associated with death also re-quickened Fort Ancient ties between kin. In a world in which only 1 percent of the population lived beyond their fiftieth birthday, death became an ever-present means by which Fort Ancient society came together. At one Fort Ancient village, 20 percent of children died by their fourth birthday. The pain of death must have been especially acute in such a village-based world, where every individual was known intimately. The dead were often buried within the homes in which they were raised. Many of the dead were buried, and later exhumed and reburied, in a multistep mortuary program. Some of these burials were in their homes, while others were inside the village itself.[56]

Protohistoric Fort Ancient Worlds on the Eve of Contact

Stretching from the falls of the Ohio, at modern Louisville, Kentucky, to the western edge of the Appalachian Mountains in south-central West Virginia, the Fort Ancient Tradition encompassed a wide cross-section of humanity. Siouan speakers such as the Quapaws, the Kansas, and the Poncas, as well as the Shawnees and the Miamis, two Central Algonquian tribes, are thought to have been a part of the Fort Ancient Tradition. There are also linguistic outliers, including the linguistically unidentifiable Mosopeleas. Some archaeologists have even suggested that the Yuchis, a people typically associated with the Southeast, migrated out of the Fort Ancient Tradition. The Ohio Valley, then, was both linguistically and culturally diverse.[57]

Eastern Fort Ancient peoples had strong ties to Dhegiha Siouans, including the Kansas, Omahas, and Poncas, and Siouans of present-day

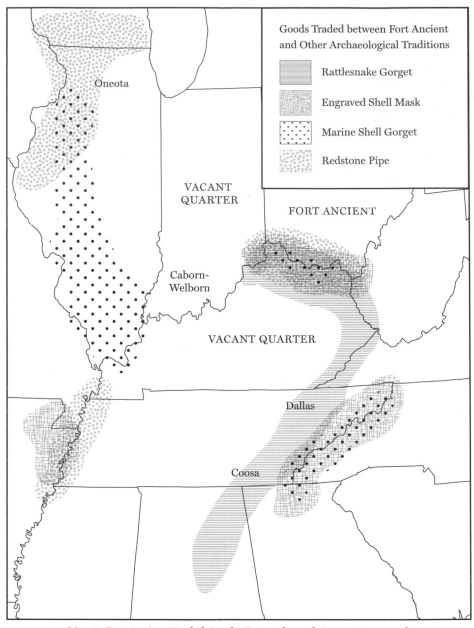

Map 2. *Fort Ancient Traded Goods. Footpaths and river systems made
the Middle Ohio Valley a center for trade from the Upper Midwest to the Southeast.
Map by Alex Gau.*

Virginia such as the Tutelo, Saponi, and Monacans. Both the Dhegiha Siouans and the Central Algonquians recall oral histories tracing the migration of Siouan speakers through the Ohio River Valley. For example, the Miami name for the Ohio River is *Kanseensa*, or Kansa River. Corn agriculture, circular villages, and shell-tempered pottery are hallmarks of the eastern end of the Fort Ancient world. But unlike the Fort Ancient Tradition at Madisonville, these villages maintained even stronger ties to the Southeast, especially to Dallas-Phase and Coosa peoples.[58]

On the eve of colonialism, these villagers lived in an increasingly integrated world. They tied themselves to distant allies, and regional "style zones" and traditions grew out of these relationships. Fort Ancient peoples saw themselves as members of autonomous villages whose allies and trade networks enabled them to survive as small-scale polities. For at least 650 years, they had avoided large-scale warfare, migration, and dislocation. Their cultures emerged slowly from the region's Late Woodland populations. Because cultural change occurred as the result of a long cross-cultural conversation, the subtle nuances separating one culture from another within the Fort Ancient region are sometimes hard to detect.[59]

By 1650, it is likely that some Fort Ancient people were trading directly with Europeans. Around this time, villagers began draining European goods of spiritual power. By 1669, when the first clear evidence of European contact with Fort Ancient villagers took place, villagers adopted a more practical and utilitarian perspective on items of European origin. Between 1650 and 1680, trade goods from Europe began appearing in trash pits rather than in the burials of esteemed people. Such irreverence would have been unthinkable in 1550. Roughly one hundred years after the beginning of down-the-line trading, it became less common for Fort Ancient villagers to associate religious values with European trade goods. From kettles and knives to guns, many of these items had become mainstays of daily life. By 1650, such trade goods became secular necessities, essential tools necessary for survival in an increasingly dangerous world.[60]

Protohistoric and early-contact sites such as the Zimmerman site, also known as the Grand Village of the Kaskaskias, along the Upper Illinois River, and Riverfront Village, near modern Augusta, Georgia, offer the best archaeological means of linking Shawnee migrants to the Fort Ancient Tradition. However, changes wrought by disease, trade, and warfare have confused the archaeological record of these societies and clouded the link between precontact and historic populations. This is especially true of the upper country.[61] At the Grand Village of the Kaskaskias, Siouan speakers associated with the Oneota Tradition coexisted with Central

Algonquians, including proto-Illinois peoples. Like the Middle Ohio River Valley, the Upper Illinois River Valley became a cultural crossroads, a meeting place for Central Algonquians and Siouans struggling with the changes wrought by colonialism. Until recently, archaeologists were fairly certain that Late Fort Ancient peoples had lived and perhaps even coalesced with the residents of the Upper Illinois River Valley at some point in the protohistoric period. In fact, the founding dean of Fort Ancient studies, James B. Griffin, once suggested that "Fort Ancient type names" might be applied to at least some of the pottery styles found along the Upper Illinois River.[62] European trade goods, including small blue glass beads, tomahawks, and compasses, were found among the pottery in question, revealing "the cosmopolitan nature of early Indian settlements and the fluid nature of ethnic aggregates" in the region. Today, archaeologists reject the notion that Fort Ancient and proto-Illinois peoples were virtually synonymous.[63] There are enough differences between ceramics on the Upper Illinois River and those found at Late Fort Ancient sites in Ohio and Kentucky to suggest that they were essentially distinct.

Just as the backhoe operator destroyed the Petersburg cite, so too did the U.S. Army Corps of Engineers destroy much of the Zimmerman site when between 1926 and 1933 it installed a lock and dam at Starved Rock, on the Upper Illinois River. In 1684, a French census described how 200 Shawnee warriors and another 1,000 of their kin settled just below where the lock and dam now straddles the river. Installation of a lock and dam just above these village sites subsequently flooded the river's floodplain, submerging these contact-era villages.[64] At first glance, this reversal seems to dash any hope of linking the modern Shawnees to both the Fort Ancient Tradition and historic sites such as the Grand Village of the Kaskaskias. The muddy waters consumed the buried remains of the 1684 Shawnee village, along with the villages of thousands of other Native people who had gathered there for mutual defense. All that remained of these coalescent villages was claimed by the surging waters of the Illinois River.[65]

Other sites of first encounter between Shawnees and Europeans, such as Savannah Town on the Middle Savannah River, provide some material evidence that illustrates the intersection of migration and social change on early-historic Native peoples. Archaeologist Tom Whitley has excavated part of Savannah Town on the Middle Savannah River. Whitley found shell-tempered ceramics that "look very similar to the descriptions [of Fort Ancient ceramics] found at Madisonville." Like the Zimmerman site, the Riverfront Village site on the Savannah River contains European trade goods, including Spanish coarse earthenware and English trade beads.

Nonlocal indigenous trade goods, including a catlinite bead deriving from pipestone quarried in either southeastern Ohio or southern Minnesota, were found in one of the burials at Riverfront Village. Dating to the period 1670 to 1730, these nonlocal items were owned by migratory newcomers who lived on the fault line between Spanish and English colonizers. Their ceramics, like their trade goods, reflect nonlocal origins. However, while their ceramics closely resemble Fort Ancient styles, the ceramics at Riverfront Village are distinctive.

Subtle differences between Fort Ancient pottery at sites such as Petersburg and Riverfront Village likely reflect the blending of identities that invariably results from migration. As colonial forces redrew maps of eastern North America, Fort Ancient peoples adapted by moving toward precontact allies, now located at great distances from their ancient homelands. It is clear that migrants to the Middle Savannah River were ethnic outliers. The proportion of Fort Ancient–style pottery increases after 1680, the time period in which Shawnees arrived at, and briefly dominated, the Middle Savannah River. But like the Zimmerman site on the Upper Illinois River, the Riverfront Village site was multiethnic and occupied by transient townspeople growing accustomed to a world on the move. Nevertheless, the location, the ceramic forms, the radiocarbon dates, and the surviving written record converge, revealing strong linkages between the Middle Ohio Valley and the Middle Savannah River.[66]

Across the Eastern Woodlands, from the southern shores of Lake Erie to the chiefdoms of the Middle Tennessee River, precontact trade networks facilitated the migration and adaptation of Native peoples in the colonial era. Ceramic styles, agricultural practices, and religious rituals changed as previously autonomous villages joined together. Styles and belief systems, like identities, drifted as people adapted to new circumstances. Some Fort Ancient peoples became Shawnees. But even as they adopted new traits, protohistoric and colonial-era groups continued to distinguish themselves from their neighbors. The people who lived at the Creek town of Mucclassee knew that their ancestors were either Koasati or Tascalusa, just as Shawnee migrants brought with them beliefs and practices associated with the Ohio Valley. Newcomers incorporated cultural elements from their new neighbors, but they did not abandon or forget who they were, as historians suggest when they employ the "new world" thesis. Shawnee migrants traveled far and wide, from the Kaskaskia to the Savannah River. The rich archaeological record of these past worlds tells us that the unique, village-based identities of the Fort Ancient Tradition persevered well into the "historic" period.

For the late prehistoric residents of the Fort Ancient Tradition, "tribe," "confederacy," and "nation" mischaracterize the parochial yet cosmopolitan nature of identity in the Middle Ohio Valley. As this description of Late Fort Ancient life makes clear, villages are the starting point for any assessment of both Fort Ancient and Shawnee identities. This basic continuity between prehistoric and historic peoples offers the best hope of understanding the moods and motivations of the people descended from the Fort Ancient Tradition. Marriage ties, trade networks, and shared religious and economic practices became the means by which Fort Ancient villagers survived, and thrived, as members of egalitarian villages. Tribal or national explanations of behavior often lead to big-picture renderings of American Indian identities. But perhaps it is better to investigate the village-level ties that bound members of distinct communities and language families to one another.

chapter 3

Nitarikyk's Slave

A FORT ANCIENT ODYSSEY

It was the winter of 1669. François Dollier de Casson, a French priest and member of the Sulpician order, spent the winter with an Indian "slave" and his captor, a Nipissing Anishnaabeg chief named Nitarikyk. Between daily mass, the baptism of dying infants, and hours of studying the An-ishinaabe language, part of the Central Algonquian language family, Dollier got to know Nitarikyk's slave. The captive and his captors spoke variants of Central Algonquian, and this enabled all involved to struggle through a conversation. Dollier learned that the slave had been a gift of the Nipissings' Odawa relatives to the west. As intermediaries in the fur trade, the Anishnaabeg, or Ojibwes, occupied villages from Lake Superior to the St. Lawrence River, and they funneled furs, guns, kettles, knives, and peo-ple from these intermarried villages to the capital of the French empire at Montreal. The Nipissings controlled one of the last stops on this vast pipeline, between Lake Nipissing and the St. Lawrence River. Nitarikyk's slave found himself more than 1,000 miles from his original homeland, which the French identified as "a great river . . . called, in the language of the Iroquois, Ohio," as a result of the Anishnaabeg's long-distance trade networks.[1]

Dollier's curiosity about the Ohio River gave Nitarikyk's slave hope that he might be able to parlay his knowledge of the region into an opportu-nity to leave the frozen woods of the Canadian North. Both Nitarikyk and his bondsman must have been aware of French desires. Indeed, Nitarikyk probably traded for the captive, knowing that slaves from the upper coun-try were as highly valued as beaver pelts. Nitarikyk might have granted this particular slave a great deal of freedom because he recognized the French desire for knowledge about the interior of the continent. He sent his slave "to Montreal on some errand," where, coincidentally or not, he managed to initiate a conversation with the head of the Sulpician order,

Gabriel, Abbé de Queylus. Seizing his opportunity for freedom, the slave offered a vivid "description of the route to his country." He convinced the French that he "could easily conduct any persons that should wish to go there with him." In a masterstroke of diplomacy, he bound his own desire for freedom to the French obsession with discovery. The Abbé came to believe that "God was presenting an excellent opportunity by means of this slave." Incredibly, the Sulpicians thought that they had manipulated the slave. A Sulpician chronicler, René de Bréhant de Galinée, wrote that they "managed so well with the man that he extracted a promise from him to conduct him to his own country."[2] The slave restored himself to freedom, and to his community of birth, by tying his destiny to the interests of the French empire. Knowledge of the continent thus became the means by which one man, perhaps a Shawnee, achieved liberation.

Sadly, Nitarikyk's slave returned to an empty land. From 1650 to the 1720s, the Middle Ohio Valley was largely destitute of people.[3] Archaeologists and historians alike have struggled to link Fort Ancient villagers to historic tribes such as the Shawnees because of this long gap in human settlement. Push and pull factors, from disease and warfare to trade, caused Fort Ancient peoples to abandon their homeland. They became parochial cosmopolitans because they chose to maintain their village-based loyalties even as they traveled toward old allies and new opportunities. Each village's unique history of trade, intermarriage, and diplomacy shaped its travels. Between 1630 and 1680—nearly two generations—Fort Ancient peoples abandoned villages that had been inhabited for more than twenty generations. They suddenly shifted from a deep attachment to place to a series of epic migrations. Their flight from the Middle Ohio Valley became the means by which villagers adapted to the seismic consequences of colonialism. For these reasons, we must reach back, into the archaeological record, if we wish to reclaim the story of Nitarikyk's slave and the people he so desperately hoped to see again.

Since Cadwallader Colden's *History of the Five Indian Nations* (1747), historians have assumed that the Iroquois bear primary responsibility for the depopulation of the Middle Ohio Valley. Following Colden, leading historians have asserted that the "huge area between the Ohio River and the northern shore of the Great Lakes [was] emptied of inhabitants by the Iroquois." But, in reality, Iroquois warriors were just one of several different invaders who assaulted the villagers of the Middle Ohio Valley. Virginia traders encouraged poorly known slavers such as the Occaneechees and the "Tomahitans" to collaborate with them during the second half of the seventeenth century. These tribes used the New River and the Kanawha River to reach the Middle Ohio Valley, where they wreaked havoc on people who did not yet possess guns. At roughly the same time, between 1669 and 1672, the main thrust of the Iroquois invasion occurred. Iroquois "mourning wars," while inherently different in motivation, had the same effect as these slaving expeditions. In both cases, Native peoples who worked with Europeans invaded the homelands of people who had not yet traded directly with colonizers. Fort Ancient villagers learned that survival depended on the ownership of guns, and by the middle of the seventeenth century, many Shawnees traveled in search of colonial suppliers. Some Fort Ancient peoples left as refugees, in response to Iroquois attacks. But still more left to trade directly with Europeans. English-allied slavers and Iroquois warriors appear relatively late in the game, at a time when most of the people had already abandoned the Ohio country. For these reasons, we must adopt a more nuanced view of the early colonial period and the Iroquois role in destabilizing the eastern half of North America. In the late seventeenth century, Algonquians did not doubt the formidable power of the Iroquois Confederacy. However, they also faced grave trade imbalances, the proliferation of the Indian slave trade, and devastating epidemics.[4]

Native peoples, from the Nipissings along the St. Lawrence, to the Occaneechees of the James River, in Virginia, carried disease, guns, and slavery deep into the Ohio country. The people who nurtured Nitarikyk's slave when he was a child confronted new people, new things, and new diseases originating from the outposts of European colonization along the Atlantic Coast. Ohio Valley villagers became wedded to Europeans in the space of two generations. Between 1630 and 1680, out-migration from the Middle Ohio Valley transformed the Fort Ancient Tradition. The Iroquois certainly contributed to this decision to leave. However, the Iroquois were far from emperors. The peoples of Fort Ancient chose to move for complex reasons, not simply in response to Iroquois mourning wars. For some, movement became an opportunity, as direct trade with colonizers, or with ancient trading partners, offered a reprieve from disease and enslavement. But in all cases, Native migrants carried with them a historical consciousness of their homeland and how it had shaped their sense of themselves as a people.

Disease and Out-Migration from the Middle Ohio Valley

Virgin-soil epidemics, from smallpox to influenza, reached the Middle Ohio Valley just as down-the-line trading came to a close. In 1616, the first recorded smallpox epidemic struck the Narragansetts, the Massachusetts, and the Wampanoags of New England. But over the next twenty years, smallpox reappeared fairly regularly, wiping out entire communities, in months, if not in weeks. Both Europeans and American Indians struggled to make sense of the destruction. For English Puritans, the disease became a symbol of both God's favor and the superiority of the English over the first Americans. The Puritan Edward Winslow explained that "the God of the English had it [smallpox] in store, and could send it at his pleasure to the destruction of his and our enemies." In contrast, the Narragansett associated epidemics with earthquakes and unhealthy air that invariably resulted from the shaking of the earth's core. But as we now know, neither God nor unhealthy "miasmas" caused the disease to spread. In fact, smallpox began devastating American Indians when large numbers of European children began arriving along the Atlantic Coast, from Massachusetts Bay to Virginia. For this reason, scholars suggest that by 1633 smallpox had gathered enough force to reach the Ohio Valley.[5]

"Crowd infections" such as smallpox depend on large numbers of sickened individuals to survive. Smallpox is the deadliest of them all because of its long life. A person sick with smallpox can communicate the disease for upward of a month, and the painful scabs of the pox, once they have fallen off the body, can carry the virus toward unsuspecting victims through bedding, clothing, or other personal items of the dead and dying. It is a tenacious and patient killer, ideally suited for diffusing across European and Indian trade networks.[6]

Smallpox moved between infected individuals in Europe, Asia, and Africa for thousands of years. It is a human-to-human infection, but one that adapted to humans only after living with — and killing — domesticated animals. Diseases proliferated in Europe, Africa, and Asia because the most important domesticated animals in the world, fully thirteen of fourteen, were bred into existence in the Old World. For at least 4,000 years, smallpox survived in densely settled agricultural communities, striking humans who lived in close proximity to their livestock.[7] Those who survived smallpox and other diseases passed their genomes on to their children, who were better able to avoid death when epidemics struck. Across generations, children still became sick, and often scarred, by these diseases. But most children inherited a degree of immunity and survived to adulthood. In contrast, American Indians had not yet encountered these diseases. And so, when sick European children arrived on "virgin soil" with these crowd infections, Native peoples' suffering began. While adults carried the disease, they were incapable of transmitting it to others. The initial *entradas* of Spanish colonizers such as Hernando de Soto and Cabeza de Vaca brought untold devastation, including forced rape, slavery, syphilis, and starvation. But smallpox would not appear in the eastern half of North America until the early seventeenth century, when English family migrations began in earnest.

In the Southeast, the so-called Great Smallpox Epidemic dates to 1696, nearly three decades after the founding of Charles Town. Both the 1616 and 1696 epidemics coincided with the arrival of children with active smallpox infections. European children arrived in large enough numbers to enable the disease to survive and to travel toward Native communities where both the young and the old would become sick and die. Among American Indians, smallpox was no respecter of persons. Young and old, men and women, able-bodied and elderly, succumbed to the disease. And as with all illnesses, smallpox used colonialism to its advantage. Indian people threatened with slavery, warfare, and European land hunger feared planting corn in remote forested clearings. Hunters often stayed home, knowing that their enemies might take advantage of their absence. Hunger and starvation became commonplace, as slaving parties and Old World diseases traveled through the land. Many Native communities dealt with the threat of enslavement by building defensive palisades around their villages. Besieged villagers, weakened by hunger, then became especially prone to virulent epidemics. Smallpox, like measles, influenza, and cholera, spreads by moving between individuals living in densely populated areas.[8]

Given what we know about the timing of the first epidemics and the "disease ecology" of Old World diseases, it is almost certain that Fort Ancient populations collapsed before the arrival of Europeans in the Middle Ohio Valley. Smallpox might have been North America's most notorious killer, as there were at least eight recorded disease outbreaks in the seventeenth-century Northeast. But influenza, measles, and whooping cough had the power to kill large numbers of Native people well before smallpox brought its own peculiar brand of devastation to Indian country. Between 1633 and 1676, eight separate epidemics "halved the population of the Five Nations, to approximately ten thousand" people. Fort Ancient archaeologists have only identified four villages that postdate 1669, the year in which the Iroquois raids began. Native traders may have unwittingly carried smallpox from the eastern seaboard to the Ohio Valley, via the Ohio River, "one of the great conduits of human civilization in North America."[9]

Village-specific migration out of the Middle Ohio Valley largely predated the Iroquois wars. Archaeologists have documented twenty-three different sites in Ohio, West Virginia, and Kentucky that were abandoned between 1633 and 1680. The end came quickly for the majority of these sites. Sometime between 1633 and 1650, Indian peoples said goodbye to their summer villages and winter hunting camps, places that had defined village life for centuries. Between 1669 and 1674, only four of these twenty-three sites remained, and none would survive into the 1680s. In 1669, when the Iroquois invasion of the Middle Ohio Valley began, their warriors entered a widowed land. American Indians would not return to the Middle Ohio Valley for another fifty years. By 1680, centuries of commitment to the Ohio Valley came to a close.[10]

Protohistoric population collapse along the Middle Ohio Valley eased the path for Iroquois invaders. Without epidemics and mass death, Iroquois war parties would have encountered populated villages within easy reach of their allies. Even well-armed expeditions with 500 or more Iroquois warriors would have faced powerful foes with intimate knowledge of the land and centuries of experience defending their territory. Ohio Valley groups who survived faced a grim choice: to remain where so many had died and to face predatory raids from a host of well-armed enemies, or to abandon their villages in search of old allies with access to new sources of trade. For all who once claimed the Middle Ohio Valley as their own, migration became the only viable path toward long-term survival.[11]

After reading Jesuit accounts of Iroquois mourning wars, some archaeologists expected to find scenes of brutality written into the land — and the bodies of Fort Ancient peoples. Some protohistoric Fort Ancient villages were located on defensible bluffs ringed by defensive palisades. Yet Fort Ancient palisades are not very impressive. They fall far short of the stockade walls common among the Iroquois during the same time period, and this suggests that Fort Ancient villagers did not settle into the reality of endemic warfare. The palisades they built might have slowed an enemy assault, but they certainly were not impenetrable. In villages of between 250 and 500 persons, everyone must have sacrificed a great deal to defend the village. But conflict-related trauma appears in less than 10 percent of protohistoric Fort Ancient burials. So, at the precise moment when historians suggest that Iroquois war parties single-handedly depopulated the Ohio Valley, evidence of major warfare is hardly in evidence. Late Fort Ancient sites on the eastern periphery of this world, particularly in West Virginia, seem to have been designed for defensive purposes. However, on the eve of colonization, most Fort Ancient villages did not reflect increasing militarization and seem to have avoided the kind of cataclysmic violence that was so common in the early colonial period.[12]

By the 1660s, we should expect to find material evidence of the Iroquois wars, signs of violent death, at sites across the Middle Ohio Valley. But widespread warfare is not evident in the archaeological record. Unlike smallpox, which leaves no trace of its impact on skeletal remains, violence can endure on the bodies of its victims. When compared to archaeological sites such as Cahokia and Norris Farm in Illinois and the Gnagey site in the Allegheny Mountains of Pennsylvania, most protohistoric Fort Ancient villages seem relatively peaceful. At the Norris Farm archaeological site and the Gnagey site, archaeologists have found evidence of scalping and beheading and other forms of violent trauma. Total warfare in which men, women, and children were killed and cannibalized is clearly evident. At Norris Farm, archaeologists have found war-related trauma in 34 percent of the burials. Crippling war-related injuries are pervasive. These protohistoric sites reveal signs of endemic violence. In contrast, less than 10 percent of protohistoric Fort Ancient burials contain evidence of violent trauma.[13] The threat of violence may have prompted many Middle Ohio Valley villagers to move away. It is also true that signs of violent trauma do not always appear on the bones of the deceased. But even with these precautions, archaeologists have not found evidence in support of the Iroquois conquest of the Middle Ohio Valley. Seventeenth- and eighteenth-century observers, and the historians who cite them, have overstated the Iroquois conquest of the region.

The Decline of Down-the-Line Trading and the Quest for Direct Trade with Europeans

Time and again, European colonists failed to see the networks that tied one village to another. The newcomers preferred seeing American Indians as dependent on their whims and largely cut off from the allies that had sustained their communities for centuries. In 1661, Jérôme Lalemant, a Jesuit missionary stationed among the Mohawk, first heard of the Shawnees. Working with Iroquois informants, Lalemant learned that "they trade with Europeans who pray as we do. From their account, we suppose these Europeans to be Spaniards." In 1668, Marquette's Illinois informants described "a nation that they call the Chaouanou [who] are laden with glass beads, which shows that they have communication with Europeans." Through conversations with the Seneca, La Salle learned that the Ohio was a "Beautiful River, which serves to carry people down to the Great Lake (for they so call the sea), where they trade with Europeans who pray as we do." The Senecas suggested that at least by the 1660s Shawnees traveled west along the Ohio, to the Mississippi, and ultimately to the Gulf of Mexico, where they traded with the Spanish.[14]

Ohio Valley villagers traded peacefully with the Iroquois for most of their shared history.[15] But as hide hunters diminished game animals in the region below Lake Ontario, Iroquoians expanded their geographic horizons. The Senecas' quest for furs intensified by the dawn of the seventeenth century. By 1600, small Iroquoian stemmed pipes appear at Madisonville. And by the late seventeenth century, pottery "reminiscent of classic Madisonville ware" begins to appear at both the Susquehannock and the Seneca sites. The Senecas and the Susquehannocks mediated the trade between Fort Ancient peoples and the French, English, and Dutch. Such down-the-line trade continued unabated until the Iroquois-Susquehannock Wars intensified during the middle decades of the seventeenth century. When the trade between Fort Ancient villagers and the Susquehannocks and Senecas collapsed, the Haudenosaunee began attacking people from the Ohio Valley. Archaeologists think that this might explain why Fort Ancient pottery begins to appear in their villages by the late seventeenth century.[16]

Susquehannock and Northern Iroquois traders brought some of the first European trade goods to the Middle Ohio Valley. Chevron, or star, beads, made from red, white, and blue glass, have been found in both the Ohio Valley and the lower Susquehanna River. The chevron style is a distinctive marker of the early seventeenth century that fell out of fashion before 1650. Dutch traders replaced chevron-style beads with distinctive straw beads, most likely manufactured in Amsterdam. By the time Susquehannock traders obtained straw beads, sometime between 1630 and 1670, trade with Ohio Valley villagers had come to a halt. We know this because straw beads are conspicuously absent from the Middle Ohio Valley. Between 1630 and 1640, archaeologists suggest, down-the-line trading between Fort Ancient villagers and the Susquehannocks must have come to an end.[17]

In 1608, when John Smith encountered the Susquehannocks at the head of the Chesapeake Bay, he immediately took note of their military abilities. Armed with clubs "sufficient to beat out the braines of a man, with bowes, and arrowes, and clubs, suitable to their greatness," he wrote, "they seemed like Giants . . . yea and to the neighbours." Though not indifferent, the Susquehannocks received Smith coolly. Smith was struck by the fact that they were "restrained from adoring the discoverers as Gods." Before the establishment of Jamestown, they lived in palisaded villages "2 daies higher" than the fall line of the Susquehanna River. Military conflict with the Iroquois and their rivals along the Potomac, the Massawomecks and the Susquehannocks, was so intense that the English described their towns as "forts."[18]

Warfare between the Susquehannocks and the Haudenosaunee caused the decline of trade in the Ohio country. Between 1615 and 1675, Northern Iroquois warriors drove the Susquehannocks from the northern reaches of the Susquehanna River, across what is now Pennsylvania, to the Chesapeake Bay. This prolonged genocidal conflict raged for at least sixty years, making it one of the longest-lasting conflicts in American Indian history. Sometimes joint, but often independent, branches of the Five Nations battled the Susquehannocks for control of the mid-Atlantic region. At the midpoint of their conflict, the Susquehannocks had at least 1,300 warriors. By 1675, only 300 fighting men remained. Battles between large armies as well as opportunistic kidnappings and killings steadily depopulated these rival powers. In 1652, Jesuit missionaries among the Five Nations described an Iroquois attack on the Susquehannocks in which a "full force" of more than 1,000 warriors "carried off 5 or 6 hundred" Susquehannock men. Archaeological evidence suggests that these rival powers devastated each other for much of the seventeenth century.[19]

War without end transformed everyday life in the Middle Ohio Valley. Prized European trade goods, used for decorative and ceremonial purposes, became scarce. For nearly one hundred years, the peoples of the Middle Ohio Valley had enjoyed access to new goods, from glass beads to metal objects, to which they assigned great power. Native hunters pursued bison and deer in great quantities in order to acquire the most pedestrian items of European manufacture. Villagers reworked strips of copper and brass from worn-out cooking pots and manufactured tinkling cones, earrings, and coiled "snakes" from these utilitarian items. They reworked European trade goods into ritual objects that described the multilayered cosmos they inhabited. Trade goods brought to the Americas by Europeans from distant Atlantic worlds became a vital part of Native Americans' aesthetic and religious identities.[20]

The desperate struggle between the Iroquois and the Susquehannocks interrupted this period of creative reinvention. As bodies piled up along the Susquehanna River, men were no longer able to cross the Allegheny Mountains to trade with Fort Ancient villagers. Sometime before 1640, warfare between the Northern Iroquois and the Susquehannocks essentially halted the trade in European goods. In the Middle Ohio Valley, important men were no longer buried with items of European origin. Deceased infants and toddlers were interred without the trade beads that had accompanied them into the afterlife for several generations. By 1650,

European trade goods were nowhere in evidence. Approximately thirty years later, in 1680, the last Fort Ancient summer villages ceased to exist.[21] When the Iroquois encountered the peoples of the Ohio Valley again, it would be as invaders. By 1669, Iroquois warriors were traveling as far as 1,800 miles from their homelands in search of people, plunder, and furs.[22] They journeyed in search of captives who might replace fallen kinsmen.

Between 1630 and 1680, some Fort Ancient villagers traveled into the Southeast along well-worn footpaths hugging the western edge of the Appalachian Mountains. Some moved east, through the Cumberland Gap, toward Carolina. Others likely reached proto-Creek towns along the Coosa and Tallapoosa rivers, in present-day Alabama. Europeans had little knowledge of the precontact trading paths that joined migrants from the Middle Ohio Valley to their southeastern allies. One exception appeared in 1684, when La Salle's official cartographer, Jean-Baptiste Louis Franquelin, drew a map that included the "path traveled by the Casquinampo and Shawnees, in trading with the Spaniards." Franquelin guessed that the Shawnees traveled with the Koasatis, the chiefdom that had such a long history of trade with the peoples of Fort Ancient. After joining with the Koasatis, these Shawnees traded with the Spanish somewhere along the Gulf of Mexico. Between 1550 and the 1680s, Spaniards traveled from Cuba to the Gulf Coast to conduct this illicit trade.[23] When French and English traders first encountered Shawnees they described seeing Spanish trade goods in their possession.[24]

During their initial encounters with the French and English, Shawnees made it clear that they had already begun trading with Europeans. They displayed Spanish trade goods to their new trading partners, showcasing their willingness to travel great distances to acquire European goods. In 1674, when the English doctor, trader, and slaver Henry Woodward first encountered the Shawnees, he was surprised to learn that they had been living "twenty days journey West Southwardly from" the Westo village of Hickauhaugau, along the Middle Savannah River. Such a location, while imprecise, would have placed them somewhere along the coast of present-day Alabama or perhaps Mississippi. Woodward noted that the Shawnees brought with them "Spanish beeds and other trade as presents, makeing signs that they had comerce wth white people." French colonizers also located the Shawnees along the Gulf Coast, where, they claimed, the Shawnees "trade with Europeans who pray as we do, and use Rosaries, as well as Bells for calling to Prayers. According to the description given us, we judge them to be Spaniards."[25] The Spanish trade did not pull the Shawnees into the Catholic mission towns of Georgia and Florida. It seems more likely that the Shawnees traded with the Spanish while living with Native peoples from the Gulf Coast. Across the upper country, Indian peoples traveled in search of precious commodities denied them by the Iroquois-Susquehannock Wars.

The Indian Slave Trade and the Middle Ohio Valley

By 1670, Virginia traders were actively encouraging Native slavers to travel beyond the Appalachian Mountains. The Occaneechees and the Westos operated independently, and Virginians rarely visited their towns. The random nature of the trade in Native slaves thus occurred largely without the knowledge or oversight of colonial officials. While Jesuit missionaries located among the Iroquois carefully recorded the arrival of mourning war captives from the interior of the continent, English officials never fully understood, or cared to ask, how Native slaves came into their colonies. Native slaves captured while at war with the English were well known to the Virginians. But the long-distance trade in slaves from the Ohio Valley and the Spanish mission towns of the Gulf Coast changed all of that. In the 1660s, when Native slavers began capturing American Indians who had not yet encountered Europeans, Indian slavery became a long-distance trade in human commodities. At this time, fifty years before colonists regularly visited the Ohio Valley, Native slavers working with English traders came to know the region intimately. In response to their raids, Fort Ancient villagers migrated out of their homelands, and survivors migrated in search of European allies.[26]

At least initially, Virginia traders operating out of individual plantations and frontier outposts such as Fort Henry, near the falls of the Appomattox River, encouraged the trade in people and furs. One such trader was Abraham Wood. Working with the support of powerful friends in London, Wood financed at least two major expeditions beyond the Appalachian Mountains. In 1671, Wood sent Thomas Batts and William Fallam on an expedition whose ostensible purpose was to "make discoveries across the mountains." Abraham Wood also had practical ambitions. Both the Occaneechees and an indeterminate people called the Tomahitans had become powerful trading partners of the Virginians by the middle of the seventeenth century. The Tomahitans, in particular, guided Wood's men into the interior of the continent. The 1671 expedition failed to cross into the Ohio Valley. But two years later, Wood learned of the river valleys that cut through the Appalachian Mountains. Traveling west, then north along the New/Kanawha River, Batts and Fallam could have followed an

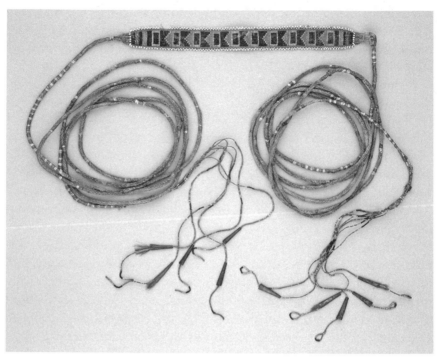

Native peoples traveled vast distances in pursuit of captives, and they used implements such as this slave halter to control their victims. Great Lakes slave halter, eighteenth century, courtesy of John D. Rockefeller Library, Colonial Williamsburg Foundation.

all-water route to the Ohio River. Shawnee migrants to the Southeast likely followed this corridor, from the Ohio Valley and on to Virginia, before finally settling along the Middle Savannah River, where they traded with the English at Charles Town.[27]

In 1673, Wood sent another team of servants, James Needham and Gabriel Arthur, into the interior. They were guided by eight Tomahitan warriors, and Wood expected Needham and Arthur to spend the next three months exploring the Appalachians and establishing trade contacts with the people beyond the mountains. But they were ill prepared for the journey. Almost immediately, an Occaneechee man encountered the trading party and began antagonizing Needham. The two men sparred for the better part of the day, until Needham decided to confront his Occaneechee accuser. Within seconds, the Occaneechee man had fatally shot Needham and cut out his heart, and he then dared the Tomahitans to do the same with Arthur. The Occaneechees may have been threatened by the Virginians' desire to expand the Indian trade beyond the mountains. While they were useful trading partners, neither the Occaneechees nor the Tomahitans seemed to be on good terms with the Virginia traders. Wood thought that the Occaneechees were "so insolent for they are but a handful of people besides what vagabonds repair to them." The Occaneechees made up for their small numbers through almost constant warfare. Wood described how "it is ye course of theire liveing to forrage robb and spoyle other natons." Constant warfare meant that their principal town was very well defended, and the Virginians took Occaneechee threats seriously.[28]

The Tomahitans aspired to replace Occaneechee slavers. When Occaneechee warriors implored them to execute Arthur, the Tomahitans rejected their demands. Arthur believed that he had been caught between rivals vying for supremacy in the slave trade. And so when Arthur and an Appomattox guide arrived at their principal town, a Tomahitan chief placed him on a scaffold so that "their people might stand and gaze" at Arthur so as not to "offend them by their throng." Arthur seems to have visited a town accustomed to down-the-line trading, because the Tomahitans treated him reverently. In Arthur, the Tomahitans gazed upon a person who might have produced some of the trade goods that they had long enjoyed. Unlike those of the Occaneechees, the Tomahitans' principal towns lay west of the Appalachian Mountains, somewhere in eastern Tennessee or northern Alabama. Scholars have variously identified them as Creek, Yuchi, and Cherokee. More recent scholars have argued that the Tomahitans might have represented a multilingual, coalescent community that ultimately migrated to the Coosa River. The Tomahitans were on good terms with the Monetons, an eastern Siouan-speaking people who controlled access to the Middle Ohio Valley through the New/Kanawha River drainage. Arthur learned that they were often at war with Spaniards. Their rivalry probably drove the Tomahitans to seek an alliance with the Virginia traders. During his year in their village, Arthur took part in at least six slaving expeditions. The Tomahitans targeted Spanish mission towns and English-allied "settlement Indians" along the Carolina coast. For Native slavers, Virginia and Carolina were distinct, even rival, powers. They felt no obligation to avoid the Indian communities of colonial Carolina. While most of these expeditions targeted Spanish-allied Indian towns in what is now Florida and Georgia, Arthur recalled participating in "a very great slaughterhouse upon the Indians," living near what is now Port Royal, South Carolina.[29]

In his last slaving expedition, Arthur crossed into the Middle Ohio Valley. After passing through a Moneton village, Arthur and the Tomahitans traveled for another three days. Somewhere along the Middle Ohio Valley, the Tomahitans hoped to "give a clap to some of that great nation" and then "fell on" their Ohio Valley enemies "with great courage." Even with guns provided by the Virginians, the Tomahitans were "curagiously repullsed by theire enimise." Wounded with flint-knapped arrows, Arthur now became their captive after an arrow to his thigh slowed his escape. His captors "scowered his skin with water and ashes, and when they discovered his skin to be white, they made very much of him." Arthur believed that the people he encountered lived in a state of nature, free from European trade and material culture. According to Arthur, his captors "knew not the use of the gun" and did not possess iron tools.[30]

His description of the land and its rivers is notoriously imprecise. Only his Tomahitan allies knew the identities of the people they attacked, and Arthur's narrative does not clearly establish who they were. But if, as some scholars suggest, Arthur had stumbled upon Fort Ancient villagers, it is very clear that they were thrilled to have captured a white man. Even as their erstwhile slaver, his captors recognized what Arthur's whiteness represented: an opportunity to engage in direct trade with Europeans. Arthur's survival depended on his captors' desire for trade goods. He reported that when he "made signes that if they would lett him return, he would bring many things amongst them . . . [they] seemed to rejoyce att it." His "knife and hatchet" were of particular interest to his captors. Through the use of signs, Wood's servant told them exactly how many furs they would need to give in exchange for the knife and the hatchet.[31]

What explains Arthur's treatment? The Tomahitans ranged widely for slaves, from the Gulf Coast to Carolina and the Ohio Valley. In a year's time, Arthur had traveled with members of one village across nearly half of the Eastern Woodlands. The Tomahitans were prepared for a world in which violence threatened. Strong palisades, complete with parapets designed to beat back an enemy assault, protected their principal village. Canoes, capable of carrying dozens of warriors into battle, lined the stream alongside their village. The Tomahitans seem to have been in the Ohio Valley before, because Fort Ancient villagers anticipated their assault. Slavers such as the Tomahitans brought English goods and their diseases and desires across the Appalachians. While the Tomahitans fought with Spanish-allied Indians along the Gulf of Mexico, the Occaneechees, a coalescent people, allied themselves with the English. By 1670, Ohio Valley villagers had not yet become allied with a European power. Those who remained seized the opportunity Arthur represented. Abraham Wood wrote that as soon as Arthur had recovered from his wounds, his captors took him to a path that "carried to ye Tomahittans." Before they parted ways, they gave Arthur "Rokahomany," unleavened corn cakes that were sometimes mixed with berries and were designed to sustain travelers on long-distance journeys.[32] His treatment was neither accidental nor naive. Confronted with well-armed, increasingly mobile enemies such as the Iroquois, Tomahitans, and Occaneechees, Ohio Valley villagers secured a valuable ally who might enable them to survive the chaos of colonialism.

Long-distance slave trading, when combined with Iroquois mourning wars, stitched together the eastern half of North America. Militarized societies now migrated hundreds of miles, often on behalf of colonizers. While some societies abandoned their homelands, as was the case with the Occaneechees, the Westos, and the Shawnees, others, such as the Iroquois, expanded their territorial claims. Migration became a survival strategy, the common thread linking these tragic histories. The Iroquoian-speaking Erie moved south in response to the Haudenosaunee assault on their homeland. They became slavers for the English. Similarly, the Illinois Confederacy's mid-seventeenth-century migration from Iowa and Missouri to the Illinois River Valley enabled them to trade more easily with the French. And in the Iroquois case, the French believed that "the lands of which they are masters stretch out as far as they want." American Indians, from the Eries to the Illinois, the Iroquois to the Shawnees, traveled great distances to cope with colonization. By the time Europeans first encountered American Indians and attempted to explain them to a curious world, migration had become a fact of life in colonial North America.[33]

Mourning Wars, the Concept of Souls, and the Complex Identities of the Eastern Woodlands

Native understandings of the soul facilitated migration and shaped American Indian warfare in the colonial period. Eastern Woodland beliefs regarding the souls of the dead and their proper treatment provided the cosmological basis for American Indians in the eastern half of North America to engage in long-distance warfare. While conceptions of the soul varied, Eastern Woodland Indians believed that souls migrated among living beings. While Christians taught that only humans possessed a soul and that each soul was unique to the individual, Algonquians and Iroquoians held that deceased relatives could be revived, could live again, if a living being could be made to embody the dead man's soul. The Innu, Algonquian speakers who were in near-constant war with the Iroquois, believed that "all beings were endowed with a life essence, which at once enlivened and animated its possessor and, upon destruction of its physical form, survived it." Among Central Algonquians such as the Miamis, young warriors led their captives to the cabins of families who had lost relatives in war, telling them that they "have brought back some men to replace, if they desire it, those whom the fate of war has taken away."[34] As these historical anecdotes make clear, Iroquoian and Algonquian conceptions of the soul made captive taking and adoption the means by which they could repair kin groups devastated by disease and warfare.

For the Shawnees and their neighbors, rituals of mourning and adoption had very real implications. Small, village-based societies became targets of larger confederacies and coalescent communities in need of replacements for their fallen kin. Victims of slaving and mourning wars turned on those weaker than themselves, and their war parties traveled vast distances in search of vulnerable towns. No other tribe rivaled the Iroquois, whose mourning-war complex became a normative means of dealing with death and destruction.

Iroquoian and Algonquian speakers alike felt a deep obligation to the souls of their fallen kin. French explorers among the Shawnees believed that they venerated their dead. In this way, Native conceptions of the soul and rituals associated with death and mourning became one of the means by which colonizers distanced themselves from Native peoples. The Shawnees, like the Innu and the Iroquois, emphasized the transitory nature of life on earth. Souls traveled west, to the land of the dead, but they maintained the capacity to shape events in the realm of the living. They could and did return to watch over their living relatives, long after the ends of their corporeal lives. The living responded by holding elaborate rituals for the souls of the dead. Frenchmen living among the Shawnees could not help but notice these mourning rituals. They complained that they held burial ceremonies and death feasts so frequently that "they prevented us from sleeping." Shawnee mourners placed the body of the deceased at the center of a wickiup, and they encircled the dead, singing to them and for them "at the top of their voices." During these rituals, Shawnee elders expected much of younger men. They were expected to stay up all night and to "sing well."[35]

Death feasts, often held on the anniversary of the loved one's death, tended to be the responsibility of the deceased's female kin. On these occasions, women asked hunters to bring in enough deer for a large feast, and invitations were sent far and wide. Shawnees believed that the deceased "eat after their death." During these feasts, the soul of the dead watches over his or her living kinsmen. Sponsors of these feasts hoped to appease the souls of the dead by inviting many friends and relatives to a ritual in which the living "rejoice" the soul of the dead. After the feast, Henri Joutel witnessed a "round dance" in which dancers kept "time with their feet." Shawnees did their best to honor the dead, and Joutel noticed that "every man is careful to wear all his finest attire." Through feasting, gift giving, and dancing, Shawnees honored their dead and acknowledged the transitory nature of life.[36]

The Indian Slave Trade, Captive Taking, and the Question of Iroquois Dominion

One Shawnee's experience of captivity and liberation shows how trade, migration, and warfare reordered Native societies across the Eastern Woodlands. In a single lifetime, he had migrated from the Ohio Valley to the Gulf of Mexico and then on to Carolina, where he was captured and subsequently liberated, on the Upper Peninsula of Lake Michigan. His story comes to us through Bacqueville de la Potherie, a French historian who interviewed Nicolas Perrot, Louis Joliet, and other French travelers in the upper country. La Potherie chronicled a failed Iroquois attack on a Saulteaux Anishnaabeg village, sometime in the early 1670s, in which forty Ojibwe scouts ambushed an Iroquois war party before it reached the Saulteaux villages. During the attack, the Ojibwes liberated a Shawnee captive who later described how he had been kidnapped by the Iroquois in "a raid against the Chaouanons, near Carolina." From there, this Iroquois war party traveled to the far north, where it hunted the Anishnaabeg. Now free, the Shawnee man regaled his liberators with "marvelous notions of the South Sea," the popular term for the Gulf Coast. The Anishnaabeg sent him "home with much merchandise, urging him to persuade his tribesmen to come and visit them."[37] As this story makes clear, migrating to Carolina, more than 500 miles from the Ohio Valley, did not guarantee Shawnee safety from Iroquois antagonists. Iroquois warriors spent months, and sometimes years, far removed from their home villages, waging war against distant enemies.

Among the Haudenosaunee, warfare was woven into the fabric of everyday life. Between 1603 and 1701, the Iroquois attacked at least fifty-one different groups of people. In this century of conflict, the Iroquois used warfare to prevent the demographic collapse of their communities. War captives assumed the identities and roles of deceased Iroquois. However, near-constant warfare guaranteed that still more of their kinsmen would die because their quest to replace fallen kin led to never-ending cycles of violence. Jesuit missionaries believed that even when victorious, warfare "cause[s] almost as much loss to them as to their enemies." By the late seventeenth century, the Onondagas included captives from seven different tribes, while among the Senecas "there are as many as eleven." Taken together, captives-turned-Iroquois made up solid majorities throughout Iroquoia.[38]

For decades, scholars have accepted the argument that seventeenth-century Woodland Indian history tells the "story of the Iroquois hammer striking Algonquian glass." The Iroquois provided ample evidence to support this conclusion. In June 1711, Onondaga leader Teganissorens explained the essential difference between European and Iroquois ways of war. According to the Iroquois war captain, the Iroquois "are not like you Christians for when you have taken Prisoners of one another you send them home." In contrast, Teganissorens explained, "we are not of that nature. When we have war against any nation Wee endeavor to destroy them utterly."[39]

But powerful archaeological evidence challenges the belief that the Iroquois are solely responsible for the depopulation of the Ohio Valley. After more than one hundred years of archaeological investigation of the Middle Ohio Valley, scholars have been unable to find time-sensitive European artifacts dating to the period between 1650 and 1720. Jesuit rings, seventeenth-century gun parts, and "distinctive indigenous artifacts" have not been found at Fort Ancient sites beyond the middle of the seventeenth century. The absence of such evidence proves that the depopulation of the Ohio Valley occurred largely before the Iroquois conquest of the Ohio Valley.[40]

And so, in the fall of 1669, when Iroquois attacks on remaining Fort Ancient villages began, the Iroquois entered a widowed land. At that time, more than 500 Seneca warriors launched a nine-month expedition against the "Ontouagannha," or the "people who cannot speak," the derisive name given to the Shawnees by the Iroquois. In contrast, the Seneca word for the Iroquois Confederacy, or Five Nations, was "Haudenosaunee," or "the Longhouse." Sacred and profane names thus informed war parties ranging across the continent. The 1669 attack became the first in a series that ravaged the Ohio Valley between 1669 and 1671.[41]

The Iroquois invasion of the Middle Ohio Valley marked a critical expansion of the mourning wars. The Haudenosaunee began a two-front war, in the mid-Atlantic and in the Ohio Valley. One French observer believed that Shawnee and Susquehannock victims had saved the Iroquois from demographic collapse. Nicolas Perrot wrote that "these tribes . . . considerably augmented their own forces, by the great numbers of children or other prisoners whose lives they spared." Illinois, Shawnee, and Susquehannock captives helped to make up for the enormous Iroquois losses of the seventeenth century. One observer noted that "this has always been their policy, to repair at the expense of their enemies the ravages caused in their nation by war." Like trade and epidemic disease, warfare contributed to the "breaking down and reconfiguring [of] identities" that was so commonplace in the seventeenth century.[42]

Epidemic disease, slaving expeditions, and Iroquois war parties converged on the Middle Ohio Valley from multiple directions. American Indians and European colonizers alike found themselves locked in a struggle for the souls of the living. Across the eastern half of North America, in village after village, people dealt with loss on a scale they never could have imagined. Rituals of warfare and mourning—and the closely related ritualized torture of enemies—assumed particular importance during the seventeenth century, as Algonquian and Iroquois survivors struggled to find socially acceptable means of dealing with grief. The psychological trauma caused by colonialism cannot be overstated. To the Iroquois, warriors captured or killed in battle became dangerous to the living, their souls barred from the afterlife and reunification with their relatives unless their kinsmen could satisfy their loss. Extensive mourning rituals, sometimes lasting a year or more, as well as ritualized torture of enemies, became the means by which the Iroquois released the souls of their slain kinsmen from endlessly wandering between the living and the dead.[43]

How, then, did the Iroquois come to understand the many thousands of captives living in their villages? By becoming something akin to reincarnated Iroquois, the Shawnees and their neighbors assumed new identities, as vital elements of Iroquois society. The Iroquois expected captives to return and fight their own people. In fact, killing one's own kinsmen became a test of sorts, a true sign that they had accepted their new, Iroquois personhood. Women were expected to marry into Iroquois society and to perform all of the duties of the person she replaced.

For captives-turned-Iroquois, this amounted to something like death and resurrection. In 1755, when white captive Mary Jemison first met the Seneca women who had adopted her, "they immediately set about a most dismal howling, crying bitterly, and wringing their hands in all the agonies of grief." "After much crying" and a "recitation" that persuaded Jemison that she was the focal point of an important ritual, she discovered that she had been adopted in place of their brother, a warrior who had been killed the year before. As a newly adopted Iroquois, Jemison dried their tears. She had restored the clan to its previous strength. By the middle of the eighteenth century, Iroquois rituals of mourning and adoption had become so widely accepted that both the French and the British actively participated in these condolence ceremonies. In fact, Jemison's Iroquois sisters had traveled to Fort Duquesne to gain satisfaction for the loss of their brother. In response, the French gave Jemison to the sisters, along with the scalps of Jemison's mother and father, as condolence for their loss.[44]

Native Migrants and the Lure of Colonial Borderlands

Colonizers introduced death on a massive scale. But their trade goods also offered the chance for a new life, albeit far removed from home. For those who survived, access to European trade goods, and guns in particular, became the means by which a fortunate few could live on. Survivors embraced violence because their lives depended on it. Shawnee migrants moved toward borderlands, to contested spaces, where they often served as mercenaries on behalf of European colonizers or more powerful and well-armed Native communities. These were not wars of choice, for remaining in the Middle Ohio Valley would have meant death, captivity, and, for the survivors, a life of perpetual slavery or the adoption of a new Iroquois identity, far removed from their homelands.

Villagers traveled out of the Middle Ohio Valley in a piecemeal fashion. Absent an overarching leader and conditioned to see themselves as part of village-based, regional cultures, Fort Ancient villagers did not respond uniformly to disease, trade, warfare, and slavery. Many Shawnees left the Ohio Valley well before the Iroquois wars, and so it is not surprising that they later resisted the notion that they had been conquered by the Iroquois. The Shawnees did not speak with one voice. Their varying responses to the Iroquois bears witness to the autonomy of their villages; those who attempted to define them as members of a unified "tribe" failed to define either their polities or their individual identities.

Beginning in 1630, Shawnees migrated because they knew that infusing new landscapes with sacred meaning was a perilous luxury. In 1779, town chiefs from Chillicothe, Ohio, admitted as much when they proclaimed that "we have always been the frontier." On the eve of the French and Indian War, in 1755, Shawnee migrants had already aroused both the suspicion and the awe of their Indian and non-Indian neighbors. In that year, the British superintendent of Indian Affairs, Edmond Atkin, described the Shawnees as "Stout, Bold, Cunning and the greatest Travellers in America." Just three years earlier, in 1752, a Cherokee named Tasattee observed that the Shawnees were "a People of no Settlement but rambling from Place to Place with nothing but Lyes." Those who knew them almost always commented on Shawnee mobility. To Atkin and Tasattee, the Shawnees were dislocated peoples, separated from their own sacred geography, and as such, they were often viewed as profane and morally suspect.[45]

The dissolution of the Middle Ohio Valley reveals important clues about the connections between precontact Native worlds and their movement into new, early American realities. East of the Mississippi River, dislocation and travel became the common lot of all Native peoples. But what happened to members of the Fort Ancient Tradition reveals broader patterns in this transition from precontact to colonial worlds. First, Fort Ancient political sensibilities, economic practices, trade networks, and alliance rituals directly informed their migrations. Second, Fort Ancient survivors traveled well-worn paths as they migrated from their prehistoric homelands. Third, long experience with ethnic difference grew out of village life. Precontact Native peoples played host to a variety of peoples, ideas, and wares. This richly layered exchange made village life possible, and it became the foundation for Native sensibilities in the colonial period.

By the early colonial period, historical sources show that Shawnees founded towns, from South Carolina to Pennsylvania, associated with or named after one of five "society clans." In the historically known Shawnee kinship system, there are five major divisions that are patrilineal descent groups, what anthropologists call "society clans." They are the Kispoko-tha, Thawekila, Chalagawtha, Pekowitha, and Mekoche, and each of these divisions "was conceived as a distinct territorial unit centering on a town that bore its name." Shawnee leaders rose out of these villages based on the society clans, so that chiefs, messengers, and other officials derived from the same patrilineally inherited division of Shawnee society. The Shawnee tendency to establish summer villages based on society clans most likely has its origins in the Fort Ancient Tradition. During the historic period, migration fragmented these society clans, and clan members no longer lived in one centralized village. Historical records indicate that between 1700 and 1730 there were at least three Pekowitha Shawnee towns in eastern Pennsylvania. Similarly, there were three Chalagawtha towns and two named Mekoche towns in southern Ohio between 1740 and 1770. From the historic period forward, the society clan "that dominated the town numerically" seems to have determined the identity and the leadership of the town itself. Each society clan was further subdivided into a common stock of twelve clans, from the loon to the deer, the bear to the wolf. During the colonial period, these smaller clans, shared by each of the five divisions, were exogamous, patrilocal units that played an important role in the Shawnee ceremonial calendar.[46]

Society clans associated with specific towns made it possible for the Shawnees to adopt symbolic and portable, rather than place-bound and unmovable, markers of identity. Contemporary Shawnee people believe that each of the five divisions is intended to fulfill different functions. For example, chiefs came from either the Thawekila or the Chalagawtha divisions, while the Kispokothas regulated war. According to contemporary tribal elder George Blanchard, "At one time we lived in different clans so if you needed something you traveled to visit them. If you needed medicine you visited the Mekoches, if you needed war you visited the Kispokothas."[47] The Shawnee towns that dotted the eastern half of North America during the colonial era were kin groups endowed with special powers.

Divisional identities seem to have organized Shawnee migrations. For example, the Shawnees who relocated to the Grand Village of the Kaskaskias, near present-day Utica, Illinois, were members of the Mekoche, Chalagawtha, and Pekowitha divisions.[48] From 1688 to 1695, when migrations to Pennsylvania occurred, these town names began to appear in the eastern half of the colony. In contrast, the Kispokotha and Thawekila divisions organized the Shawnee diaspora in the South. In the 1730s, métis trader James Le Tort explained that the Carolina Shawnees were, in fact, Thawekila Shawnees. There is no evidence to suggest that either the Mekoche or the Chalagawtha Shawnees migrated to either Alabama or South Carolina following the Iroquois wars.[49]

It is clear that these kin groups fragmented and coalesced with each other as they moved. Like all human families, the Shawnee divisions were porous and unstable markers of identity. While movement between Shawnee villages did take place, the Shawnees did not move as a unified people during, or after, the colonial period.[50] Their world was simultaneously parochial and cosmopolitan, driven by kin groups that shared a language and a host of cultural practices.[51]

We are tempted to view Indian people in isolation, as residents of coherent polities with obvious homelands. Long-distance migrants became even more cosmopolitan as they moved hundreds of miles from their homelands. And yet they remained attached to their villages, even as slavery and warfare tore at their parochial loyalties. Ties forged by Fort Ancient villagers shaped the choices they made. In the chapters that follow, I explore the Shawnee expression of those networks during the early colonial period. Their wide-ranging migrations reflect the variety of unique ties forged by Fort Ancient villagers. To illustrate how village-based autonomy became even more pronounced during the colonial period, we will follow three separate Shawnee migrations: to the Savannah River Valley, the Grand Village of the Kaskaskias, and the head of the Chesapeake Bay. In each of these contexts, prehistoric alliances and trade networks informed Shawnee migrations. The Shawnees were far from a people without history. Reaching back into the archaeological record offers a deeper understanding of the material, cultural, and linguistic affinities that shaped these varied migrations. By combining the archaeological, documentary, and oral evidence on the prehistoric and colonial periods of North America, we can bear fuller witness to not only the crucible of colonial North America but also the ways in which ancient alliances and religious practices enabled American Indians to survive.[52]

By 1680, Fort Ancient villagers had abandoned their last villages, bringing an end to 700 years of commitment to the Middle Ohio Valley. Some Fort Ancient survivors, including many Shawnees, never returned to this region. The remaining chapters of this book trace one branch of the Fort Ancient Tradition, the Shawnees, as they migrated from, and in some cases returned to, the Ohio Valley. Between 1630 and 1680, Shawnees migrated widely, and the varying contexts to which they were drawn shaped their culture in profound ways. Their long sojourn as both opportunists and refugees furthered the distinctiveness of their villages. Simultaneously parochial and cosmopolitan, the Shawnees became even more culturally varied during the colonial period.

part 2

The Lure of Colonial Borderlands

At first glance, violent borderlands do not seem like places of opportunity. But Shawnee villagers recognized that their survival depended on both their ability to trade with Europeans and their capacity to serve as guides, porters, slave hunters, mercenaries, and traders. Between 1673, when the first "Shawnees" appeared in the historical record, and the beginning of the eighteenth century, English and French colonizers competed for their allegiance, and Shawnee people lived in a range of seemingly inhospitable places. Separated by hundreds of miles, Shawnees appeared in zones of conflict, places of intersection where Europeans hoped to gain strategic advantage. In these early years of colonialism, American Indians and Europeans needed each other. Shawnees, Westos, Yuchis, Iroquois, Mahicans, and a host of long-distance migrants established villages at fall lines of important rivers and warrior paths that connected regional powers to one another. Native migrants and colonizers needed each other the most at these strategic centers of trade and war. The Shawnees traveled toward these zones of intersection, and these places became especially significant in the colonial period. At locations such as the Upper Illinois River Valley, the Middle Savannah River, and the head of the Chesapeake Bay, Native migrants often mediated the borderlands between colonizers and powerful Native confederacies that struggled to remain within their homelands.

Shawnees who migrated to these contested borderlands helped to reorder and reimagine colonial worlds. When Shawnee guides led French explorers to the Gulf of Mexico, and when Shawnee slavers captured and enslaved people bound for places as wide ranging as the kitchens and dining rooms of colonial New England and the sugar plantations of St. Kitts, they helped to integrate diverse regions and peoples into a shared Atlantic World. Shawnee migrants settled in close proximity to colonizers with whom they could trade, and thus they became wedded to new colonial worlds whose reach extended back to centers of power in London and Paris. And yet precontact allies often inspired the Shawnees to migrate to violent borderlands. Ancient allies thus encouraged Shawnee migrants to relocate and thus to reorder the eastern half of North America. Familiar allies lived at places such as the Upper Illinois River Valley and the northern reaches of the Chesapeake, but as these old and new worlds came together, it was the newcomers who often redefined the land and its people. In the chapters that follow, I argue that we must explore the connections between precontact and colonial-era worlds because most American Indian histories overstate the ruptures of colonialism.

chapter 4

A Ranging Sort of People

MIGRATION AND SLAVERY ON THE SAVANNAH RIVER

In March 1670, John Carteret, an owner and governor of colonial Carolina, sailed with a delegation of Englishmen from their colony at Bermuda to modern Beaufort, South Carolina. Carteret was amazed by the friendliness of the Indian people who greeted them. He was "carried ashore by the Indians," inhabitants of a town they called Sowee, one of many Siouan-speaking villages along the Carolina coast that would over time become known as the "Catawba." In the seventeenth century, Sowee was located along the coastal plain, just north of Charles Town, and its residents "gave them [the Englishmen] the stroking compliments of the country and brought deer skins to trade with." Indian women offered them "a pretty sort of bread and hickory nuts," as they were escorted to "the hut palace of his majesty," a village headman Carteret mistakenly described as an Indian "King." After offering the Englishmen still more "nuts and root cakes and water," the Indian "King" described "a ranging sort of people," named the Westos. The people of Sowee described them as "man eaters" who "had ruinated that place, killing the Indians and destroying their habitations."[1]

Nearly forty years later, Indian agent and slave trader John Lawson portrayed the Shawnees as a "shifting, wandering people" who have "changed their settlements many hundred miles." Another tribe then located along the Savannah River, the Yuchis, or *Coyaha*, tell an origin story that describes how they "came from the sun" and believed it would be best for "each tribe going its own way and living alone."[2] The Shawnees, Westos, and Yuchis were migratory outliers who placed their villages between the collapsing Mississippian chiefdoms of the interior and the new English settlements of the coastal plain. Their villagers saw migration into the valley, where they worked as slavers, traders, and diplomats, as an opportunity. Carteret and Lawson witnessed a world in motion, as Indian people across the eastern half of North America searched for allies and stable places to call home. In the 1670s, Muskogean speakers continued to occupy towns descended from larger Mississippian chiefdoms. Like all Native people, Muskogeans moved in response to colonization. However, they remained in the colonial Southeast and they shared a common language and ritual life with most of their neighbors. Migratory villagers such as the Westos, the Shawnees, and the Yuchis maintained their independence. As slavers and mercenaries of English traders, ranging parties from the fall line of the Savannah River forced coastal villagers such as the Catawbas and interior tribes such as the Creeks to coalesce. The smaller, transient communities of the Middle Savannah River compelled Muskogean-speaking townspeople to form confederacies. In contrast, the Westos and the Shawnees maintained strikingly autonomous towns.[3] In 1708, soldier, slaver, and Carolina Indian agent Thomas Nairne described the "progression of on[e] village out of another." He wrote that "as for authority," southeastern Indians "look on their own Village to be independent . . . and free to manage their affairs as best pleases themselves." Following Nairne, this chapter explores how independent and migratory villagers such as the Westos, the Shawnees, and the Yuchis used the Indian slave trade to build alliances with the English. These newcomers initiated processes that led to the formation of larger, more powerful, confederacies that came together to resist enslavement.[4]

Between 1659 and 1715, the Middle Savannah River became a place of importance for small numbers of long-range migrants to the Southeast. Westo, Shawnee, and Yuchi people lived on the fall line of the Savannah River, approximately 140 miles from the English at Charles Town. These migratory villagers participated in the enslavement of American Indians, only to be enslaved as the Indian slave trade metastasized. In 1670, Sowee Indians complained about new immigrants to Carolina, many of whom had abandoned the Ohio country. Over time, the Middle Savannah River became home to transient people who moved there by peculiar combinations of choice and force. People from modern-day Ohio, Tennessee, Florida, and Georgia congregated at the fall line, the point at which the coastal plain meets the Piedmont. The fall line was an important ecological and imperial boundary. For Native peoples, the region was a borderland between English and Spanish colonizers to the east and south and larger, Muskogean-speaking tribal towns in the interior Southeast. The English recruited well-armed migrants capable of defending their settlements from more powerful and numerous interior tribes. Fall-line villagers mediated imperial and intertribal rivalries on behalf of their English benefactors. Native newcomers soon became well-armed mercenaries who used their affiliation with English slavers to carve a space for themselves in the Southeast. War captives came into the fall-line villages from across the Southeast, and most resident tribes distrusted migrant villagers.

Westo, Shawnee, and Yuchi histories illustrate how participation in the Indian slave trade became a survival strategy for smaller Indian societies living in the shadow of indigenous communities that were coalescing into formidable regional powers.[5] The slave trade pulled smaller tribes such as the Westos, Shawnees, and Yuchis toward English towns, even as it pushed the victims of Indian slavery away from colonizers. In the second half of the seventeenth century, the slave trade triggered innumerable migrations and tied Native peoples to the global traffic in human commodities. A hallmark of the Indian slave trade was the instability of intertribal alliances, and the Savannah River villages illustrate just how contested and ephemeral they became. The newcomers' towns along the Middle Savannah River employed violence and the rituals associated with it to define who they were and to carve out a valued place for themselves in the Southeast.

Thomas Nairne understood that in the seventeenth century Indian people identified themselves by their tribal towns. We must now seek to explain the symbiotic relationship between long-distance migrants and townspeople descended from the larger Mississippian chiefdoms. Algonquian-speaking Shawnees, Iroquoian-speaking Westos, and Uchean-speaking Yuchis migrated toward new colonizers in the colonial Southeast. The sheer inventiveness of these small societies is staggering.

Long-Distance Migrations and the Example of the Westos

Between the late 1650s and the early 1720s, the Middle Savannah River became a haven for survivors of disease and warfare. Some of those who withstood death, captivity, and the loss of identity at the hands of Iroquois, Occaneechee, and Tomahitan warriors established towns in the region. In the late 1650s, the Eries, Northern Iroquoian speakers who originally inhabited the region south of Lake Erie, between what is now Buffalo, New York, and Toledo, Ohio, began appearing along the James River in colonial Virginia. Their arrival came in the aftermath of wars with the Five Nations. From 1654 to 1656, the Iroquois devastated people living along the southern shore of Lake Erie. Survivors abandoned their homeland and moved to the Southeast, where they became known as the Westos.[6] The possibilities of the slave trade seem to have drawn the Westos southward, as there is little archaeological evidence linking them to either Virginia or the Savannah River prior to the arrival of Europeans.

We do know that Iroquois devastation of the Eries prompted them to abandon their towns in northern Ohio and to migrate into the colonial Southeast. Between 1630 and 1660, as a tobacco economy spread rapidly in the Tidewater region, Virginians traded guns to the Westo newcomers for Indian slaves. Virginians also sold Indian slaves to faraway places such as New England, or to sugar planters in Bermuda, St. Kitts, and Jamaica.[7] The transformation of the Westos—from victims of the Iroquois to slavers—paralleled the development of cash-crop agriculture in the English colonies.

As tobacco and sugar became the principal cash crops of Virginia and the British Caribbean, the planter class reached far and wide for sources of cheap labor. During the seventeenth century, approximately 315,000 indentured servants traveled from England to the Chesapeake and the Caribbean. By the end of the seventeenth century, nearly 29,000 Africans had endured the middle passage to North America. Out of that number, some 20,000 African slaves were sent to Virginia and, to a lesser extent, Maryland.[8] The first Westo town in the Southeast, Rickahockan Town, was located just west of this immense traffic in human beings. Located at the falls of the James River, Rickahockan Town was built at the point at which the deep, navigable waters of the coastal plain are interrupted by the rocky and impenetrable shoals and waterfalls of the Piedmont. From north to south, the foothills of the Appalachians transformed the ecology of the Atlantic seaboard and the rivers that emptied into the Atlantic. Western trails paralleled the fall line because its shoals allowed for easy river crossings. The fall line also became the effective head of boat traffic along the rivers. Below the fall line, river channels deepen. Native paddlers brought canoe loads of furs and slaves to Europeans settlers along the Atlantic Coast.[9]

The Westos established their town at the falls of the James because this geographic position enabled them to regulate the flow of Indian peoples— and their trade goods—to the English settlements of the coastal plain.[10] Warrior paths stretching from Iroquoia in the North to the low country of Carolina cut through the towns along the fall line. From their town on the James, the Westos followed trails into the Shenandoah Mountains and beyond, where they attacked American Indians who had not yet acquired guns.

The Westo experiment on the James River became a trend that other long-distance Native migrants would follow. In the coming decades, would-be Native slavers from outside of the Southeast moved to the spaces between large, rival populations. The Middle Savannah River was devoid of people when the Westos settled there. In May 1540, Hernando de Soto and his men nearly met their end along this stretch of the Savannah River. They described the country as "wasted and without maize," an endless series of sand hills that effectively barred Native peoples from living in the region. Along the coastal plain, the Savannah River offered few tributaries on which to plant villages. Below the shoals of the fall line, the Savannah River runs shallow and wide, and swamps and side channels allow for cypress forests and other trees capable of thriving in this wetland environment. Large sections of the river's banks are poorly drained, and Native peoples struggled to farm in this floodplain. The land was not rich enough to support societies that depended on corn for survival. Native peoples learned this firsthand when, during the middle of the fourteenth century, climate change brought with it record droughts. Grand chiefdoms below the fall line had to abandon this region after a prolonged drought caused a series of devastating crop failures. This is the region that nearly killed de Soto and his men when they traveled for seventeen days, from Georgia to the Carolina Piedmont, without encountering people, and the food they had hoped to wrest from them. They were relieved to finally reach Cofitachiqui, an abundant chiefdom above the fall line on the Wateree River. At the time of contact, the fall-line region was a perilous borderland between rival chiefdoms. When the Westos ultimately established their village, the region had been abandoned for more than one hundred years.[11]

Carolina's rulers, the Lords Proprietors, wanted the Westos to procure slaves and to mediate the flow of people and trade goods above and below the fall line. The English colony at Charles Town presented an opportunity for the Westos, and the Middle Savannah River quickly became a region of strategic importance. Georgia governor James Oglethorpe described the fall line of the Savannah as the "key to the country." In his journal, naturalist and travel writer William Bartram marveled at how Savannah Town was "seated at the head of navigation and just below the conflux of several of [the Savannah's] most considerable branches." Bartram described how the town "command[ed] the trade and commerce of vast fruitful regions above it and from every side to a great distance." Like Hickauhaugau on the James, Westo Town, and later Savannah Town, became an entrepôt for the Indian trade. Routes to Charles Town, the seat of English power in Carolina, cut through their villages.[12]

By 1670, the year in which the colony of Carolina was founded, Hickauhaugau, or Westo Town, was more than a decade old. Paradoxically, Hickauhaugau became a model for survival, even as it was situated on a vital crossroads of the traffic in human beings. The Westos became a portable slaving society, having moved from what is now Ohio, then to Virginia, and finally to Carolina. These slavers, like ongoing virgin-soil epidemics, compelled their human targets to migrate and coalesce to survive. By 1715, when the onset of the Yamasee War ended the large-scale enslavement of American Indians across the eastern half of North America, at least 50,000 Indians had been enslaved. Scholars estimate that at least three additional people died for every one person who was captured and enslaved. Between 1659 and 1715, the peoples of the Middle Savannah River presided over this vast reordering of the colonial Southeast.[13]

Westo warriors paddled down the Savannah River to the vulnerable Indians along the coastal plain and the Spanish mission towns of Georgia and Florida. As many as 30,000 Indians from Florida were enslaved in the seventeenth and eighteenth centuries.[14] In 1675, Bishop Gabriel Díaz Vara Calderon, like the Sowee Indians encountered by Carteret, described Westo slavers as "cruel and barbarous pagans" who "assault the towns of Christians as well as pagans, taking their lives" with little regard for age or sex. Westo attacks on the peoples of Guale and Mocama played a central role in the demise of the Spanish mission system. A Westo force of from 500 to 2,000 men enslaved and depopulated a region with tens of thousands of inhabitants, across hundreds of miles of what is now north Florida.[15]

The Indian slave trade became the centerpiece of an informal economy in the last decades of the seventeenth century. Native peoples often acted as mercenaries for English settlers. Native men also traded everything from deerskins to cattle to colonizers. Indian hunters often killed "tame hoggs and cattle," then sold the meat to ordinary Englishmen. In response, colonial officials passed laws prohibiting Indians from selling "any flesh dead or living Except venison wild fowl or other vermine." By the last decades of the seventeenth century, an extensive and unregulated trade with American Indians threatened the authority of colonial officials. In 1685, Carolina's Lords Proprietors admitted as much, writing that "the dealers in Indians are the greatest sticklers against having the Parliament elected according to our instructions."[16]

From the 1690s to 1715, colonial leaders alternated between establishing martial law to offering trade monopolies to colonial elites in an attempt to regulate the Indian trade. Officials in Maryland and Pennsylvania tried a licensing system, and they threatened to impose heavy fines on "whosoever that shall intice surprise Transport or cause to be transported or sell and dispose of any friend Indian or Indians whatsoever." In contrast, Virginia planter and member of the House of Burgesses William

Byrd offered the king one hundred pounds per year in exchange for the right to manage "such persons as shall be employed by me" so that "the Indian trade might be taken into his Majesty's hands." Their efforts failed to curb the Indian slave trade. But then, in 1712, Massachusetts passed a law against the importation of slaves. At the same time, diminishing Native populations along the Gulf of Mexico and the Florida Peninsula curbed the supply of slaves. Buyers and sellers found themselves at a crossroads.[17]

The Indian slave trade startled even those Englishmen who promoted and managed the human traffic. Planters became enmeshed in slaving in ways that they could not have anticipated. And in this regard the enslavement of Africans, removed as it was from New World planters, might have offered a more palatable alternative to the Indian slave trade. Men such as Henry Woodward received a 20 percent share in all profits derived from the Indian slave trade for his labors. And yet, on a visit to Hickauhaugau, Woodward noted that the Westos "hang the locks of haire of Indians that they have slaine" from the rafters of their longhouses. Under threat of constant attack, they built a double palisade along the inland side of the town and a single one facing the river's edge. Even with a minimum of 500 warriors, Westo slavers were surrounded by 6,800 American Indians in South Carolina alone. Another 130,000 people lived beyond the Appalachian Mountains.[18] As a people without allies, other than English slavers from Carolina and Virginia, palisaded villages—and interminable warfare—became the common lot of these long-range migrants.

The Westos had been slaving throughout the Southeast for a little more than twenty years when Carolina established a permanent colony. In 1674, Woodward wrote that "they are well provided with arms, ammunition," from "the northward." The Chesapeake colonies exchanged guns and other trade goods for "skins, furs, and young Indian slaves." The Carolinians noted that "our Indians are more afraid [of the Westos] than little children are of the Bull beggars in England." All along the coast of Carolina, the Westos targeted the people who eventually became the Catawbas. The Sowees, Wanniahs, and Edistos were "afraid of the very footstep of the Westoe" living "to the westward" of their villages.[19]

The Virginians' primary need might have been labor, but Carolinians worried principally about how to secure their colony. In Carolina, both the English and the Westos faced a common predicament. And both newcomers, keenly aware of their vulnerability, found common cause. Carolina occupied a precarious spit of land along the Atlantic Coast. Planters from Bermuda, with the support of English investors, had founded the colony more than sixty years after Jamestown had been established. They wanted to avoid the kind of Indian wars that had nearly destroyed their counterparts in both Virginia and Massachusetts. In this way, colonial ambitions intersected with those of the Westos. In exchange for English guns, the Westos provided Carolinians with the security they desperately needed. The Lords Proprietors understood that "our trade with the Westoes so far has not been merely out of a design for gain." Rather, the Lords Proprietors believed that "by furnishing a bold and warlike nation with arms, ammunition, and other things," the Westos would "keep all other nations in awe." Terror and enslavement became the means by which Carolinians hoped to control Indian peoples throughout the Southeast. Like the Westos, the English used violence to carve out a space for themselves on the southern rim of English settlement. "Being by us exalted over their neighbors," one Englishman wrote, long-distance migrants "terrify these Indians."[20] The English wanted Westo slavers to intimidate and ultimately to destroy the Spanish missions on the Florida Peninsula. But the Indian slave trade was beyond their capacity to control. The Westos attacked Spanish mission Indians as well as settlement Indians allied with Carolina. Violence became more commonplace and unpredictable throughout the Southeast.

The Westos, the Shawnees, and the End of Their Long Alliance

By 1674, when the Shawnees first met Henry Woodward at Hickauhaugau, the Westos had already become a problem for the English. Their attacks on mission Indians threatened the colony's security in the greater Southeast. For more than a decade, Westo slavers had expanded their reach, attacking disparate peoples ranging from the Creeks and Cherokees to the proto-Catawbans of coastal Carolina. These raids contributed to the formation of the Creek and Catawba confederacies.[21] The trade in Indian slaves compelled far-flung villages to coalesce into defensive alliances. Some of these peoples had already established alliances with the English, but Carolinians wanted to challenge French and Spanish colonizers by drawing these confederacies into their alliance. Near-constant Westo attacks jeopardized these strategic aims.

Carolinians were unable to control whom the Westos besieged or with whom they traded. By 1674, Anthony Ashley Cooper, the first earl of Shaftesbury and the head of the Lords Proprietors, considered asking the Cussitas, "a powerful and warlike nation," for help in "root[ing] out" the Westos. The town of Cussita played a central role in the coalescence of the Lower Creek Confederacy. The Lords Proprietors hoped that "some nation whose government is less anarchical" than that of the Westos might be willing to settle along the Savannah River, where they would act as a kind of protective buffer for English settlements. Shaftesbury thought that Westo intransigence might come to an end if they could attract a rival power to the region.[22]

Shawnee visitors to Hickauhaugau had impeccable timing. In 1674, Shawnee migrants visited the Westos and warned them of an impending Cussita attack. Their warning came as Henry Woodward visited Westo town. During their encounter, Woodward described the Shawnees as carrying "Spanish beeds & other trade as presents." Shawnees then accompanied Woodward on his return journey, and they hunted on his behalf. In November, they parted company at his plantation on the Edisto River. Woodward expected them to return in March, "wth deare skins, furrs, and young slaves."[23] The Shawnees may have been looking for a more robust trading partner. With little more than trade beads to show for their travels, the Shawnees must have hoped for more than the English. Woodward seems to have provided the spark that prompted a large-scale Shawnee migration to the Savannah River. A seismic change in the Shawnees' economy and identity occurred as a result of the move.

The Shawnees' warning saved the Westos, albeit temporarily, from certain destruction. Chickasaw and Cherokee warriors had promised to join men from Cussita in an attack on Hickauhaugau. Initially, the Westos and Shawnees were allied against the Creeks and the Cherokees. But their allegiance to each other proved temporary. In 1679, the Westo War erupted between the Westos and the Shawnees. Within a year, the Westos lost control of their monopoly on the trade. Carolinians aided the Shawnees in the destruction of their former allies. The Shawnees emerged from the Westo War as the new regional power. According to Episcopal minister Francis Le Jau, the Shawnees "settled near this province Even before the Nations of the Westos were destroyed and to this day they keep about the places where the Westos lived."[24]

Long-range migrants such as the Shawnees appealed to the Lords Proprietors. They believed that newcomers "tyed . . . to soe strict a dependence on us [will] owe their strength . . . and absolutely depend on us." Migrants' access to guns and ammunition guaranteed English power. The Lords Proprietors' decision to abandon the Westos and to replace them with Shawnee migrants worked very well. When the war ended, colonial officials estimated that there were "not 50 Westohs left alive." After surviving Iroquois mourning wars, it was the slave trade that caused the ultimate ruin of the Westo people.[25]

The Westos may have encouraged the Shawnees to migrate to Carolina. Nevertheless, their alliance fell apart because of the pressures of the slave trade. During the Westo War, Shawnees captured Westo peace messengers, who "were taken & sent away to be sold." Westo survivors left Carolina in chains. The Lords Proprietors wondered "where shall ye Savanahs get Indians to sell ye Dealers in Indians." The Shawnees' answer to this question, like that of the Westos before them, was to capture Indian slaves wherever they could find them. Indiscriminate slaving had caused the Westos' downfall. But their Shawnee successors also noted their exclusive dependence on English allies. Unlike the Westos, Shawnee migrants came to the Southeast as allies of many resident populations, primarily the Upper Creek towns of Mucclassee and Tukabatchee.[26]

Between 1671 and 1708, Shawnees built a life for themselves along the Savannah River by obliging Woodward's request for Indian slaves. They established three villages on or near Beech Island, on the east side of the Savannah River, across from modern Augusta, Georgia. South Carolina's former governor, John Archdale, seemed pleased with the Shawnees' ascendancy. He noted that by 1680 the Shawnees in Carolina accounted for such numbers that they were able to reduce the Westos "from many thousands . . . to a small Number." Archdale believed that "the Hand of God was eminently seen in thin[n]ing the Indians, to make room for the English." He credited their defeat to divine justice, noting that the Westos, when compared to the Shawnees, were "the more cruel of the two." The Shawnees had become "good Friends and useful Neighbours to the English."[27]

Shawnee migrants must have sensed their vulnerability. By 1683, officials at Whitehall had learned that the Shawnees had "united all their tribes," and as a result it would be "dangerous" for Englishmen "to disoblige them." The Shawnees seem to have become mediators of the trade in Indian slaves. While some Shawnees certainly participated in slave raids, it was more common for allied tribes to bring captives to Savannah Town for shipment to English plantations. English laws encouraged the Shawnees' status as middlemen in the Indian slave trade. The English prohibited "buying slaves of any other but ye Savannahs." By granting the Shawnees such an exclusive right, allied tribes were compelled to trade their slaves to the Shawnees in exchange for "Gunns powder bullet and all things they have need of."[28] Savannah Town's geographic position on the fall line, coupled with the legal structure of the trade, made Shawnee migrants a formidable power.

The harrowing experience of Lamhátty, a Timucuan-speaking man captured somewhere west of the Apalachicola River, on the Gulf Coast,

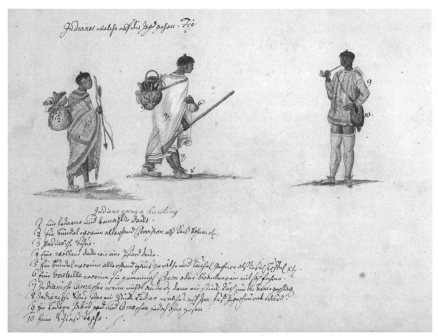

During his time as a slave of the Shawnees, Lamhátty traveled with a Shawnee family as they hunted in the Carolina backcountry. "Indians going a hunting," drawing by Philip Georg Friedrich von Reck, courtesy of The Royal Library, Copenhagen, Denmark.

provides a rare example of the Shawnees' role in mediating the Indian slave trade. Although Lamhátty did not identify his initial captors, some contend that it was the Tuscaroras, while others believe that the Creeks must have taken him. Whatever the identity of his captors, Lamhátty was one of 10,000 to 12,000 Indians from Florida who were enslaved during the first decade of the eighteenth century. Lamhátty's captors dragged him through Creek country for months, passing slowly from one town to another. The Tallapoosa Creeks "made him work in ye groun" before he was taken to the Shawnees, who "took him out a hunting." Lamhátty had been traded to a Shawnee hunting party that included six men, two women, and three children. His Shawnee captors bound him as they traveled north, along the eastern "ledge of Lower Mountains." Lamhátty eventually escaped, probably in the Piedmont of the Shenandoah Mountains. He then wandered onto the plantation of Colonel John Walker, who, like his various Indian captors, treated him as both a slave and a curiosity.[29]

The Shawnee hunters might have traveled north to trade Lamhátty to Virginia planters. Two slave owners, John Walker and Robert Berkeley, recorded Lamhátty's narrative. Throughout his captivity, from the Gulf Coast to Virginia, Lamhátty traveled through Indian and English settlements whose customs had been shaped by the slave trade. Lamhátty eventually fled Walker's plantation. He chose to take his chances alone, rather than face life as the slave of either the Shawnees or the Virginians.[30]

Slave raids in the Southeast were so frequent and unpredictable that alliances often came and went in the blink of an eye. Few Carolinians traveled beyond Savannah Town in the late seventeenth century, and their absence encouraged slavers to kill and capture both friends and enemies of the colony. The Westos and then the Shawnees largely determined with whom they were allied. By controlling the fall line, first the Westos and then the Shawnees managed Native desires for guns and other trade goods, and for a time Savannah Town became the most important center for trade in the Southeast. In 1675, the Westos attacked and enslaved the Yuchis. But five years later, the Yuchis joined the Westos in an assault against the mission Indians. In 1692, Shawnee warriors enslaved Cherokees. But in the coming years, at least some Shawnees at Savannah Town lived among the Cherokees.[31]

During the 1680s, at the height of Shawnee power, townspeople from the proto-Creek towns of Coweta and Cussita, in addition to the Yamasees, brought their slaves to Savannah Town. By reaching out to Muskogean, Yuchi, and Apalachee peoples, Shawnees created a formidable network of trading partners. English traders feared the fall-line villages, and they worried that they might become sites of pan-Indian resistance. In 1685, trader Caleb Westbrooke wrote that he believed that the leaders of ten different towns along with "3 nations of Spanish Indians" in Florida might be engaged in some "evil designed." Shawnees at Savannah Town murdered Westbrooke nine years later after he had alerted colonial officials about a possible anti-English alliance. Long-distance migrants at the Savannah River towns used the slave trade to become a formidable regional power. They became cultural brokers, capable of using trade goods and guile to threaten their English benefactors.[32]

By the eighteenth century, Shawnee had become a trade language in the Southeast. The English and French often used it to communicate with Muskogean, Iroquoian, and Uchean speakers in the Southeast. Le Jau, the Anglican minister, described the Shawnee language as "fine, smooth, and easy to be got." But the adoption of Shawnee reflects more than simply the ease of learning the language and the importance of the Shawnees to the Indian slave trade. The use of Shawnee—a linguistic outlier—speaks, quite literally, to the range of Shawnee migrations. According to Le Jau, "That language [the Savannah tongue] is understood all over these Northern Parts of America, even in Canada."[33]

In 1700, Jesuit missionary Jacques Gravier noted that both Yuchis and Shawnees could speak each other's language. On a trip down the Mississippi, probably near modern Memphis, Gravier encountered "a pirogue of Taögria," or Yuchi. Gravier noted the Yuchis' affinity for English trade goods and was surprised to learn they could "say a few words of Illinois." However, the exchange between the Yuchi and the Jesuit improved considerably when they both began speaking "the Chaouanoua tongue."[34]

Francis Le Jau served as the Episcopal minister for Goose Creek Parish, and many of his parishioners were notorious for their participation in the slave trade. "Goose Creek men" were particularly invested in the Indian slave trade, in part because they viewed Native peoples as little more than commodities. Men such as James Moore lived between the Ashley and the Cooper rivers, well beyond the rice plantations of the coast and the port city of Charles Town. While thinly populated and relatively remote, Goose Creek did have its advantages. By 1695, Moore owned property at the intersection of two vital roads, both of which connected Charles Town to Savannah Town and to a palisaded Catawba village, known as the Santee Fort, northwest of the city. Moore and one of his neighbors, Maurice Matthews, received commissions to destroy tribes that attacked Englishmen. Both men saw the advantage in prompting wars with the Indians, and Native villagers accused of committing depredations became their favored targets. Moore and others like him used accusations of violence to initiate wars against Native peoples. Anglicans in and around Charles Town supported these tactics because war captives could be legally sold as slaves. As with the Pequot War of 1637 and King Philip's War of 1675, Carolinians used warfare to legitimate the Indian slave trade.[35]

English officials worried about the ill effects of "Private Gaines . . . by buying slaves." However, stopping the slave trade seemed next to impossible. Carolina governor Joseph Morton tried to do something about it, and he doomed his political career as a result. Morton struggled to enforce the trade and navigation laws that would have limited the human traffic. For his efforts, the Carolina Council ruled that Morton was incapable of governing. His primary opponent, Captain James Moore, saw the Indian slave trade as the way to wealth.[36] The Goose Creek men defended themselves by claiming that some tribes were "transported" into slavery for the common good, to protect public safety. Colonial officials acquiesced to

Moore, but they demanded that Native people living within 200 miles of Charles Town would remain safe from his mercenaries and slavers.[37]

James Moore went on to become the governor of Carolina and reached the height of his power during Queen Anne's War (1702–13). English traders ventured beyond the Appalachian Mountains, driven by the desire to check French and Spanish ambitions. Imperial rivalries redefined the fall-line towns of the Savannah River. The Shawnees' ability to mediate the slave trade weakened as traders relocated to Savannah Town or moved west of it. Moore and a handful of rival traders aggressively courted the Creeks and the Chickasaws, hoping that they would challenge tribes allied to the French and the Spanish in the region. Moore's pastor, Francis Le Jau, described the motives of his parishioners in this way: "It is evident that our traders have promoted bloody wars . . . to get slaves." Moore used the slave trade to build great wealth for himself and his family. His own ascendancy, from overseer to colonial governor, pivoted on twin invasions of Spanish Florida in 1702 and 1704.[38]

Moore attacked the Apalachees, Muskogean speakers who lived between the Aucilla and Ochlockonee rivers along the Gulf of Mexico, because they had settled in a series of Spanish mission towns early in the seventeenth century. The Apalachee towns formed a barrier to Carolinians hoping to claim the Florida Peninsula. But Moore saw this as an opportunity. War with the Apalachees might yield thousands of slaves and promote English territorial claims. Native peoples from Florida and the Gulf Coast were far from partisans of the Spanish. The Spanish had convinced them to relocate to mission towns after disease had devastated their communities. Apalachee towns, now formally allied with the Spanish, became targets of the English. Worried about the French outpost at Mobile and the "capacity [of the French] to raise an Indian army," the English encouraged the confederacies of the southern interior to conduct slave raids along the Gulf of Mexico. The Shawnees' well-armed rivals in the interior Southeast now circumvented Savannah Town.[39]

In the 1702 invasion, conducted by sea and land, a force of 1,000 men, evenly divided between Englishmen and Indians, attacked St. Augustine. Moore's force was "obliged to retreat" by superior Spanish forces. In 1704, Moore reconfigured his army. With just 50 Englishmen and 1,300 Creek, Chickasaw, and Shawnee warriors, Moore launched a ground invasion on the vulnerable mission towns and forts of the Florida Peninsula. The invaders destroyed six Apalachee towns, and Moore estimated that they had enslaved 325 men and another 4,000 women and children. Most of the Apalachee slaves came from towns that had resisted Moore's forces. Another 300 men and 2,000 women and children surrendered. According to Moore, the "King of Attachookas" initiated the surrender by bringing Moore and his army "horses loaden with provisions." The defeated king explained that "the Spaniards were no longer able to protect or assist him." Moore compelled those who surrendered to join with their Creek and Shawnee attackers. Together, they relocated to the fall line of the Savannah River, where they established new Apalachee towns alongside Savannah Town. Moore regretted his decision to free some of the Apalachees. He complained that "my mens part of the plunder" would be small because of the forced relocation of the Apalachees. However, he acceded to the will of the Commons House of Assembly, which wanted to bolster the number of Indian allies on the Savannah River. Moore disputed the assembly's decision, pointing out that he alone raised the funds for this mercenary army and that the subsequent sale of Apalachee captives had made the invasion possible.[40]

The warriors who joined forces with Moore had their own motives for devastating the Apalachees. Apalachee assaults on "friends of the English" as well as the "settlements of Carolina" had challenged Shawnee, Creek, and Chickasaw authority. In the decade prior to the 1704 invasion, epidemic disease and slave raids contributed to demographic collapse in parts of the southeastern interior. Confederated tribal towns responded by initiating a kind of mourning war complex. Among the Ocheses and Tallapoosas, Thomas Nairne described Creek methods of captive taking that seem to be consistent with Iroquois practices. He wrote that "the first slave they take in his place [of a fallen kinsmen], to make up the number of the fameily." For Native peoples and the Goose Creek men alike, Queen Anne's War marked the apex of enslavement, captive taking, and migration in the colonial Southeast. The European dimensions of the conflict mattered little along the borderland between English and Spanish colonies. Creeks and Shawnees now had to make a space for their former enemies amid their own people. Decades later, in 1738, South Carolina governor William Bull attempted to convert Moore's invasions of Spanish Florida into a territorial dispute between rival empires. Bull claimed that the conquest, enslavement, and exile of the Apalachees amounted to the English conquest of Florida. But for Moore and the Native warriors involved in the invasion of the Gulf Coast, the quest for slaves and captives to replace fallen kinsmen was the primary motivation. Bull tried, and failed, to claim Florida and the Gulf Coast by right of conquest.[41]

Profits from both the Indian slave trade and the deerskin trade grew dramatically in the first decade of the eighteenth century. Increasingly ambitious traders had reached the interior Southeast by the close of the seventeenth century. Sustained trading relationships with the Chickasaws and the Muskogeans began in 1698 when Thomas Welch set up a trading post west of the Mississippi, among the Quapaws. In that same year, English traders moved to Savannah Town, where they gradually undermined Shawnees who had mediated the trade from their town. The Middle Savannah River became a frontier outpost, a place where traders and mercenaries rested and resupplied before setting out for the interior. Illegal French traders, as well as Indian hunters and guides, often worked for English traders at Savannah Town.[42]

By 1710, Apalachee and Yuchi migrants, along with English traders, had relocated to the fall line of the Savannah River. This region became a much more diverse place, and people from across the Eastern Woodlands were drawn to it through a combination of fear, force, and the lure of English goods. Following their forced relocation, the Apalachees became English mercenaries. But the Shawnees and the Yuchis chafed at the English notion that they had become little more than soldiers for hire and guides. They now witnessed the transformation of the Middle Savannah River. It was no longer a borderland in which Indian migrants could live with a degree of autonomy. By the eighteenth century, Savannah Town was an outpost of the English empire.[43]

Migrants to the borderland towns of the fall line traded extensively with the British. Archaeologists have found evidence of English goods strewn about the fall-line towns. The human traffic brought with it a degree of material comfort for long-distance migrants. In fact, Spanish trade goods are present at these sites as well, but they are nowhere near as abundant. The material evidence reveals a broader pattern of migration and trade that is consistent with the archival record. Native people moved vast distances to trade with Europeans, but the Spanish trade never amounted to what they had hoped. In response, Native migrants turned to the English and, to a lesser extent, the French. The Indian slave trade became an important element in migration and the quest for European goods.[44]

In the first decade of the eighteenth century, the English tried to bend the Shawnees to their will through a mixture of diplomacy and force. In response, Shawnees began secretly leaving the colony. Carolina Shawnees migrated to the northern reaches of the Chesapeake Bay by the last decade of the seventeenth century. As Algonquians originally from the Ohio Valley, these Savannah River Shawnees called upon long-standing ties with northern tribes, including the Iroquois, Susquehannocks, and Delawares. Their journey northward was prompted by a devastating attack on Savannah Town by the Catawbas. Carolinians probably overstated the numbers, but they claimed that the Catawbas had killed 450 Shawnees in a single battle.[45] Catawba proxies of the English now devastated the Shawnees in ways that resembled Shawnee actions in the Westo War. Shawnees abandoned the region to avoid the fate of their Westo predecessors.

The Carolina proprietors did what they could to stop Shawnees from leaving. Traders, new arrivals, and spies at Savannah Town kept the English informed of their movements. In 1707, rumors circulated about Shawnee intentions after "Cundy, an Indian Woman and Wife to one of the traders, reported that the Savanas intended to goe away."[46] The following year, Francis Le Jau confirmed these rumors when he reported that "one of the Savannah Town's Inhabitants went away from us . . . and are joined with our enemies." In 1710, Le Jau observed that some Shawnees continued to "keep about the places where the Westos lived, but perhaps are not so numerous."[47]

Carolina sent a delegation north to Maryland to induce the Shawnees to return. Later, in 1707, Governor Moore led what amounted to an "armed posse" of Creek Indians against the runaway Shawnees. Moore feared Shawnee reprisals against his new allies, the Catawbas and the Creeks. After they migrated to the contested borderland between Maryland and Pennsylvania, Carolina passed the Indian Trade Act of 1707. With a board of commissioners, an Indian agent, and the power to issue lucrative trade licenses, the legislation was designed to put a stop to slave raids against English-allied tribes. Thomas Nairne was the first Indian agent under the Indian Trade Act of 1707, and his grand tour of the Southeast was an attempt by the Carolinians to adopt a more muscular, assertive role in the greater Southeast. The act bolstered the position of the Catawbas and other English-allied towns by forbidding their enslavement.[48]

Like previous attempts at regulating who, where, and under what circumstances people could be enslaved, the 1707 act revealed the essential weakness of colonial governments. By 1707, slavers and mercenaries had depopulated many of the Indian villages of Carolina. Native slavers became desperate as their search for slaves narrowed. But more important, militarized slaving societies such as the Chickasaws became the main slavers of the English, and the slave trade moved westward, to the Mississippi Valley. Chickasaw slavers decimated neighboring groups such as the Quapaws and the Choctaws. Similar transformations were taking place in other parts of the South. By 1710, in Georgia and Alabama, "60 percent of Tallapoosa warriors, 33 percent of Abeca warriors, and perhaps all Alabama warriors" had acquired guns. These proto-Creek townspeople, like their Chickasaw neighbors to the west, now dominated the Indian slave trade. As the slave trade moved westward, intermediaries such as the Shawnees became expendable.[49]

From Slavers to Refugees: The Collapse of the Fall-Line Migrants

Southeastern tribal townspeople confronted the reality that if they chose not to become slavers they would almost certainly be enslaved. This simple calculation triggered vast migrations and compelled many tribal towns to coalesce in order to survive. By the second decade of the eighteenth century, English traders lived among coalescent populations such as the Cherokees, Creeks, and Chickasaws. These confederacies now targeted small societies such as the Yuchis, Shawnees, and French-allied tribes of the Gulf Coast. Traders allied with larger, coalescent communities encouraged this transition, from the Middle Savannah River towns to the confederacies of the interior Southeast. The most spectacular reflection of this reality came in 1714, when a Yuchi town, Chestowe, situated near the Cherokees on the Middle Tennessee River, was attacked by a Cherokee force. A rogue British trader named Alexander Long inspired the slaughter over a soured trade relationship with the Chestowe Yuchis. When Cherokee warriors surprised their village, the Chestowe Yuchis understood that those who survived the attack would be enslaved and sold into slavery, most likely in the British West Indies. This was a fate worse than death, and it was all too familiar to tribes such as the Yuchis. According to a trader named James Douglas, "The Euchees killed their own People in the War House to prevent their falling into the Hands of the Cherikees."[50]

The attack on Chestowe threatened to engulf the entire region in a general war, as allied tribes on both sides considered retaliation. Both Alexander Long and the Cherokees nearly waged a surprise attack on the Yuchi and Shawnee villages along the Savannah River in order to prevent them from retaliating on the Chestowe Yuchis' behalf. The Cherokees claimed that "they were told by the white people since Chestowe was cut off they ought to goe cut off the other Euchees att the Savana Town or else there would be no Traviling." Long and his Cherokee allies knew that allied towns frequently came together for mutual defense. While the Middle Tennessee River and the Savannah River seem geographically distant to us now, colonial Americans understood that "the headwaters of the Savannah interlaced with the sources of the Tennessee." Yuchis and Shawnees on the Savannah River thus had easy access to Chestowe. They could—and would—seek justice for their fallen kin. It was only through long hours of careful diplomacy, what Indian people called "covering the dead," that the British were able to avert further bloodshed.[51]

Even the Chickasaws, the ascendant slavers of the Lower Mississippi Valley, sometimes fell victim to slavers from the upper country, whose war parties ranged all the way to the Gulf Coast. The Chickasaws complained that the "Paywallies [or Illinois] . . . are the slyest and most patient men stealers of the World, for they sculk close by the Towns untill they have done some murther, and Fly off with all speed." Like Nairne, the Chickasaws understood that security against Illinois attacks could only come with English guns. Nairne encouraged the Chickasaws, once armed, to attack "their Bow and Arrow Neighbours," along the Gulf Coast. Nairne convinced a Chickasaw chief "that slave Catching was much more profitable than formal haranguing." In his view, the Chickasaws could be "as good a man hunter as the best of them."[52] The slave trade tied people from different regions and empires to a common fate, one in which access to guns and trade goods became the means of survival.

English travel writer and slaver John Lawson witnessed the Shawnees' place in the region at this crucial moment in their history. He described them as a "famous, warlike, friendly Nation of Indians." Lawson aptly characterized the Shawnees' multiple roles as slavers, traders, and intermediaries between tribes. As he traveled through the Carolina Piedmont, among proto-Catawban people, he learned that the reputation of the Shawnees varied considerably. Lawson was astounded by the particular differences between the Native peoples he encountered along the Pee Dee and Santee rivers. He wrote that "altho' their Tribes or Nations border one upon another, yet you may discern as great an Alteration in their Features and Dispositions, as you can in their Speech, which generally proves quite different from each other, though their Nations be not above 10 or 20 miles in Distance."[53] The threat of Shawnee attack had moved these Catawban villagers toward a military alliance. By the second decade of the eighteenth century, reprisals between the Catawbas and the Shawnees had become so intense that a "Catawba Trail" leading warriors to Shawnee villages in Carolina and Pennsylvania became well known. Centuries after these wars, Catawba elders told their children tales of Shawnee warriors so fierce that even wolves feared them.[54]

In these years, Shawnees now located in the mid-Atlantic, along the fall line of the Susquehanna River, attacked Indian towns allied with Charles Town and sometimes killed or made slaves of those they captured. Carolinians swiftly retaliated. In February 1708, the Carolina assembly paid the "Northward Indians," probably the Catawba, "fifty guns a Thousand flints

200tw of powder 400 tw of Bulletts . . . to attack the said Indians our Enemies." Catawbas who brought in either a scalp or a Shawnee prisoner got to keep their gun. Long-distance warfare between Shawnees and Catawbas made it almost impossible for large numbers of Shawnees to remain at Savannah Town. Shawnee migrants took advantage of the rivalry between the British colonies, and reprisal killings up and down the eastern seaboard proliferated. In 1708, Carolinians conducted a census of Indian towns in their colony, revealing that some Shawnees had stayed behind, residing in one of their three towns, and still could field a combined force of 150 warriors.[55]

Carolina's Indians sensed that indebtedness to traders further weakened their bargaining power. Faced with diminishing supplies of deer and slaves, Indian hunters became little more than debt peons. To cite one example, the Yamasees, a coalescent population of Muskogean speakers who lived along the southern coast of Carolina, were 50,000 pounds in debt to traders by 1715. Across Carolina, groups ranging from the Tuscaroras to the Yamasees came to grips with their diminished status.[56]

Shawnees who remained in Carolina assisted British traders in some of the most dangerous work of the Indian trade, including mercenary slaving. During the Tuscarora War of 1711–12, Yuchi, Shawnee, and Apalachee warriors defended colonial plantations from possible attack. In 1711, the Carolina assembly created a force of Indians for protection, to include "100 from the Savannahs and Appalacheas and Tohogoligo [Yuchis]." The Shawnees, Yuchis, and Apalachees became armed defenders of British settlements in order to remain in Carolina. Their warriors coordinated a defensive buffer between Tuscarora warriors in North Carolina and settlements such as Charles Town.[57]

Constant war transformed the ritual lives of American Indians in the Southeast. The tactical use of violence ensured their continued relevance to English colonists, but it also meant that rituals of war came to dominate their ceremonial lives. Colonists involved in slaving sometimes attended war rituals because they sanctified the taking of life in warfare. European observers left behind some written descriptions of these ceremonies. For example, in 1736, Lower Creek chief Tomochichi, the leader of the Yamacraws, joined the Yuchi chief Umpeachy in performing a war dance prior to their attack on St. Augustine. Tomochichi's and Umpeachy's people "made a ring, in the Middle of which four sat down, having little Drums made of Kettles, cover'd with Deer-skins." The four men "beat and sung" while "others danced . . . naked to their Waists." The ritual culminated when the "chief warriors . . . stood out" and "describ'd (by Actions as well as by Words) which way he had vanquish'd the Enemies of his Country." This

Native mercenaries assisted colonizers often enough that they sometimes witnessed rituals associated with war. "A War Dance," probably Yuchi, 1736, Georgia, watercolor by Philip Georg Friedrich von Reck, courtesy of The Royal Library, Copenhagen, Denmark.

particular war ritual, while performed by southeastern tribes, resembles Algonquian war rituals, including those of the Shawnees, Kickapoos, and Delawares. Yuchi war rituals manifested the common bonds shared between them and their Shawnee neighbors. Linguistically and culturally, the Shawnees and the Yuchis were outliers in the Muskogean-speaking worlds of the Southeast.[58]

Across the Eastern Woodlands, music, dance, and descriptions of war exploits were central to rituals associated with war. But within this shared custom, tribes set themselves apart from each other in subtle ways. For example, Creek rituals of war typically included fasting and purification, and women were excluded from these ceremonies. In 1772, while on a diplomatic mission among the Upper Creeks, David Taitt witnessed a series of ritual events designed to bring success for men "going off to war the next day." Central to the evening's ceremonies was the powerful emetic, the black drink, or *ilex vomitoria*. After taking black drink, Taitt joined the men in a sweat lodge, followed by the "usual Ceremoney of Smoking Tobacco." In everything from warfare to planting, the complementary, but sex-segregated, world of the Creeks contrasted with that of the Yuchis.

The Indian agent Benjamin Hawkins was struck by the fact that at Yuchi Town "the men take part in the labors of the women." As a keen observer of the Muskogee people, Hawkins noticed that the Yuchis were outliers, in terms of both gender and language.[59]

The Yamasee War and the Decline of the Indian Slave Trade

By 1715, the English hunger for Indian slaves had diminished Native populations throughout the Southeast. English-allied tribes remained vulnerable to kidnapping and enslavement. Rogue traders, encouraged by the planter elite, fueled the cruelty. Aggrieved Indian communities joined forces against the Carolinians. On Good Friday, April 15, 1715, the Yamasee War began with a massacre of settlers around Port Royal. Thomas Nairne attempted to stem the bloodshed on the day before the attack. Nairne, along with two other men, rushed to the Yamasee town of Pocataligo, only to be taken hostage by the people he visited. Nairne's compatriots were quickly put to death. The Yamasees saved their rage for Nairne. After tying him to a post, they thrust hundreds of wood splinters into his body, which they then lit on fire. He died slowly, consumed by fire, over a period of days. Le Jau observed that Native peoples who had been allied with the English, including "Crick Indians, to whom the Yamoussees, Savana, and Apalachi Indians are joined," suddenly became their enemies. For years, Carolinians feared such an alliance. With "2,000 stout men" against them, Carolina's Indians remained formidable.[60]

The Yamasee War featured intimate violence between Indian slavers and their English buyers. In July 1715, Le Jau described how approximately 600 warriors from the "Yamousees, Apalachee's Savanas & other Southern Indians . . . burn'd about 30 houses, Destroy'd all the Horses Cattle and Plantations they could." The Yuchi and Lower Ochese Creek fought against the English in the southern arm of the Yamasee War. Uchee Island, located "16 miles above Fort Augusta," was a short distance north of Savannah Town, on modern Beech Island. While only 67 Shawnee warriors and another 166 women and children remained at Savannah Town in the 1715 census, 130 Yuchi men lived with their wives and children at two Yuchi settlements above modern Augusta, Georgia, in that same year. In 1716, Carolinians ultimately turned the tide of the war against the Shawnees and the Yuchis and their more numerous and powerful allies, the Creek and the Yamasee. Cherokee and Tuscarora warriors allied with Carolina fought alongside African slaves pressed into service to save the colony from destruction.[61]

By the 1720s, Shawnees continued migrating to Maryland and Pennsylvania. In 1725, the Savannah Town trader Charlesworth Glover conducted a census of Indian towns in the Southeast. He noted that there were thirty Shawnees remaining at Savannah Town, only eight of whom were men. In contrast, there were 530 Yuchis at the time. For Glover, the 1725 census confirmed that "the Indians [seemed to] decay every where." The lone exception to this demography of decline, for Glover, was the "Youches." Surprisingly, in 1725, they represented the "highest Number of Souls in the 3 provinces."[62]

The thirty Shawnees who remained at the town that bore their name may have coalesced into any number of the Indian towns along the Savannah River. There were simply too few of them to have survived independently. In contrast, the Yuchi seem to have rebounded from the massacre at Chestowe. Some degree of political centralization seems to have occurred as well. As late as 1737, the Chickasaw war chief Mingo Ouma created a map of the Southeast that defined the Yuchis' place in this world. While Mingo Ouma identified Muskogee towns such as Coweta and Okfuskee, he did not locate these towns within an overarching "Creek" national synthesis. His preference for locating various southeastern Indian identities in *talwas*, or towns, reflects the real limits that the Creek people placed on centralized power. Individual towns remained the primary marker of identity, the means by which one sorted out the difference between an ally and an enemy. Mingo Ouma believed that the Yuchi were allied with both the British and the lower Creek town of Cussita. In contrast, Mingo Ouma did not include Shawnee towns on his map of the colonial Southeast. His silence regarding the Shawnees illustrates the extent of upheaval and migration endured by Native peoples in the eighteenth century. Regional contexts changed frequently in the colonial world.[63]

Shawnees who stayed behind remained allied to the Yuchis and Creeks. Their historic alliance is so extensive that many colonial observers erroneously believed that Yuchi was a dialect of Shawnee. The travel writer and naturalist William Bartram, writing in the 1770s, described the Yuchi language as "altogether or radically different from the Creek or Muscogulge tongue, and is called the Savanna or Savanuca tongue." Bartram was right to clearly differentiate Yuchi from Muskogee. But local traders led him to believe that Yuchi was "a dialect of, the Shawanese."[64] Ties between the Yuchis and the Shawnees were so close that Bartram, along with local traders, often thought of them as a single people.

Colonizers tended to identify people by their primary language. But Native people often used distinctive hairstyles and material ornamentation to draw boundaries between themselves and others. The 1736 drawings of Philip Georg Friedrich von Reck illustrate the Yuchis' distinctive "top-knot hairstyle." In 1753, Shawnee warriors wore a single feather attached to a roach haircut. When asked to explain, the Shawnees simply replied that "all our Indians dress the same way." Hairstyles helped warriors differentiate between friend and foe. According to von Reck, "They cut the upper part of the head hair from those they have conquered in order to see from what nation and tribe they are." Shawnee men further distinguished themselves by partially severing the auricles of their ears and by applying trade silver and other metal wrappings, stretching them down toward their shoulders over time.[65]

Across Indian country, language, hairstyle, and dress embodied striking differences between contiguous tribal towns. Bartram noticed incredible variation in the Creek Confederacy's influence over the sixty to seventy towns in its sphere of influence. The Yuchis possessed "a very extensive territory over which they claim an exclusive property." Bartram did not challenge Yuchi understandings of their territory, perhaps because he noticed that members of the Creek Confederacy were "cautious of affronting the Uches so generally yield for their common interest and safety."[66]

When the Indian slave trade subsided after the Yamasee War, Yuchi and Shawnee villagers continued to work as mercenaries and auxiliaries of both the British and the Creek Confederacy. Then, as before, the Shawnees and the Yuchis converted their knowledge of the eastern half of North America into an asset. Both were well armed and both had the linguistic and diplomatic skill to make sense of intensely mobile Indian villagers. Unlike the Westos, the Shawnees and the Yuchis would survive the chaos and disorder of colonialism by holding fast to their unique traditions in semiautonomous towns that were an extension of the larger multiethnic confederacies. Mobile tribal towns became proving grounds in their long struggle against genocide and assimilation.

chapter 5

The Grand Village of the Kaskaskias

OLD ALLEGIANCES, NEW WORLDS

In September 1680, "a Chaouanon, Confederate to the Illinois," rushed to the Grand Village of the Kaskaskias with an urgent message. He arrived just ahead of a war party led by the Iroquois but supported by Miamis and his own Shawnee kinsmen. He warned that more than 500 warriors were preparing to attack the Kaskaskias, the foremost tribe of the Illinois Confederacy. The Kaskaskias scrambled to protect the aged and infirm, as well as the women and children of their village, sending more than 1,500 people down the Illinois River toward a village of Tamaroa allies located ten miles below the confluence of the Illinois and Mississippi rivers. The Iroquois held the advantage, and the Illinois knew it. The French described how the Illinois hid their people in a wetland so inundated that it was "almost inaccessible." Those who stayed behind berated Henry de Tonty, a Frenchman and a lieutenant of the Sieur de La Salle. They said that it was Tonty "who made them come."[1] Tonty listened to their chastisement and walked out onto the prairie to greet their attackers with the calumet pipe and an offering of corn. The Iroquois ignored these peace gestures. Iroquois gunmen fired on them as they approached but missed their targets. Frustrated, a young Onondaga warrior ran toward the Frenchmen and stabbed Tonty near the heart, the blade glancing off his rib cage. When Tonty fell to the ground, the Iroquois discovered that he was French "by his ears, which were not pierced." Only then did they accept the calumet pipe and the corn offering. His attackers then "embraced him and covered him, telling them to excuse them." Tonty, Father Gabriel de la Ribourde, Father Zénobe Membré, a young man of the lesser nobility named Sieur de Boisrondet, and two other unnamed French *engages*, hired canoe men, were taken by the Iroquois "under a false pretence of peace."[2]

Now captives of the Iroquois, the Frenchmen had no other choice than to abandon their confederates to their fate. Half dead, and with little ammunition, they began walking eastward, along the Illinois River, to its confluence with the Des Plaines River, then north toward the St. François Xavier Mission at the base of Green Bay. After a three-month journey with little food, in which the seasons changed from fall to winter, Tonty and four others were discovered by Potawatomis near the French mission. Father Gabriel had been killed by an unknown assailant along the way after he separated himself from the group to pray.

Tonty and the French survivors of the 1680 attack had been stationed at the Grand Village of the Kaskaskias, a place at the center of the upper country, a region riven by warfare, disease, and migration in which Native peoples' home villages guided their response to these cataclysms. Whole "tribes" did not create alliances with either the French or the Iroquois. Instead, villagers reached ephemeral agreements with confederacies and colonizers connected to distant trading centers at Charles Town, Jamestown, Montreal, and Albany. In the 1680 attack, which devastated the Kaskaskias and the Tamaroas, Membré described "a hundred Chaouanons, armed with bows and arrows only," who had joined the Iroquois in the attack on Grand Village. They joined forces with Iroquois warriors who were "armed with guns, pistols, and sabres." Wearing shields made of wood and leather, the Iroquois were formidable enemies whose dress and arms made plain that they were well supplied by colonizers and, as a result, militarily superior to the Illinois.[3]

Shawnees and Miamis fought for and against the Iroquois in the attack on Grand Village. The 100 Shawnees allied with the Iroquois may have decided to join forces with them after the Haudenosaunee invasions of Fort Ancient territory between 1669 and 1671. We will probably never be able to fully recapture their motivations. But we do know that as the Kaskaskias tried to save their people, another 150 Shawnees did their best to help them. In 1680, two distinct Shawnee bands met in battle near the Grand Village of the Kaskaskias. Such conflicts were common throughout the upper country in the seventeenth century. And in moments in which members of the same tribe fought against one another, a historian cannot simply "make the crooked ways straight" and ignore the evidence. It is clear that members of the five Shawnee divisions, the Chalagawtha, Thawekila, Kispokotha, Mekoche, and Pekowitha, occasionally fought each other. When confronted with this evidence, a historian might conclude that Shawnee and Miami villagers were engaged in a civil war played out in and around the Grand Village of the Kaskaskias. After all, Native peoples in the upper country lived in a world in which warfare and migration created competing alliances. Shawnees allied with the Iroquois joined with them as villagers, just as Shawnees who fought alongside the Kaskaskias and the French followed their own local predilections. For these reasons, the 1680 attack cannot be described as a civil war. Neither the Miamis nor the Shawnees thought of themselves as a "tribe" in which widely accepted leaders set policy and led a series of interconnected villages. They were not members of Native nations torn apart by colonialism. The violence of 1680 stemmed from the parochial cosmopolitanism that characterized the Native peoples of the upper country. Central Algonquians maintained divided loyalties, and their unique allegiances frustrated the French and the Iroquois alike, accustomed as they were to more far-reaching systems of authority.[4]

The Shawnees' Role in French Exploration

In the historic period, the first Shawnees to have reached the Upper Midwest probably arrived as captives-turned-guides of the French. Three different contingents of Shawnees were involved in the 1680 attack, including guides whose captivity had estranged them from the villages of their birth, confederates of the Kaskaskia, and partisans of the Iroquois.

Captives from distant villages eased the way into the interior for French explorers. In 1673, when Marquette and Joliet first arrived at Grand Village, they became the first Europeans to live among the Kaskaskias. Like Native people then moving across the continent, Marquette, Joliet, and others like them traveled constantly. However much Catholic missionaries professed a desire to convert Native peoples, it seems that an unwritten vow of adventure compelled them to travel for months at a time into the interior of the continent. In the 1670s, French traders journeyed between Fort Frontenac, at the mouth of the Cataraqui River, to Fort Michilimackinac, at the juncture of Lake Huron and Lake Michigan. From Fort Michilimackinac, the French descended Lake Michigan, where they portaged to the Illinois River basin. The Illinois River—and the Grand Village of the Kaskaskias—became the staging ground for the discovery and exploration of the Mississippi River. La Salle spent the majority of his time on the Mississippi in search of a "northwest passage." As with the Virginia traders, La Salle hoped to discover an all-water route to Asia, the real El Dorado of European dreamers. La Salle's obsession was so great that he was largely blind to the endemic warfare that had overtaken the Illinois country. Trade, conversion, and the concentration of Native people at refugee centers fell to Tonty and those missionaries willing to martyr themselves in this difficult land.

For a number of other Shawnees who were being held captive, guiding French explorers became the means by which they escaped possible death and, at best, the loss of their identity to their captors. Working with Europeans enabled captives to return to their people and their homes. Some Shawnees traveled to the Illinois country as guides and hunters for French expeditions, along with some captives who had been liberated from the Iroquois. It is clear that these forays lured some to the Grand Village of the Kaskaskias. These Shawnee guides joined with Shawnees then living on the Illinois River in 1673, when Joliet and Marquette arrived.[5]

For the French, captives became an essential tool in their exploration of the continent. Among the Senecas, La Salle planned on offering French "presents" to "procure slaves of the tribes to which he intended to go, who might serve him as guides." Near the Irondequoit River, in central New York, their party was greeted by Seneca villagers, who gave him small gifts, including "Indian corn, squashes, blackberries . . . and fruits that they have in abundance." La Salle decided to "try to get a slave of the tribes to which we wished to go for the purpose of conducting us thither." To gain these captives, he presented the Senecas with a double-barreled pistol, "so that with one shot they could kill . . . the tribes against whom they wage a cruel war."[6]

Captives of the Iroquois cleared a path to the interior of the continent. The French described the two captives as Shawnee and "Nez Perce," or "Pierced Nose." As an ethnic marker, nose piercing most likely meant that this captive was either Potawatomi or Ottawa. For Dollier, the Nez Perce's hunting skills mattered almost as much as his ethnic affiliation and his ability to guide his expedition. Dollier believed that "both were good hunters and showed that they were well disposed." La Salle became the de facto owner of the Shawnee slave, while the missionary traveling with him became the owner of the Nez Perce.[7]

On July 6, 1669, "a fleet of seven canoes, each with three men," departed for the upper country. Almost immediately, La Salle disagreed with the missionaries over which route to take to the interior. They divided their canoes, and historians now believe that La Salle traveled south from Montreal, into the *pays d'en haut*. However, his claims to have reached the falls of the Ohio (modern Louisville) are almost certainly false. In contrast, the Sulpician headed north, toward the Jesuit mission at Sault Sainte Marie. No longer content with servility, the Nez Perce guide got drunk, destroyed a canoe, and abandoned the missionaries as soon as they were clear of the Seneca villages.[8]

The 1680 Attack and the Complex Social
Worlds of the Upper Country

The attack on the Grand Village of the Kaskaskias occurred while Tonty's benefactor, the Sieur de La Salle, explored the lower reaches of the Mississippi River. In December 1680, on his return to the upper country, La Salle finally learned what had happened to his men and his Indian allies. When he reached the Tamaroa village, all he discovered was death and destruction. A sense of foreboding took over his party after Tamaroa runners failed to greet La Salle and his men on the prairie leading up to the village. Once in the village, the official historian of the expedition, Abbé Claude Bernou, wrote that "nothing was left but the ends of burnt poles . . . and on most of them the heads of corpses had been fixed and picked by crows." The village, which had stretched for three miles along the riverbank, was entirely deserted, save for "a quantity of calcined bones." Wolves and crows had gorged themselves on the corpses left to rot in the adjoining cornfields. Storage pits brimming with corn, beans, and squash had been thrown open, the remnants of summer labor strewn about the destroyed village. Curiously, about three miles from the village, he found "six stakes . . . painted red, with a drawing on each of a black man with his eyes bandaged." La Salle guessed that it was an Iroquois custom to "put up such stakes at the places where they have captured or killed some of their enemies."[9]

Upon leaving the Tamaroa village, La Salle traveled northeast, up the Illinois River. In this leg of his journey, the broad outlines of the Iroquois attack became clear. The Iroquois first destroyed the Grand Village of the Kaskaskias before pursuing those sent to the Tamaroas. La Salle's men described how the Iroquois "vented their rage on the dead bodies of the Illinois, which they disinterred," or threw down from their platform burials. The bodies left to the dogs, the Iroquois beheaded some of the dead, fixing their skulls on stakes throughout the village.[10] At both the Kaskaskia and the Tamaroa village, everything from food stores to burials had been desecrated.

La Salle's sense of the carnage became clear to him because, as he and his men moved north and east along the Illinois River, they camped at the temporary shelters of the Iroquois and their allies, composed in haste as they pursued the Illinois. At one such camp he found 113 "huts." The attackers had carved "portraits of their chiefs and the number of men under the command" onto the bark of trees. La Salle counted 582 warriors. Of the Illinois women and children, less than half survived the long journey back to Iroquoia. Bernou estimated that nearly 400 people had been captured, while another 800 had been killed.[11]

Iroquois mourning wars reached deep into the upper country. In response, towns such as the Grand Village of the Kaskaskias became important sites of French and Indian confederation. At its height, more than 8,000 American Indians from thirteen different tribes settled at or near Grand Village. A "Chaouanon chief" led 150 warriors, part of approximately 500 Shawnees, to the Grand Village of the Kaskaskias. The French learned that the Shawnees came from "a great river which falls into the River Ohio." This geographic location supports the contention that some of the historically known Shawnees migrated out of the Middle Ohio Valley and into the Illinois River Valley. The French described how the Shawnees allied with the Iroquois first appeared along the Vermilion River, near modern-day Danville, Illinois. Shawnees and Miamis had joined with the Iroquois to the east of Grand Village as they moved toward their targets on the short-grass prairies of Illinois. In contrast, members of the Illinois Confederacy were allied with Algonquians and Siouans from Wisconsin, Iowa, and Missouri. The Grand Village of the Kaskaskias sat on a fault line between competing alliances.[12]

La Salle was preoccupied largely with exploring the Mississippi River, so Tonty was left with the task of building French forts in the Illinois country. Tonty was a soldier-adventurer who had lost his right hand to a grenade while fighting the Spanish in Italy. His Indian allies called him "bras-de-fer," or "Iron Arm," because of the iron-fisted prosthetic he wore. Tonty was no stranger to violence. A month before the Iroquois-Miami attack, twenty-three French laborers and would-be traders helped build the first fort on the Illinois River, Fort Crevecoeur. It was built on Lake Pimitoui, near modern-day Peoria, and the fort was burned to the ground by the same men who built it. Evidence suggests that La Salle drove his men ruthlessly during construction. A revolt occurred, and his workers burned Crevecoeur to the ground. These men then deserted Tonty, leaving him and five others to an uncertain fate among the Illinois, whose primary village, Grand Village, lay to the northeast, toward Lake Michigan. Tonty and his remaining men made Grand Village their temporary home, and while they were there they made plans for the construction of Fort St. Louis, across the river from Grand Village. One of the Frenchmen who helped build, and then burn, Crevecoeur was Martin Chartier. The burning of the French fort marked a turning point in his life and introduced a new era in Shawnee relations with colonizers as well. Chartier became a notorious *coureurs de bois*, or "runner of the woods," the French term for men who traded among the Indians without a license from the empire.[13] For the remainder of his life, Chartier journeyed with Shawnees as they moved from Illinois to Pennsylvania. For Chartier, marrying into Shawnee society became a better path toward survival than remaining with La Salle and Tonty. His Shawnee kinsmen valued his intercultural skills as they moved between French, English, and Native worlds, from Grand Village to the Lower Susquehanna River.

Chartier traded canoeing the interior of the continent for French explorers for a life as a partisan of a Shawnee band that refused to choose sides in imperial contests for power. Their refusal to become permanent allies of New France explains why French officials often executed illegal traders when they caught them. The colonizers with whom he dealt always treated him with suspicion. But the Shawnees valued him because he effectively brought his knowledge of European colonizers to Shawnees struggling to make sense of these newcomers. Chartier became their cultural broker.[14]

In the 1670s and 1680s, Shawnees converged on the Upper Illinois River Valley. At the height of their tenure in Illinois, French observers estimated, there were "a hundred families of Shawnee." Scholars have used this figure to estimate that as many as 800 to 1,000 Shawnees then lived near the Grand Village of the Kaskaskias. However, a more likely figure seems to be between 400 and 500 people. Tonty placed an extraordinary level of trust in the Shawnees living near Fort St. Louis. Since the late 1660s, Shawnee guides and hunters had accompanied La Salle and Tonty on most of their explorations of the Mississippi River. At Fort St. Louis, Tonty relied on the Shawnees to help with the shipment of trade goods across the cultural and geographic divides of the upper country, and he cited the "Honesty of the Chahouanous" when asked to explain his preference for their assistance. Shared struggles, as outsiders and migrants, might have quickened the ties between them. For Shawnee migrants, proximity to colonizers, from Martin Chartier to Henry Tonty, was a matter of survival.[15]

La Salle mistakenly believed that the Shawnees had "quitted" their villages "in order to become French." As evidence, he cited the fact that "they have obeyed me as to all the movements I have wished them to make." Shawnees consistently answered French requests for porters, laborers, and guides. Tonty valued their stout defense of Fort St. Louis as well as their willingness to haul supplies to Fort St. Louis. La Salle's high opinion of the

Shawnees likely came from the firsthand experiences of Tonty and another valued lieutenant named Henri Joutel. Joutel thought that the Shawnees were the most extraordinary of the tribes allied against the Iroquois. Like Tonty, Joutel was a military man who was accustomed to authority and intrigued by the possibilities of exploration. But, unlike Tonty, Joutel was a native of Rouen, France, La Salle's hometown. Joutel probably helped recruit Shawnees into the alliance at Grand Village. He enjoyed an extraordinarily close relationship with both La Salle and the Shawnees. Joutel often worked alongside Shawnees at Fort St. Louis, across from Grand Village, and he was surprised by the fact that "they were often among us, and in the warehouse, but nothing was ever observed to be missing." Later, in 1687, Joutel and Shawnee guides accompanied La Salle on his final journey down the Mississippi River, to the Gulf Coast. Beginning in 1688, the year Joutel returned to France, Shawnees steadily abandoned the Upper Illinois River Valley. Nevertheless, in 1698, when Pierre Le Moyne d'Iberville followed in La Salle's footsteps and attempted to found a permanent settlement in east Texas, he considered Joutel's journal of the La Salle expedition. In it, Joutel lauded the Shawnees' intercultural skill and trustworthiness. Not surprising, Le Moyne sent for a Shawnee "who can speak the language of the Indians," on what is now the Colorado River, in modern-day east Texas. Even before Shawnees led La Salle to the Gulf Coast, their people had become known for their geographic and linguistic range.[16] But after the 1687 expedition, the Shawnees' abilities became a settled fact, a matter of public record.

Between 1680 and 1688, when large numbers of Shawnees lived in and around Fort St. Louis, the French hired Shawnees for all sorts of tasks, including arduous journeys to and from French forts on Lake Michigan when supplies at Fort St. Louis ran low. Their commitment to the French caused an "unfriendly feeling" between the Shawnees and their Native neighbors at Grand Village and may have contributed to the dissolution of the confederacy. Joutel participated in a rich trade for goods and labor between the Shawnees and the French stationed at Fort St. Louis. When their labor was not needed, Shawnees traded corn bread and other foods to the French. Unlike the Illinois, who redistributed trade goods, most likely in an attempt to maintain the alliance they had helped to create, the Shawnees "keep what they possess." Joutel favored the Shawnees because they seemed to share French values associated with work and property.[17] Their customs and their loyalty made them familiar to the French in the strange world of the upper country, and the French granted the Shawnees special privileges as a result.

The Shawnees' emphasis on communally owned property surprised Joutel again and again. He described how "all their goods are kept always among their own men." Shawnee elders reinforced their authority by controlling access to European trade goods. Joutel once witnessed a game in which elders divided village property "into several lots" after a feast. An elder then held aloft a carved stick that had been smoothed and greased to such an extent that it was difficult to grasp. He then threw the stick as far as he could in front of a throng of young Shawnee men. These younger Shawnees rushed to grab the stick and return it to the elder, and they fought over it as they struggled toward the man who had initiated the competition. Whoever returned the stick to the elder won the largest "lot" of trade goods.[18] Such contests must have been one of the ways in which men sorted out who might lead them in this highly egalitarian, village-based world. But more important, this contest, like the feast that preceded it, emphasized loyalty to the village. Masculine displays of speed and strength and the trade goods they fought over reinforced the Shawnees' sense of community, often to the exclusion of their Native neighbors.

Warfare, Death, and Survival in the Upper Country

Epidemic disease contributed to the virulence and size of the Iroquois attack on the Kaskaskias and Tamaroas in 1680. Just one year earlier, Iroquois communities across the Finger Lakes region and the lower St. Lawrence River had died by the hundreds from smallpox.[19] No one was safe. And as the Iroquois sought to replace their fallen kin in a series of mourning wars waged across the Lower Great Lakes, their warriors usually killed double or triple the number of those they captured. The French estimated that at least 800 Illinois had been killed in the 1680 attack alone.

These were genocidal wars. The Iroquois destroyed whole villages in a single day. Survivors often starved, as retreating warriors laid waste to food stores. After the 1680 attack, the Miami switched sides and returned to the French alliance, joining with their Central Algonquian relatives, the Illinois and Shawnees, at Fort St. Louis. Having chosen to settle, and to fight, alongside their long-standing enemies, the Miamis now became Iroquois targets. Shortly thereafter, an Onondaga chief named Outreouate told the governor of New France, Antoine le Fèbvre de la Barre, that the Illinois and Miamis had become targets of the Haudenosaunee because they had "engaged the Chaouanons in their interest and entertained them in their country." The brief inclusion of the Shawnees within the French alliance at Fort St. Louis had enormous consequences for the Miamis. The

People of the Longhouse saw the Miamis' decision to relocate to the Upper Illinois River—and to join with the Shawnees—as the ultimate betrayal. By the winter of 1682, when the French began building Fort St. Louis, the Iroquois had extended the western door of their confederacy from the colony of New York to the tall-grass prairies of Illinois.[20] For the Illinois Confederacy generally and the Kaskaskia in particular, Iroquois attacks became a new and grievous threat to their survival.

Ancient ties between the peoples of the Upper Illinois and Ohio rivers helped sustain Central Algonquian peoples under siege. While some Shawnees moved south, to the Savannah River, others migrated to the Upper Illinois River Valley. Central Algonquians briefly coalesced at places such as the Grand Village of the Kaskaskias in the final decades of the seventeenth century. It had simply become too dangerous to inhabit vast stretches of the upper country. One such refugee center grew out of the Grand Village of the Kaskaskias, near modern-day Utica, Illinois. The Kaskaskias, members of the Illinois Confederacy, resettled there in the 1670s. In 1673, Marquette and Joliet found 74 cabins there. But by 1680, this same village had become a multitribal town, with 400 to 550 cabins and a population that ranged from 6,000 to 9,000 persons.[21]

Tonty and twenty-five Frenchmen built Fort St. Louis during the winter of 1682–83, across from the Grand Village of the Kaskaskias. As the parent village of the Illinois Confederacy, Grand Village had the ability to attract large numbers to the community. The Algonquians who came there in the 1680s were part of a much older alliance that predated the Iroquois wars and French incursions into the Illinois River Valley. Rapprochement with the French, toward a cultural middle ground, certainly played a defining role in Illinois culture during the eighteenth century. But in the seventeenth century, large population centers such as the Grand Village of the Kaskaskias were fairly common. La Salle and Tonty were not responsible for the coalescence of the Illinois and their neighbors. This thriving village had long been a center for trade, and the French chose the site of Fort St. Louis because of its strategic importance. The French alliance with Central Algonquians, predicated on rituals of integration such as the Calumet Ceremony, gift exchange, and intermarriage, took place at precontact centers of exchange such as the Grand Village of the Kaskaskias.[22]

Central Algonquians called upon centuries-old allies in order to deal with the threat of Iroquois attack. They were not unwitting participants in a crude experiment in the reconfiguration of identity. Rather, they were peoples with a keen sense of their own history and of the alliances that had long been essential to their survival in the upper country. In the last several decades of the seventeenth century, dozens of multiethnic confederacies emerged on the northern and western fringes of the upper country. The Grand Village of the Kaskaskias was one such site. Long accustomed to travel and exchange across cultural and linguistic frontiers, Kaskaskia villagers shared much in common with their Shawnee allies.

In navigating their way through the stream of history, smaller tribes traveled toward precontact allies. People from the Grand Village of the Kaskaskias had fostered multiethnic alliances between Fort Ancient and Oneota peoples. In the 1680s, the diverse communities that gathered together on the Upper Illinois River grew out of these ancient alliances. Familiar multiethnic allies rallied together in response to Old World diseases, Iroquois mourning wars, and the trade in guns and slaves. Traditions stretching back to the fifteenth century helped Central Algonquians survive in the late seventeenth century. For at least two generations, Grand Village had been an important site of down-the-line trading. Fort St. Louis brought together precontact and early colonial worlds at a familiar site of multiethnic exchange and alliance.

The Upper Illinois River: An Abundant Land

Grand Village's strategic position made it a likely target for Iroquois attacks. From its origins at the confluence of the Des Plaines and Kankakee rivers, the Illinois River runs due west. Descending from what is now southern Wisconsin, the Fox River merges with the Illinois River near modern Ottawa, Illinois. Grand Village was situated just below this confluence. Approximately twenty miles to the west of Grand Village, the river cuts diagonally across the state, where it drains into the Mississippi River at modern Grafton, Illinois. The people of Grand Village thus enjoyed easy access to diverse populations to the north, south, east, and west. The Des Plaines and Fox rivers connected the people of Grand Village to both Algonquian and Siouan speakers, from the Potawatomis to the Ho-Chunks, while the Kankakee River flows into what is now northern Indiana, joining the Illinois to their Miami and Wea kinsmen. To the west, the Illinois River watershed linked members of the Illinois Confederacy to Chiwere Souians, including the Iowas, Otos, and Missourias. To the south, below the confluence of the Illinois and Mississippi rivers, lived Caddoans and Siouans. And by the second decade of the eighteenth century, this region—known as the American Bottom—joined the Illinois to the French at New Orleans.[23] *Nipi*, the Central Algonquian word for water, ruled the land. Rivers were the great highways of human interaction in the seventeenth century, linking people and their cultures.

In the second half of the seventeenth century, the Illinois River Valley had much to offer Shawnee migrants. Large swaths of central Illinois had been depopulated between the fifteenth and seventeenth centuries, and as a result the region abounded with wildlife.[24] When Henry de Tonty's nephew, French commander Pierre Deliette, first entered the region surrounding the Grand Village, he marveled at its beauty. To him, Grand Village was located in "undeniably the most beautiful [land] that is known anywhere between the mouth of the St. Lawrence River and the Mississippi." Situated on the north bank of the Illinois River, Grand Village sat on a narrow spit of land where the Upper Illinois River basin fuses together the lowland rivers joined to Lake Michigan. Here the river valley is not more than a mile and a half across, and it cuts through sandstone bedrock, creating a fair amount of whitewater. Just across from Grand Village, a towering stone outcropping with a summit that is defensible on three sides rises out of the river. Henry de Tonty built Fort St. Louis at this strategic location. Located adjacent to the Grand Village of the Kaskaskias, Fort St. Louis became the center of French and Indian resistance to the Iroquois.[25]

Grand Village's true strength lay in the merging of diverse habitats that converged near the town. Because the Des Plaines and Kankakee rivers are only slightly lower than Lake Michigan itself, "water drained the land only grudgingly" in the region east of Grand Village. Vast wetlands cleansed the Illinois River, providing clear, healthful water for local villagers. The Upper Illinois River basin supported ninety-seven fish species and thirty-eight different mussel species. Oak-hickory forests thrived in the floodplain, while bluestem prairies covered the flat uplands. The river was often too shallow to navigate, and Native paddlers frequently had to portage their dugout canoes. Without horses and undermined by the shallow waters of the Illinois River, Illinois women used headbands or pack straps to carry supplies across the land. The shallow streams of the Upper Illinois River basin created the perfect habitat for game animals. Deer, elk, bear, and wolves thrived on this interconnected network of prairie, forest, wetland, and island habitats. Like Deliette, La Salle struggled to describe the abundance he witnessed. La Salle found that the land was "overrun with bears, deer, roebucks, and wild turkeys," on whom gray wolves made "relentless war."[26]

Ancient foodways linked these societies to their pre-Columbian past. The Illinois, like their Shawnee relatives, gathered together in large, agriculturally minded summer villages. And by late October, extended families splintered away from the summer village and occupied smaller winter hunting camps of not more than fifty people. While deer made up the majority of the meat in their diets, the Kaskaskias and their neighbors exploited a range of animal life, consuming everything from elk and bear to smaller species, including raccoons, squirrels, and muskrats. Inhabitants of Grand Village also feasted on both trout and catfish, and waterfowl ranging from mallards to grebes also found their way into their cooking pots. Indian men preferred to hunt the wild turkeys that fattened themselves on the mast from the nut-bearing trees that proliferated along the river's banks.[27]

Bison hunters of the tall-grass prairies and maize agriculturists to the south and east came together along this section of the Illinois River. By 1600, vast herds of buffalo had populated the interior of the continent. Perhaps encouraged by these western hunters, the Illinois adjusted and made bison hunting their central focus. Over time, the Illinois shared a host of common traits with their Siouan neighbors. During the first half of the seventeenth century, they followed the buffalo herds westward, into present-day Iowa and Missouri. Jesuit Claude Dablon wrote that the prairie "affords ample sustenance to the wild cows, not infrequently encountered in herds of four and five hundred each. These, by their abundance, furnish adequate provisions for whole villages, which therefore are not obliged to scatter by families during their hunting season." Bison thus enabled villagers in the Illinois country to concentrate their numbers. Villages that once peaked at 500 persons now concentrated 6,000 to 9,000 people. Indians who once depended on corn for at least 65 percent of their diet now found that meat—and the protein necessary for good health— allowed for unparalleled population growth. By the seventeenth century, "bison provided approximately 56 percent of the total meat supply."[28]

Like Fort Ancient villagers, the Illinois burned the wooded lands to foster the ideal habitat for the animals they preyed upon. Ecologists estimate that they set fire to the prairie as well as the oak-hickory forests surrounding the Illinois River every six to seven years. Controlled burns destroyed the understory of the forest without killing larger, nut-bearing trees such as oaks and hickories.[29] Fires thus created ideal conditions for white-tailed deer and other animals that preferred the forest edge. In addition, fire helped along fruits ranging from grapes to blackberries and pawpaws. The human use of fire enabled the prairie to expand deep into the Illinois and Ohio river valleys.

Fed by anywhere from thirty-six to forty inches of rainfall per year, these prairie grasses developed thick root systems that only the steel plow could remove. Stone and bone farming implements could not cut through these root systems. Floodplain farming thus made sense for the Kaskaskias.[30] Predictable spring floods occurred annually or semiannually, reinvigorating the bottomland soils. Kaskaskians continued to grow maize at Grand Village. But unlike their Shawnee relatives, the Illinois made hunting the central focus of their economy.

Algonquian families joined together to procure and cook ancient foods, linking precontact and colonial-era foodways. At the Grand Village of the Kaskaskias, archaeologists have unearthed much evidence of subsistence practices that were subsequently witnessed by French colonizers. For example, archaeologists have found enormous pits and attendant floral remains associated with the roots of yellow water lilies. Deliette witnessed a similar process during his time at Grand Village. He described how women waded out into the shallow marshes, collecting the rhizomes, or roots, of yellow water lilies for a grand feast. All told, the effort took at least a week to execute, and it combined the labor of women and men. Men from several wickiups joined forces, digging an enormous hole five to six feet deep and sometimes as wide as ten to twelve feet square. The women then placed a layer of wood in the bottom of the pit, which they set on fire. They then covered this with a layer of rock and grass, on top of which they placed the lily roots. These roots were then covered with grass and tree bark and were smoked for three days. At the end of the smoking, the roots were ready to eat, and the families that shared in the effort feasted on the lilies.[31]

The Archaeology of Mobility and Exchange at Grand Village

Archaeologists describe the period after 1300, and especially after 1450, as an era of "great mobility." So many different people lived along the Upper Illinois River Valley that associating the site with a single modern tribe, such as the Kaskaskias, is impossible. Grand Village was a multiethnic center for trade on the prairie peninsula. In the spring of 1680, when La Salle encountered this village, he found 1,800 warriors from ten different branches of the Illinois Confederacy as well as Siouan-speaking Quapaws in residence there. The immediate cause of their coalescence might have been the Iroquois, but allies gathered there well before the Iroquois wars.[32]

After 1300, when the Mississippian chiefdom of Cahokia collapsed, the smaller tribes associated with it moved away to survive. Large swaths of their former homelands became vacant. Major Mississippian societies such as Cahokia vanished between 1300 and 1450. Cahokia's demise left an enormous void in the Lower Great Lakes, and this enabled historically known tribes and confederacies, from the Kickapoos to the Illinois, to move into Illinois. Central Algonquians "with little connection to the prehistoric inhabitants" now possessed the land.[33] On the eve of colonization, Native peoples moved toward allies and ecotones, and their migrations fostered coalescence in the continental interior.

Ethnic mixing occurred as a result of bison hunting, seasonal migration, and maize agriculture. Like their Siouan neighbors, the Kaskaskias built scaffold burials. Their mortuary rituals also included practices common among Algonquians and Mississippians to the east and south. For example, the dead were often taken down from the scaffolds and their bones cleaned and then reburied with other esteemed members of the village in a common grave. Archaeologists at the Zimmerman site, now associated with the Grand Village of the Kaskaskias, found "an adult male [who] had received special handling." Cut marks were found on many of the bones. Portions of the flesh appear to have adhered to the bones, and muscles had to be cut to separate the bones. Probably the body had been placed on a scaffold initially and portions of the flesh might have been mummified by the sun. The bones were then removed from the body and cleaned prior to burial.[34]

The Grand Village of the Kaskaskias thus illustrates the incorporation of many different ritual practices. It was part of an "open system," a place in which cultural pluralism often superseded discrete tribal or ethnic polities, made possible by Cahokia's collapse as well as the abundance of the Upper Illinois River. The Kaskaskias adopted many Siouan traits, everything from the Calumet Ceremony to platform burials. Their shared history, in both peace and war, is reflected in the "mixed content" of their archaeological sites.[35]

Down-the-Line Trading and the Impact of Guns on the Upper Country

By the 1640s, the Illinois had made peace with the Dakota Sioux in order to smooth the flow of French trade goods moving south. At the same time, Illinois slavers attacked their Ho-Chunk, Osage, and Pawnee neighbors to the north and west and Chickasaw and Choctaw villages to the south. Guns became an unparalleled source of terror for Illinois warriors. Through guns, and "their noise and smoke," Marquette wrote, they "make themselves dreaded by the distant tribes to the south and west."[36] Guns were particularly important to the rise and fall of rival tribes during the protohistoric period, when French traders had not yet reached the Illinois country.

French and Dutch traders had exchanged smooth-bore guns for furs and people since the beginning of the seventeenth century. By the 1640s, both the Iroquois and the Huron were well armed, and they dominated down-the-line trading in European guns, giving them a marked advantage over their rivals. The Iroquois used guns to shock their adversaries into submission. The Dutch called shooting weapons *donrebussen*, or "thundering guns." Lead balls fired from these muskets left gaping holes in Indian bodies. And most trade muskets were accurate at upward of fifty feet.[37]

Trade guns dramatically increased levels of violence. Armed with guns, people began going to war impulsively, with little to no planning. Armed with bullet molds and gunpowder, Native warriors decided on war more easily than they could with bows and arrows. In contrast, the skill, effort, and planning involved in making arrows made warfare deliberate and organized. With the introduction of guns, ready access to European gunpowder was all that was needed. In addition, guns often led to stalemates that prolonged engagements and increased the number of casualties. Skilled marksmen could fire four to six shots per minute, and larger numbers of women, children, and the elderly were shot as a result.[38]

In the first half of the seventeenth century, William Bradford of Plymouth Plantation wrote that the Indians "saw the execution that a piece would do" and decided that "their bows and arrows [were] but baubles in comparison." Many European observers, like Bradford, assumed that American Indians readily sacrificed their own weapons in exchange for European weaponry. But evidence from the Illinois country suggests a much more gradual process. Well into the eighteenth century, Native hunters used both guns and bows and arrows. This potent mix of power and stealth made American Indian warfare more lethal than it had been in the past. As late as 1693, Peoria archers impressed the resident Jesuit priest among them, Sébastien Rale. He observed that "arrows are the principal weapons that they use in war and hunting." After witnessing Peoria men in their dual role as guardians and hunters for their people, Rale understood why they had little use for French guns. A proficient Peoria archer "will have discharged a hundred arrows sooner than another person can reload his gun." Twenty years earlier, Father Jacques Marquette noticed that the Illinois were "active and very skillful with bows and arrows."[39]

As with French guns, the Illinois slowly incorporated French kettles and cooking utensils into their daily lives. It took several generations for

French brass, copper, and earthenware to replace Native ceramics. The Illinois preferred wood and bone implements well into the historic period. According to Marquette, "They make all of their utensils of wood, and their ladles out of the heads of cattle [bison], whose skulls they know so well how to prepare that they use these ladles with ease for eating their sagamité."[40]

Most protohistoric trade goods were used for ceremonial and ornamental purposes, and they tended to be buried with important men. Native artisans refashioned everything from cooking pots to iron nails into familiar material forms. Huron, Ottawa, and Illinois people converted brass kettles into tinkling cones for buckskin leggings. Kettle strips were often rolled into tight, serpentine spirals, resembling snakes. Illinois artisans reworked blue glass beads by melting them down and then cutting them as if they were precious stones. Blue, red, and alabaster glass became decorative elements in earrings and necklaces. Native peoples equated firearms, brass, and iron tools brought by the French with spiritual power. In 1683, Ottawa traders told a French trader that "thou art one of the chief spirits, since thou usest iron; it is for thee to rule and protect all men."[41]

French traders working out of trading centers such as Chequamegon Bay on Lake Superior inspired the Illinois to migrate. However, by 1670, the terms of this return migration had changed. Writing in the summer of 1670, Dablon described how the Miamis had joined with the Illinois and the Mascoutins. He attributed their coalescence to the need for a defensive alliance, and he estimated that their united village included at least 3,000 people. As a result, they "are able to furnish each four hundred men for the common defense against the Iroquois, who pursue them even into these remote districts." Occupying a variety of "cabins" resembling everything from Meskwaki wickiups to Kickapoo longhouses, even their dwellings reflected the incongruous legacy of Siouan, Algonquian, and Iroquoian occupations of the upper country.[42]

At least initially, these coalescent migrants thought of the French as "extraordinary spirits." According to Dablon, "They had conceived so high an opinion of the things of the Faith, and of those who published it, that they invited us to many feasts." Dablon wrote: "We availed ourselves of this advantage to instruct the people everywhere, and to seek out sick persons in all the cabins." The Illinois associated with the Jesuits out of regard for their power. Even their "thundering guns" demonstrated their supernatural capacities.[43]

In 1653, the Iroquois began launching massive assaults against Ottawa and Illinois traders and hunters who participated in the French trade.[44] Iroquois attacks intensified over the next three decades, except for a brief moment in which the Haudenosaunee focused the full extent of their power on their Susquehannock enemies at the head of the Chesapeake Bay. Across the Eastern Woodlands, mourning wars and slaving expeditions created vast stretches of vacant land, as terrorized villagers migrated to safer places. Most of what is now Ohio, Indiana, and Illinois became devoid of human settlements. War refugees tended to move to the north and west, to multiethnic population centers in and around Green Bay, Wisconsin, and Michilimackinac on the Upper Peninsula.

Near-constant warfare remade gender roles among the Illinois. In the second half of the seventeenth century, the Iroquois wars and the Indian slave trade enhanced the power of Illinois men. Marquette estimated that by 1668 the Illinois had a combined population of 8,000 to 9,000 people, including perhaps as many as 2,000 warriors. Of Illinois warriors, Marquette wrote that they "take a great many slaves, whom they trade with the Outaouaks for Muskets, Powder, Kettles, Hatchets and Knives." Down-the-line trade between the Illinois and the Ottawa refashioned gender roles and transformed the Illinois way of life.[45]

Like their Shawnee counterparts on the Savannah River, the Illinois became middlemen in an intertribal trade network that joined the Illinois country to the French at Montreal. Grand Village was positioned between Ottawa traders at Chequamegon Bay on Lake Superior and Indian people to the south and west who lacked access to European trade goods. Well before Henry de Tonty began drawing up plans to build Fort St. Louis, old and new alliances linked Native people to the French. Illinois, Miami, Meskwaki, and Kickapoo hunters traveled beyond the Illinois prairie in pursuit of people, bison, and white-tailed deer. The French reported that "after they had planted their fields . . . they went to hunt cattle." Potawatomi intermediaries accepted bison, beaver, and deer pelts at the base of Green Bay, where they were hauled north to Ottawa traders at Chequamegon. For much of the seventeenth century, French officials depended on Ottawa traders for beaver pelts. In 1681, the French intendant, Duchesneau, wrote that the Ottawas "are those of the greatest use to us because through them we obtain Beaver." According to Duchesneau, the Ottawas no longer hunted. Rather, they "exchange [beaver] for . . . our merchandise which they procure at Montreal."[46]

Warfare and the Transformation of the Upper Midwest

Warfare transformed an abundant land into a place of hardship and want. Jesuits living in the upper country understood how war had drained the land of its riches. Nevertheless, they continued to condemn Central Algonquian religious practices. On the eve of a second Iroquois assault on Fort St. Louis, the Jesuit missionary Thierry Beschefer lambasted the religious practices of the Miami and Illinois peoples he hoped to convert. He abhorred Miami "superstitions," particularly vision quests, which "the old men cause the youth to undergo." Beschefer drove a rift between the old and the young, the latter of which were "delighted to be freed" from the requirement to undergo days of fasting while alone in the wilderness. Miami elders protested. For one, they argued, the vision quest was designed to help young men "discover . . . the object upon which their good fortune depends." Quite apart from the religious dimensions of the quest, the logic of fasting made particular sense in the demanding environment of the Great Lakes region. How else, the elders wondered, would they "inure their young men to fatigue . . . and prevent them from becoming too heavy?"[47]

Beschefer admitted to the wisdom of the vision quest after making it through a full winter among the Miamis. As the fall cold settled in during late October, he traveled along with a mixed band of Miamis and Shawnees, numbering "eighty cabins." On any given day, they passed through damp prairies and marshes. The marshes were particularly challenging because Beschefer sank up to his knees in the icy water as they hunted. "With sufferings and fatigue which might have overcome the most robust," the people he hoped to convert offered him only a few "moments that they could give him for their Instruction." Beschefer proselytized on the rare occasions when everyone rested, and he struggled to disabuse the men of their beliefs as the women served "only a few miserable roots" in these moments. The rigors of life after the harvest, during those times in which wild animals were scarce and Iroquois war parties were near, forced Beschefer to admit to the sense of vision quests. Hunger and fatigue were common. Writing in Latin, as if to keep the extent of his suffering between himself and his God, Beschefer wrote that he was so hungry that "he wanted to fill his stomach with pig slop, but no one would give it to him."[48]

Beschefer's discretion paid off. His traveling companions noticed that he had endured the hardships of the winter hunt with equanimity. The Shawnees were particularly impressed, remarking that Beschefer "was very different from [other] Europeans." The English, they said, offer "no tokens of friendship . . . and take no trouble to instruct them." Migrants to the Illinois country developed a keen eye for the differences between colonizers. The Shawnees drew on firsthand experience with Spanish, English, and French colonizers. Each colonizer had his own errand into the wilderness, and Native peoples understood how Europeans' competing aspirations shaped the course of their relationships with them.[49]

Migration, endurance, and the possibility of violence shaped the lives of all who lived in the Upper Midwest. During the 1680 attack, the story of a captive Illinois girl bears witness to the far-reaching consequences of colonialism and the mourning wars. After being taken by the Senecas in the 1680 attack, a seven-year-old Illinois girl managed to run away from her captors. She survived alone, in the woods, before being discovered by Huron hunters, who brought her to the French-Kiskanon Ottawa trading center at Michilimackinac. Illinois men who had married into Kiskanon Ottawa society asked her who her parents were, and upon learning their names, found out "that she was an Ilinoise." Happily reunited with her people, the girl's story might have ended there. But days later, her captor, a Seneca war captain named Annanhec, had been captured near Green Bay while in pursuit of the girl. The Ottawa brought him to Michilimackinac. Incredibly, Annanhec "insisted on having her." The Ottawas recognized that they could not disrespect their Illinois allies by simply returning her to captivity. Hurons living at Michilimackinac castigated the Illinois for letting Annanhec live in their presence. Perhaps the taunting worked. It might also have been the case that the Illinois feared that the Ottawas might bow to Iroquois pressure and return the girl to Annanhec. Tense negotiations followed. Amid one heated exchange, an Illinois man took a knife from Henry de Tonty and stabbed Annanhec to death "before any of those who were in the cabin had the power to prevent it."[50]

Annanhec's death, triggered by a dispute over a captive child, might have escalated the war between the Iroquois and the peoples of the upper country. Annanhec had dared to challenge his enemies—the Ottawas, the Illinois, and the French—at their most important trading center, Michilimackinac. He risked, and ultimately lost, his life by walking into the heart of enemy territory, alone, an individual bereft of his community. Hubris alone does not explain Annanhec's suicidal tendencies.

Annanhec was a man of such importance that the French governor, Louis de Baude, Comte de Frontenac, summoned a delegation of Ottawa, Huron, and Miami chiefs to Montreal to discuss the repercussions of his death. For three days, from August 13 to August 15, 1682, these men argued about what to do next. Everyone knew that Annanhec's kinsmen would soon avenge his death by launching a mourning war on their villages. Alimahoué, a "Miami Captain," complained that his people "were daily slaughtered by the Iroquois." Frontenac blamed the Algonquians for these attacks. Their failure to further concentrate their forces into a defensive alliance was to blame. "Were there not Frenchmen in his country?" asked the governor. Frontenac contended that La Salle had "exhort[ed] them to build a fort to defend themselves with the Ilinois."[51]

The Kiskanon Ottawa delegates rejected Frontenac's criticism. Did the concentration of thousands at the Grand Village of the Kaskaskias spare them from the Iroquois, they asked? Second, the Miamis and Ottawas distrusted the Hurons and refused to live among them. The Ottawas accused the Hurons of working as double agents, conducting a kind of whisper campaign against them while visiting the Iroquois. Third, the Illinois could not overlook the fact that some Miamis had participated in the siege of the Grand Village of the Kaskaskias. Frontenac may have hoped for a grand alliance in the upper country. But his dreams of unity failed because of antagonisms between villagers.

The Kiskanon Ottawas recognized that the Illinois would not allow the Illinois girl to be taken again. And so they offered another child in her place. The Kiskanons "spread a small mat in the middle of the room, and placed thereon a little boy between 8 and 9 years of age, with a belt of wampum before him and a robe of beaver on his body." Frontenac was appalled by the Kiskanons' gesture. Child slavery was not the issue. Rather, it was the Ottawas' suggestion that the little boy was somehow "equivalent for the loss of so great a captain as Annehac [Annanhec]."[52]

It was clear to Alimahoué, the Miami war captain, that Frontenac did not understand the exchange, and that he would not support an Algonquian counterattack on the Iroquois. The French refused to join the Ottawas, Hurons, and Miamis in their war against the Iroquois. Frontenac argued that "they should confine operations to their own country." Alimahoué countered that "he was weary of this, and wished not only to bite them in his turn but also to eat them."[53]

Frontenac knew that his failure to coordinate the defense of the upper country gave the Iroquois "reason to believe that we fear them dreadfully, and that it is in their power to dictate the law to us." Jesuit Father Jean de Lamberville, then stationed at Onondaga, chastised Frontenac for failing to travel personally to Iroquoia. Because of his absence, "the brunt of the war must fall on the Illinois." Lamberville believed that "the Oumiamis will be swept away." The problem, according to Lamberville, was that the "Upper Iroquois," especially the Senecas, did not fear the French. In fact, "they profit every year by our losses. They annihilate our allies, whom they convert into Iroquois, and . . . enrich themselves by our plunder."[54] Lamberville used the language of conversion to describe Iroquois mourning wars.

The 1680 attack became the first of several battles, featuring hundreds of warriors, which shook the foundation of the French empire in North America. The French intendant, Jacques Duchesneau, also used the 1680 attack to challenge Frontenac's authority as the leader of New France. He believed that the Iroquois victory doomed the French because of the vital role the Illinois played in the fur trade. Duchesneau only slightly exaggerated when he argued that "all the peltries that come into the country" are gathered by the Illinois from "the Far nations." By 1680, Grand Village had become a vital trading center, a place where western hunters brought pelts to exchange for French trade goods. Indeed, Iroquois attacks on the Illinois devastated the economy of New France. In 1683, Algonquian hunters managed to deliver 95,000 pounds of beaver hides to Montreal. But two years later, they brought in just 23,000 pounds. Indian hunters feared leaving their women and children alone and defenseless and hunted only for subsistence. Those with hides to sell stopped journeying to trade centers such as Grand Village and Michilimackinac because they might fall victim to the Iroquois on the trails northward. Between 1680 and 1700, Iroquois war parties captured approximately 2,500 people, a 60 percent increase from the years 1640 to 1669. Central Algonquians such as the Illinois and Shawnees faced a stark choice, for while Iroquois ethnicity was inclusive, it was also exacting. The mourning war process, a process of death and rebirth, amounted to something more than conversion.[55]

Intercolonial Competition and the Failure of the French Plan for the Upper Country

The French offered a second alternative. Some Algonquians hoped that Jesuit and Franciscan Recollect missions might protect them from their Iroquois attackers. But most refused conversion to Catholicism and consolidation as French Indians, under the direction of French fathers. The French, like their Spanish counterparts, dreamed of consolidating their people into tightly knit, hierarchically organized societies. Jean-Baptiste Colbert, one of Louis XIV's favored advisers, implored La Salle to "consolidate, collect, and form" Indian people "into towns and villages." The Grand Village of the Kaskaskias seemed like the perfect place for La Salle to fulfill Colbert's vision. Like Colbert, the French governor, Frontenac, worried that France's inability to organize a well-armed and coordinated defense of the upper country would give the Iroquois "reason to believe that we fear them dreadfully, and that it is in their power to dictate the law to us."[56]

With little more than 6,000 French people in all of Canada, French officials depended on American Indians in the upper country. The French believed that Native people would prefer town life and the hierarchies of power that came with them. They imagined a series of refugee centers in which French absolutism would determine American Indian actions. But such imagined power had little application in the upper country. More than 500 *coureurs de bois*, or French "runners of the woods," undermined their plans. Illegal traders encouraged Indian hunters to travel great distances in pursuit of fur-bearing animals for European markets. They promoted a kind of individualism that was anathema to French absolutists. One French official wrote that "people who went to trade for peltries . . . ruined the colony" because they were the fittest, most able-bodied men in the colony. In his opinion, these men squandered their earnings from the fur trade on "drunkenness and fine clothes." Colbert hoped that his close allies, including La Salle, would support the king's goal of rationally organizing Indian villages such as the Grand Village of the Kaskaskias. Louis XIV asked Frontenac to "labor incessantly and during the whole time you are in that country to consolidate, collect and form them into Towns and Villages, that they may be placed in a position the more easily to defend themselves."[57]

La Salle and Tonty struggled to re-create the coalition that was originally inspired by the Illinois at the Grand Village of the Kaskaskias. In 1683, La Salle encountered Shawnees living among the French-allied "petit nations" on the Gulf of Mexico, and he persuaded them to return, northward, where they could live "near the St. Louis fort I had erected." Migrating from what is now Louisiana to the Illinois country, these Shawnees joined with their kinsmen already residing among the Kaskaskias and the Miamis. Their villages lined the north bank of the Illinois River, amid the ruins of the Grand Village of the Kaskaskias, across from Fort St. Louis.[58]

Illinois, Miami, and Shawnee warriors predominated in and around the site of Fort St. Louis. The Shawnees seemed to arrive in several different contingents, suggesting that most had made contact with the Kaskaskias, La Salle, Tonty, and Joutel independently. By the spring of 1683, La Salle had persuaded "nine or ten villages" from a range of tribes "to become French" and migrate from their homes along the Gulf of Mexico. According to La Salle, these multiethnic villagers included some Shawnees who traded with the Spanish. Missourias and Mitchegemeas moved from west of the Mississippi to the vicinity of Fort St. Louis in the aftermath of the 1680 attack as well.[59]

French travels across the country led to some surprising long-distance additions to the confederacy at Fort St. Louis. At least fifty Mahican and Wampanoag survivors of King Philip's War (1675) fled "the district of the Indian chief Philippe, so much feared by the colonists of Massachusetts." The Mahicans and their neighbors were no friends of the Iroquois. The Iroquois alliance with the New England colonists had turned the tide of the war against the Mahicans. La Salle promised them "oxen, horses, and all the other conveniences which they had had in New England," to encourage their migration. La Salle was thrilled at adding the Mahicans and Wampanoags to the confederacy. He believed that "they have the bodies of Indians from New England, but the minds and hearts of Miamis."[60]

The Illinois had become the most important trading partners of the French, and they simply had to be defended. To that end, the king replaced Frontenac with Joseph-Antoine de La Barre. La Barre prepared for war by gathering intelligence from Jesuits stationed throughout Iroquoia and the upper country. And after consulting with them at their home monastery, in Quebec, he learned that with 1,200 warriors, the Senecas alone could "exterminate the Illinois altogether," destroy French posts, "and deprive us of all the trade drawn from that country."[61] A preemptive strike was necessary. Lamberville, writing from Onondaga, explained that the Iroquois were then planning a mourning war against the Miamis and Illinois, to be launched that August, to avenge Annanhec's death.

In May 1683, an Iroquois war party composed of sixteen men and one woman "disguised themselves as Ilinois both in their language and their dress . . . and carried a white flag and called to them they had nothing to fear, that they were all their brothers." The disguised warriors may have been Illinois captives turned Iroquois warriors, men who felt compelled to attack their kinsmen as proof of their loyalty. The ruse worked, for they were able to deceive a party of fourteen French traders and get away with seven canoes laden with furs and supplies. According to the traders, who were eventually left with nothing more than "two worthless guns and a little lead" near the Chicago River, the Iroquois had fanned out in smaller groups across the Illinois country. After taking them prisoner, the traders learned that the Iroquois "had 200 men six day's journey away, inland, and 500 more on the Great River of the Mississippi, below the Illinois."[62] Continued Iroquois attacks on the peoples at Fort St. Louis compelled most of these warriors to remain at home, rather than to mass near Montreal, as La Barre had hoped.

As Iroquois warriors closed in on Fort St. Louis, Tonty and his Native allies became convinced that they had been forsaken by French Canada.

By the spring of 1684, Native members of the confederacy knew enough about the government of New France to see that they had been left largely on their own. The siege confirmed their suspicions. In retaliation, Tonty barred French traders from the fort and worked to create his own defense of those who remained in the old alliance. Tonty chose to "not permit the French to trade in the direction of the Illinois." French officials reacted angrily, arguing that "it is a ridiculous pretence on the part of Tonty." Final proof came in March 1684, when the Iroquois massed their forces and lay siege to the fort for six days. With "300 cabins, near the Fort Illinois, as well as Miamis and Chawanons [Shawnees]," the confederacy that had massed along the Illinois River repulsed their Iroquois attackers.[63]

As an Italian working on behalf of the French state, Tonty maintained a precarious existence. Nevertheless, his near-death experience in the 1680 attack and his years in the upper country had taught him about the limits of French power. Tonty was not an apologist for the state, though he did appreciate the symbolic power of the French monarchy. His ultimate loyalties were personal and local, and absolutists in Montreal found this maddening. Tonty consistently challenged the authority of French officials. In 1685, they sent Captain Richard Pilette to Fort St. Louis to relieve Tonty of his command. When Pilette attempted to assume command of his new post, Tonty "swung at him with his famed iron hand and knocked out the man's front teeth." Pilette remained, but he lived outside the gates of the fort as a farmer and illegal trader.[64]

La Barre ultimately conceded to Iroquois power and played for time by reaching multilateral agreements with the Haudenosaunee and the English. Residents of the upper country knew better than to trust such treaties, and the proof of their failure came shortly thereafter, when La Barre was replaced by Jacques-René Brisay de Denonville, the Marquis de Denonville. Denonville, like La Barre before him, seemed unaware of frustrations within the French alliance. That November, he summoned Tonty and others charged with managing the western forts. He hoped that Tonty and his colleagues in the west could gather a force large enough to defeat the Iroquois.[65]

Shawnee Out-Migration from the Upper Country

Wedded by trade and by custom to the French, the Illinois, Miamis, and Ottawas had no choice but to support Denonville. The Shawnees were different. Relative newcomers to the region, they had migrated to the Grand Village of the Kaskaskias from the south, north, and east. They departed from the upper country in a similarly piecemeal manner. Shawnees slowly abandoned the Upper Illinois River Valley between 1688 and 1693, when they grew tired of the Kaskaskia-French alliance and set out to find new trading opportunities or alternative sources of European trade goods.[66] Following their departure from the Illinois country, most Shawnees migrated to a number of different villages in what is now Maryland and Pennsylvania. By casting their lot with the English and their Iroquois allies, these Shawnees initiated a new chapter in their people's history.

In January 1687, during La Salle's final, and fatal, journey to explore the Gulf of Mexico, his party "perceived two Indians running after us." They "were greatly surprised" when the two men fell on La Salle "and almost stifle[d] him by their embraces." La Salle's party stood in disbelief. The two men were La Salle's former Shawnee guides. During one of his previous expeditions, the men described how they had "gone out to hunt" only to be "surrounded and taken by thirty or forty warriors." To their surprise, they were not bound. Rather, their captors "honored them and held them for something more than men on account of the power of their guns." They chose to remain and to marry into the village because "they had no difficulty in learning their language." La Salle tried to persuade them to return to the upper country with him, but the Shawnees replied that they "were not unnatural enough to abandon their wives and children." After having traveled across most of the eastern half of North America, they had found a "most fertile, healthy and peaceful country." Both men felt that they "would be devoid of sense to leave it [only] to be tomahawked by the Illinois or burnt by the Iroquois on their way to another where the winter was insufferably cold, the summer without game, and ever in war."[67]

Their assessment of the upper country was prescient. Incessant warfare between the Iroquois and the Illinois had destroyed much of the wildlife on Illinois prairies, as hundreds of warriors from the Northeast searching for captives sustained themselves on the wildlife of the Upper Midwest. La Salle described how "the buffalo are becoming scarce here since the Illinois are at war."[68] It was not uncommon for hundreds of well-armed men to live for months at a time on game animals, large and small, while they were fighting. Indeed, warfare reduced American Indian reliance on food crops such as corn, beans, and squash. Floodplain farms attached to summer villages became prime targets for genocidal war parties.

American Indians became caught up in market forces linking them to decision makers in London and Paris. And in the seventeenth century, the English did a better job of promoting and organizing the trade in fur-bearing animals. English prices were so superior to French prices that it is no wonder that Algonquians desired proximity to the English. In 1689, a gun was worth two beaver at Albany, whereas a gun was worth five beaver at Montreal.[69] Iroquois access to British arms largely predetermined the outcome of the violence between competing tribes.

Colonial powers might have hoped for a world in which Indian "kings" and "emperors" ruled over subject populations, but the Upper Illinois River Valley tells a different story. Village sites on both the Illinois and the Ohio rivers were multiethnic in content and character. Imperial powers, obsessed as they were with the nation-state, attempted to impose their understanding of political theory onto Native peoples, who were accustomed to a kind of parochial cosmopolitanism. At Grand Village and other places like it, Native peoples lived in a confederated world. While village chiefs spoke on their peoples' behalf, they lacked the coercive authority of European kings. Such small populations were always vulnerable to attack. These villages ceded some of their authority, often balancing local needs against the pressures of outside forces. Transient townspeople understood that their survival depended on alliance networks that radiated out, like spokes on a wheel, from the places they called home.[70]

chapter 6

"Mixt Nations" at the
Head of the Bay

THE IROQUOIS, BACON'S REBELS, AND

THE PEOPLES IN BETWEEN

In the spring of 1692, a mysterious band of Indians arrived at the head of Chesapeake Bay. They were an alarming collection of "strange Indians," who seemed to be led by a Frenchman with the letters M C tattooed to his chest. Residents of Cecil County, Maryland, where the Susquehanna River drains into Chesapeake Bay, believed that this Frenchman was the notorious Michel Costeene. His arrival coincided with a report from New York describing how a French and Indian force, including Costeene, had devastated New England, resulting in the "slaughter and death of many hundred souls." Folks in Cecil County believed that Costeene epitomized the evils of France in America, for he had crossed over profound cultural and ethnic divides. He had embraced savagery by marrying into an Indian community that now considered him their kinsmen. For the English, Costeene's actions led to social disintegration because he had abandoned civilization, and as such he represented man in his primal state. Costeene was an agent of "violent disorder." French, Catholic, and kin to the Indians with whom he traveled, Costeene's arrival terrified local Englishmen.[1]

To make matters worse, Costeene's band now lived on Bohemia Manor, an estate owned by a Dutch colonist–turned–Maryland settler named Augustus Herrman. Herrman had lived at the head of the bay for many years and had chosen to remain there after 1664, when the English seized control of Dutch possessions in North America. Costeene and a host of Seneca, Shawnee, and Susquehannock newcomers asked Herrman to advocate for them before colonial officials in Annapolis. The newcomers made it clear that they "desired peace with this province & that they might bear [word illegible] trading with us." Hoping for a stake in this lucrative trade, Herrman brought their request to the capital. Maryland's leaders made it clear that the head of the bay could not and would not become a haven for dispossessed Native migrants and their French intermediaries, and Herrman left without the license to trade that he desired. He failed, at least in part, because Englishmen remained ambivalent about men such as himself. Many of them were important players in the Indian trade along the lower Susquehanna River and the Delmarva Peninsula. English residents of Cecil County trafficked in stories about rival European powers bent on conspiring with Native peoples to halt their progress. Herrman must have been aware of these stories. Since 1664, his 4,000-acre estate, Bohemia Manor, had grown, in spite of rumors about his loyalties.[2]

The alleged Michel Costeene had fallen victim to one such seventeenth-century whisper campaign. His accuser, a man named Henry Thompson, had deliberately led colonial officials astray. Thompson had survived a previous French and Indian attack when he lived in New England, and he wanted to implicate the new arrivals. Fortunately for the Frenchman and the Indian community he represented, Thompson's neighbors challenged his understanding of the person and the "strange Indians" traveling with him. The Maryland Colonial Council admitted its mistake, making clear that the accused was not Michel Costeene, "the grand Enemy of the English."[3]

He was, in fact, Martin Chartier. And while he was not guilty of any crime in the English-speaking world, French officials wanted him dead. Maryland's colonial officials feared Chartier and the "strange Indians" traveling with him. As people on the move, it was impossible to discern the intentions of these refugees, and the English vigorously interrogated Chartier as a result. Through him, they learned that the Shawnees had abandoned the Illinois country in 1688, when for unknown reasons their alliance with the Illinois and the Miamis dissolved. Their expulsion triggered a five-year exodus from the Great Lakes. According to Chartier, "They were two years traveling to the Southward." Perhaps in search of their relatives, these Shawnees lived in the South before arriving at the head of the bay.[4] Chartier's testimony certainly helped the Shawnee cause. For the English, it was crucially important that the Shawnees had migrated to Maryland from somewhere in the Southeast, where, from their perspective, Native peoples had broken from the French alliance. Both the origins and the extent of their migrations remained a mystery to them. All that mattered was their geographic and economic distance from the upper country and, by extension, from New France.

Native Migrants and the Lure of the Head of the Bay

Chesapeake colonists initially believed that Native peoples, from the Iroquois to the Piscataways, acted largely in response to European demands. This belief made it difficult for them to discern how Native alliances, trade networks, and long-distance migrations shaped the Tidewater region. Even so, Chesapeake planters were surrounded by newcomers whose stories of travel, trade, and warfare tied one region to another. As early as 1685, Piscataway Indians predicted that "far away Indians . . . will be united with us." New arrivals such as the Shawnees and older residents of the mid-Atlantic, including the Iroquois, the Susquehannocks, and their Eastern Algonquian neighbors, understood that the head of the bay was a site of enormous strategic importance.[5]

The confluence of the Susquehanna River and Chesapeake Bay became a place of opportunity for Chartier and the Shawnee migrants. For much of the seventeenth century, the Iroquois and the Susquehannocks had battled for control of the region. These rivals for power used the Susquehanna River as "the main artery of transportation between New York and Maryland." Through them, powerful men in Pennsylvania and Maryland, including William Penn, Daniel Coxe, and James Logan, learned what the Iroquois and Susquehannocks already knew: that the lower Susquehanna River might be an ideal hub for the Indian trade. The English trading center at Albany compelled Native hunters to haul their furs over land. It was an arduous journey, one that exacted a heavy toll on the hunters. Flowing more than 400 miles to the north, the Susquehanna River reached deep into Iroquoia, connecting their warriors to their southern enemies. As the main rivals of the Iroquois Confederacy, Susquehannock warriors effectively controlled the Chesapeake and its tributaries. The Susquehannocks also controlled another important river, the Potomac, which cut into the Appalachian Mountains. For at least the last 200 years, Susquehannock traders had followed trails along the Potomac River into the Ohio Valley, where they had established trade relations with the peoples of the Middle Ohio Valley. The Lower Susquehanna River offered a much easier route to the English trading posts. The Iroquois, after defeating the Susquehannocks, made it clear that "wee have wonn by ye Sword and as owners of ye same wee have Transported it to this government." Many Senecas, in particular, seemed determined to relocate permanently to the Lower

Susquehanna River. They intended to "settle amongst the Susquahan-nough Indians, here upon ye Susquehannough River." Perhaps in recognition of the region's strategic importance, "Forreign Indians" and "French people," including Martin Chartier and Shawnees from the Grand Village of the Kaskaskias, joined with a sizable number of Iroquois resettled at or near the head of the bay.[6]

The physical geography of the region helps to explain why the region became such an important site of migration and coalescence. The Piedmont of the Appalachian Mountains converges near the confluence of the Susquehanna River and Chesapeake Bay, making the northern shore rugged and hilly. Indeed, the fall line of the Susquehanna is less than five miles from the mouth of the Chesapeake. The head of the bay became a narrow corridor in which diverse peoples, languages, and trade goods intersected. Eastern Algonquians used the Susquehanna River and its many branches to travel up and out of the coastal plain and into the hunting grounds of the Appalachian foothills. Conversely, Iroquois warriors canoed down the Susquehanna River as part of their longer journeys southward, to their Susquehannock enemies and beyond to the Catawba villages of Carolina. The Susquehannocks occupied six villages above the falls of the river, the most populous of which was Carristauga (later formalized as Conestoga). It was a place of convergence, a resource-rich zone in which Iroquoian-speaking Susquehannock and Five Nations peoples and their Eastern Algonquian rivals, including the Lenapes (Delawares), Piscataways, Choptanks, and Pamunkeys, interacted. Networks of rivers and footpaths ran through the head of the bay, connecting these populations to other Indian peoples to the north, south, and west of the region. The most well-traveled north/south route, the Great Indian Warpath, hugged the Susquehanna River before cutting through towns such as Carristauga, on the lower Susquehanna, just above the fall line. From there, the path moved to the west, where it followed the Upper Potomac River near modern-day Cumberland, Maryland. At this point, some warriors followed the eastern slope of the Appalachian Mountains, into the Ohio country.[7]

Dutch and Swedish settlers residing near Fort Amstel and Fort Christiana conducted a lively trade in furs in this region. It was a sparsely populated land settled by non-English-speaking peoples such as Herrman, who were interested in the Indian trade. Tobacco growers located to the south and east of Cecil County viewed the region with suspicion, and they feared the borderland culture there. English planters depended on tobacco agriculture by the second decade of the seventeenth century, but the residents of Cecil County labored as fishermen, and in the eighteenth century they

Map 3. *Warrior Paths. Warfare stitched together Native peoples along the Atlantic Coast, and colonial officials began coordinating their efforts in an unsuccessful bid to halt the traffic. Map by Alex Gau.*

shipped timber down the Susquehanna toward the shipyards of Baltimore. Monocrop agriculture and slavery did not redefine Cecil County until well into the eighteenth century. And unlike Carolinians, who depended on the Indian slave trade, members of the planter class were less interested in the region's Indians.[8]

Tidewater planters learned that they could not ignore French, Swedish, Dutch, and Native migrants at the head of the bay. As Native newcomers from the west and south settled in the region, violence between Indians and whites became commonplace. Distrust between migrants and colonists had particularly serious consequences for the French, Dutch, and Swedish colonists who lived near them. By the close of the seventeenth century, Indian migrants helped to redefine the ways the English thought of themselves because they caused colonial officials from New York to Virginia to engage in a regular conversation. In 1675–76, King Philip's War and Bacon's Rebellion undermined their particular ambitions. The presence of migrants on the northern perimeter of the Tidewater helped to bring about a shared understanding of the mission, purpose, and identity of English colonization. In response to the "strange Indians" at Bohemia Manor, Englishmen had to consider distant lands and events and their impact on everyday life in North America.

The fall line of the Susquehanna River, like those along the James and Savannah rivers, became an important site of trade and migration in the mid-Atlantic. Englishmen protested against American Indian warriors who crossed over the fall line and then made their way through English farms and plantations. They demanded an Indian "bullwarke" against the "strange" and "forreigne Indians" who traveled along the many footpaths that bisected their planted "clearings." Shawnee migrants recognized the opportunity these tensions presented. First, the Iroquois-Susquehannock Wars, which concluded in 1675, made it possible for the Shawnees to enter into an alliance with those who survived. Bacon's Rebellion further weakened the Susquehannocks, and the Iroquois reimagined their territory as a refugee center. "Mixt Nations," including the Shawnees, became part of the southern door of the Iroquois Covenant Chain. Their warriors became useful to both the Iroquois and the English, and they became a significant part of the regional fur trade. In these ways, the "Mixt Nations" adapted to the intercolonial circumstances that the region presented. By acting as mercenaries, traders, and hunters, the Shawnees, Susquehannocks, and Piscataways shielded the Iroquois from southern tribes, particularly the Catawbas, who traveled north to attack them. After living among the French at Grand Village and the "Goose Creek men" at Savannah Town,

Shawnees now adjusted to the use of tactical violence and regional diplomacy to carve out a space for themselves at the head of the bay. They had already learned that survival in the space between colonizers and Native powers was contingent on the strategic use of violence. Cecil County also helped to foster the Shawnees' long-standing alliance with the Delawares and the Senecas, two peoples who would later migrate with the Shawnees in successive removals across the continent. The Susquehannocks made these longer-term alliances possible. Ties between the Shawnees and the Susquehannocks reached back into the protocontact era, when Susquehannock middlemen brought European trade goods into the Ohio Valley. Susquehannock peoples now invited Shawnees to the head of the bay and guaranteed their good behavior to skeptical colonial officials. For the English and for their Native counterparts, the Lower Susquehanna River became a place of reinvention, as peoples on the move adjusted to a region that fused a series of regions together.[9]

Interregional Violence along the Mid-Atlantic Borderlands

By choosing sides, Maryland became actively involved in the suppression of the Iroquois Confederacy. In response, the Iroquois expanded their attacks on Tidewater settlements. The Senecas, in particular, killed several Englishmen after Maryland concluded its alliance with the Susquehannocks. By carrying their attacks to Maryland's capital at St. Mary's, the Iroquois began to undermine colonial authority. This was more than the frontier violence Englishmen had come to expect. It was a war between rival imperial powers. Maryland redoubled its efforts with the "Kings of the friend Indians" in the region, including the Susquehannocks.[10]

The Great Indian Warpath cut through Maryland and Virginia, and both colonies compelled resident tribes to halt the traffic. In one treaty, Maryland paid "one hundred armes length of Roanoke [wampum]" for the "Right Eare" of every Iroquois killed or "every prisoner they shall deliver." Mid-Atlantic villagers always needed gunpowder and ammunition, and the tribes allied with the Tidewater colonies acquired these precious commodities by fighting "agt any Indians now held and declared Enemyes" of Maryland. The Piscataways and Susquehannocks fought with the Iroquois and Catawbas to retain their homelands. Piscataway leaders "revive[d] the League" between themselves and the English so "that they may sleep by their wives quietly and take their Tobacco."[11]

No one, not even well-armed settlers who organized themselves into "ranging" companies, could stop hundreds of warriors moving along the

Great Indian Warpath. Large war parties continued to travel through the Chesapeake and forage on settlers' farms. Bounties for Iroquois scalps and ears did reduce the number of attacks on white settlers in the region. But seemingly random attacks on African American slaves and livestock remained commonplace. In response, Maryland and Virginia developed a pass system that obligated Indian people to "haue ticketts if they haue occasion to come further among the English plantacons."[12] Colonial officials worked diligently to circumscribe Indian people to specific lands and to limit their migrations. Warriors traveling to and from Iroquoia sometimes engaged in opportunistic stealing and killing in the Chesapeake region. Indians captured without a pass were either killed by English allies such as the Susquehannocks and Piscataways or sold as slaves.

Maryland rangers patrolled the backcountry for "skulking" enemies, and allied tribes joined with them to secure their lives and their lands. Maryland's dream of a multiethnic defense of its frontiers languished because of centuries-old rivalries.[13] While Indian slavery in Carolina triggered a wide range of migrations, Maryland's Indians tended to remain attached to their homelands. These small societies diminished over time, as disease, warfare, and English land hunger steadily eroded their territory.

Colonial officials created the pass system not simply to restrict the movements of Indian people. Marylanders complained about "such distractions as take the people from planting." As cash-crop agriculture became the great obsession of the seventeenth-century Chesapeake, settlers became largely unaware, if not unconcerned, with the region's Indians. Cattle and hogs regularly trampled the fields of Indian corn planted by allies of the English. The English lacked any real cultural knowledge of the Indian people in their midst. Such passes offered a visual means by which settlers distinguished between friends and enemies. A Maryland official admitted that Indian-white violence proliferated because "the English cannot easily distinguish one Indian from another."[14]

Native peoples traveling north and south through the head of the bay regularly attacked frontier settlers, compelling colonial officials to coordinate their efforts. The English noticed the success of Jesuit missionaries in drawing large numbers of Iroquois converts closer to Montreal in Catholic Indian towns such as Kahnawake. The formidable power of the Iroquois over the eastern half of North America became one engine driving English officials to consolidate their efforts along the Atlantic Coast. Officials in Maryland and Virginia abandoned the Susquehannock and became allied with the Iroquois because they recognized the growing power of the Haudenosaunee. Colonial officials, from New York to Maryland, consolidated diplomatic relations. By the close of the seventeenth century, regional allies such as the Susquehannock became an afterthought. The English recognized that these regional powers could no longer protect them from the Iroquois. As a result, the English switched sides and became allied with the Iroquois.[15]

The reversal of Susquehannock fortunes is surprising given their long history with the Tidewater planters. Susquehannock warriors had always inspired their awe. Writing in 1666, the writer George Alsop, like John Smith before him, described them as giants "stately and majestick, treading on the Earth with as much pride, contempt, and disdain to so sordid a center, as can be imagined from a creature derived from the same mould and Earth." In 1676, Maryland governor Thomas Notley portrayed them as one of the "bloodiest people in all these parts of America." Implicit in all of these accounts is English frustration with the Susquehannocks' autonomy. Unlike the Piscataways, Pamunkeys, and Choptanks, who pledged obeisance to the English so that their nation "may not be Scorned and Chased out of our Protection," the Susquehannocks lived just out of reach of English settlements, and they remained somewhat unfamiliar to the English as a result.[16] While Algonquians along the Eastern Shore and the Potomac accepted de facto reservations and life as subsistence farmers and hunters for the English, the Susquehannocks hoped for something different. From their village at Carristauga they traded with the Dutch, Swedish, and English, people for whom loyalty to the crown was secondary to personal interest. Iroquoians, from the Senecas to the Susquehannocks, avoided English dominion. By the time Shawnee migrants arrived, the Chesapeake colonies had adopted two separate Indian policies. Subjugated tribes, such as the Piscataways and the Pamunkeys, remained loyal to the English.

In contrast, the independent villages of the lower Susquehanna River and Delaware Valley continued to frustrate colonists' ambitions for a secure and racially segregated zone into which they might expand plantation agriculture. After the Haudenosaunee defeated the Susquehannocks, colonists worried that an alternative, Iroquois-led alliance might emerge "that may corrupt Our Indians and Mould them So to their own future." Now part of the Five Nations' Covenant Chain, the Susquehannocks joined their new allies and turned their guns on the smaller Algonquian tribes of the region, including the Piscataways, Choptanks, Pamunkeys, and Mattawomans.[17] When they became part of the southern door of the Longhouse, Susquehannocks served Iroquois interests by keeping the Great Indian Warpath, from New York to Carolina, open. The Iroquois' desire to travel freely through this corridor was more important to them than a temporary alliance with the English. The Chesapeake colonies had no alternative but to rely on the remnant Algonquian communities that were no match for their Iroquoian-speaking rivals. Without English support, the Susquehannocks had little choice but to acknowledge defeat and accept Iroquois authority over them. The Iroquois displayed a kind of soft power over those they conquered. They did not compel the Susquehannocks to abandon their villages and to migrate north to Iroquoia. By gaining such a formidable ally, the Seneca-Susquehannock alliance presaged the incorporation of the Delawares into the Covenant Chain. For the Piscataways and their neighbors, their alliance signaled an escalation of their long war with the Haudenosaunee.

The Parable of Jacob Young and the Failure of Intercultural Diplomacy in the Mid-Atlantic

There were few, if any, reliable cultural brokers in the Chesapeake colonies. Anglicized Dutchmen, including Jacob Young and John Hans Steelman, became important to colonial officials, who struggled to regulate Indian-white relations after Bacon's Rebellion. Maryland's lead negotiator, Henry Coursey, admitted as much, writing that without Jacob Young, "I cann doe nothing, & what truth is to be had is from him & none else."[18]

Colonial officials used men such as Young to pursue a regional solution to the violence. Maryland governor John Llewellin wrote that "we are never safe from the Northern Indians as long as they have any pretense of war with our ffriend [*sic*] Indians." Under the guise of war with the Piscataways, Seneca warriors might "hide their owne faults and lay it upon their Enemies."[19] The governments of Virginia and Maryland had to stop the mourning wars in order to enjoy continued economic growth. Frontier settlers would continue to suffer attacks against livestock and slaves as long as Indian men used the Great Indian Warpath to attack their enemies. Young persuaded Coursey to use Palmer's Island, at the head of the bay, as the site for negotiating an end to Bacon's Rebellion. Senecas and Susquehannocks joined with Native migrants at this important trading center. Palmer's Island had always been strategically important to Iroquoian and Algonquian peoples, whose homelands ranged from the Delmarva Peninsula to the Potomac River.

Henry Coursey was a newly appointed royal governor, and his ignorance of Indian ways had consequences for years to come. Without the economic incentives to educate themselves, and wary of befriending Indian peoples in the conspiracy-driven world of the Chesapeake, men such as Coursey struggled to make sense of Indian people. With Young's help, Coursey did learn that the region's Indians used gift exchanges as a way to measure the sincerity of the people with whom they negotiated. The "Mixt Nations" at the head of the bay believed that presents revealed whether or not "the peace betwixt us shall be justly kept." Maryland's Indians understood that gifts of gunpowder, silver medallions, and rum were accompanied by a demand that they offer additional proof of their loyalty. These "friend Indians" delivered hostages to the Maryland General Assembly in the years after Bacon's Rebellion. But risking everything on their behalf was not enough.[20]

Planter elites raised in a monarchical society had little patience with Native diplomacy. Born to rule, Englishmen used words and deeds to exaggerate their power over Native peoples. The taking of hostages and other overt displays of their newfound authority reflected the diminishing status of the Piscataway, Mattawoman, and Pamunkey communities. Maryland's Algonquians recognized their descent when colonial officials focused their energies on the head of the bay. Monatquund, speaker of the Piscataways, articulated his people's fears when he came to "revive the league" with Maryland. Too poor to offer presents, Monatquund realized that the English would abandon them "when their Nation may be reduced to nothing." While Maryland expanded its control over "our Indians liveing with us," they virtually ceded their authority over the head of the bay to the Senecas and the Susquehannocks.[21]

Iroquois warriors occasionally acquiesced to Maryland's demand that they request and receive a pass to travel through their settlements. Maryland officials sometimes permitted the Iroquois to "go through the country" to fight their enemies. But more often than not, the Iroquois ignored English wishes. They used Carristauga, a Susquehannock fort, in what is now Lancaster County, Pennsylvania, as a resting place before traveling through Maryland and Virginia.[22]

Frustrated by their powerlessness, planter oligarchs turned to the use of force against their allies. In Cecil County, the Maryland General Assembly required "Frequent Musters and Appearances in Arms" in an attempt to intimidate long-distance war parties. But this was a dangerous game. The Iroquois had extended the league to include their former enemies. The English were, in effect, surrounded by potential enemies. If the Iroquois abandoned them, the colonists would be "left as friendless as faithless, and utterly unable to deal with this Sckulking Enemy."[23]

In this climate of insecurity, assemblymen blamed their principal intermediary, Jacob Young, for the unrest, and they imprisoned him on charges of treason. As proof of his treachery, they cited his marriage to a Susquehannock woman and the several children he had had with her. They inferred that "the said Iacob is more nearly Concerned for those Indians . . . [than] the good Christian People of this Province."[24] By marrying into Susquehannock society, Young became so untrustworthy that he was jailed and nearly killed for challenging the emerging racial divide.[25]

During his trial, Young denied both his marriage and his paternal relationship to the Susquehannocks. Instead, he claimed to be a "Cecil County planter" rather than an Indian trader and intermediary. The legitimacy of Young's claims to membership in the planter class reflect a clear play to save his own life or at the least to avoid an extended jail term. Tidewater planters remained largely ignorant of Indian affairs. And the success of tobacco agriculture often came at the expense of the Indian trade. Young's trial contributed to the Maryland General Assembly's decision to vastly restrict the Indian trade. In their view, the trade encouraged "severall forreign and unknown Indians" to settle at the head of the bay.[26] They reasoned that an expanding population of Indian refugees further jeopardized their security. Iroquois war parties were trouble enough. Adding new Native migrants to a volatile region through a permissive trading regime would only further complicate the colony's affairs.

While Young was in jail, his behavior seemed to confirm English fears of a broad anti-English conspiracy. He delivered drunken, bellicose speeches while he was jailed. In one episode, Young boasted that he could make the Susquehannocks and other "northern Indians . . . do what he please[d]," declaring that if the English dared to put him in irons, "they should pay Dearly for it." Invariably, when the alcohol wore off, Young resumed his pretensions of membership in the planter class. He lamented that "the evill Effects of Drink" caused him to claim powers over Indians he did not have. But in the climate of the late seventeenth century, even a drunken man's grandiosity was taken seriously. As recently as 1673, Dutch residents of New York had briefly reclaimed the colony from the English. Such realities added depth and weight to the most ridiculous conspiracy theories.[27]

Without men such as Young, Maryland and Virginia ceded much of their involvement in Indian affairs to New York governor Edmund Andros at Albany. Their decision to make Albany, New York, the de facto capital of English-Indian relations represented more than a concession to the growing power of the Iroquois. New York's ascendancy as the diplomatic center of the Covenant Chain made sense. Chesapeake planters were not interested in building their fortunes through the Indian trade. Rituals of reciprocity, respect, and intermarriage failed utterly in their world, for the authority of planter-oligarchs depended on the racial caste system of the slave South.

Martin Chartier, "Inland" Indians, and the Onset of Iroquois Dominion

When Martin Chartier's band appeared at Bohemia Manor in 1692, it became part of a vast migration of "inland Indians" and other migrants to the mid-Atlantic. As Indians moved into the region, colonists realized that their dreams were linked to the "farr," "strange," and "foreign" Indians who appeared on the lower Susquehanna River in the final decade of the seventeenth century. Native migrants from distant places caused mid-Atlantic settlers to think continentally. Native newcomers had lived on the fault line between France, England, and the Iroquois, and so they were doubly vexing to Englishmen along the mid-Atlantic. Not only were their identities and origins difficult to determine, but their allegiances suggested that they might very well have treasonous intentions. The English knew that migrants possessed a great deal of knowledge about the eastern half of North America. In fact, many of these newcomers had already traded directly with their Spanish and French opponents, at great distances from Pennsylvania.[28]

Chartier's band of Shawnees seems to have encouraged Marylanders to reach out to Native peoples beyond the mountains. After journeying from South Carolina to Maryland, some Chaouanon [Shawnee] Indians "chalk[ed] out ye way to those settlements, & so to ye river Maschasipi [Mississippi], to ye parts adjacent, and down to ye Bay of Mexico." After they "made a small rude draught" for Maryland's governor, Chartier and his Shawnee allies wanted the English to "furnish ye in-land Indians with such quantitys of Goods, and so cheap, yt they may get the trade from ye French."[29] Their knowledge of the continent made them attractive, though dangerous, mediators. The English had to cultivate their friendship, even though they suspected that men such as Martin Chartier could never be completely trusted. Shawnee mapmakers reminded mid-Atlantic colonists that they lived in an integrated world traversed by Native peoples and the traders associated with them. The Shawnees and their neighbors traveled easily between regions claimed by competing colonizers and amassed a geographic and cultural knowledge that became increasingly valuable as French and English worlds came together.

As Native migrants from the "Ohyo River" and the "western Inland frontier" moved into the mid-Atlantic, colonists began to see them as essential to their struggle with France for control of the continent. Crushing French ambitions required an extensive Indian trade and ready access to European manufactured goods. A colonial official from Maryland believed that a "small fort or trading houses . . . in convenient places" might enable the English to "hinder the French from extending their colonys on the back of the kings provinces."[30] Trading houses and forts beyond the Appalachians, in their view, were essential to the long-term ambitions of the English empire.

Marylanders actively discouraged Native migrants from settling at the head of the bay. Nevertheless, Governor Francis Nicholson described how "foreign Indians" known by "diverse names" continued settling there. Nicholson knew that they "come down by ye falls of potomoke & Susquahanah Rivers." But the "parties of rangers" he posted at these places rarely halted migrants' progress. A suspicious lot, Englishmen believed that Indian migrants were tainted by their alliance to the French. Nicholson guessed that Shawnees, Miamis, and other "Naked" Indians "are supposed to inhabit upon ye river Ohio." However, many of these migrants seemed to come from "ye southward," suggesting that they had been dislocated from the Ohio River for some time.[31]

Shawnee migrants recognized that indigenous hierarchies of power would determine their ability to establish villages along the Lower Susquehanna River. Like Chartier, who was interrogated by the English for moving to the region, Shawnee travelers negotiated with both the Susquehannocks and the Senecas to settle there. These treaties forbade the Piscataways, Choptanks, and Mattawomans from making agreements with foreign Indians without the governor's approval. In contrast, Maryland did not compel the Susquehannocks to sign a similar treaty. The Susquehannocks' return to their old fort, above the falls of the Susquehanna River, might have made such a provision unenforceable. It is clear that by migrating out of Maryland, the Susquehannocks effectively removed themselves from Maryland's control. The region above the falls became a place of exile, a place where tribes voluntarily removed to avoid crushing subservience to the Chesapeake planters. And the lower Susquehanna River offered many natural advantages. Lured by better hunting and easier, all-water trade routes, the region became a haven for Native peoples from a wide range of locales. During Chartier's interrogation, a Susquehannock head man intervened on his behalf and explained that, "being reduced to a small number," his people hoped that Chartier and the Shawnees would "come and settle upon their own land at Susquehannoh Fort." The Susquehannocks and the Shawnees had been separated by hundreds of miles and divided by significant linguistic differences. And yet, in 1692, Susquehannock familiarity with the Shawnees, built as it was on centuries of trade, enabled Shawnee migrants to live among them along the Lower Susquehanna River.[32]

The Susquehannocks offered the Shawnees a place to settle. But traders in New York, using Munsee Delaware and Mahican intermediaries, drew some Shawnees from Grand Village to the mid-Atlantic. The Albany merchants worried that the English colonies might fall to New France and its Indian allies if they managed to defeat the Iroquois. They hoped that the Shawnees might fill the void left in the event of Iroquois defeat. By 1692, Arent Schuyler had become a prominent merchant in Albany, and he encouraged at least two different Shawnee bands to migrate from the Illinois country to Pennsylvania. Schuyler orchestrated their migration with the support of New York's governor, Thomas Dongan. New Yorkers knew that this migration would anger the Iroquois, who were then "in a public war" with the Shawnees. Schuyler also knew that the Iroquois would be incensed if the Albany traders reached an agreement with the Shawnees "without their knowledge." To make matters worse, Shawnee migrants from Illinois refused to acknowledge that they had been conquered by the Iroquois. The leader of one of the Shawnee bands, Kakowatchy, believed that they had migrated eastward for better trading opportunities. But when the Iroquois learned of their migration, they demanded that the Shawnees acknowledge defeat as a precondition of settlement on the Lower Susquehanna River. The Senecas, in particular, chastised New Yorkers for encouraging the Shawnee migration. One of their speakers stated that he could not "understand how the Christians can be so drunk in their minds as to negotiate a separate peace now without their knowledge." Schuyler hoped that a meeting between "10 or 12 of the most important Schowaenos [Shawnees]" and an Iroquois delegation would resolve the differences between them. He ignored Iroquois wishes and negotiated with the Shawnees, because he worried that if the French were able to defeat the Iroquois, it would "bring us trouble here."[33]

Arnout Viele, one of Schuyler's principal traders, seems to have made the journey to the upper country, along with Munsee Delawares associated with Chief Matasit and Mahicans living in allied towns in the Delaware Water Gap. Viele was, at heart, an entrepreneurial trader who wanted new arrivals to shift the riches of the fur trade from Montreal to Albany. He believed that Shawnees associated with Kakowatchy would ultimately resettle in eastern Pennsylvania. Not surprisingly, Arnout Viele became their principal trader. One Shawnee migrant from the Illinois country corroborated the story, claiming that the Shawnees had migrated because of the trading opportunities offered by the English along the Susquehanna River. He admitted that "we are people yt Lives only upon hunting." The hide and fur trade now dominated their economy, for it was the means by which his people bought "English goods to Clothe oure Selves." Pennsylvanians received them enthusiastically, noting that the Shawnees were "a nation of Consequence."[34]

With so many villagers, each with their own history of being on the move, it became impossible to tell a shared story about the Shawnee people. A century after their migration, Mahican diplomat Hendrick Apaumat challenged this narrative about trade and migration. Apaumat affirmed the Iroquois interpretation of the Shawnee migration to the east. He believed that the Iroquois had defeated the Shawnees on the battlefield and that the Iroquois compelled them to move to Pennsylvania as a result of their subjugation. Apaumat remembered that "our ancestors near 200 years ago rescued them [the Shawnee] from . . . the Iroquois . . . who were ready to swallow my younger brother, Shawany." Like Apaumat, a Pennsylvania trader from Pennsylvania believed that "ye five nations [Iroquois] had a design of carrying off the Shawanah Indians." Without the diplomatic efforts of the Delawares, Mahicans, and Susquehannocks, they argued, the Shawnees could not have settled on the Lower Susquehanna River, within the southern door of the Iroquois Confederacy. The Shawnees had a slightly different interpretation. They explained that "we come to renew the Covenant chain of peace with you." Whether they were manipulated by the English, motivated by trading opportunities, or compelled by Iroquois overlords, these competing narratives reflect the piecemeal nature of long-distance migration in early America. When the Shawnees arrived in Pennsylvania, they explained that they "desire[d] that we may be as one heart, one blood, and one soul with the English, the Mohawks, and the Mahikanders, and all of the Indians of this Government." These Shawnees understood the Covenant Chain as a kind of multiethnic "government."[35] The Iroquois and their English allies remembered Shawnee migrations differently, and it is their memory of Shawnee migrations that has defined Shawnee history since the late seventeenth century. In 1692, when Shawnees began arriving at the head of the bay, Iroquois explanations of Shawnee migrations caused the Shawnees to lose control of their sovereignty. When they set foot on Bohemia Manor, they did so as refugees.

The "Mixt Nations" of the Lower Susquehanna River

Shawnees, Susquehannocks, and Delawares on the Susquehanna enjoyed considerable autonomy from the Iroquois. Each tribal village in the region had a small number of warriors. But when combined, these allies became formidable. With only forty warriors remaining, the Susquehannocks would have been annihilated by their enemies. But the Shawnees founded a village just four miles below Carristauga, their last remaining village. In 1707, a Shawnee king named Opessa led another group of Pekowitha Shawnees from Carolina who ultimately settled along the headwaters of the Potomac River. Thirty miles from Carristauga was Minguannan, a Delaware village near the Elk River. This was the largest of them all, with 300 warriors. Iroquoian-speaking Susquehannocks joined with Central Algonquian–speaking Shawnees and Eastern Algonquian–speaking Delawares in this borderland between the Haudenosaunee and their southern enemies. They resided there, free from Iroquois attacks, for as long as they agreed to serve as a kind of military buffer for the Iroquois. The Susquehannock town of Carristauga became the diplomatic center of the migrants' alliance. They absorbed many of the retaliatory blows delivered by the Catawba and other enemies of the Iroquois. In fact, Iroquois and Susquehannock animosity toward the southern tribes became a kind of intercultural glue, bonding disparate peoples into this new alliance. After the Treaty of 1701, which created peace between the French-allied tribes of the Old Northwest and Canada and the Iroquois, the Five Nations focused their warfare on the southern tribes. Pennsylvania governor William Keith explained that Iroquois "projects of war" were now directed "against the Indians who are in amity with Virginia and Carolina."[36]

Pennsylvanians puzzled over the allegiance of the Indians at the head of the bay. They asked the governor of New York if he could determine "whether they do not belong to the nations or any other Indians under his Government?" In the ascribed world of the seventeenth century, to whom one belonged was a matter of critical importance. The English scarcely understood personal or national independence. This was the logic of empire. Surely the villages seated at or near the head of the bay had either English or Indian masters? Such questions point to the conceptual failure of the English to properly understand the Iroquois Covenant Chain. The Iroquois Confederacy was not an empire, nor was it a monarchy, and English

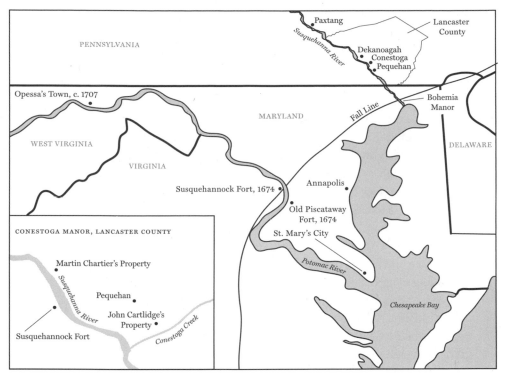

Map 4. Chesapeake and Lancaster County Indians. Susquehannock diplomacy and Penn's rhetoric of peace and trade combined to make southeastern Pennsylvania a haven for Native migrants in the early eighteenth century. Map by Alex Gau.

hierarchies of power could not explain Haudenosaunee understandings of diplomacy and war. The decades-long war between the Susquehannocks and the Iroquois had permanently altered tribes such as the Senecas. By the 1690s, many Seneca people had permanently relocated to the head of the bay, where they lived largely among the Susquehannocks and the long-distance migrants allied with them.

By joining the Covenant Chain alliance, Shawnee migrants from Grand Village and Savannah Town entered into a peace agreement with the Iroquois and ended decades of warfare between them. At a conference with Pennsylvania governor John Evans, Opessa explained that "he was happy to live in a country at peace." Initially understood as "part of a nation of Indians at the head of the bay," Opessa's Shawnees help to explain their rationale for migrating toward the southern door of the Iroquois. With Carristauga as their diplomatic center, Shawnee and Seneca diplomats offered Pennsylvania eight wampum belts to ensure that "room to sport and play without danger of slavery might be allowed them." Opessa acknowledged that they had been "strangers to this place," before this migration. In spite of coming "as people blind," Opessa hoped that the Pennsylvanians would "take them by the hand and lead them." If so, the Shawnees might finally be able to "lift up their heads in the woods without any danger or fear."[37]

The Shawnees and their neighbors had to address the competing interests of both the Iroquois and the English in order to remain on the Lower Susquehanna River. Maryland continued to regard the Indians at the head of the bay as formidable, and they desired "that the friendship of the Susquehannah and Shavanore [Shawnees] be secured." Taken together, both peoples were "of considereable moment and not to be slighted." Ultimately, the "Mixt Nations" at the head of the bay moved out of Maryland, to the new colony of Pennsylvania, where the Indian trade dominated the economy. By 1700, residents of Cecil County, Maryland, were busily establishing town sites and plantations. The head of the bay was no longer a trading center.

Those who stayed behind the English frontier were not so lucky. The Piscataways, Nanticokes, Choptanks, and Mattawomans lived in a circumscribed world without allies. They faced the Iroquois alone. Marylanders continued to require them to participate in ranging parties, where they worked as scouts on behalf of the English. Colonists made sure that if they aided slaves they too would become enslaved, and colonial officials did little to check settlers' power. In fact, new laws were written, so that if "any Indian so meeting an English man shall refuse to throw down his arms . . . he shall be deemed an enemy." Barred from entering into alliances with "strange Indians," Maryland's Algonquians lost control of both their internal affairs and their relations with other Indian peoples. In both law and practice, Maryland was now a fully segregated society.

The Piscataways fled from Maryland to forestall these drastic limits on their freedom and safety. By moving to the Shenandoah Mountains of Virginia, they hoped to "secure themselves their wives and children from the English who dayly threatened them." Constantly blamed for the death of slaves, hogs, and cattle, the Piscataways had become a hated minority. Neither free nor enslaved, they complained about being "called Rogues & dogs." Their English neighbors regularly pulled down their fences and destroyed their cornfields. In spite of their complaints, both Virginia and Maryland threatened to use force against them if they did not return. "Settling there is not advisable or safe," officials warned, because neither colony could protect them from their settlers. The Piscataways' short-lived experiment with migration out of their homeland ended after one growing season. Most returned to Maryland, though some chose to migrate to Seneca villages in western New York. The English later reported that the Piscataways were "now all one people" with the Iroquois.

For American Indians from the Chesapeake Bay, voluntary absorption into the Iroquois Confederacy seemed a better alternative to harassment and servitude among the English. Virginians noted that their "weake towns" were often attacked by "foreigne Indians." Indian villagers complained about opportunistic slavers among the Englishmen. Small hunting parties sometimes found that one or two members of their group did not return. In one instance, an Englishman named Daniel Pugh captured and sold two Tuscarora hunters to a Barbadian shipmaster named Thomas Tyler. Pugh sold them to Tyler as his ship, the *Swallow*, shadowed the Virginia coastline. The constancy of war and the frequency of migrations up and down the eastern seaboard made it relatively easy for men such as Daniel Pugh to capture and enslave Indians. Without badges or other visual markers of their status as "friend Indians," Virginia made it legal to capture and sell Indian migrants to West Indian planters. It is hard to know exactly how Pugh captured them, but it is almost certain that he acted with others. As late as 1720, Virginia governor Alexander Spotswood complained about English colonists who offered guns and ammunition to local Native peoples if they attacked and captured southern Indians. Pugh's story suggests that settlers employed Indian people to hunt for Indian slaves well into the eighteenth century.[38]

Small bands of Algonquians sometimes abandoned their "ancient seats" in the Chesapeake before enslavement, assault, and harassment overwhelmed them. In one instance, a Nanticoke "emperor" named Panquash chose to leave his people behind. Nanticoke representatives traveled to Annapolis to explain that "if he had stayed he might have remained" their emperor. After he left them, "they would have nothing to say to him." Perhaps chastened by their earlier attempt to flee to the Shenandoahs, the Piscataways "resolved not to leave the Country where they had so long lived but to live with the English as if they had one Father and mother." Faced with the agony of exile from their homelands, the Piscataways remained on what was left of their lands. Their collective choice offers one of many poignant examples of Indian people living in a region that offered few viable paths to survival. Panquash—and those at the head of the bay—preferred to leave Maryland and Virginia behind than to face the uncertainties of life behind the English frontier. We now take up the stories of these Native migrants who searched for a home, from Pennsylvania to Ohio.

part 3

Becoming Strangers

THE LONG HISTORY OF REMOVAL

As Native sojourners who moved every generation for more than 250 years, the Shawnees adopted a wide range of identities, and the differences among them accelerated over time. Within the parochial cosmopolitanism that had shaped their migrations lay new understandings of American Indian unity that were an inevitable by-product of long-distance migration. The Shawnees were at the forefront of these new expressions of identity, which in the eighteenth century reflected their increasing estrangement from Europeans. Land hunger and the decline of both the slave and the fur trade drove a wedge between Native and European residents of colonial-era borderlands. Mid-Atlantic colonies such as Maryland and Pennsylvania no longer believed that Native peoples were vital to their survival. The Shawnees and their neighbors began moving out of borderland towns on the edge of colonial settlements as their importance diminished. They moved west of the Appalachian Mountains, and their return to the Ohio Valley became a kind of homecoming. But those Shawnees who returned were at the vanguard of a new way of thinking in an imperial age. Among them were Shawnees such as Peter Chartier. He had discovered valuable lessons in movement and reinvention, and he turned Shawnee histories of migration and violence toward the adoption of a new racial consciousness for Indian peoples in the eastern half of North America.

Between 1720 and 1754, Peter Chartier robbed British traders and rejected French demands for consolidating his people at Detroit. These audacious examples of independence infuriated Englishmen and Frenchmen alike. At the same time, he encouraged pan-Indian expressions of unity. Behind a failed temperance movement on the Upper Ohio and an interregional commitment to neutrality among the Upper Creeks were Shawnee intermediaries. By the middle of the eighteenth century, the Shawnees knew more about the eastern half of North America than anyone else. Their migrations and their ongoing commitment to adaptation posed a real challenge to the imperial ambitions of both the French and the British.

In the following chapters, I argue that we must situate the Indian Removal Act of 1830 into a much longer history of forced relocation. Beginning in the 1720s, the Shawnees and their neighbors abandoned their villages in response to settler colonialism. They became the first participants in acts of violence and estrangement caused by European land hunger and massive demographic shifts in British North America. I argue that we must understand these long-term continuities in Indian-white relations if we are to understand the social movements pioneered by Native peoples on the eve of the Seven Years' War. By the 1720s, advocates for race-based understandings of identity competed with those who preferred older notions of village-based autonomy. The conflict between these groups foreshadowed the Seven Years' War as they responded to the increasing social and geographic distance between Native peoples and Europeans.

chapter 7

One Head and One Heart

MIGRATION, COALESCENCE, AND PENN'S IMAGINED

COMMUNITY ON THE LOWER SUSQUEHANNA

Between 1676 and 1710, Native peoples from the mid-Atlantic, the upper country, and South Carolina coalesced in colonial Pennsylvania. Indian migrants saw it as a refuge for oppressed people well before European immigrants redefined it as "the best poor man's country." William Penn certainly promoted their understanding of his colony. In 1701, while negotiating a treaty with the Susquehannocks, Penn hoped that Indians and colonists might live "as one head and one heart." Penn's repeated promises to defend the rights of Native peoples must have resonated with migrants from borderlands that had been remade by warfare, slavery, and vigilantism. Pennsylvanians assured Indian migrants of their safety by passing "a law to prevent any injuries to them from the Christians, and laying greater punishments on those that should commit them, than if they were done to the English themselves."[1]

Fourteen years later, in a council meeting held at Philadelphia, the Delaware leader Sassoonan recalled Penn's vision. Sassoonan desired "that they should be joyn'd as one, that the Indians should be half English & the Indians make themselves as half Indians." Sassoonan described "how hard [it] was upon them, for that they knew not what they were to expect for their goods, and that they could scarce purchase ours." Sassoonan hoped to restore fairness to the Indian trade, but he did so by evoking the kinship terms first articulated by William Penn. A generation of Indian people had been raised in the belief that Pennsylvania stood apart from the other English colonies, particularly Maryland, Virginia, and South Carolina. Sassoonan's metaphors reflected his desire to enjoy the religious and ethnic pluralism championed by William Penn. However, by 1715, the limitations of Penn's vision became impossible to ignore. The economics of the Indian trade revealed the ethnic and cultural limits of Penn's peaceable kingdom.[2]

At least initially, Penn and the officials he appointed attempted to marry the radical reformation to their economic ambitions. As a member of the Society of Friends, Penn subscribed to the notion of the Inner Light, that every person, regardless of gender, social rank, or race, had access to "direct revelation from God." Such radical egalitarianism caused innumerable conflicts for Penn after October 1682, when he founded the proprietary colony of Pennsylvania. In that year, at a council with Native Pennsylvanians, he expressed his ardent wish that he "intend[ed] to order all things in such manner, that we may all live in Love and peace one with another." Penn strove to apply Quaker principles in his government's dealings with American Indians. His first experiment in reconciling his ideals to the realities of making a colony began with Native migrants attached to the diplomatic center of Conestoga, in southeastern Pennsylvania. In 1690, Penn proposed founding a city on the Lower Susquehanna that would serve as the hub for the Indian trade in the mid-Atlantic. Penn knew that the Susquehanna River's strategic importance would enable him to wrest control of the Indian trade from New York and that the Iroquois were central to the success of his plans. He recognized that many Iroquois hunters had grown tired of hauling furs and skins via overland routes to Albany. Many preferred the Lower Susquehanna and the all-water routes it made possible.[3]

Penn inspired thousands of Indian people to migrate to Pennsylvania in the first three decades of its existence by linking the Indian trade to metaphors of kinship and security. New York's governor, Thomas Dongan, responded decisively to their migrations. He viewed Penn's ambitions as a threat to the very survival of New York. Dongan used his alliance with the Iroquois to check Penn's ascendancy. Acting in concert, the Iroquois and the New Yorkers tried to compel Indian migrants to answer to their imperatives. Dongan and Penn struggled for control of the Susquehanna Valley in London and the mid-Atlantic. In 1683, Dongan signed an agreement with the Iroquois for all of the lands surrounding the Susquehanna River. Dongan reasoned that the land was the Iroquois's to sell, by right of conquest. The Iroquois had sold Susquehannock lands from under their feet.[4]

Penn ultimately triumphed over Dongan, but not before challenging the Iroquois and the hierarchies of power that connected vast numbers of Indian people to British North America. First, in 1697, Penn paid Dongan a nominal fee for the rights to the Susquehanna River. Then, in 1700 and 1701, Penn signed two agreements with the Susquehannocks and the Shawnees for those same lands. After Penn's death in 1718, his successors returned to Dongan's policy and expanded Iroquois dominion over the migrant communities of Pennsylvania. Proprietary officials, insecure about their land claims, forced the Shawnees, Delawares, Conoys, and Susquehannocks to accept Iroquois dominion, and they argued that the Haudenosaunee had earned this by right of conquest. Pennsylvania's rivals in New York, Maryland, and the migrant communities of Lancaster County challenged its sovereignty. In response, proprietary officials aggressively promoted the 1737 Walking Purchase. Based on the fiction of Delaware subordination to the Iroquois, the Walking Purchase effectively divested yet another Indian claimant of lands in eastern Pennsylvania. Finally, at the Treaty of Lancaster in 1744, both the Iroquois and the Pennsylvanians acted as "sole recognized spokesmen" for the diverse Indian peoples of Pennsylvania.[5]

William Penn instinctively challenged Iroquois and New York claims to Pennsylvania's land and people. He negotiated directly with Native peoples wherever he found them. To Penn, rights of conquest mattered less than the social realities on the ground, at places such as Conestoga. In the Treaty of 1701, Penn negotiated directly with the Susquehannocks and the Shawnees along the Lower Susquehanna, reflecting his belief in direct negotiations with those peoples living on the land in question. Surprisingly absent from the proceedings were the Iroquois themselves. By ignoring the Iroquois, Penn implicitly questioned their jurisdiction over the land and its peoples. Second, by acknowledging both Shawnee and Susquehannock claimants, Penn granted their communities a degree of legitimacy that both had lacked. For the first time in their recorded history, Shawnee migrants participated in treaties for land within the English colonies. And in so doing, they assumed a central role in the region. Indians and colonists ultimately failed to live "as one head and one heart." But even in losing, Shawnee migrants had established their legal sovereignty and had distinguished themselves from the Iroquois as a result.[6]

French and Indian Migrants and the Backlash against Penn's Peaceable Kingdom

As in Maryland and Virginia, Native newcomers caused a great deal of anxiety for proprietary officials. Pennsylvanians feared that French and Indian war parties would lay waste to their homes and villages. Harrowing examples from New England came in regularly. French traders formerly associated with the Sieur de La Salle, including Martin Chartier and Peter Bizaillon, invited scrutiny. Pennsylvanians suspected them of being "very dangerous in their Traffique with the Indians." Other French traders such as James Le Tort had moved to the colony after 1685 and the revocation of the Edict of Nantes. French Huguenots such as Le Tort settled alongside illegal traders such as Chartier and Bizaillon. Le Tort had much in common with the dissenting Christians who had immigrated to Pennsylvania. Nevertheless, proprietary officials struggled to separate French Calvinists such as Le Tort from men such as Chartier and Bizaillon. Proprietary officials compelled Chartier, a man who had "long lived among the Shawanah Indians & upon Sasquehannah," to periodically swear his fidelity to the British crown and to openly reject the supremacy of the Holy See as a condition for residency. After making one such loyalty oath, Chartier was "dismist under solemn engagements, to be true to the Government, & Inform of whatsoever might come to his knowledge worth notice."[7]

Across British North America, Indian-settler relations became a flash point for criticism of colonial governments. Pennsylvania was no exception. Penn's plans for economic growth through the fur trade made his colony fundamentally different from the Chesapeake colonies. And Pennsylvania was unlike New York, which depended on the Iroquois to defend its backcountry. From the beginning, Penn made the contrast explicit. In 1681, he was "very Sensible of the unkindness and injustice . . . too much exercised towards you by the People of these Parts of the world." Penn promised that his colony would be different. Its settlers would be "plain and honest people that neither make war upon others nor fear war from others." He believed that the principles of nonviolence espoused by the Society of Friends would make "friendly termes" possible. As a safeguard, Penn promised to create a "society of Traders" that would sell European goods "at reasonable rates." Penn imagined that an ever-expanding Indian trade, built on fairness and mutual understanding, would adequately protect his colony from tribes allied with New France. The proprietary government refused to raise a militia, even after the Glorious Revolution of 1688–89, which, in America, manifested itself in ongoing warfare between partisans of France and England. Quaker intransigence on matters of defense became so pronounced that the Crown placed Benjamin Fletcher, the former governor of New York, in the Pennsylvania governor's office from 1692 to 1696.[8]

Robert Quarry, a judge in the Vice-Admiralty Court and a prominent Anglican, used the arrival of Indian migrants as evidence in support of Pennsylvania's becoming a royal colony. In a literary battle refereed in London by the Board of Trade, Quarry accused Penn of promoting "a very great dread and Furor" among colonists. Anglican settlers, particularly those from the tobacco-growing region of the Delmarva Peninsula, supported Quarry through a series of petitions chronicling his alleged sympathy for "French" Indians. Much like Nathaniel Bacon's anti-Catholicism, which was based on an alleged conspiracy between Virginia's Indians and Governor William Berkeley, Pennsylvania's settlers described how "Mr. Penn hath Lately reced into his Government severall strange Indians, some of those being supposed to have Murdered many of her Majesties subjects."[9]

Queen Anne's War added legitimacy to their accusations. Discontented with religious toleration and unhappy with Penn's interest in the Indian trade, Quarry melded anti-Quakerism to antipathy toward Indian migrants. Quarry and his supporters charged that "Mr. Penn Endeavors all he can to invite Forreigne Indians known to be villainous and but lately come from Canada to settle in their country only for ye benefit of a trade with them." In response to these charges, Penn wrote: "I never to my knowledge invited or entertained one French Indian in my life: But discouraged French men . . . from treiding with our Indians." Penn rejected the notion that Chartier, Le Tort, Bizaillon, and the French traders of the Lower Susquehanna had committed treason. He argued that they were "great factors" and that the Indian trade was their sole interest. Penn did not sacrifice the French traders of the Lower Susquehanna to appease his critics. However, many Pennsylvanians continued to resent Native peoples and the French traders who lived among them.[10]

Some of Penn's allies in his proprietary government questioned his decision to promote the Indian trade. Tonty and La Salle had learned that working with men such as Martin Chartier had its risks. A cooperative trader in the spring often became a rebel by the winter. Not long after receiving helpful intelligence from Chartier, officials became convinced that he "intend[ed] shortly to depart this Govmt." As a consequence, the provincial council ordered that the sheriff of Newcastle "diligently . . . observe their motions and Designs." In the case of any "probable grounds," the council ordered that the sheriff must "apprehend & secure the said Martin."[11]

Most Englishmen feared that "inland Indians" could roll back the English empire. Quarry and his supporters had little faith in Indian diplomacy. Preferring an organized militia over a Covenant Chain lightly regulated by the Iroquois, Penn's critics hoped for greater imperial control of the colonies. In their view, Quaker resistance to an organized defense seemed particularly foolhardy given the number of migrants who had, until recently, traded with New France. For Quarry, a series of internal and external foes threatened to bring down the colony. Penn's supporters insisted that Native diplomats, individuals who believed in Penn's promise to live as "One Head and One Heart," would identify treasonous newcomers and separate them from well-meaning migrants. Faith in the Susquehannocks guided their remarks. Penn and his placemen created a process by which the Susquehannocks and later the Shawnees vetted new arrivals before sending them to Philadelphia for further cross-examination. Council members believed that "our proprietary [government] would not admit [new arrivals] till ye sd Susquehannats Indians our known friends became Guarantees for ye others good Behaviour."[12]

William Penn's personal secretary and family representative in Pennsylvania, James Logan, knew that Quarry enjoyed widespread support, and Logan used his considerable political and economic power to defend Penn's policies. He went on to become "a chief justice of the Supreme Court and an unofficial superintendent of Indian affairs in Pennsylvania." Across his long career, Logan achieved influence through land speculation and his dominance of the Indian trade. Nevertheless, he struggled to implement Penn's vision of Indian-settler relations in the colony. Even before the second decade of the eighteenth century, when German and Irish migrants flocked to Pennsylvania, the settler population was simply too diverse and geographically dispersed to contain. New immigrants, especially those interested in farming and in skilled trades, challenged Logan's authority. With such a significant investment in the Indian trade, men such as Logan reflected an older economic order, based on the manorial system Penn had established in his colony. German and Irish immigrants often refused to pay quitrents and ignored the land claims of important men. In contrast, Native peoples depended on Frenchmen such as Chartier, Le Tort, and Bizaillon, who were then caught between feudal lords such as Logan and the Native people they represented. French intermediaries were crucial to the Native villagers of Lancaster County, who defended their right to live among them.[13]

Conestoga Manor: A Place of Importance

The Lower Susquehanna River became a center of both diplomacy and trade in spite of these protests. Susquehannock villagers made the region a place of importance, particularly after survivors of Bacon's Rebellion migrated to the region. Shawnee, Delaware, Nanticoke, and Conoy migrants joined with the Susquehannocks, reinforcing its significance.

While Conestoga was the diplomatic center of this coalescent world, a Shawnee town, Pequehan, and a Conoy town sometimes called

Dekanoagah were seated nearby. Conestoga sat between the east bank of the Susquehanna River and its confluence with Conestoga Creek. Martin Chartier owned 300 acres that abutted the Susquehanna, on the northern edge of the manor. Prominent figures in the Indian trade, including James Logan and John Cartlidge, held adjoining property at the southern end of Conestoga Manor. Pennsylvanians described the Conestoga, Shawnee, and Conoy villages as the "3 Nations," and some believed that, taken together, they were "in a perfect good understanding with us." Shawydoohungh, or "Harry the Interpreter," a Susquehannock spokesman from Conestoga, served as both translator and diplomatic advocate for the coalescent communities of the Lower Susquehanna. Even though the Susquehannock had been vastly diminished, the migrant Indians of Conestoga Manor chose Harry the Interpreter because of his tribal affiliation. Further, as an English speaker, his linguistic skills and diplomatic acumen more than made up for the void left by the Susquehannocks' declining military power.[14]

The Susquehannocks, who increasingly went by the name of their principal town, Conestoga, set an example for many other tribes when they fled Maryland after Bacon's Rebellion. The Conoys, a coalescent people composed primarily of Piscataways and other Algonquian survivors of backcountry violence in the Chesapeake, described how "some of the Virginians had much disturbed them, killed one of their men, & abused several others." Violence between them and the Tidewater settlers was so pronounced that "they thought it not safe to Continue there, & were now come hither where they hoped they might live peaceably." But Pennsylvania was far from a peaceable kingdom. Warrior paths cut through their villages, and violence remained an everyday reality. European settlers often formed irregular militias that menaced their towns. Indian migrants feared a repeat of Bacon's Rebellion. Lieutenant Governor John Evans attempted to allay their concerns, assuring them that the militias intended "to help [rather] than to hurt them."[15]

Indian migrants based their coalescent community on the legal and diplomatic history of the Susquehannocks. In the Treaty of 1701, four Susquehannock sachems sold the Susquehanna River "and all the lands . . . on both sides of the said river" to "our friend and brother, William Penn" for "a parcel of English goods." Later, Pennsylvanians remembered that "in this sale the Susquehannocks as a nation practically ended their existence." By the 1730s, Pennsylvanians treated the Susquehannocks as if they were "completely under" the Iroquois. The Pekowitha Shawnee chief named Opessa signed this treaty. His people later moved into western

Maryland, and they established a village on the upper reaches of the Potomac, then a vital passageway from the interior of the continent to the
Atlantic Coast. The move may have been prompted by the 1701 Treaty,
which gradually converted migrant communities into tenants of the colony. Nearly twenty years after Pennsylvania's founding, Penn's plans for a
robust Indian trade that would bring an end to violence had become untenable. Addressing immigrants' land hunger had become a more immediate and intractable problem. Proprietary officials faced the impossible
task of reconciling Penn's vision with the realities of settler colonialism.[16]

The Treaty of 1701 had a chilling effect on the coalescent tribes of the
Lower Susquehanna River. Any hope that the Shawnee people might congregate and unify in the region vanished. While Opessa's people moved
to the Upper Potomac, others moved to the Wyoming Valley and farther
north to the Delaware Water Gap. Lancaster County remained an important trading center, but over time Conestoga Manor, in particular, became
known as a site of trade and diplomacy rather than as a population center
for Indian migrants.

After 1701, Native peoples crafted their own alliances, and their loyalties often frustrated colonial officials accustomed to the Covenant Chain
alliance. There were at least fifty Indian towns east of the Allegheny Mountains prior to the French and Indian War. Iroquois "half-kings," some
heavy-handed, others not, presided over many of them. Indian migrants
affiliated with the town of Conestoga lived at peace with the Iroquois if
they deferred to them in matters of diplomacy and war. Seneca and Cayuga diplomats lived at Conestoga and intermarried with tribes under
their control. These ties led the Nanticokes, Conoys, Susquehannocks,
Tutelos, and Tuscaroras to eventually join with the Iroquois Confederacy.
But others, particularly the Shawnees and Delawares, resisted permanent
coalescence into the Iroquois Confederacy. For example, Opessa seems to
have resisted the rules of Longhouse diplomacy. His ambivalence about
the Covenant Chain and Penn's 1701 treaty was evident even to the English, who imagined that Iroquois authority was absolute.[17]

The Iroquois did not adopt a single rule of engagement with Indian
newcomers to Pennsylvania. The Haudenosaunee varied their diplomatic
efforts, and the nuances of warfare and colonialism shaped their relations
with other tribes. At least some Iroquois joined Shawnees and Susquehannocks in attacks on the Catawba. But in another instance, Bizaillon
described how "ye five nations . . . had a design of carrying off the Shawanah Indians, both those settled near Conestogoe, & those near Lechay." In
this case, Pennsylvanians decided to intervene on the Shawnees' behalf.

Echoing Penn's metaphor of the shared head and heart, provincial officials declared that "ye Shawannahs are as of our selves." The long-distance journeys of Seneca, Cayuga, and Oneida warriors, in particular, often determined particular Haudenosaunee responses to Shawnee migrants in Pennsylvania. On one occasion, Arent Schuyler reported that Iroquois men "hunting towards ye farr nations" had been killed. In response, Iroquois warriors returning from the upper country wanted to avenge their kinsmen by attacking relatives of the "farr nations" in Pennsylvania.[18]

Colonial officials from New York ignored the fragmented perspectives of the Iroquois. It served their interests to project the belief that the Iroquois spoke from a single, unified perspective on the various migrants to Pennsylvania. Even after the Grand Settlement of 1701, a series of treaties in which the Iroquois declared their neutrality in the wars between England and France, New York continued to subscribe to the myth that they were the "sole custodians" of the Iroquois. New York colonial secretary Robert Livingston wrote that a "considerable number" of Iroquois lived near Conestoga and that more than 2,000 Indians in the region acknowledged that they were tributaries of the Iroquois. Following Livingston, one historian has argued that the "Shawnees were under Iroquois control, and Shawnee trade went where the Iroquois directed it."[19]

Colonial leaders in Pennsylvania were far less certain of Iroquois authority. For example, it was the Susquehannock rather than the Iroquois who guaranteed the good behavior of Opessa's Shawnees. The Shawnees had to answer to the Susquehannocks, who "shall answer to the said William Penn, his heirs and Successors, for the Good Behaviour and Conduct of the said Potowmeck Indians." The provincial council insisted that Opessa's Shawnees "shall not Suffer any Strange Nations of Indians to Settle or Plant on the further side of the Sasquehannah, or about Potowmeck River." Residents of Opessa's Town could not offer support and shelter to Indian migrants without first seeking permission from both the Susquehannock and the provincial council. Migrant communities established villages in the spaces between these unstable hierarchies of power.[20]

Native migrants to Pennsylvania brought with them a wealth of experience with colonizers. They had enough knowledge regarding the instability of colonial alliances to resist acquiescing to Iroquois and English authority. The Covenant Chain was particularly unstable in Pennsylvania because migration, warfare, and linguistic differences frustrated diplomats working toward a grand alliance. Even after the Iroquois defeated the Susquehannocks, violent reprisals at Conestoga continued. Diplomats from the Three Nations struggled to assert their sovereignty. Iroquois warriors continued to target smaller tribes such as the Nanticokes. In 1706, Nanticokes left "a very large Wampum Belt of 21 Rowes" at Conestoga and Philadelphia in order to avert an Iroquois attack. Not accustomed to wampum diplomacy, provincial council members wondered "what might be intended by the Indians in leaving that Belt here." Nanticokes believed that the Three Nations, united at Conestoga, mediated their relationship with the Iroquois. The Shawnees at Pequehan also felt threatened. They "owned themselves under some apprehensions from the 5 nations."[21]

Violence sometimes brought the Indian migrants and the Iroquois together. United by the Catawbas' ongoing attacks on their towns and angered by Virginia's attempt to regulate and enslave their people, Algonquian newcomers often joined with the Iroquois. In the spring of 1704, Catawba warriors "set upon some of those of Potowmeck." Old animosities from their time in Carolina contributed to Catawba attacks on Opessa's Town. However, the Shawnees' situation was made all the more difficult by their proximity to the Great Warrior Path, the primary north-south route east of the Appalachian Mountains. Opessa's people managed to repel their attackers. But the shared need for survival cultivated a sense of unity. James Le Tort later reported that "Senecars & those of Potomock & Conestogoe . . . were resolved to be revenged, & that all three nations had Joyned" for the purpose of destroying the Catawbas.[22]

The Tidewater colonies—Virginia in particular—further complicated the violence between Native warriors along the eastern seaboard. Virginians tried to stop war parties by posting irregular militias at the heads of rivers. Paths to and from the Southeast often crossed over these locations, and the militias, or "ranging parties," sometimes captured "strange Indians" descending from the Piedmont. The Virginia House of Burgesses passed laws legalizing the sale of Indian migrants traveling without a pass. All along the Atlantic colonies, Native peoples shared stories of captivity and enslavement. When whole villages relocated, they developed an acute understanding of the differences between the colonies. For example, in 1722, when the Tuscaroras, Iroquoian speakers then living in Virginia and North Carolina, abandoned their villages and migrated northward, where they became the sixth member of the Haudenosaunee, they shared their knowledge of the colonial Southeast with their allies.[23] Iroquois warriors adjusted by moving their trails farther west, beyond the mountains. When colonists captured and enslaved warriors traveling through their farms, they weakened the commitment of the Haudenosaunee to British North America.

Interregional violence did not diminish Native peoples' belief in Penn's peaceable kingdom. Tuscaroras from North Carolina longed to settle in

Pennsylvania. In 1710, a Tuscarora delegation gave eight belts of wampum to the Pennsylvania authorities in the hope of migrating to the colony. The Tuscaroras explained that "the second belt was sent from their children born, & those yet in the womb, Requesting that room to sport & play without danger of slavery might be allowed them." Four of the eight belts made some reference to slavery, the fear of it, and the desire for protection from it, as the motivating factor for leaving the Southeast.[24] Their Iroquoian-speaking relatives, the Senecas, sponsored their migration.

Colonial officials tried in vain to stop retributive violence among the Catawbas, the Iroquois, and the peoples of the Lower Susquehanna. Bands of ten to fifty warriors continued to slip through their settlements. Deganawidah, the Great Peacemaker, made the cessation of clan revenge the basis of Iroquois identity. Each member of the Iroquois Confederacy pledged to halt the violence between them and other members. Similarly, the Iroquois halted military action against the Susquehannocks and their neighbors when they acquiesced to Iroquois power. These and other examples show that tribal societies such as the Five Nations could and did halt warfare when the need or the circumstances called for it. Colonists' failure to end raids on the Catawbas reflected their relative weakness vis-à-vis the Iroquois. The English lacked the coercive power to end the conflict, and the Iroquois essentially condoned hostilities toward enemies such as the Catawbas. Nevertheless, Virginians declared that "none of the said Tributary Indians are to pass to the westward of the great Mountains, or cross potowmack River without a passport from the Govr' of this dominion." In an effort to control the movement of Native peoples, Virginia claimed sovereignty over a vast expanse of western lands beyond the Appalachian Mountains and the known limits of its colony. Virginians warned that if northern Indians crossed the Potomac, they would be "condemned to Death or transported and sold for slaves."[25]

Enemies often encountered each other along the warriors' paths. In one such event, Virginians complained that a joint Seneca-Shawnee war party attacked some Catawbas in Virginia. They claimed that "some of the Shawnois Indians in the province of pensilvania, & in amity with this Governmt, were present & Concern'd in the murder & Insult aforesd." Virginians looked for justice from Pennsylvania. But Shawnees rarely assented to their demands. In one instance, the provincial council demanded that the Shawnees return a Catawba boy who had been taken captive. In reply, the Shawnees explained that "he had now forgot his native language . . . and they did not think themselves obliged to return him at this time."[26]

Virginians' complaints about warriors amid their settlements pushed the warriors' path further westward. To reach Iroquoia, Catawba warriors now traveled along the western slope of the Appalachians to the head of the Potomac River and Opessa's Town, before moving further east, across Pennsylvania, to the Susquehanna River. Shawnee villagers thus lived at a violent crossroads. By 1720, Pennsylvanians finally realized that "it seems as if [the Iroquois] intended to make us a Barrier" between the Catawbas and their towns in New York. Opessa's Shawnees and the allied town of Conestoga Manor absorbed much of the violence between the Catawbas and the Iroquois along the southern edge of the colony. Years after Governor William Keith protested their involvement with military raids against the Catawbas, he learned that "the young men of Conestogoe had made a famous Warr Dance" before launching yet another attack on the Catawbas. On this occasion, Keith blamed the Shawnees, believing that their "Ears are thick." As a result, they "do not hear what we say to them." The violence involved all of the tribal towns associated with the Shawnees. Conestoga chiefs regularly complained that their "Indian hunters have been attacked near the Head of the Potowmack River, by a considerable body of Southern Indians Come out to war against the ffive Nacons [sic], and the Indian settlements on the Susquehanna."[27]

The western border between Maryland and Pennsylvania became increasingly violent as hunters and traders rediscovered the natural abundance of the Ohio Valley. The hunting grounds of southeastern Pennsylvania had been in decline for a decade, but deerskins continued to account for 30 to 40 percent of all exports through the 1720s. Indian hunters now traversed the Allegheny Mountains to meet the European demand. Many long-distance hunters entered the Ohio Valley through the Upper Potomac River. This gap in the mountains soon became a flash point of violence, as hunters competing for new territory encountered each other in the backcountry. In May 1717, a Delaware hunting party was attacked by a "Large Company, made up of Christians & Indians." The Delawares had been hunting "beyond the furthermost branch of Potomack" when one of the Delaware hunters found his brother "shot with two Arrows in his side, & his Head Cutt off, & Carried away."[28]

The Collapse of Conestoga Manor

Warriors passing through Opessa's Town had to strike a balance between violence and economic necessity. As colonists increased economic and diplomatic pressure on Native migrants, the Ohio Valley became an alternative to Conestoga Manor. Some migrants returned to places that had been abandoned by their people more than two generations earlier. But all who crossed over the Appalachians and descended the Upper Ohio River carried with them a changed worldview. By 1720, the Three Nations were often described as "the Mingoes or Conestogoe Indians." Since 1692, when Martin Chartier and Shawnees arrived at Bohemia Manor, Shawnees, Conoys, Senecas, and Susquehannocks had lived together. Englishmen ignored the interdependence that had developed between them when it was convenient to their interests. James Logan often described the Three Nations as independent nations. He chastised the Shawnees for joining the Senecas in their war with the Catawbas, and he blamed the Iroquois for encouraging the raids. He complained that they "come through your Towns and bring back their prisoners through your Settlements." Logan believed that the Senecas had simply manipulated the Shawnees to their advantage, declaring that "while those of the five Nations are safe at home at a great Distance with their wives and children . . . you may be the only sufferers."[29] Logan vacillated between describing the Three Nations as sovereign and, on other occasions, as subjects of Iroquois dominion. Logan's wavering understandings likely reflect the tensions of trying to manage a diverse population in a period of profound change.

Pennsylvania, like Carolina and New York, had extraordinarily close relations between Indian traders and the most powerful leaders of these colonies. Like Logan, Governor John Evans also invested in the Indian trade. All of these leaders depended on the same cast of métis traders who later ran Logan's fur-trading empire. Prominent traders on the Lower Susquehanna, including Martin Chartier, James Le Tort, and John Cartlidge, used their role in the fur trade to purchase land from Logan. About a decade later, most of these men were so hopelessly in debt to Logan that he foreclosed on their farms. In this way, Logan and other government officials, including Edward Shippen, Logan's personal secretary and the man charged with divesting Indians and traders of their land, presided over an Indian trade that closely resembled a debt peonage system.

Even after they migrated to Pennsylvania, Native peoples continued to fear enslavement. In 1707, Harry, an intermediary sent by "the Queen and the Principal men of the Conestogoe," traveled to Philadelphia to lodge a protest on his peoples' behalf. According to Harry, "divers Europeans," including Chartier, Bizaillon, and Le Tort, had "built Houses upon the branches of the Patowmeck, within this government, and pretended that they were in search of some mineral or ore." Harry accused the traders of compelling them to provide a labor bounty or quota of men from their communities who would "assist them" and be "serviceable to them." Traders promised that the governor would pay them for their labor. But when these payments did not materialize, Harry wondered whether or not this was "consistent with their past treaties and leagues of friendship." Following Harry's complaints, the Pennsylvania provincial council noted that only Peter Bizaillon was licensed to trade. They required that all of them come to Philadelphia to "give an acct. of the Reasons of their seating themselves" near Opessa's Town.[30]

James Logan corroborated Harry's accusations. Logan accused former governor Evans of "making 100 pounds, if not twice that, each week out of a mine somewhere back of Conestoga." William Penn seconded Logan's opinion, writing that "the Indians chiefly discovered the mine and worked it." Penn credited a "Shawnoe King," most likely Opessa, with finding the "ore." The Shawnees might have been searching for an alternative to the fur trade, because "the spirit of securing valuable minerals had gotten among the Indians." Unfortunately for the Shawnees, the governor of Pennsylvania, Colonel Evans, had taken an interest in the mine. Months later, "subjects" of the "Shawnoe King" found themselves laboring on his behalf. Logan doubted that Evans was acting "honourably about the mines," and he and Penn agreed that while "settlement is the pretence" for securing the lands around Conestoga, "the mines are the thing." The Shawnees' swift reversal of fortune, from mine owners and workers to mine laborers, occurred almost overnight. Fortunately for the Three Nations, flakes of gold never led to a major strike, and the frenzy of interest in mining the Susquehanna passed.[31]

Native migrants knew that physically resisting unscrupulous traders was futile and might lead to retribution and even exile from their homes. Weary of travel and eager to make a life for themselves in Pennsylvania, Indian people often submitted to their demands. In 1709, Lieutenant Governor Evans described "an Indian boy called Mingo" who had been "imported into this province" by unknown persons. Evans cited the case as evidence of the need for a comprehensive law designed to halt the importation of Indian slaves.[32] William Penn might have hoped to distinguish Pennsylvania from other English colonies. But even his lieutenants subscribed to forms of debt peonage. Captive taking and Indian slavery took place in Pennsylvania as well. By 1710, the rhetoric of brotherhood had been replaced by the reality of dependency.

Harry's complaints about forced labor drafts coincided with growing complaints about the rum trade. Rum traders avoided Conestoga and took their business "into the Countrey beyond their Towns, to meet the Indians returning from Hunting." Traders exchanged alcohol for furs and cheated Native hunters from the "fruits of all their labours . . . before they get home to their wives." As hunters turned their profits from the trade in furs to alcohol, the impact on Native towns became obvious. A chorus of leaders from the Three Nations and beyond, including the Delawares and Senecas, called for Pennsylvanians to regulate the trade, to issue licenses, and to limit the number of traders on the Susquehanna River.[33]

Opessa's Rise and Fall from Power

As traders came and went and mining turned from promise to fool's gold, the Shawnee "king," Opessa, tried to solve the riddle of early America. He reached the height of his power in the first decade of the eighteenth century, when Shawnee newcomers settled with him at Pequehan, named for the Pekowitha clan which he led. Within the Shawnee tribe, the Pekowithas are known as "helpers," charged with supporting the efforts of the other divisions. Opessa's newfound authority thus represented something of a revolution in Shawnee leadership, for they were not expected or encouraged to speak for all of the Shawnee people. Opessa sanctioned subsequent migrants when they moved into Pennsylvania, and he then encouraged them to seek the approval of the provincial council at Philadelphia. Opessa became a gatekeeper for Shawnee migrants to Pennsylvania, in much the same way that in 1692 the Susquehannock had spoken for Chartier and his Shawnee allies. He became an essential mediator between the colony and Native migrants, and his diplomatic efforts greatly enhanced his power. Even one of the two divisions responsible for supplying chiefs capable of speaking for the Shawnee people, the Thawekilas, had to meet with Opessa and receive Pekowitha support. The same is true for the Mekoche, the division responsible for medicine and healing, as they moved into the mid-Atlantic.[34]

In 1710, Pennsylvanians noticed that the Susquehannock and Delaware had resolved "not to plant corn this year." Panic set in, and some speculated that France had finally won over the Indians of the Lower Susquehanna. The Indians complained about unlicensed traders who "waylay their young men returning from hunting, making them drunk with rum, & then cheat them of their skins." As a result, the Indians "must be forced to remove themselves or starve."[35] Disgruntled Shawnees blamed traders rather than the Iroquois or the British for their misfortune. In conversations with colonial officials, the Haudenosaunee downplayed the ill feelings among Native migrants. They tried to convince agents of the crown that "even as far as ye Shawenhes are thankfull for his majes. good inclination."[36] Provincial officials were not fooled by Iroquois reassurances. The Shawnees and the Delawares were pulling away from Conestoga and from the old alliances that emanated from there.

Opessa seems to have lost much of his prestige when the colonists took over the mines and exploited Indian laborers from Conestoga Manor. In 1711, Pennsylvanians accused him of murdering a trader, and, if guilty, they wanted Opessa to hang for the crime. His accusers believed that a rival trader had hired Opessa to murder Francis de la Tore. Opessa went into hiding, and Susquehannock emissaries tried, and failed, to bring him to Philadelphia for questioning. For the next three years, Conestoga villagers could not persuade Opessa to turn himself in, and they took to describing him as "the late king of ye said Shawanoise." In his absence, the Shawnees elevated one of their speakers, a Shawnee diplomat named Cakundawanna, to the position of *hokema* (chief). But in council meetings, even Cakundawanna acknowledged that he "had only the name [of king] with no authority; and could do nothing."[37]

Then, in June 1715, Opessa returned in the company of Sassoonan, a Delaware leader from Paxtang, just north of Opessa's former town, Pequehan. Both men traveled to Philadelphia so that "there might be a firm peace" between them. Sassoonan opened their meetings with "ye Calamet with great Ceremony of their rattles and songs." He affirmed his support for Opessa, saying that he "lived at a great distance and entertained them with victuals and provisions when they went that way." Since 1711, Opessa and a small band of followers had founded a town on the Upper Potomac, near what is now Cumberland, Maryland. The Delawares at Paxtang "desired that when he came among us he might be received as one of themselves, with the same openness that he reced. Them." But for Cakundawanna and the Shawnees who remained at Pequehan, Opessa had ceased to exist. Not only did they describe him as a socially dead person, they heaped blame on him for his exile along the Upper Potomac. By 1720, Cakundawanna explained that the break occurred because "the people differed with him" and, as a result, "he left them."[38]

Opessa and Sassoonan spent at least a week in Philadelphia. In meeting after meeting, they complained of rum sales, linking this nominally illegal practice to their desire to move away from the Lower Susquehanna River. Philadelphians feared that the Delawares at Paxtang were preparing to abandon the colony. Opessa's decision to move west threatened the Pennsylvanians, who worried about their security if and when the Three Nations chose "to leave Conestoga." Provincial council members provided gifts to secure their loyalty. Sassoonan and Opessa received stroud matchcoats, colorful blankets used as a kind of body wrap, "the better to cover them from the night dews in their travels." While Sassoonan hoped to be "half English," it had become clear that Pennsylvanians did not share his wish.[39] The coalescent peoples remained important, but the diminishing significance of the fur trade, ongoing backcountry violence, and the pernicious effect of the rum trade undermined their alliance.

Opessa gave up his leadership role and became a Delaware in order to save himself from English systems of justice. He almost certainly would have hanged for killing de la Tore. But by moving westward and joining with the Delawares, Opessa avoided becoming yet another example of the failure of Penn's peaceable kingdom. Even after the murder of de la Tore, Opessa remained a frustrating symbol of Indian autonomy in the mid-Atlantic. Increasing numbers of black slaves ran away to Opessa's new town. To recapture runaway slaves, the provincial council now employed Cakundawanna, the "Shawanna king" of Pequehan. Cakundawanna promised to take at least ten men with him on a raid against Opessa's Town as soon as their winter hunt had ended. He recognized that "there will be hazard in seizing them for they are well armed." Speaking from Conestoga, Cakundawanna promised to "take them by Guile."[40]

The Three Nations did what they could to demonstrate their commitment to the Covenant Chain. But renegades such as Opessa offered a desirable alternative to Native people. In the second and third decades of the eighteenth century, German and Dutch immigrants further strained their commitment to Lancaster County. Arable land in southeastern Pennsylvania, in the heart of the Three Nations territory, attracted the majority of these new immigrants. By 1760, some 50,000 German immigrants had settled in this region. They became the largest ethnic group in the area stretching from the west bank of the Lower Susquehanna to Opessa's Town, near modern-day Cumberland, Maryland. Pennsylvania's deputy governor, Charles Gookin, worried that alienating these immigrants might further undermine their relations with "the Indians of America[, who] seem so unsettled." But structural changes in the economy had a far greater impact on the Three Nations. As the economy shifted from the fur trade to farming, immigrants' land hunger could only be sated by the taking of Indian lands. New arrivals coveted the towns and territories that used to be essential to Pennsylvania's economy as well as its security.[41]

Martin Chartier, Sawantaeny, and
Out-Migration from Conestoga Manor

Martin Chartier's death, in February 1718, foreshadowed larger changes in southeastern Pennsylvania. James Logan used Chartier's indebtedness to him to liquidate Chartier's land and belongings within days of his death. Chartier's son, Peter, became the first of many Lancaster County traders to lose his land and property to Logan. Similar proceedings against James Le Tort, Edmund Cartlidge, and others took place as the trade moved westward. During the first three decades of the colony's existence, powerful men had depended on French traders such as Chartier and Le Tort to cement their alliance to migratory bands of Native people. Their linguistic and cultural skills had been indispensable.[42]

By 1718, their assistance was no longer essential to the economic and military survival of the colony. James Logan personally divested these traders of their land. He had been closer to William Penn than any other provincial official, and he did more to secure the cooperation of these same traders than any other representative of the government. Viewed in this light, the swiftness of these foreclosure notices is surprising. Logan offered extensive, easy credit to both his traders and prominent Indian diplomats and friends, including the Oneida leader Shickellamy. Colonial officials, including Logan, often overstated Shickellamy's power. As a longtime resident of the Lower Susquehanna, he "served as the eyes and ears of the Longhouse." While he was something less than a viceroy, he had few diplomatic rivals. Nevertheless, Shickellamy found himself economically beholden to James Logan. Like the Oneida leader, virtually all of the Lancaster County traders were indebted to him.[43] Edmund Cartlidge's predicament nicely illustrates how Logan amassed so much power. Logan complained that Cartlidge had "told me lately in town that his Peltry this year would come to near 600 pounds, and all he has talk'd of to us or given us to expect is 200 lbs." To make up for the discrepancy, Logan pressed Cartlidge to acquire lands from Indian hunters who had failed to bring him the 600 pounds of pelts that Cartlidge required to pay his debts. Traders thus assisted Logan in acquiring land from the Native inhabitants of southeastern Pennsylvania. Land had become the only commodity left to Native people faced with declining hunting opportunities and new waves of European immigrants.[44]

Logan used debt to force the Indians of Conestoga Manor westward. Newer immigrants to Pennsylvania introduced an agrarian vision for the colony. Chartier's passing thus signaled the beginning of the end of the Indian trade on the Lower Susquehanna. But in divesting Indians and traders of their lands along the river, Logan jeopardized the security of Pennsylvania's frontiers. Logan was well aware of how his actions impacted Indian-white relations in the colony. Settlers made it known that "borderers are in the most danger" when alliances between the colonies and Native peoples broke down. Logan's financial goals often conflicted with his roles as diplomat and representative of Pennsylvania. For these reasons, Logan used delegates such as Edward Shippen when dealing with the traders and the Native communities of Lancaster County. In one instance, Logan asked Shippen to foreclose on a trader's land and property in "a very private manner, for I hate to have it said that J L takes his Traders Plantations."[45]

The murder of Sawantaeny, a Seneca man who lived at Conestoga Manor with a Shawnee wife, furthered the end of the coalescent experiment in the mid-Atlantic. In January 1722, Edmund and John Cartlidge traded him some rum. On awakening, Sawantaeny accused the Cartlidge brothers of cheating him. There is no way of knowing the truth of Sawantaeny's accusations. But it was common practice for traders to water down rum sold to Indians. Regardless, the Cartlidges resented Sawantaeny's accusations, and a fight broke out. The Cartlidge brothers beat Sawantaeny so badly that he died soon after the fight ended. Sawantaeny's death triggered a diplomatic crisis that culminated in the imprisonment, trial, and eventual acquittal of John and Edmund Cartlidge. In a council leading to the trial, Governor Keith described how the peoples of the Lower Susquehanna "are the same flesh and blood with us, and we are all men, sometimes wise & sometimes weak." Violence between Indians and whites increased as the alcohol trade became more difficult to control. Keith acknowledged that "we have heard that it is a custom amongst you, when an Indian happens to be killed, that his relations often demand and expect money or goods for satisfaction." The calumet, gift exchange, and wampum diplomacy became increasingly irrelevant, as British systems of justice replaced indigenous systems of justice and alliance making. However, Keith continued, "The laws of our great king will not suffer any such thing to be done amongst us." At the conclusion of the trial, the Cartlidges returned to Conestoga, where they lived and worked as traders among Sawantaeny's kith and kin. At the conclusion of their trial, Iroquois diplomats ceded their claims to the land in and around Conestoga. Sawantaeny's death became yet another moment in which the Iroquois asserted their right of conquest over the land and the peoples of the Lower Susquehanna River.[46]

After Sawantaeny's death, the breakdown of Penn's peaceable kingdom became irreversible. During the council, a Conestoga leader named Tawenna proclaimed that "they & all William Penns people are as one people, that Eat, as it were, with one Mouth, & are one Body & One Heart." Shippen recognized the emptiness of this rhetoric. In a letter to his wife, Shippen assured her that there was "no danger of Indians however my grandmother has given me a pair of pistols worth 6 or 7 pounds and I fear no man." Shippen clearly had cause for worry. In 1730, Logan demanded that he "receive of all and every person and persons dwelling in the County of Lancaster . . . all such sums of money or other Effects as they now stand indebted to me for." Not surprisingly, Delaware leaders Allumapies and Opakhassit no longer wanted to hold diplomatic meetings at Conestoga. They explained that "we have nothing but love and good will toward the Governour." However, they would not travel to Conestoga to meet with provincial officials.[47]

Some Iroquoians and Algonquians moved west of the Allegheny Mountains, where they could continue to hunt and trade beyond the disapproving eyes of the settlers who now surrounded them in the Susquehanna Valley. Others moved up the Susquehanna River to the Wyoming Valley and the multiethnic village of Shamokin, where the Covenant Chain remained important. Older, kin-based understandings of the Delaware people—emanating from the Munsee, Unalachtigo, and Unami branches of the tribe—became less apparent. Similarly, the lines between the Thawekila, Mekoche, and Pekowitha divisions that used to determine village settlement and chiefly authority became less important. Increasingly, Native people in the eighteenth century made choices about where to live based, in part, on particular villages' disposition toward colonizers. The unique histories of long-distance migrants shaped their perspectives on colonization and how best to deal with their European counterparts. Shawnees and Delawares in and around Logstown, a multiethnic town on the Upper Ohio River, now lived within the orbit of the French outpost at Detroit. Villagers moved toward Te' o' chanontian, "toward the place of the beaver dams," and had forsaken their villages in eastern Pennsylvania. Communities such as Conestoga, Pequehan, and Dekanoagah—associated with the Susquehannocks, Shawnees, and Conoys, respectively, blended together at Logstown. In contrast, those who stayed behind were sometimes called Wompanosch, or easterners, by colonists who knew them. Easterners could no longer resist Iroquois subordination. And so, for example, villagers living in the Wyoming Valley, at places such as Shamokin, thought of themselves as tributaries of the Haudenosaunee.[48]

In 1727, Shawnees, Susquehannocks, Conoys, and Senecas from Conestoga Manor founded Logstown in response to land hunger and violence between Indians and whites. Logstown was known as Shenango in English and Chiningué in French, and Shawnees began returning to their precontact homeland after a fifty-year exodus from the Ohio River Valley. Its multiethnic character made Logstown a diplomatic center. Situated approximately eighteen miles downstream from the confluence of the Allegheny and Monongahela rivers, Logstown marked the return of the Shawnees to the Ohio River Valley. It was one of several migrant Indian villages in the region, from the Delawares at Kittaning to Chartier's Old Town, both of which were on the Allegheny River, just above what became Fort Duquesne, or modern-day Pittsburgh. The coalescent villages of the Lower Susquehanna fell apart, as multiethnic towns on the Ohio River offered a better alternative to the tribally affiliated villages of the Lower Susquehanna River.[49]

Chiefs along the Upper Ohio, including Opessa's old friend Sassoonan, now openly challenged proprietary officials. Sassoonan charged Logan with unfairly selling their lands, especially Tulpehocken, just west of the Schuylkill River, above Philadelphia. Sassoonan also accused Governor Keith of violating diplomatic protocols associated with gift giving. Rumor had it that he had taken presents intended for the Susquehannock and sold them in exchange for furs. Sassoonan's accusations against Logan and Keith reflected the new reality, which is that land speculation returned a greater profit than the fur trade. Logstown became the Shawnee and Delaware response to the new economic and social conditions in eastern Pennsylvania.

The migration of Native peoples to Logstown strained Logan's ability to control the fur trade and brought renewed fears of war with France to Pennsylvania. Unlicensed traders working out of Montreal and New York frustrated Logan's efforts as the trade moved westward. Logan chastised his traders, telling them "that it is exceedingly wrong and unjust that people should come from other governments to carry away their furrs and skins." Logan complained about traders from New York and New Jersey, those "who we do not know," to the Oneida diplomat Shickellamy as well. The exodus from the Lower Susquehanna temporarily disrupted Pennsylvania's fur trade. An anxious Logan wrote that everything from raccoons to deer hides "yielded a better price this last sale than ever I knew them bear before." In a fit of desperation, Logan asked Edmund Cartlidge to travel to Logstown and to persuade Peter Chartier to return to Lancaster County. He wanted Cartlidge to use "any means [to] get some furs of Chartiere."[50]

When Chartier refused to return, Logan had to concede that the Shawnee and Delaware migration to the Ohio was permanent. As frustrations with Chartier, Cartlidge, and Le Tort mounted, he turned to a German immigrant, Conrad Weiser, for trade and diplomacy with now-distant Shawnee and Delaware peoples. Logan wanted Weiser to investigate the Shawnees at Logstown. He wrote that "some of our traders coming home from Ohio" believed that the Shawnees "put up a french flagg or Colours in their town, as if they would say, they are in league with the french and all are one as french men." Logan rejected the notion that the Shawnees could declare independence from the Covenant Chain in this way. After all, the "Shawanah Indians have been in league with our Government above thirty years, and the land on Ohio belongs to the 5 Nations." Logan wanted them to return to Pennsylvania, and to accept life within the Iroquois Confederacy.[51]

The Lure of the Ohio Valley

As Shawnees and Delawares departed for the Ohio River, they foreshadowed the Seven Years' War and reinvigorated French ambitions in both the Ohio country and the Southeast. Logan sensed that their departure signaled deeper troubles for the British colonies. He remarked that the French "are naturally so well fitted to gain upon the Indians by accommodating themselves to their manners." In addition, "they have lately gain'd the Shawanese a considerable & warlike nation from the English over to their interests." Sassoonan, Allumapies, and Shawnees associated with Peter Chartier were less committed to the French than Logan suggested. In fact, the Shawnees and Delawares continued to seek redress for their lands in eastern Pennsylvania. Logan and many other prominent Pennsylvanians understood that "they will insist on satisfaction for their lands about Conestoga and Sasquehannah about which they are much dissatisfied."[52]

The 1737 Walking Purchase and the 1744 Treaty of Lancaster formalized a longer, haphazard removal from the eastern half of Pennsylvania. These land cessions reshaped relations among Native migrants, the Iroquois, and their English patrons. First, in 1737, "a great land fraud" occurred in which a branch of the Iroquois Confederacy signed away more than 12,000 square miles of Delaware land from below the forks of the

Delaware and Lehigh rivers. Delawares east and west of the Appalachians protested the move, complaining that "we are very much Wronged & Abused of having our Lands taken & Settled." An Onondaga speaker, Canasatego, was unsympathetic. He again repeated that the Delawares, like the Shawnees, "had no land left to sell," and that the Iroquois, by right of conquest, had the authority to do away with their lands. But as historian Gregory Evans Dowd points out, "no such conquest is known in the record."[53] Indian villagers found that life along the Lower Susquehanna had become untenable. When James Logan foreclosed Martin Chartier's property, he set in motion the erasure of the coalescent villages of Conestoga Manor. But more important, Shawnees no longer migrated toward borderland zones that enabled them to live as useful neighbors for colonizers. For two generations, Shawnee migrants had built a way of life based on their proximity to colonizers.

As this history of the Lower Susquehanna makes clear, the coalescent villages of southeastern Pennsylvania moved west in response to a host of factors. Each village had a unique history and an even more particular understanding of its relationship to the Iroquois. This was true for various Shawnee villages. These separate histories of migration account for some of the differences between the Shawnees and their neighbors, including the Nanticokes, Delawares, Conoys, and Susquehannocks. When Shawnees returned to the Ohio Valley, they modeled themselves after men such as Martin and Peter Chartier, men who moved between regions and empires in a single lifetime. Like the Chartiers, the Shawnees refused to acquiesce to French, English, or Iroquois "overlords." Frustratingly independent, Shawnee migrants made deliberate choices based on the realities of Indian slavery, intertribal warfare, and access to European trade goods.

chapter 8

One Colour and as One Body

RACE, TRADE, AND MIGRATION TO THE OHIO COUNTRY

In 1733, an Iroquois diplomat named Sagohandechty, "a great man" of the Senecas, was murdered along the Allegheny River. He and four other representatives of the Iroquois Confederacy had been sent from their capital, Onondaga, to the mixed Shawnee, Delaware, and Iroquois towns along the Allegheny and Upper Ohio rivers to try to compel them to return east of the mountains. From the very beginning, Sagohandechty mishandled the negotiations. Iroquois diplomats who witnessed the negotiations described how he had "pressed them so closely that they took a great dislike to him." Even so, the westward migrants withheld their anger during the council meetings. Several months after these negotiations, at councils in which Sagohandechty tried to endow the Covenant Chain with coercive power, the Shawnees seized their opportunity and "murdered him cruelly." The Iroquois wanted to avenge Sagohandechty's death, but the Thawekila Shawnees fled to South Carolina after committing the murder. The Iroquois knew that they had "returned to the place from whence they came." Composed of only "thirty young men, ten old men, & several women & children," the Thawekila Shawnees had been much diminished by the slave trade in colonial South Carolina. The Iroquois described how this "Tribe of Shawanese" had abandoned the Allegheny River and returned to the Savannah River, to avoid near-certain retribution.[1]

Just two years earlier, in 1731, the Thawekilas had been "true to the English." Most had resided east of the mountains, on lands set aside for them along the eastern foothills of the Allegheny Mountains.[2] Since then, they had joined their kinsmen, an increasingly motley assemblage of Pekowitha, Mekoche, and Chalagawtha Shawnees, west of the mountains, along the Allegheny and Ohio rivers, near modern-day Pittsburgh. They had become disenchanted with the assertion of Iroquois power, and

Sagohandechty's murder occurred because of the disintegration of the relationship between the Thawekilas and the Iroquois. Rather than attack Shawnees randomly in retaliation for Sagohandechty's murder, the Iroquois chose to pursue the Thawekila Shawnees, the society clan responsible for the crime.

By voting with their feet and moving beyond the mountains, at least some Shawnees refused to accept Iroquois and British domination. Even so, the assertion of Iroquois sovereignty continued after Sagohandechty's death. Of the Delawares and Shawnees in the Ohio country, the Iroquois believed that they "have no where a Fire burning . . . for they have no land remaining to them." Sagohandechty died because the English and the Iroquois understood "tributary" tribes such as the Shawnees differently than their Algonquian counterparts. To the peoples of the Allegheny River, it meant that "one tribe accepted the protection of another and then acknowledged the relationship by token gifts of wampum." Nevertheless, between 1698 and 1737, both the Pennsylvanians and the Iroquois came to believe that the Iroquois were emperors of tribes throughout the eastern half of North America. The Thawekila Shawnees murdered Sagohandechty and abandoned Pennsylvania, in a stunning rejection of their perspective on history.[3]

Neither the Iroquois nor the British thought of the migrants to the Ohio Valley as socially dead slaves, without any legal right to own property. However, the hardening of the Covenant Chain's understanding of history occurred just as Pennsylvanians, Virginians, and New Yorkers created companies that speculated in Middle Ohio Valley lands. Migrants to the Ohio Valley learned that their legal status emanated from the British perspective on Iroquois history. These historical and legal understandings denied Shawnees and Delawares, Nanticokes and Susquehannocks, "the right to achieve the necessary conditions of liberty." And without land rights, "freedom becomes a hollow concept," particularly in the property-driven mind of colonial British North Americans. Covenant Chain understandings of warfare and history thus introduced a new category of person to eighteenth-century America: the refugee. Only migration beyond the rim of British colonies delivered these refugees from the servility that English society associated with the absence of real property.[4]

The Covenant Chain Understanding of History

Historians have generally accepted the Iroquois and British contention that the Shawnee and Delaware migrants to the Ohio Valley were refugees. In fact, most claim that the Iroquois imposed this refugee status on the peoples of the Ohio Valley during the seventeenth century, when the Iroquois supposedly won the land from Central Algonquians, such as the Shawnees, and asserted their "right of conquest" over their ancient homelands. New York's lieutenant governor at the time, Cadwallader Colden, described the Iroquois as the "Romans" of Indian country, divesting interior rivals of their land and coercing the survivors to either join with them or face further attacks. Following Colden, historians have argued that by right of conquest, and later as proxies of the English, the Iroquois asserted their authority over much of the Atlantic Coast and present-day Midwest.[5]

English colonial officials, from New York's governor, Thomas Dongan, to William Penn's secretary, James Logan, helped to develop this narrative of Iroquois conquest. As migrants abandoned Conestoga Manor, James Logan worked closely with trader Conrad Weiser and Oneida diplomat Shickellamy "to inflate the Six Nations authority over the lands and affairs of the Shawnees, Delawares, and other allies in the region." Just as Iroquois preeminence in the fur trade began to decline, Logan and the Pennsylvania traders increased their diplomatic and legal authority exponentially. Powerful people in New York and Pennsylvania helped bring about this transformation in accepted understandings of the Covenant Chain and of the nature of Iroquois power. Fluent speakers of the Mohawk language such as Conrad Weiser, who was also considered a member of the tribe, signed important land cessions—the 1737 Walking Purchase, for example—on the Mohawks' behalf. He was given a Mohawk name, and Weiser became James Logan's principal intermediary before the Onondaga Council.[6] Covenant Chain understandings of conquest, history, and land became joined just as Native migrants from Conestoga Manor came to distrust neighboring whites. Rumors of a French and Indian conspiracy capable of destroying British North America began almost immediately after Shawnees and Delawares moved beyond the Allegheny Mountains.

Pennsylvanians suspected that residents of Logstown were behind this conspiracy. One backcountry settler became convinced that Native peoples living beyond the backcountry settlements had "been put on by the french to stir up mischief." Another settler believed that "the Indians will fall down on us very suddenly." Their fear was palpable and fueled by the hundreds of Indian migrants passing through their farms on their way from Indian towns in the east such as Shamokin to the western backcountry. Colonists reasoned that communication between "Christians and Indians" had broken down because there was "a great dissatisfaction amongs them."[7]

Peter Chartier's Response to the Covenant Chain

Like all Shawnees struggling to retain their rights to land they had settled and improved for more than a generation, Peter Chartier carried his memory of how Logan had gained control of his father's estate in Lancaster County, and he continued to fight against Logan's seizure of his land. Logan well knew that Chartier "expects land of us and may clearly see his interest to be concern'd with me." The loss of his father's estate taught him that land title was the only real means of combating English land hunger. The settlements on the Conemaugh River may have been designed, as proprietary officials promised, to "defend them from all Incroachments." But absent real title to the land, Pennsylvanians had provided the Shawnees with little more than refugee camps.[8]

The Shawnees' association with the Chartier family added depth and weight to backcountry rumors. Peter Chartier himself was a curious mix of backcountry settler and Shawnee renegade. Born to a Shawnee mother and a French trader in Lancaster County, Pennsylvania, he straddled multiple worlds. At the time of his departure from Pennsylvania, Peter Chartier was the "Master" of at least one English servant, James Cunningham, a man who allegedly witnessed Chartier accept a French commission. Fluent in English, French, Shawnee, and other Indian languages, Chartier also understood the ways in which the English tied land ownership to freedom. His multiethnic background and competencies caused Pennsylvanians to overstate his influence. They believed that he was capable of "defeat[ing] any future attempts we shall make to revive" the friendship between the Shawnees and Pennsylvania.[9]

Between 1730 and 1733, Peter Chartier was very much on Logan's mind. The shortage of furs, combined with Chartier's now-elusive Shawnee relatives, frustrated Logan. Logan asked Edward Shippen to lure "P. Chartiere" back to Pennsylvania through presents of English goods. Logan believed that such acts of generosity might cause "Peter to shew something of his Gratitude to me." The ultimate measure of Chartier's loyalties was with whom he traded. Logan must have doubted his own mastery of the trade because of the distance between his estate on the outskirts of Philadelphia and villages such as Logstown. Traders from rival English colonies and New France further undermined his confidence. In a letter to Shickellamy, James Logan complained about traders from New

York and New Jersey "who we do not know." Everyone noticed that migration had changed the rules of the fur trade and brought on intense competition, so much so that Logan was willing to be paid half as much as he thought he deserved for Chartier's skins.[10]

Throughout the 1730s, Logan saw "a fair prospect of a considerable trade with the Shawannese." He instructed Shippen to offer Chartier trade goods, including gunpowder, in exchange for continuing his trade with Pennsylvanians. Like his father before him, Chartier had become a shrewd trader, one who would not be intimidated by a skilled businessman such as Logan. Diminishing supplies of fur-bearing animals in western Pennsylvania placed increasing pressure on Native hunters to travel deep into the Ohio country. Logan became desperate, but he held on to the hope that Chartier would deliver the furs and skins necessary to keep his trading empire afloat.[11]

Logan complained bitterly about Peter Chartier and the cat and mouse game that had developed between them. Shickellamy, the Oneida diplomat and "overseer" of the Shawnees and Delawares, despised Chartier. He fomented rumors about Chartier carrying rum "in very large quantities" to the towns on the Allegheny. Shickellamy also complained that Chartier had persuaded migrant Indians that "the Proprietor of Pennsylvania, Onas, would have a chief hand in their destruction if they remained loyal to the British."[12]

As if to illustrate his growing weakness, Logan turned to Sawantaeny's murderer, Edmund Cartlidge, in an attempt to repair the breach between Chartier and Pennsylvania. Logan asked Cartlidge to "pray get some furs" from Chartier "by any handsome measures." Logan actually believed that Chartier would be willing to form a partnership with Cartlidge and save his trading empire. He knew that Chartier suspected Cartlidge of coordinating the dispossession of the Shawnees and Delawares from eastern Pennsylvania. In fact, traders favored by Logan, such as the Cartlidge brothers, had received land deeds from the Delawares along Conestoga Creek. To make matters worse, Sawantaeny had been married to a Shawnee woman, and her people remained outraged about his murder. Logan seemed to be unaware of this history, and he relied on Edmund Cartlidge to carry "Divers messages to the Indians."[13] Such obvious diplomatic gaffes revealed the essential weakness of Logan's Indian trade. Without friendly intermediaries to sustain his business and largely ignorant of Native communities, Logan depended on alcohol and cheap goods to retain their allegiance. Nevertheless, Logan did recognize that Chartier was a shrewd businessman. He anticipated that Chartier would "obstinately insist" on cheaper goods in exchange for his skins, and he seemed to accept Chartier's demands. Logan tended to be less accommodating with other traders in his employ.[14] But Chartier's case reveals that Logan's influence had begun to weaken. After more than thirty years in the Indian trade, the Native peoples who used to live along the Susquehanna River considered abandoning him for the French.

British and French Competition for Native Migrants

Non-English Indian traders remained essential to increasingly out-of-touch businessmen such as Logan. While James Le Tort remained important, a new generation of traders, including Scots-Irish immigrants such as George Croghan and German newcomers such as Conrad Weiser, began to replace the older traders of Lancaster County. It was an exceedingly risky business, one that was both physically grueling and financially perilous. One of Croghan's biographers pointed out that in his time as a trader, Croghan "was tomahawked, shipwrecked, alternatively rich and poor, despised and praised, rejected and sought after."[15] That he survived such tumult is a testimony to the grit and fearlessness that were necessary prerequisites of the Indian trader.

Amid Logan's agony, Jonah Davenport reported that the Shawnees living along the Allegheny River might soon "break off from the English interest." Davenport had had several conversations with "a French Gentlemen [who] spoke the Shawanese language" at Logstown. These conversations led him to report that "they intended to goe & live among the French." James Le Tort corroborated Davenport's testimony. Le Tort knew that "a certain French Gentleman . . . fixes his abode amongst the Shawanese" every spring. Le Tort suggested that he was an ambassador of the French at Montreal, and that through his efforts "the French have gained a great Influence over the Shawanese." In a savvy move, the "French Gentleman" in question had sent a blacksmith from Montreal to Logstown, where he fixed guns, hatchets, and farming implements. These goodwill gestures greatly improved French fortunes among the migrants.[16] Blacksmiths and cheaper trade goods, rather than political principles and proselytizing, secured their allegiance.

In 1731, traders in James Logan's employ learned that "the Shawanese . . . went to Canada . . . with some French men [and] came back to their town on Ohio." The traders described how the Shawnees "put up a french flagg or Colours in their town, as if they would say, they are in league with the french and all are one as french men." There was some substance to the English rumor mill. In 1729, Charles de la Boische, the Marquis de Beauharnois and governor of New France, hosted three Shawnee leaders, yet the meetings did not go as Beauharnois would have preferred. He struggled to find someone who knew the Shawnee language, and their diplomatic venture became difficult as a result. The general absence of Shawnee speakers in Montreal revealed the extent to which the Shawnees had become estranged from the French since leaving the Grand Village of the Kaskaskias.[17]

The French continued to make progress in spite of these diplomatic missteps. "French Emissaries" did make inroads among the Shawnees and Delawares. But the "Indians at Alleghany" quickly developed a reputation for independence. In 1729, Pennsylvania's governor, Patrick Gordon, told Indian traders working the backcountry that "it is of the highest importance to the Peace and Tranquility" of Pennsylvania to "treat them with Courtesy and Humanity." Gordon's open letter to the traders evoked Penn's memory by asking traders to treat Native people as Penn would have preferred. Gordon's message was designed to correct the very real damage done by land acquisition and abusive trading practices.[18]

In this context of alienation and mistrust, real and perceived misdeeds became signs of impending warfare. In one incident, Allegheny Delawares reported the deaths of two traders. The first trader was killed "above a hundred miles Down" the Allegheny River, well within what is now eastern Ohio. The Delaware hunters wanted the traders to stand aside because they had planned "to fire huntt by makeing a ring." It was a dangerous though highly productive means of hunting at night—white-tailed deer were surrounded in flames and then killed as the circle of fire narrowed around them. The traders refused to sit out of this hunt in spite of the danger, as some traders had grown accustomed to hunting alongside their trading partners. Amid the flames, the first trader was shot in the mouth by the Delaware hunters. The second trader died during a drunken revelry after the hunt. Governor Gordon expressed "deep concern" about these suspicious deaths, and he explained that "justice requires nothing less than blood for blood."[19] Pennsylvanians recognized that migration ended their ascendant legal position, wherein Native communities resigned themselves to British laws. Gordon might have hoped that there would be "blood for blood," but the Allegheny tribes no longer abided by British systems of justice.

Native migrants to the Ohio Valley became a source of frustration for traders and diplomats associated with the British colonies. Pennsylvanians could not ignore them, for their hunters ranged deep into the Ohio country, procuring large numbers of deerskins. But Native hunters now had a special advantage, in that they entertained traders from Montreal, Albany, and Philadelphia. The Ohio Valley Indian trade became very democratic, competitive, and unpredictable. In the middle decades of the eighteenth century, the Ohio Valley became a "heaven for hunters [and] a purgatory to chiefs." Just as Governor Gordon conceded the economic and military limits of his power, so too did older chiefs from Pennsylvania who struggled to lead increasingly multiethnic migrants to the Ohio Valley.[20]

At the same time, French voyageurs to the Ohio country feared British-allied traders, and they traveled north of Lake Ontario rather than down the Allegheny River to reach the Ohio country. Sieur de Noyan, the French commander at Detroit, recognized that migrant Indians saw voyageurs' fear of traveling through the Ohio country and equated it with French cowardice. For Noyan, "fear, or the right of the English," explained why French traders were unwilling to confront British-allied traders who were "scattered as far as the sea, trading with the Chaouenons." Croghan and Weiser unleashed a torrent of cheap goods in order to undermine the French. Materialism, rather than morality, would keep the Covenant Chain intact.

British colonial officials saw these migrants as traitorous allies of "their first father," the French. But men such as Noyan knew that the Shawnees and the Delawares were "very weary of the English yoke." At the same time, Noyan and others acknowledged that they were frustratingly independent. In the 1730s, they hoped that they could turn migrants' dissatisfaction to New France's advantage. Like the Pennsylvanians, the French placed a high value on regaining their allegiance because the Shawnees were "the most industrious and the most peaceable [tribe] known on this continent." The French imagined that a "considerable trade with them" might be conducted in the Ohio country.[21]

Migration to the Ohio Valley made it increasingly difficult for French and English colonizers to determine the identities and leanings of the migrants. Beauharnois concurred with Noyan's general assessment of the Shawnees. Like Noyan, the governor of New France described them as a "hardworking, docile and faithful nation." Were it not for Peter Chartier, whom he suspected of "acting on behalf of the English," Beauharnois was convinced that Shawnee migrants to the Ohio Valley would return to the French alliance. In contrast, James Logan attached the most pejorative meanings to Shawnee migrants. He described them as "a considerable & warlike nation" whom the French had lured "from the English over to their interests."[22] Both the French and the English struggled to make sense of the people who had been, at various times and places, a vital part of their respective empires.

The New Face of Shawnee Leadership in the Ohio Country

Shawnee migrants explained that they moved beyond the mountains for local, village-based reasons. In 1732, at a meeting in Philadelphia, a Shawnee leader from Logstown named Opakethwa described how they left Opessa's Town because "they knew not what to do" when their chief died. After relocating their village to Logstown, they acknowledged that they had been to Montreal. However, Opakethwa made his position of neutrality clear, declaring that he "had no intention to leave their Brethren the English." After their negotiations ended, the Logstown Shawnees became less certain of neutrality when Opakethwa and another Shawnee leader from Logstown named Quassenung contracted smallpox during their stay in Philadelphia. The disease took Opakethwa quickly. But Quassenung, the son of Chief Kakowatchy, one of the Shawnees who had migrated from the Grand Village of the Kaskaskias to Pennsylvania, was "seized with violent pains, and languished" until mid-January, when he lost his battle with the disease. In its aftermath, the Allegheny Shawnees became less willing to travel to Philadelphia, much less return to the reservation-style communities set aside for them on the Conemaugh River. Seven years later, a Shawnee delegation explained that they disliked traveling to Philadelphia because when they "came near this Town our Hearts were likewise full of grief."[23]

A coherent assessment of the Shawnees and their motives had become impossible to ascertain by the middle decades of the eighteenth century. Even the Cayugas who had lived among them in Pennsylvania described these migrants as "a Republic composed of all sorts of Nations." As Shawnees became divided between French- and English-allied towns, colonial loyalties played an increasingly important role in defining their respective identities. The multiethnic towns of the Ohio Valley brought with them a new kind of chief. Lower Shawnee Town, at the confluence of the Ohio and Scioto rivers, where Peter Chartier lived, had leaders who were not members of a Shawnee patrilineage. Bereft of clan ties through his father, Martin, Peter Chartier depended on trade and diplomacy to secure his status among his mother's people. Similar changes were at work throughout the upper country, as hereditary chiefs gave way to charismatic and well-connected leaders with increasingly assertive points of view regarding the role of colonizers in their lives. This revolution in the social order grew

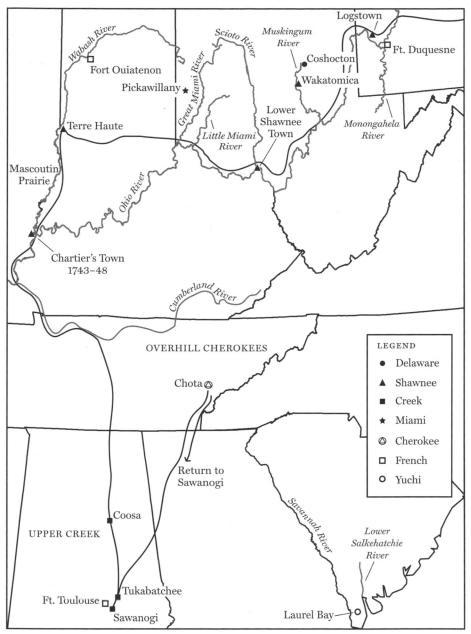

Map 5. Chartier's Journey. Peter Chartier's journey from Conestoga Manor to the
Southeast mirrored the growing separation between colonizers and Native migrants,
and in response Shawnees began calling for racial unity and revitalization in the
backcountry of North America. Map by Alex Gau.

out of the increasingly selective and voluntary nature of Indian identities. Migrant villages west of the mountains represented another choice, an alternative to life within the Covenant Chain.[24]

Census data from the time period reflects the increasing fragmentation of Shawnee villages. In 1731, there were three Shawnee towns in central Pennsylvania, between the Conemaugh River and the west branch of the Susquehanna. These towns were affiliated with the Thawekila division that later abandoned the Conemaugh and returned to South Carolina. Pekowitha Shawnees associated with Opessa's Town had migrated to the Conemaugh River as well. At Conemaugh, there were an estimated 45 families and 200 Thawekila men, along with 50 families and 100 Pekowitha men. At "Choniata," or Logstown, there were 20 families and 60 men. An English census taker believed that the Thawekilas were "true to the English" while a Shawnee chief named Okowelah was a "favourer of ye French interest." In 1736, Beauharnois estimated that there were 200 Shawnee men in the Ohio country. A year later, James Logan dispatched one of his traders, a man named George Miranda, to Logstown and two other Shawnee villages on the Allegheny. Miranda found only 79 men living there at the time. By then, only 130 Shawnees remained near the Conemaugh River. Such small numbers of men reflected the enormous demographic imbalances common in villages in which men were often absent for long periods of time. The constancy of war had left these villages with large numbers of women and children, all of whom depended on declining numbers of men for protection and economic support.[25]

Out-migration from the coalescent villages of southeastern Pennsylvania had a devastating impact on the Eastern Algonquians who had fled Maryland in the aftermath of Bacon's Rebellion. Conrad Weiser described how "the six nations had invited the nanticook and Delaware Indians living about Shamokin to come up to the heads of the Susquehanna River to live." Most Nanticokes chose to accept the Iroquois offer, while the Delawares at Shamokin remained committed to what little independence they had left in eastern Pennsylvania. Native migrants no longer feigned interest in Penn's peaceable kingdom. Even so, Pennsylvania's governor recounted the Shawnees' painful history of migration and described how Penn "took the Shawanese by the hand, and admitted them as friends" when they first arrived on the Lower Susquehanna River. The Shawnees' departure from the colony betrayed Penn's generosity and amounted to a rejection of the alliance he created. Gordon was "much griev'd that so many of my Friends are removed to so great a distance." Colonial leaders in New York and Pennsylvania contributed to out-migration from the mid-Atlantic by tirelessly linking William Penn's kindness toward the Indians to the Iroquois right of conquest. New York's lieutenant governor described how the Senecas and the Cayugas had "settled" the Shawnees on the Susquehanna and had put them "under their protection" as a result.[26]

New France took advantage of migrant resentment and drove a wedge between the Iroquois and the Algonquians of the upper country. Noyan reported that "they hate and fear the fierce temper of the Iroquois." Allegheny Shawnees were sometimes attacked by Iroquois warriors on their way to and from the Southeast. Shawnees looked to the French "to seek deliverance" from the Iroquois. The French complied by drafting plans for the concentration of Native peoples at points of strategic interest, from Detroit to Fort Ouiatenon to Vincennes. They hoped to engineer a multiethnic Indian community at Detroit, composed primarily of Hurons, Delawares, and Shawnees. Beauharnois mistakenly believed that the Shawnees would consolidate as a nation at Detroit, where they would join with similarly aggrieved tribes. The Shawnees would take the place of the Hurons, whose demographic collapse was nearly complete by the middle of the eighteenth century. Intelligence gathered from French traders traveling through their towns convinced Beauharnois that "the Chaouanons will come and take their [the Hurons'] place . . . for they are very docile, and the man Chartier appears very well disposed."[27] French officials clearly hoped that Chartier's French roots might bring the Shawnees back into the French orbit, but facts on the ground suggested otherwise. Chartier's migrations, and his unwillingness to move decisively into either the French or the English orbit, reflected Shawnee values of independence, honed by years of proximity to colonizers. Their awareness of European customs — their moods and desires — outmatched Beauharnois' understanding of the Shawnees. Beauharnois regarded them as "docile," in spite of the fact that they had rejected French calls for their people to relocate.

The French continued to believe that concentrating Indian migrants in large, strategically located villages was essential if they were to thwart "the English who are established on the upper part of the Ohio River [and] are working incessantly to win nations to their side." A smallpox epidemic offered one opportunity to rearrange the cultural map of the Ohio Valley. In 1733, Beauharnois learned that smallpox had devastated Miami villagers living along the Wabash, in what is now Indiana. The Iroquois reportedly lost "five hundred warriors in their five villages, without counting women and children." Several villages were "entirely destroyed" by the disease, and some Miamis considered "receiv[ing] the Chaouanons into their number" to make up for their losses. The French hoped that the Shawnees would "desire to form but one village with their brothers," the Miamis. They imagined a confederacy of Shawnees, Weas, and Piankashaws tied to the French interest, and they hoped that the Shawnees would relocate to Fort Ouiatenon, near present-day Lafayette, Indiana.[28]

Shawnee migrants stubbornly refused these demands for relocation. By 1735, it had become obvious to the French that the Ohio River was a strategic liability, a region full of people who undermined their authority in the upper country. Pennsylvania traders used the Ohio to move through well-placed Shawnee villages, from Logstown to Lower Shawnee Town, and these villages took advantage of the traffic. It was a borderland between New France and British North America, and Shawnee villagers mediated the traffic between empires. While some villages were predominantly Shawnee, the Ohio River villages were even more multiethnic than the "imagined communities" that Beauharnois and others dreamed of at Detroit and Ouiatenon.[29]

Like Logstown on the Upper Ohio River, Lower Shawnee Town had become "a sort of republic." Populated by a diverse array of migratory peoples, from the Iroquois to the Delawares, and supplied by British traders, Lower Shawnee Town had become a formidable threat to French ambitions. With a "fairly large number of bad characters of various nations," Lower Shawnee Town posed a significant challenge to France and Great Britain alike. The community was less a village and more of a "district, extending along the wide Scioto River and narrower Ohio River floodplains and terraces." It was a sprawling series of wickiups and longhouses, and George Croghan maintained a storehouse there. At the northern end of the district, the various coalescent peoples met in a ninety-foot-long, bark-covered council house. French and British-allied traders regarded Lower Shawnee Town as one of two capitals of the Shawnee tribe. The other branch of the Shawnee tribe "decided to go and join the Alibamons," most likely at Sawanogi, in the Upper Creek Confederacy.[30]

Shawnees at Lower Shawnee Town stalled for time as the French pressed them to move to Detroit. "Frequent talks" and "divers interviews" had not yet produced the desired result. In August 1741, Shawnee diplomats met with Beauharnois and firmly rejected his requests. The Shawnees explained that "they never thought of going to settle at Detroit," for "some of them were burnt there, and they wish[ed] to keep away from a land where their blood has been shed." But for Beauharnois, Shawnees could not be allowed to remain at Lower Shawnee Town. He wanted the Shawnees to abandon the Ohio River entirely because "they were in great danger there[,] being upon a war route." The French did not know that

Shawnee migrants had chosen "war routes" on which to settle before, from Illinois to Pennsylvania. Lower Shawnee Town thus represented a continuation of the Shawnees' mediation of violence and trade in multiple colonial worlds. The meeting convinced Beauharnois that he had been betrayed by Chartier, who had promised nothing less than the relocation of the Shawnee people to Detroit. Beauharnois now understood that Shawnee migrants maintained some form of contact across their villages, even those as distinct as Logstown and Lower Shawnee Town. In response, Beauharnois tried to save face by forbidding them "to communicate anything to the man Chartier" because he "had not kept faith with me."[31]

James Logan and the Fate of the British Empire

James Logan recognized that the fate of these empires ran through "the Ohio, a gateway into the heart of French territory." Once again, Indian migrants to the Ohio country compelled the British to coordinate their activities. Logan saw the French as the chief threat to his own wealth and privilege, and, by extension, that of British North America. The Shawnees' decision to return to their homeland foreshadowed the impending conflict between the Covenant Chain alliance and Native migrants to the Ohio country. Between 1713 and 1744, a long Anglo-French peace had existed between these competing empires. But with the withdrawal of Shawnees, Delawares, and other disgruntled Native peoples from Pennsylvania, Logan convinced himself, and colonial officials like him, that these migrants desired to be "in league with the French."[32]

Pennsylvanians began coordinating a shared vision of the interior of the continent in an attempt to deal with the French and Indian threat. They planned a series of forts manned by traders affiliated with the various colonies, from New York to South Carolina. Proprietary officials encouraged their counterparts in Virginia "to extend their settlements beyond the Mountains" and to "build some forts on Lake Erie." Similar efforts by South Carolina might challenge French traders and diplomats working out of New Orleans and Mobile. When Native warriors traveled through Virginia's backcountry, the Virginia House of Burgesses turned to Logan, and to Pennsylvania, for help. Logan instructed Conrad Weiser to tell the Iroquois, via Shickellamy, that "none of their young men or warriors as they call them, shall in any manner attack or goe near those Southern Indians." Logan forbade them from going "near the inhabitants of Virginia." Pennsylvania now rivaled New York as it used diplomacy and trade to fight for the hearts and minds of Indian people west of the Appalachian Mountains.[33]

But in many ways Pennsylvanians found that they could not serve two masters. History, memory, and land rights in Pennsylvania continued to shape events in the Ohio River Valley. In 1737, James Logan learned that the Shawnees on the Susquehanna River had sent a "Belt of Wampum," perhaps signifying war, "to the French Indians" at Detroit. After the Walking Purchase, many Shawnees and Delawares developed a keener understanding of their shared destiny than they had known in Pennsylvania. The Ohio country became their home, and they migrated there in search of autonomy. Playing the French and English off of one another in these regions became the preferred strategy of these migrants. Their neutralist stance reflected a sea change in Shawnee history. Previously, Native peoples migrated in search of direct trade with colonizers, and they sometimes became mercenaries on their behalf. After 1737, Shawnee migrants abandoned such close connections with traders and other agents of competing empires. The prevailing interest of their villages was no longer tied to the needs of their colonial patrons. Rather, a new generation of Shawnee leaders who were little known to either the English or the French made decisions that affected the course of empires. "Trading directly with Pennsylvanians and Virginians operating well beyond Iroquoian control" became the means by which the Shawnees and Delawares established their independence.[34]

The Walking Purchase, which had been orchestrated by James Logan, further strained the Covenant Chain alliance. The Iroquois felt that the Pennsylvanians deserved all of the blame because "we think there is an old misunderstanding between the Schawenoes and Governor Penn and they have Conceived some disgust against Governor Penn."[35] For forty years, Logan cultivated the image of Penn as the embodiment of Pennsylvania's Indian policy. In practice, Logan saw himself as the de facto head of Pennsylvania or, at the very least, as the person in charge of Indian affairs. On a visit to the Onondagas, Logan told Weiser to "acquaint them that our late Governor Patrick Gordon who was Governor here for ten years past is lately dead at a great age above 72 years." Ultimately, Logan did not think that Gordon's death mattered very much, because "their old true friend & father William Penn's own son is here, and so is James Logan." Logan reminded them that "their said father Penn" chose Logan "to take care of his brothers the Indians, and that through all that long tract of time, he has observed his Master's commands in treating with the Indians."[36]

Logan built his fur-trading empire with the goal of acquiring Indian lands. He did so with meticulous precision, by turning traders and Indians alike into debt peons. Hopelessly in debt, traders and hunters saw their plantations, villages, and hunting grounds pass into his hands. Logan's distance from the actual work of empire, from the exchange of European goods for furs to the eviction of traders from their lands, enabled him to cultivate the myth of William Penn. Opportunistic and often illiterate traders might have been partly to blame for the unhappiness of Native migrants. The Iroquois were also partially to blame for their falling out with the Delawares and the Shawnees. But both scenarios hide the fact that James Logan was behind the steady acquisition of Indian lands in Pennsylvania.

Motivation to return to their homeland was not the Shawnees' primary reason for leaving Pennsylvania. Rather, the Shawnees desired to protect their economic and cultural sovereignty. Logan sought to make them into lifelong, inherited serfs, servants of his fur-trading empire. They refused, and Logan guessed that his aggressiveness might ultimately lead to war with France. Nevertheless, he continued to pursue his self-interest. After the Walking Purchase, Native people in Pennsylvania understood that land-hungry settlers would inevitably consume their estates. The Ohio country became the only remaining alternative for those seeking economic and cultural freedom.

Alcohol, Empire, and Revitalization

Shawnee villagers had moved across the eastern half of North America, and they had consistently migrated out of places in which they had been threatened with servility and death. In contrast, the Delawares had remained in the mid-Atlantic region, and their primary allies had been the English. Nevertheless, both the Shawnees and the Delawares began to search for a path toward independence from European colonizers and the Iroquois Confederacy. They worked together to begin a revitalization movement that sought a means by which Native people might avoid dependence on colonizers and subjugation by the Iroquois. The Ohio country offered a kind of sovereignty that they had not known since the middle of the seventeenth century. The rum trade, combined with ongoing land cessions, caused some to blame themselves for the disasters that had befallen their people. In March 1738, one hundred "Alleghany" Shawnees, including Peter Chartier, pledged that any kegs of rum brought into their towns "shall be broak and spilt." Signers included Opessa's son, Laypareawah. These Shawnees had made clear their desire for neutrality. In a letter to Thomas Penn and James Logan, they described a "Good Correspondance with the French, the five nations, Ottawas, and all the French

Indians." Shawnees seeking an end to the alcohol trade attributed their success to their temperance pledges, "that we would live in peese and quietness and become another people."[37] Shawnees interested in temperance sent messages to the Iroquois and the Delawares and to their relatives remaining on the Susquehanna, asking them to stop bringing rum into their towns. The trade was simply so widespread that it came from all sectors of society—Indian and non-Indian, backcountry trader and Philadelphia diplomat.

Shawnees described how "monthly some new Upstart of a Trader . . . comes amongst us." "Bringing nothing but rum," these traders quickly deprived Shawnee people of their wealth. Many of these "Upstarts" were former servants of Cartlidge and Davenport. Governor Gordon complained that "the woods are so thick and dark we cannot see what is done in them."[38] An excess of democracy in the Indian trade doomed the Allegheny Shawnees to a futile war against the scourge of alcohol. Even migrating beyond the Appalachians did not protect them.

Their inability to halt the rum trade in the Ohio Valley convinced Indian people from many different villages that they were inheritors of a common history, and they began to turn that inheritance toward new, pan-Indian identities. They spoke of becoming "another people," and they believed that this revolutionary desire might bring about an end to decades of violence and subservience. Their struggle against Iroquois dominion was another common element of their history. New York's governor described how "these Refugees of the Six Nations (if I may use the Term) the Shawonese & Delawares, with their new allies the Owendats [Wyandots] and Twightees [Miamis] make a body of fifteen hundred if not two thousand men." The multiethnic villages along the Ohio River massed enough warriors to pose a threat to French- and British-allied traders. But the Shawnees and their neighbors did not wish to antagonize either the Iroquois or the British. In 1739, Ohio Shawnees acknowledged that they were "scattered far abroad from the Great Island to the Alleghany." However, they hoped that they might "cling close to one another as long as the World endures." When confronted regarding negotiations with the French, the Ohio Shawnees acknowledged that they had made contact with them. However, they "told them they might live where they pleased." They desired to "continue in friendship with their Brothers, the English, for they had better goods than theirs to furnish them with."[39]

Many of the Haudenosaunee agreed with these sentiments and came to believe that life east of the mountains was untenable. Warriors who traveled through Virginia continued to do so under threat of enslavement and death. For example, in 1743, thirty Iroquois warriors traveling through Virginia on their way to the Catawba towns battled with backcountry settlers in the Shenandoah Valley. Survivors told Weiser that they "travelld along in great want of Victuals." When they decided to approach the settlers for food and shelter, "the white people would not permit them to go but sent out a captain with a sword." After further negotiations, the Virginians seemed poised to attack them. The Iroquois tried to flee, but the settlers blocked their escape and fired on them. The warriors then counterattacked, killing many. The Iroquois gathered up their wounded and ran for the mountain paths leading northward to the relative safety of Pennsylvania. They stopped at the Shawnee towns on the west branch of the Susquehanna River, where they relayed their story and tended to their wounds.[40]

Oneida diplomat Shickellamy prevented the Susquehanna River Shawnees from exacting revenge on the Virginians. Speaking directly to them, Shickellamy commanded that they "not pretend to Revenge our people that have been killed in Virginia." He forbade them from taking action, stating that "we are the Chief of all the Indians." After this incident and the Iroquois response, Shawnees could no longer ignore the changing face of Indian-white relations in the region. They were so incensed by the melee in Virginia that they became convinced that "the white people are all of one colour and as one Body, and in case of war would assist one another."[41] Shawnees astutely recognized that Pennsylvania no longer sought to distinguish itself from its colonial neighbors through Quakerism and nonviolence.

Years of living on the fault line between empires had convinced some Native people of their shared history. Long-distance migrants had direct experience with the alcohol trade, land loss, and Iroquois-English domination. Looking back on decades of migration, many now understood that they shared a common racial heritage that had supplanted tribal and village-based identities. To the settlers, and perhaps now to themselves, a kind of "Indian" racial identity bound them together in a common fate.

King George's War and the End of Neutrality

In March 1744, France declared war against England, and the first of two global wars for supremacy between these rival colonial powers began. Most residents of the Ohio Valley would not know peace in their, or their children's, lifetime, as King George's War initiated backcountry violence and outright rebellions that continued well after the conclusion of the

American Revolution. In 1744, The king of France tasked the Marquis de Vaudreuil with the mission of destroying Lower Shawnee Town. It was "His Majesty's wish" that Vaudreuil break up the "republic." The French hoped that if Vaudreuil succeeded in "inducing the Chaoüanons to leave, it will be weakened to such an extent that it need no longer be feared." Villagers at Lower Shawnee Town made it clear that they were neither part of the Covenant Chain nor subjects of the Iroquois. "Those savages claim to be and in fact are independent of all nations," the French foreign minister wrote. Therefore, Beauharnois pinned his hopes on the "rights" of the peoples at Lower Shawnee Town. If New France acknowledged their sovereignty, they might be persuaded back into the alliance. Beauharnois preferred to see the Shawnees as independent, while Vaudreuil believed that "the Indians of the Ohio country, having formed themselves into a Republic and Confederacy," migrated to the region "by the consent of the five Nations."[42]

The Iroquois had much to lose if the Shawnee vision of neutrality became a reality in the interior of the continent. In 1744, Pennsylvanians noticed that "there was but one of the Shawonese from their principal town upon Ohio" at the Treaty of Lancaster. The British learned that the "Six Nations and the Shawonese are far from being on good terms" and that the Shawnees were determined to persuade the remaining Pennsylvania Delawares to come to their towns on the Ohio.[43]

Meanwhile, after the attacks of 1744, a peace treaty with the Iroquois became the only means by which the Tidewater colonies could avoid open warfare with the Haudenosaunee. Later that year, Pennsylvania coordinated a vast treaty between the Six Nations and Virginia, Maryland, Pennsylvania, and New York. In it, Maryland and Virginia reconciled themselves to ceaseless warfare between the Iroquois and Catawbas by granting the Iroquois "free passage through Virginia" for their warriors. In exchange, the Six Nations gave to Virginia the lands to the west, "to the setting sun." This second, and more important, element of the Lancaster Treaty enabled the Iroquois Confederacy to extend its claim, by right of conquest, to what became the Old Northwest, the heart of the continent. Later, with the 1768 Treaty of Fort Stanwix, the Iroquois agreed "to bulge the Proclamation line westward," into the Ohio Valley. Shawnees, Delawares, and other migrants from Pennsylvania protested the treaties of 1744 and 1768 because they extended British and Iroquois claims into the Ohio country. They waged war with the British for a generation in an attempt to combat the imposition of British and Iroquois understandings of history, and, by extension, land rights.[44]

British North Americans were at the weakest point in decades when the Treaty of Lancaster became law. Peter Chartier sensed this when in the spring of 1745 he robbed a pair of English traders working for George Croghan. Two men in Croghan's employ, Peter Tostee and James Dinnen, described Chartier as leading "a great company of Indians (including women and children) to Seven or Eight Hundred." Before letting them go, with only the clothes on their backs, Chartier told them that if they "were incline[d] to stay with the Shawaneese" they were welcome to do so. Three of the traders' servants and a "Negro man" jumped at the opportunity and remained with Chartier's band. Deference and authority died quickly in the Ohio country. Beauharnois described how Chartier's band of Shawnees had "tied and plundered the English traders on the Belle Rivére, to the number of eight" and have "carried the others along with them to their winter quarters."[45]

The brazenness of Chartier's robbery convinced the British that Chartier and a party of 500 Shawnees planned to attack their settlements. Pennsylvanians interpreted Chartier's robbery as a declaration of war. Chartier did seem eager to know whether or not the Miamis had "accepted the tomahawk." Delawares and Shawnees still loyal to Pennsylvania distanced themselves from Chartier and warned the colonists of a possible attack from "French Indians living at a Town or Fort on a Branch of the River Mississippi." Pennsylvania militiamen believed that Peter Chartier led a band of marauding Indians from the South and that he had stored a "large house full of snow shoes" so that they could attack the frontier settlements of Pennsylvania and New York in the winter. Chartier was "capable of any villany" from their perspective, and colonial militias prepared for an assault. Under normal circumstances, the provincial council would have dismissed these outlandish rumors. But remaining Susquehanna River Shawnees had alerted Pennsylvanians to the threat posed by Chartier. They believed him to be a man "of a savage, treacherous Disposition."[46]

The Marquis de Vaudreuil coordinated French efforts to consolidate power in the Ohio Valley. Chartier's robbery of Tostee and Dinnen seems to have reflected his policy of encouraging Native migrants to attack English traders and forts. He planned to thwart English "aggrandizement" by exploiting old antagonisms between Native villages to further the ambitions of New France. For example, Vaudreuil encouraged Illinois warriors to attack English-allied Chickasaw towns. And on the Ohio, Vaudreuil offered a substantial sum of money to anyone capable of taking off Croghan's scalp.[47]

The Shawnees, like their Kickapoo, Miami, Wea, Piankashaw, and Delaware neighbors, placed conditions on their alliance with New France. They "demand[ed] to be taken care of at a reasonable price." Based as they were near the Ohio River, which acted as a boundary between French Canada and French Louisiana, they found that French forts, from Ouiatenon, in northwest Indiana, to Vincennes, in southwest Indiana, to Toulouse, in Alabama, were chronically undersupplied. Their hunters sometimes responded by moving closer to English traders such as George Croghan, whose territory ranged from Pennsylvania to the falls of the Ohio River, at modern-day Louisville, Kentucky. Their constant presence along the Ohio River, the region Vaudreuil described as the "heart of the colony," posed a clear challenge to French ambitions.[48]

In 1745, Beauharnois could finally report that the "emigration of the Chaouanons has at length taken place; they have removed from their former location to the place I allotted them at the prairie of the Maskoutins," along the border between west-central Indiana and Illinois. As if to confirm his genius, Beauharnois believed that Mascoutin Prairie was free from the influence of English traders. Before leaving Lower Shawnee Town, Chartier's band performed a "Death Feast," a ceremony common among both the Iroquois and the Algonquians across the *pays d'en haut*. Native peoples conducted this ceremony prior to abandoning their villages, and so this ritual must have been particularly common among Ohio Valley migrants. A French trader then in residence at Lower Shawnee Town witnessed the event, and he described how the ceremony itself lasted "from two in the afternoon to eleven o'clock at night." There are several different translations of the central event of this two-day ceremony, including "draw[ing] the waters of the feast," to "go[ing] through their formal leaps," to "gather[ing] up the bones of the feast." Unfortunately, it is impossible to discern the ultimate meaning of the ceremony based on the translation itself and the limited description of the event as a whole. However, we do know that Chartier's band would not depart Lower Shawnee Town until they had conducted the ceremony. Performing the Death Feast effectively closed this chapter of their history, a necessary step before moving closer to the French-allied towns along the Mascoutin Prairie.[49]

It is possible to partially reconstruct the eighteenth-century meaning of the Death Feast among Shawnee migrants by describing similar ritual events practiced by their neighbors. For the Hurons, the Feast of the Dead was their most important ceremony and was conducted every time a village was relocated. But unlike the Shawnees, who chose not to return once they abandoned a village, the Hurons returned to their old town and retrieved the bones of their dead relatives. Once they were disinterred, the Huron buried the remains of their relatives, along with those from satellite villages, in a common burial in the new village. Now released from their village cemetery, the souls of the dead were free to "travel westward to the land where Iouskeha and Aataentsic lived." Burial in a common ossuary in which the bones of the dead intermingled for eternity symbolized the common destiny of the village, a physical reminder of the need for unity and harmony among its members. Once reburied, the souls of the dead were reunited with the two most important figures in the Huron belief system.[50]

Both the English and the French were hampered by the mobility of smaller tribes and the increasing competitiveness of the fur trade. Native peoples, like British and French colonizers, claimed the Ohio country. And as they struggled with each other, everyone involved in the trade became vulnerable. Delaware hunters reported being robbed by Pennsylvania traders they knew personally. In another incident, a French trader was "knocked in the head" for offering too little in exchange for a Native hunter's skins. And in 1747, black wampum belts, which signified war, had been sent from French-allied Indians to Lower Shawnee Town and Shamokin, carried across the Appalachian Mountains by Delaware and Shawnee messengers. These were interconnected worlds, brought together by long-distance migrants and the long-distance traders who sought their business.[51]

In these years, it took French traders twenty days to travel from Detroit to Lower Shawnee Town. Sometimes guided by Abenakis from what is now Maine, French traders typically left Detroit by the end of May. They encountered Hurons and Potawatomis, Ottawas, Miamis, and Iroquois along the way. Such a profusion of people on the move caused them to guard their encampments by night and to travel briskly by day. The Ohio country had become incredibly diverse, as migrants from the St. Lawrence River Valley, as well as what is now Michigan and Illinois, took advantage of abundant game and the traders who competed for their loyalty.[52]

Conrad Weiser aptly described the turbulence of the age. The constancy of the French threat and the growing fragmentation of the Iroquois convinced Weiser that "we live in an age where the steadfastness of mankind is not to be depended on and most of all nations are guided by self-interest." He was not surprised by the fact that "poor Indians" such as the Shawnees and Delawares "look out for gain and more so as the French are for ever busy about them." War strained already-fragile ties between the migrants and the Pennsylvania traders. Weiser recommended that "the Present intended for the Indians on the River Ohio should be larger." Because the "Indians at Ohio are much nearer Neighbours," Weiser reasoned, they "should not be pass'd over without something."[53]

Land and Sovereignty in the Ohio Country

Native migrants sometimes acknowledged Iroquois power in order to gain compensation from Pennsylvania for the loss of their lands. Iroquois diplomats delivered a "string of wampum from the Connays," who were then seeking compensation "for their settlement at the Connoye town" in Lancaster County. Like the Iroquois, George Croghan believed that their town "had been reserved for their use," rather than owned by the Conoy people. The Conoys chose to work with Pennsylvania through Iroquois mediators. Some "Ohio Indians" approached the provincial government directly. They argued that "they were entitled to part of the goods paid for . . . [lands] on the east side of the Sasquahannah." In their opinion, "the lands belonged as well to them as the Onondaga Council." As late as 1748, the "Ohio Indians" continued to fight their subordinate status as they pursued land claims in Pennsylvania.[54]

Ohio Valley villagers contested the legal and historical foundations of the Iroquois right of conquest. The Iroquois Confederacy, the Seneca, Cayuga, Mohawk, Onondaga, Oneida, and Tuscarora, became divided between France and England. By the 1740s, English trade goods had become increasingly scarce, and this contributed to division and decline among the Iroquois. In 1747, Iroquois warriors from the Ohio Valley visited the provincial council with a complaint. At Philadelphia, the Iroquois explained that "the French have hard heads, and we have nothing strong enough to break them. We have only little Sticks and Hickeries." As a result, they asked for "better weapons, such as will knock the French down." The Iroquois wondered "how comes it to pass that the English, who brought us into this war, will not fight themselves?" Pennsylvanians' commitment to pacifism clearly bothered the Iroquois. While the Pennsylvanians had supplied them with an abundance of European goods, far more than had the French, their unwillingness to engage with them as military allies had become a problem. Weiser saved the day for the Pennsylvanians. In separate meetings with the Iroquois warriors, Weiser learned that "the Governor of Canada had sent the Hatchet to the Indians about the Lakes and on the branches of the Ohio." More ominously, "It was always the Custom in war time to put the management into the hands of the Young People." Weiser clearly worried over their allegiance to the British, and he persuaded the provincial council to make a large gift in trade goods to cement their loyalty. He wanted to correct the long decay in the relationship between Pennsylvania and the "Ohio Indians." In 1749, Weiser asked the proprietors "to build a couple of villages for the good of the trade with the Indians" somewhere in the "endless mountains."[55]

That same year, a French military man, Pierre Joseph Céleron de Blainville, a French Canadian marine officer, traveled from Montreal to the Ohio country. He led a party of two hundred, including thirty Iroquois and Abenaki warriors, on an expedition against Logstown. After a three-week journey, Céleron chose not to attack Logstown because it was "composed of Iroquois, Chaouanons, and Loups [Delawares]. Mingled with these were Indians from other tribes, making a very bad village seduced by the cheapness of English goods." He described how "the Indians in council made a very conciliatory reply," in spite of their allegiance to the British. Céleron's war party left Logstown with vague reassurances regarding some future visit to Montreal and only the faintest hope that they might ally themselves with the French. Soon after his departure, Native residents of the Upper Ohio Valley dug up the lead plates that Céleron had left at important points along the river. Such plates amounted to sovereign claims by the French, and Indians from the Upper Ohio would not entertain such fanciful notions.[56]

Céleron was supposed to drive Ohio Valley Indians from the British interest. But they encountered nothing but multiethnic villages, and their precise loyalties were hard to discern. In most, some combination of Shawnee, Iroquois, and Delaware peoples predominated. However, Céleron was struck by the fact that "nearly all of the tribes of the Upper Country" were represented in the villages they passed through along the Ohio. Circumstances seemed to have compelled their union, and the French resorted to describing them as a "republic" or as "Ohio" Indians, for lack of an adequate means of capturing their precise loyalties and tribal identities.[57]

Native discontent with the French trading system had spread throughout the Ohio and Upper Mississippi Valleys, and this complicated Céleron's task. New France provided trade monopolies to fur-trading companies working exclusively out of Montreal. This fixed location and the fixed prices offered for furs and skins meant that French traders were chronically undersupplied. Appeals to patriotism failed to persuade these monopolies to offer more goods. Native hunters tied to the French received about half as much for their efforts as they could among the British. Under the constraints of the French system, Native peoples believed that "almost any type of British alliance was better than starvation." France struggled to maintain its alliance, in large part because of the problems with its system of trade. As Vaudreuil himself admitted, "An ample supply of merchandise is needed in the stores to prevent revolutions and obtain peace for the colony."[58]

Logstown, Lower Shawnee Town, and Pickawillany, in western Ohio, all carried on a robust trade with the British. Nevertheless, Céleron repeated the wish that these villagers relocate to French forts in what is now Indiana and Michigan. Most followed Logstown's example and made a series of false promises to move at a later date. As Céleron traveled down the Ohio, he encountered Miamis who had been allied to New France for much longer, and more consistently, than either the Iroquois or the Shawnees. This might explain why New France placed such extreme demands on the Miamis, Weas, and Piankashaws. For example, La Demoiselle, or Old Briton, the Piankashaw chief at Pickawillany, paid the ultimate price for ignoring French commands. Céleron tried to compel Old Briton to remove from Pickawillany, along the Great Miami River in southwestern Ohio, and move closer to French outposts in Indiana. His objective was to stop the trade between the Miami and the English along the Ohio River, so that "the English who are the authors of all evil designs may not approach this territory which belongs to me." In council, Céleron warned that "if you fail, fear the resentments of a father who has only too much reason to be irritated against you." The French blamed Old Briton for his subsequent demise. "La Demoiselle and other Indians of the Beautiful river [the Ohio]," they explained, "had pushed their rebellion to excess, had adopted the English and had openly declared themselves the sworn enemies of the French." Such open declarations of allegiance were somewhat unusual for the Indian migrants of the Ohio Valley, most of whom strove to remain neutral. Philippe-Thomas Chabert de Joncaire, an expert frontiersmen who had lived among the Iroquois and later advised Céleron, believed that "not a party of Indians goes to the Beautiful river but leaves some there to increase the rebel forces."[59]

In 1752, after La Demoiselle parlayed the Céleron expedition, another French and Indian force, led by Charles Langlade, a métis leader with ties to the Ottawas, attacked Pickawillany. Langlade led a surprise attack that resulted in the capture and killing of several British traders. After laying siege to Pickawillany, Old Briton saw that his situation was futile, and he surrendered. Langlade then executed Old Briton before all of the surviving members of Pickawillany. To reinforce French displeasure, Langlade butchered Old Briton's corpse, threw his remains into a large cooking pot, and then he and the 200 warriors who joined in the attack ate the resulting stew.[60]

Like all Native peoples from the upper country, war divided the Miamis. Since 1692, at least some Miamis had been migrating to and from Pennsylvania and New York, where they secured cheaper trade goods. One Miami leader, Le Pied Froid, did relocate. And he warned Céleron of the differences between his people. Le Pied Froid explained that "la Demoiselle lies" and that, like "all the nations of the South," La Demoiselle was "exasperated against the French." Le Pied Froid described himself as "the only one who loves you [the French]." He made clear that the economics of the fur trade, and the near-constant migrations of his people, had made reconciliation between them impossible.[61]

Céleron acknowledged that "our traders can never give our merchandise at English prices on account of the costs that they are obliged to incur." These structural problems aside, the French railed against individuals such as George Croghan, whom they described as "The English Man" who has conspired "to have us attacked." Croghan, more than any other trader, held the Ohio Valley tribes to the British. For this reason, the French tried, and failed, to persuade the Ohio Valley tribes to scalp and murder him. In fact, Croghan regularly corresponded with prominent officials and businessmen in Pennsylvania. Croghan knew that "Ingans are very much Led by self Intrest, and will think a Great Dail of a Litle powder & Lead." He used trade goods to draw French-allied villagers to the British interest.[62]

The Shawnees and the Advantages of Mobility

French commanders, from Detroit to Montreal, recognized that the Miamis "received a speech from the English" through Shawnee intermediaries. Indeed, Lower Shawnee Town had become a hub for English traders and diplomats who wished to draw Native people away from the French orbit. The French tried, and failed, to destroy the Shawnees. First, they encouraged the Ottawa, and then the Illinois, to attack Lower Shawnee Town, but neither tribe elected to fight them. What caused this failure? The French hoped that an ongoing conflict between the Piankashaws, the Illinois, and the Shawnees might spread, because "it would be in our interest to destroy these Chaouanons by getting the nations to wage war against them." A French official associated with Céleron was convinced that the Shawnees "are always trying to disturb the nations that are our allies."[63]

The Shawnees, the Delawares, and the Iroquois of Logstown and Lower Shawnee Town managed to avoid Old Briton's fate. These villagers were spared the genocidal ferocity of the French toward the Meskwaki

(Fox) people, against whom they fought two wars during this time period. As the Meskwakis learned, there was a price to pay for challenging the authority of New France. But the Shawnees seem to have avoided this fate.[64] New France responded differently to the Shawnees in the Ohio Valley for several reasons. First, they had not been longtime allies of New France. In fact, their long relationship with men such as Martin and Peter Chartier, both of whom were estranged from New France, reveals the limits of the Shawnee engagement with the French alliance. Second, the French knew that Shawnees at the Alabama towns of the Upper Creek Confederacy visited Fort Toulouse and strategized with Vaudreuil. An assault against Lower Shawnee Town might threaten French inroads in the greater Southeast. French commanders in Montreal and Detroit remained wary of attacking Shawnee towns on the Ohio River, lest they undermine gains they had made in French Louisiana, at nominally Creek towns such as Sawanogi.

These "greatest travellers in America" had been misunderstood for a long time. Both the French and the British tried to impose their own meanings on Shawnee villagers living at great distances from each other, from the Ohio Valley to the greater Southeast and the eastern Piedmont of the Allegheny Mountains. George Croghan told the Shawnees that he hoped that they might be "coming home . . . again, that you may become once more a people and not as you were dispersed thro' the world." Croghan argued that it was "the French that the Indians call their Fathers that deceived you and scattered you about the woods, that they might have it in their power to keep you poor." The Shawnees' Ohio Valley homeland had become the center of a global power struggle and the sight of the next world war. Once again the Shawnees found themselves at the crossroads of empires. Shawnee villagers already possessed an enormous geographic range, and the knowledge gained as a result of it helped them challenge the authority of empires. By asserting their rights to the land, they hoped to shake the growing consensus that they were refugees, "a people with no where a fire burning."[65]

Perhaps, as Croghan suggested, they were "scattered" about the world. Shawnees such as Peter Chartier and the thousands of villagers from Logstown to Sawanogi saw the advantage in dispersal. By 1754, the Shawnees claimed multiple homelands, and they migrated between them. By returning to the Southeast, to villages such as Sawanogi, we can examine how migration between these homelands advanced Shawnee sovereignty and challenged the authority of empires. Ohio Valley villagers from Wakatomica, Lower Shawnee Town, and beyond traveled between regions and empires. These journeys made the Shawnees essential participants in the revitalization movements that swept across the eastern half of North America in the second half of the eighteenth century. Moreover, Shawnee migrants made up for their small numbers by using their considerable diplomatic skills, gained through generations of mobility, to their advantage. As we return to the Southeast, we will see why the Shawnees became so pivotal in early American history.

chapter 9

Race, Revitalization, and Warfare in the Eighteenth-Century Southeast

The Shawnees and the Creeks have been telling stories about each other for as long as either community can remember. Indeed, the relationship between them stretches back into "deep time," to the period before Europeans began recording their histories. Archaeological and archival evidence shows that Shawnees have been living within the various Creek *talwas*, or towns, since the seventeenth century. Many of the colonial-era stories feature the Creek towns of Tukabatchee and Abihka, both of which are widely regarded as the "foundation towns" of the Upper Creek Confederacy.[1] Louis LeClerk de Milfort, a Frenchman living among the Upper Creeks at the end of the eighteenth century, had heard stories about "an Indian tribe which had just been destroyed by the Iroquois and Hurons [which] came to implore the protection of the Muskogees." According to Milfort, sometime late in the seventeenth century "the Creeks took them in and assigned them land in the center of the nation" at Tukabatchee.[2] In the nineteenth century, Creek métis George Stiggins recalled hearing stories about a second group of Shawnee migrants who had moved into the Upper Creek towns sometime in the eighteenth century. Stiggins described how, at the time, the "Ispocogas" (Kispokothas) and Shawnees were two different "nations" brought together at Tukabatchee through an elaborate ritual exchange.[3]

Stiggins believed that the "Shawnees" were a large nation that coalesced with, and later subsumed, the five society clans. "Shawnee" thus became the umbrella term by which the Thawekila, Chalagawtha, Kispokotha, Pekowitha, and Mekoche identified themselves in the nineteenth century. According to Stiggins, coalescence between the Shawnees and Kispokotha took place during the Busk or Green Corn Ceremony, typically held in late July or early August. Stiggins's understanding makes sense given the fact that the Green Corn Ceremony brings together a whole series of ritual events whose purpose is to renew the world by renewing the *talwa* in which the ceremony takes place. As a peace ceremony, the Busk, or Green Corn, is a ritual in which townspeople reaffirm their commitment to each other. During the late eighteenth century, naturalist and travel writer William Bartram described a Green Corn Ceremony he witnessed in the Alabama town of Mucclassee, within the Upper Creek Confederacy. Bartram noticed that on the fourth day of the ceremony "the high priest, by rubbing dry wood together, produces new fire in the public square, from whence every habitation in the town is supplied with the new and pure flame." Every Creek *talwa* "had a hearth with a fire burning that represented the entire community and the people's connection to their ancestors." This sense of homeland, of place, symbolized by the sacred fire, became the means by which various community members reconciled their differences and bound themselves, on a yearly basis, to the land on which their town was located. Associated with the "ripening of the second or late crop of corn," the Busk also marked the end of the agricultural season. As such, it became a kind of thanksgiving ceremony in which the Creek people, and the Shawnees living among them, offered thanks for life, which was symbolized by corn, their primary means of sustenance.[4]

During the Green Corn Ceremony at Tukabatchee, ceremonialists displayed sacred brass plates described in their origin stories and often linked to the Shawnees. In the nineteenth century, Creeks recalled that the Kispokothas "deposited with the keepers of the national square of one of their groups their calumet Tobacco Pipes Belts and war club called by them *Attussa*," along with the twelve sacred brass plates of the "Ispocoga" nation. According to Stiggins, the union between the "Ispocogas" (Kispokothas), the Shawnees, and the Tukabatchee Creeks did not last. "Through some unknown reason," the Shawnees abandoned their Kispokotha Shawnee kinsmen and "formed a resolution to recede from the union." Stiggins learned that the Shawnees abandoned Tukabatchee, leaving behind their Kispokotha relatives. Before they departed, the Shawnees "carried off six of the sacred brass plates . . . which the Shawanose have retained possession of ever since." Creek people did not see these sacred brass plates again until the War of 1812, when Muskogees sympathetic to the revitalization movement led by Tecumseh, himself a Kispokotha, saw them in "the care of the old prophet at tippaconoe," the multiethnic village associated with Tecumseh's brother, Tenskwatawa, on the Tippecanoe River in northwest Indiana. Ties between the Kispokotha Shawnees and the Tukabatchee Creeks are so profound that Tecumseh "once described himself as a man of

Tuckabatchee." Native people who knew him later related that his mother was a Creek, and, as such, Tecumseh and Tenskwatawa possessed clan identities in both Shawnee and Creek society.[5]

In the 1930s, relic hunters unearthed several sets of Tukabatchee plates that have since been investigated by professional archaeologists. Discovered near the falls of the Tallapoosa River, near where Tukabatchee once stood, the plates were clearly imported from outside of the Southeast. They were almost certainly made from French copper basins traded to the Neutrals, Iroquoian speakers from Lower Ontario. According to archaeologist William A. Fox, "There was communication ca. A.D. 1600–1650 between what is now the Niagara region of Ontario and central Alabama, either direct or indirect, and perhaps through Shawnee 'middlemen.'"[6] From the seventeenth through the nineteenth centuries, Shawnee migrants linked the Southeast to the Northeast. In ritual as in trade, they bridged regions and cultures. The protohistoric archaeological record offers this kind of suggestive evidence of Creek and Shawnee origins.

But even by the end of the eighteenth century, the various Shawnee villages in the Southeast had not coalesced into the Upper Creek Confederacy. This might have stemmed from the fact that Creek *talwas* are often considered "mother towns" of newer *talwas*. It is often the case that "clusters of buildings," or *talofas*, become associated with Creek *talwas*. In this way, distinct Shawnee villages, or a handful of Shawnee migrants, often became affiliated with Creek *talwas* such as Tukabatchee, Abihka, and Mucclassee. Shawnee villages in Creek country might have been affiliated with specific Creek towns but not fully integrated into Creek society. By the close of the eighteenth century, the southern superintendent of Indian Affairs, Benjamin Hawkins, certainly thought that this was the case. Hawkins noted that the Shawnees at Sawanogi, within the Upper Creek Confederacy, still retained "the manners of their countrymen to the N.W."[7]

Some Shawnees had remained in the Southeast since at least 1674, when Henry Woodward met them at Hickauhaugau, or Westo Town. Newer Shawnee migrants from Pennsylvania, including the Thawekila Shawnees responsible for murdering Sagohandechty, moved back to the Southeast in the eighteenth century. By 1730, there were at least three distinct clusters of Shawnee migrants in present-day Alabama. The most important of these was Sawanogi, near the Alabama-Coushatta town of Mucclassee. By the 1740s, British trader John Spencer was operating a trading post dubbed "Little Savannah House," and he served a multiethnic community that included Shawnees, Alabamas, Creeks, and Yuchis. Further to the east lay the Creek town of Ecunhutke. The resident trader, John Eycott, noted that he served Creeks "and the Savanoes." Finally, a third contingent of Shawnees settled far to the north, on a tributary of the Coosa River, near the Creek town of Coosa. This last town was affiliated with the Abihka people, one of three ethnic groupings that composed the Upper Creeks. However, most Shawnees seemed to have particularly strong ties to the Alabama towns, particularly Mucclassee, in the middle of the eighteenth century.[8]

Fort Ancient villagers had conducted a lively trade with Koasati and Coosa villagers from Tennessee. They seemed to have joined forces and traded with the Spanish along the Gulf Coast during the protohistoric period. During the early historic period, the Indian slave trade drew still more Shawnee migrants to Savannah Town. However, by the middle decades of the eighteenth century, Shawnee migrants moved into the interior Southeast in defense of their sovereignty. They preferred villages among the Upper Creek, rather than the fall-line towns that had been typical of the borderland between Native peoples and colonizers. Among the Creeks, new Shawnee arrivals promoted a neutralist stance toward French and English traders and diplomats vying for their allegiance. For example, in 1736, a small band of Shawnees moved into Chickasaw towns. Jean-Baptiste Le Moyne, Sieur de Bienville, the French commander at New Orleans, described how "sixty Shawnees . . . are said to have retreated" to Chickasaw territory, where they joined a force of "at least four hundred and fifty [Chickasaw] warriors and the Natchez to one hundred and fifty."[9] Shawnees migrating to Chickasaw country might have been related to or inspired by La Salle's Shawnee guides, who lived among the Chickasaw in the late seventeenth century. Finally, after 1748, Peter Chartier's band joined their kinsmen and moved into the Upper Creek Confederacy as well.

Sawanogi became the de facto capital of the southeastern Shawnees. While other Shawnee communities seem to have been little more than *talofas*, small clusters of people attached to larger Creek mother towns, Sawanogi was a self-consciously Shawnee town, or *talwa*. This village was situated near the confluence of the Coosa and Tallapoosa rivers and the Upper Creek town of Mucclassee. Sawanogi's relationship to the Alabama-Coushatta people seems to have been particularly important. Diron d'Artaguette, the French commander at Fort Toulouse, built in 1736, opposite Mucclassee, learned from the Alabama-Coushattas that seven Shawnee villages would eventually join with the Upper Creeks. The Coushattas determined their ultimate location, for it was their right to "place [the Shawnees] where they judge proper."[10] The French believed that the "Kauachatis" (Coushattas) had an "ancient" alliance with the Shawnees that had been renewed by these eighteenth-century migrations into the Southeast.[11]

Sawanogi first appears in the archival record in 1737, when French traders took note of new Shawnee arrivals among the Upper Creek towns of Alabama. They were few in number, for Pierre de Rigaud, Marquis de Vaudreuil, the governor of French Louisiana, noted that "seventy or eighty" Shawnees had "come from Canada . . . to settle among the Alabamas." Almost immediately, the Shawnees had an outsized impact on the region. They applied their geographic and cultural knowledge to long-standing regional antagonists, such as the Cherokees and Creeks, who had been at war for more than a generation. Sawanogi Shawnees first mediated peace talks between the Cherokees and the Lower Creek town of Coweta. The Shawnees acted "as mediator and introducer, and as guarantors of peace" between these communities. In 1743, Vaudreuil reported that Shawnees living among the Alabamas should be asked to escort the Cherokees to Montreal for a "settlement."[12]

Their long history of migrations made Shawnee diplomats especially important to New France and British colonial officials on the eve of King George's War. With villages among the Creeks, Alabama-Coushattas, and Yuchis, as well as "Indian republics" such as Logstown and Lower Shawnee Town, the Shawnees had an influence that far outstripped their small population. Shawnees assured French diplomats that "they wish[ed] to make a long term peace among all the Nations of this continent." Their foremost goals included guarantees of safety for migrants. "Peace on the river" and "free access to all travel routes" might enable Native travelers to settle where they liked.[13]

For more than a decade following their arrival, Vaudreuil dreamed of a peace agreement between French-allied villagers in the upper country and the Southeast, brokered by Shawnee middlemen. However, Algonquians and Muskogeans alike remained loyal to their villages, and they resisted French directives. They were parochial cosmopolitans whose migrations taught them to remain skeptical about French plans for a grand alliance. In 1744, Vaudreuil himself admitted that "each village has its own chief who, with his warriors, follows the course that seems good to him, so that they are so many small republics."[14]

Fort Toulouse and the Structural Weakness of the French Trading System

French traders at Fort Toulouse never had enough merchandise to satisfy Creeks and newer migrants. It was a lonely outpost of New France, and it reminded Native people of French weaknesses. Vaudreuil had promised

Shawnee migrants "a complete supply" of trade goods in exchange for their loyalty, and the Sawanogi Shawnees had come to expect a French trader who would "supply them all their needs." Shawnees disappointed with Fort Toulouse turned to English traders. D'Artaguette described how "the English who were in the neighborhood of the fort have all returned to Carolina to fetch trade merchandise." He assumed, incorrectly, that "these Indian nations are completely devoted to the English."[15] In Sawanogi, as in Lower Shawnee Town, Shawnees preferred neutrality to subordination.

In fact, nearly every year, Shawnees moved from the Ohio country to Creek *talwas*, bringing with them anti-British sentiment. In 1744, Vaudreuil described how "about 80 Chaouanons came and set up with the Abekas." Some Shawnee migrants to the Southeast had had enough of men such as James Logan and the settler colonialism he promoted. They hoped that the trade with France would make it possible for them "not to have any dealings with the English." After Chartier's robbery of Tostee and Dinnen, Vaudreuil described how Shawnee migrants "came to blows" with English traders on the Ohio. Since then, the Shawnees had taken approximately fifteen English traders captive along Lake Erie, at Sandusky Bay. They had refused to turn them over to the French at Montreal.[16]

The Shawnees, as much as any tribe in the Southeast, understood how the slave trade and violence had undermined their villages. Cherokees, Chickasaws, and Creeks alike hoped for an end to the raiding and violence that had structured relations between tribes since the beginning of the slave trade. Vaudreuil wanted the French to be the linchpin of a grand, interregional alliance between the major southeastern tribes. But they worried about "a peace achieved without Onontio's [New France's] mediation." They may have hoped that Shawnee diplomats had accepted French plans for them, but Shawnee migrants knew better than to ally themselves with the French. The French wanted to expel English traders from the lands between the Appalachian Mountains and the Mississippi River. They hoped to "see an ultimate, complete integration of the Indians into the social and economic life of the French settlements," from Montreal to Mobile.[17] Vaudreuil misunderstood Shawnee motivations for their attacks on traders such as Tostee and Dinnen. French officials did not understand the Shawnees' history along the Lower Susquehanna River and so they mistook revenge for something more, for a sign that Shawnees were finally willing to surrender themselves, as a nation, to New France. This explains why Vaudreuil continued to believe in the possibility of a grand alliance. He pursued a peace agreement between the Choctaws and the Chickasaws, whose villages lined the Mississippi River drainage. Such a peace would allow for the "free navigation" of the Mississippi, thereby creating an all-water route through lands claimed by New France.[18]

Shawnee Diplomacy in a World of Villages

Villagers west of the Appalachian Mountains had always used the trails and rivers of the interior to foster a series of connections between different regions. After two centuries of colonization, these rivers and footpaths had become even more important, and Native peoples and colonizers alike tried to regulate travel along them. No one knew these routes better than Shawnees, who had traveled the length and breadth of the Eastern Woodlands. In a letter to French statesman Jean-Frédéric Phélypeaux, Comte de Maurepas, Vaudreuil conveyed his confidence in Shawnee diplomacy, and he described using them as ambassadors as a "true . . . method of conciliation." Shawnees had brought representatives of more than forty southeastern towns to New Orleans to discuss the possibility of unity.[19] But all of these efforts led to an inconclusive peace, one marred by occasional spasms of violence and mistrust. Migratory townspeople possessed such different histories, making grand alliances difficult. Some, such as the "red English captain of the Shawnees," moved between neutrality and outright antagonism of the French. But at the same time, a rival band of Shawnees "attacked a troop of Choctaws and Chickasaws," even though there were Shawnees living among the Chickasaws at the time. Some Alabamas spoke against their Coushatta relatives and demanded that the Sawanogi Shawnees leave the Upper Creeks and rejoin their kinsmen in the Ohio country. Vaudreuil continued to support "the project of the general peace that the Shawnees have proposed," but these rivalries undermined their attempts at a grand alliance.[20]

King George's War further divided the Native peoples of the Southeast and the upper country. The French now recognized that hopes of preserving their empire ran through the many villagers who migrated between French, English, and Iroquoian worlds. The dynamic nature of tribal societies, from their ephemeral unity to their shifting and seemingly contradictory alliances, constrained their grand plans. Vaudreuil depended on yearly meetings at New Orleans and Mobile to "probe their true sentiments." The French came to depend on unnamed Shawnee mediators, who sought a "general peace" in the eastern half of North America.[21]

In the spring of 1746, tribes as different as the Shawnees, the Chickasaws, and the Cherokees gathered at New Orleans, and they promised to expel British traders as soon as the French supplied them with all of their needs. Similarly, the Shawnees, the Kickapoos, and the Mascoutins would "secure the continent" and protect the Mississippi River trade so long as France delivered on the promise of robust trade. English traders among the Cherokees mocked Shawnee efforts. But the Shawnees persevered and claimed that "they wanted peace for a long time." When Vaudreuil learned of this exchange, he commended the Shawnees for being "always ready to establish peace on the continent." Perhaps recognizing the diversity of Shawnee villages, he worried that the Shawnees would "cause revolutions and unrest" if they failed to adequately replace British traders and the cheaper goods they offered.[22]

Vaudreuil's ambitious plan to link French Louisiana and the upper country was doomed by the long-term characteristics of the Indian trade. The French had never been interested in the deerskin trade that was so central to both the Ohio Valley and the greater Southeast. The fur trade thus became a "strategic tool" for France in America. But its economic irrelevance to French traders in the upper country, who remained primarily interested in beaver pelts and other small game animals, complicated French diplomacy. Their situation was made worse by an effective British naval blockade during King George's War that prevented many French ships from resupplying their posts in North America. As a result, prices for trade goods, including shirts, guns, mirrors, and combs, rose by 150 percent during the war.[23]

The English trading system featured ruthless competition among traders, colonies, and Native villagers. Men such as James Logan certainly dominated the fur trade in Pennsylvania, but Logan faced British competitors from New York to South Carolina. Métis traders such as Peter Chartier often mingled trade goods from New York with those from Charles Town. It was a decentralized trading system, and the absence of authority provided Native peoples with many opportunities to take advantage of intercolonial competition. In contrast, New France coordinated "a closely knit chain of government control in the disbursement of goods." Merchandise moved slowly, from north to south, and frustrated Native consumers, who complained incessantly about the shortfall in goods. This system was so inflexible that it weakened Vaudreuil's designs in the Southeast. Indian hunters tied to French traders received about half as much for their efforts as they could among the English. The chronic limitations of the French trading system meant that France struggled to maintain its alliances. As Vaudreuil himself admitted, "An ample supply of merchandise is needed in the stores to prevent revolutions and obtain peace for the colony." He worried that the chronic deficiencies in the Indian trade might cause the Alabama-Coushattas to leave the French fold altogether. Vaudreuil knew that "they will become disgusted in the end if they do not receive the merchandise that I have caused them to expect."[24]

Shawnees continued to make progress toward peace in spite of these challenges. In 1746, a Frenchman traveling through Creek country learned that "the peace was made, both on the upper part of the river and in the lands of the Wabash." He observed that "twelve Shawnees had come to confirm it [the peace] also with all the nations," including Cherokees, "Alabamas, Talapoosas, Abihkas, Kawitas, Kasihtas." French officials lauded the Shawnees' diplomatic efforts and credited them with a peace " reigning in all the nations." Footpaths that had once carried slavery and disease into the Southeast had been transformed, or "whitened" into roads carrying diplomacy and peace to peoples who had traveled on the red road of war for generations.[25] French diplomats used Creek metaphors to describe this fragile peace, and the Alabama-Coushatta towns seemed to have been at the center of this new beginning.

While among the Choctaws, the twelve Shawnee ambassadors described how "they had just made peace with the Cherokees" and that, among the Illinois, the French had "whitened the earth of the whole northern quarter." The increasingly commercial nature of the fur trade clearly informed their rejection of English traders. An Alabama speaker, Tamatlémingo, described how "the Englishmen gives no presents to red men, that he gives nothing except for skins, and that those of the village where he lived were obliged to furnish him with food." The lack of gifts coming from the English, their callous demands for food and shelter, and their obsession with financial gain had made the French a popular alternative to a whole series of southeastern villagers.[26]

New France had always desired control over the various networks of interrelated villages that stretched from Montreal to New Orleans. However, it seems more likely that the Shawnees and their neighbors desired neutrality rather than overt declarations of loyalty to the French. The relationships among Alabama-Coushattas at Mucclassee, Sawanogi Shawnees, and a Choctaw chief named Red Shoe offer some clues regarding their motivations in promoting an intertribal peace agreement. The Shawnees knew that the French preferred professions of loyalty but that they often accepted advocates of neutrality as well. At the same time, the French waged war against pro-British chiefs and did everything they could to terrorize their supporters. Like his Piankashaw counterpart in the upper country, Old Briton, a Choctaw chief named Red Shoe became a cautionary tale in matters of trade and alliance. As early as 1734, Bienville learned that Red Shoe, a prominent Choctaw leader, had "remained at the Shawnees" on what they suspected was a Choctaw diplomatic mission to the English colony of South Carolina. When questioned, Red Shoe admitted to a kind of double game in which the Choctaws declared neutrality from both the French and the British. At least initially, Bienville suspected that Red Shoe was much like the Alabama-Coushattas and the Shawnees in that he preferred to remain neutral. He learned that Red Shoe "would not abandon at all the word of the French; that he knew well that the Alabamas saw the Englishmen and the Frenchmen."[27]

But Vaudreuil could not accept the fact that some Choctaws, like the Shawnees and the Alabama-Coushattas, played colonizers against one another, and he began to plot Red Shoe's assassination. He wanted seven or eight of Red Shoe's kinsmen to prove their loyalty, and he requested that "one of them . . . bring me the head of Red Shoe." Vaudreuil asked the Choctaws to "risk everything in order to rid themselves of a man who up to the present had sowed nothing but dissention among them."[28] One French envoy described giving "a red coat" and "two fine shirts" to an Indian warrior who might "rid us of this monster." In June 1747, Red Shoe's professions of neutrality ended when a Choctaw assassin stabbed him in the stomach while he slept. "The tensions of the Anglo-French rivalry" led to Red Shoe's untimely demise, "making a dispute between chiefs into a colonial affair of considerable dimensions." Red Shoe's assassination illustrated how imperial rivalries often became civil wars in Indian country, furthering the divisions within Indian villages.[29]

By 1748, Vaudreuil despaired of achieving a peace favorable to French interests. Like Creek *talwas*, the differences between Shawnee villagers had been enhanced by a century of migration and violence. Peter Chartier's band epitomized the dilemma of Shawnee identity. Vaudreuil advised his commander among the Illinois, M. de Bertet, "to distrust the Shawnees [who had] settled at the fork of the Wabash." Vaudreuil was unaware of Chartier's long-standing disdain for James Logan and the Pennsylvania traders associated with him, and he mistakenly believed that Chartier had "always been accustomed to trade with the English." In 1748, when Chartier's band chose to move near "their [Shawnee] brothers" among the Alabamas, Vaudreuil continued to suspect that they had "harmful intentions toward us," intentions that could only be mitigated through delivery of the high-quality trade goods to which they were accustomed.[30]

For Peter Chartier and many Shawnees like him, the Southeast was a kind of safe haven from British land hunger and Iroquois dominion. They moved toward French Louisiana, first to near what is now Terre Haute, Indiana, and then to Shawnee Town, in southern Illinois. From 1743 to 1748, Shawnee Town villagers became rivals of the Illinois, who had long been the primary trading partners of the French in the prairie-plains. Regional allies such as the Kickapoos and Mascoutins also relocated to the region, increasing the threat to Illinois hunters and traders. Chartier's band lived on the boundary between French Louisiana and French Canada. Piankashaw and Illinois attackers burned their new village and exhumed the graves of their deceased while the Shawnees were hunting. The violence between them jeopardized the French alliance. According to Vaudreuil, such an attack was "past atonement" and beyond his capacity to correct. Shawnees exacted revenge on the Illinois, from whom they took "scalps and slaves in full daylight." Chartier did not agree to halt the reprisals until 1750, when Vaudreuil brokered a peace agreement between the Shawnees and the Illinois at Mobile. [31]

Economic interest also compelled Chartier's band to hunt beyond the Mississippi in search of hides, oil, and tallow. Vaudreuil sometimes called Chartier "the Arkansas Hunter," and he believed that economic competition between the Shawnees and the Illinois in and around the Wabash had "a bad effect" on the French alliance. [32] By the middle of the eighteenth century, Shawnee hunters traveled hundreds of miles beyond their home villages in search of enough fur-bearing animals to support their needs. Saddled with the responsibility of supplying their people with European goods, Shawnees began to travel west of the Mississippi to hunt.

After 1750, Shawnees continued to challenge the Illinois, as well as the Miamis, Weas, and Piankashaws, along the Wabash, for dominance in the Indian trade. Vaudreuil recognized the extent to which Shawnee hunters and diplomats had upset the dynamics of the French and Indian alliance. He noted that the Illinois and Miami tribes along the Wabash were "seeking to avenge themselves for the inroads that the Shawnees have been making upon them in recent years." On the eve of the Seven Years' War, many Shawnees no longer thought of their Central Algonquian relatives as kinsmen. They began joining Upper Creek war parties when they attacked their regional rivals, particularly the Choctaws, in the years preceding the Seven Years' War. In 1754, the French commander at New Orleans, M. de Kerlérec noted that Cherokees and Shawnees had joined Chickasaws in a series of attacks on French traders on the Mississippi River. This particular band of Shawnee and Cherokee allies had not committed treason. Even

Kerlérec had to admit that "they have married among the Chickasaws" and, as a result, fight "under the[ir] name."[33] After King George's War, the French gave up on the dream of unity in Indian country.

Chartier's band may have become estranged from the Miami and the Illinois. But the French knew that the Ohio Shawnees were "relatives of their brother Shawnee with the Alabamas." They relocated to a "refuge near the Alabamas, at a place called the Abikudshis [Abihka]." At this time, the British estimated that 120 men had migrated with Chartier. Sawanogi Shawnees who had been working toward a peace agreement with France now had to incorporate Chartier's people into their community. Chartier quickly became one of the Shawnees' most outspoken ambassadors during annual visits to meet with Vaudreuil at Mobile. He encouraged French officials to think of the Shawnees as a unified nation, even though facts on the ground proved otherwise. During a 1750 visit to Mobile, Chartier assured Vaudreuil that "his entire nation . . . was entirely devoted to us [the French]." Vaudreuil had become suspicious of the Shawnees and less optimistic about a grand interregional alliance. But Vaudreuil played along, because he recognized the esteem in which the Shawnees were held. He cautioned that "it is well to show this nation certain considerations in view of the fact that it has always been strongly attached to us, as well as that of the Alabamas."[34]

While Chartier wanted the French to see the Shawnees as a nation, others described a decentralized polity in which the peculiar demands of colonization and kinship shaped village-based identities. As one Shawnee from Wakatomica, a village along the Muskingum River in eastern Ohio, explained, "I am a Shavanah, and Head of a Town," but "we are distributed by different Names." Shawnee villages composed of both kith and kin made intensely local decisions. These local decisions often imperiled other Shawnee towns because warfare between France and Great Britain had become normative. Shawnees among the Upper Creeks struggled to draw boundaries between themselves and their Shawnee kinsmen in the Ohio Valley.

Violent Encounter and the Centrality of Shawnee Peoples on the Eve of the Seven Years' War

By the middle of the eighteenth century, even those Shawnees who remained in Ohio traveled into the Southeast. Wakatomica Shawnees interested in captive taking descended the Muskingum River, heading south to the Overhill Cherokee town of Chota, before moving against the Catawbas and, in some cases, the Laurel Bay Yuchis. Shawnees affiliated with Sawanogi distanced themselves from these attacks, recognizing that both the British and the French assumed that Shawnees acted in concert, as a nation. For this reason, ten Shawnee headmen living among the Abihka Creeks tried to convince South Carolina governor James Glen of "their good affection for the English upon any occasion."[35]

"Settlement Indians," Native peoples living behind the frontier who were clearly allied with the British colonies, had become easy targets for Cherokee, Iroquois, and Shawnee war parties from the Northeast. In 1751 alone, a single Seneca war party killed twenty-five Laurel Bay Yuchis and dragged ten captives back with them, to western New York. Northern Indian attacks increased in the years leading up to the Seven Years' War, caused in part by the 1744 Treaty of Lancaster, which made it easier for Native warriors to travel through British colonies on their way to attack distant enemies. In 1753, a local militiaman near Laurel Bay named David Godin captured six Shawnee warriors from Wakatomica along the Lower Salkehatchie River, not far from Yuchi settlements. They told Godin that "they were Cherokees and looking for Utchees." Godin then turned the warriors over to Governor Glen, who ordered them jailed. After being imprisoned in Charles Town, the Shawnees acknowledged their true identities. In fact, they were Chalagawtha Shawnees from Wakatomica, and as such they claimed the right to speak on behalf of the Shawnee people. Native peoples from the Ohio country as well as the Southeast recognized the Chalagawthas' status as one of the two Shawnee divisions capable of speaking on their people's behalf. As such, their capture had repercussions throughout Indian country. Itawachcomequa, their chief, denied hunting Yuchis, claiming instead that he "came to find my friend Shirtier [Peter Chartier]." In a separate interrogation, a Shawnee boy admitted to carrying a slave halter with him, in case he "took any prisoners and tied him, I might put it round his neck." Though the Shawnees had been unsuccessful, they admitted that prior to their being captured they had conducted six different raids on the Laurel Bay community. A planter named Morgan Sabb recognized them, testifying that he had seen these same Shawnees in 1751, in an encounter along the Salkehatchie River. Governor Glen became further convinced of their guilt when a Yuchi named King Tom came to the Charles Town jail, pointed to Itawachcomequa, and claimed that the Shawnee chief had taken him prisoner twice. On both occasions, King Tom described how Itawachcomequa had "carried [him] to the Cherokee country."[36]

Governor Glen defended settlement Indians such as the Yuchis because they were "upon many Accounts very serviceable to us." Glen's

King Tom, the Yuchi "king" targeted by the Shawnee warrior Itawachcomequa, may well have been the subject of this painting. "The Indian King and Queen of Uchi," 1736, Georgia, watercolor by Philip Georg Friedrich von Reck, courtesy of The Royal Library, Copenhagen, Denmark.

explanation suggests that the Laurel Bay Yuchis provided the British with intelligence regarding Indian country. The Yuchis understood the dynamics of the backcountry in ways that the British did not. But, more important, the British called on settlement Indians to hunt down runaway slaves. According to Edmond Atkin, those "still living in our settlements" played a vital role in perpetuating the slave economy by insuring that black slaves could not escape, and unite with, Indians of the interior Southeast.[37] Yuchis, Catawbas, and coastal groups allied with Carolina remained necessary to the security of the colonies because "they form part of our Barrier, and if they are cut off, a Door will be left open to the French Indians." Prior to the Seven Years' War, "French Indians," "settlement Indians," and people such as Chartier's Shawnees, whom the British believed were "capable of any Villany," came into collision.[38] The Wakatomica Shawnees now jailed by Governor Glen had crossed paths with all of these townspeople as they moved to and from the Southeast. Early American migrants lived in an increasingly integrated world, and yet they resisted national and interregional unity. They remained parochial cosmopolitans.

The Overhill Cherokees tried to free Itawachcomequa and his Shawnee kinsmen. They warned Governor Glen that holding the Shawnees in prison would surely imperil Carolina and the rest of British North America. Little Carpenter of the Cherokees did not vindicate their actions. However, he warned Glen that "for the sake of the white people that come among us," he would be wise to set them free. If, instead, Glen chose to hold the Shawnees for their attacks on the Yuchis, "the 5 Nations will join these people, and some of the Cherokees" will do the same. Sure enough, when three Shawnees managed to escape from the Charles Town jail, they laid waste to frontier settlements as they made their way back to Wakatomica. Old Hop, the headman at Chota, blamed Governor Glen, who "did not do well by the Savannahs." As if to illustrate his point, the Chalagawtha headman, Itawachcomequa, died shortly after breaking out of jail in Charles Town. Old Hop chided Glen, explaining that he should "have killed them" or done something more so that "they could never return back to their own people." After their escape, the Overhill Cherokees understood what the British did not. The Cherokees knew that the Shawnees, as the "greatest travellers in America," were known and respected by thousands of tribesmen. A chain of interrelated and allied towns would mobilize for war against the British. Glen hoped that Woodland Indian "nations" would yield to his will. Instead, Glen watched with horror as Indian towns, from Alabama to New York, learned of Glen's ill-treatment of the Shawnee prisoners.[39]

For their part, the Wakatomica Shawnees could not understand Governor Glen's defense of the settlement Indians. In the proving ground of slavery and American land hunger, Shawnees had adopted racialized notions of identity. They complained that "their business was with red and not white people." And unlike their Yuchi victims, who chose to live behind the frontier, the Wakatomica Shawnees had migrated west and had forestalled dependence on the British. But after they had been captured and imprisoned, they had to admit that even those Shawnees who desired a measure of autonomy remained wedded to colonizers. For Skiagunsta of the Cherokees, "red" and "white" worlds were inseparable. He conceded that "every necessary thing in life we must have from the white people."[40]

The Indian slave trade that had so decimated the Middle Ohio Valley in the seventeenth century had become an integral part of Shawnee identity. The killing and capture of Indian people remained central to manhood and the achievement of respect. Well into the 1760s, Shawnees sometimes referred to their victims as slaves. Initially, Shawnees viewed their captives as little more than war trophies. But if they survived the ordeal, the captives' humanity was restored and they became full-fledged members of Shawnee society. For much of the eighteenth century, Shawnee captive taking resembled Iroquois models of warfare.[41]

Among historians, the Shawnees are most well known for their diplomatic and military efforts on behalf of pan-Indian resistance movements between the Seven Years' War and the War of 1812. Tecumseh's grand tour of the Southeast on behalf of his revitalization movement has garnered a significant amount of attention. But a longer history of warfare, trade, and migration laid the groundwork for the revitalization movements that proliferated across the Eastern Woodlands between the Seven Years' War and the War of 1812. The Shawnees became vital participants in these social movements because they managed to convert travel away from their homeland into one of their principal strengths. By the eighteenth century, Shawnee had become a trade language, and Native peoples and colonizers alike recognized Shawnees as the principal architects of intertribal alliances east of the Mississippi River. By migrating out of their Fort Ancient homeland and adapting to new colonial circumstances, the Shawnees used their parochial, yet cosmopolitan, origins to maximum effect.[42]

epilogue

Reconsidering the "Literary Advantage"

The appropriation of a past by conquest carries with it the risk of rebounding upon the conquerors. It can end up sacralizing the past for the subject people and encouraging them to use it in their effort to define and affirm their own identity.
—Ranajit Guha, Dominance without Hegemony, *1997*[1]

Since the eighteenth century, eyewitnesses and historians have misunderstood both the causes of migration in the Eastern Woodlands and the varied motivations of migrants. For many American Indians and colonizers, long-distance migrants were inherently treacherous. The Shawnees have lived with these misconceptions for centuries. And because the Shawnees typically occupied perilous borderlands between competing colonizers, they developed a reputation for violence. When faced with oblivion, through combinations of coalescence and military defeat, Shawnees moved on. Each new location seemed to illustrate that an "innate sense of tribalism" inclined the various Shawnee villages toward "collective violence."[2]

Colonizers laid the groundwork for this literary assault on the Shawnees and their migratory neighbors well before the founding of Jamestown. Armed first with the written word, the English made "the civilizing mission" a rationale for conquest. Europeans depended on science and technology to support their essential superiority.[3] In contrast, American Indians were thought of as barbaric because they migrated often, especially as warfare became endemic. English cultural assumptions regarding technology, warfare, and mobility provided the lens through which the English justified their authority over Native peoples. Settler societies had long equated associated societies that depended on seasonal migrations with barbarism. The Elizabethan colonizer Sir John Davies used the seasonal round of the Gaelic Irish to justify the English conquest of their homelands. In 1612, Davies explained that prior to Roman conquest, ancient Britons were "rude and dispersed" people who, because of their mobility, were "prone upon every occasion to make war." Ever in debt to their Roman conquerors, reformed Englishmen in the early modern world believed that it was their duty to compel people who migrated seasonally to adopt the virtues of settled life. The English colonization of Ireland thus became the opening act in the longer history of English colonization. The conquest of Ireland provided the intellectual—and legal—basis for the assertion of English sovereignty over Indian lands, particularly those beyond the Appalachian Mountains, because the interior of the continent had become a haven for dispossessed and migratory peoples from the mid-Atlantic to the Upper Great Lakes.[4]

Historians and cartographers of British North America, from Cadwallader Colden to John Mitchell, argued that the Iroquois had conquered the Shawnee people and that they had secured, by right of conquest, the ability to sell their lands. As historian Jill Lepore points out, "War is, at least in part, a contest for meaning." The Shawnees avoided conquest, but they lost the larger battle over their rights to the lands of the Middle Ohio Valley. They survived without legal sovereignty. Europeans, and the British in particular, justified this legal conquest because they believed that transience and violence were antithetical to civilization. Central Algonquians such as the Shawnees, the Miamis, and the Illinois watched as the British and their Iroquois allies used the power of the written word to define what the chaos of colonization meant. The "literary advantage" of colonizers became the Achilles' heel of oral societies that were on the move. For most of the eighteenth century, the English used the written word to resolve questions of sovereignty and land ownership to their advantage.[5]

During the Seven Years' War, nearly one hundred years after the Iroquois allegedly defeated the Shawnees in the Middle Ohio Valley, the British and the Iroquois signed a series of treaties that formally divested the Shawnees and the Delawares, among others, of their land in western Pennsylvania and beyond. Between 1754 and 1760, the British laid claim to Iroquois military history and used it to creatively imagine British sovereignty, from the Atlantic Ocean to the Mississippi River. British cartographer John Mitchell explicitly linked Iroquois and British military history, from the seventeenth to the eighteenth centuries, in his 1757 map of North America. In the Lower Great Lakes region, Mitchell explained, "the Six Nations have extended their Territories to the River Illinois ever since the year 1672, when they subdued, and were incorporated with the antient Chaouanons." Mitchell believed that through the Iroquois, the

"Ohio Indians" came "under the Six Nations," and, by extension, the British empire.[6]

Cartographic sparring between colonizers was commonplace in the eighteenth century. In 1720, the governor of New York, William Burnet, complained of "Mapps published at Paris" because they made "encroachments on the Kings territories." The British were particularly incensed about Guillaume De l'Isle's maps of 1703 and 1718 because they named the land and its people from the Great Lakes to the border with Pennsylvania. As Governor Burnet and the English well knew, the power to name became the power to own. De l'Isle, like John Mitchell, may have speculated on behalf of his sovereign, but in the competition between empires, such cartographic assertions became the means by which colonizers laid claim to the land and its people.[7]

James Logan also acted as the official historian of Indian-white relations for the colony of Pennsylvania. In his rendering of the past, he described the Shawnees as "Southern Indians," who migrated to Pennsylvania in 1698. He described how the Shawnees "had joined themselves to the Sasquahannah Indians who were dependent on the Five Nations." Because the Susquehannocks became "answerable for their good behavior," the Shawnees had become "dependents" of the Five Nations. From 1698 onward, Pennsylvanians treated them as "our Indians." Logan described how the Shawnees had "bound themselves" to the Susquehannocks and the Iroquois. Since then, proprietary officials recalled how "about the year 1727," Shawnees had committed "outrages" in Pennsylvania. In response, Shawnees fled to the Ohio country, where they "put themselves under the protection of the French, who received them as their children." Pennsylvania's governor, Robert Hunter Morris, agreed with this understanding of history and concluded that "this Province has ever been remarkable for its just and favourable Treatment of the Indians."[8] Governor Morris and his provincial council viewed the thousands of Indian migrants to Pennsylvania as squatters and as dependents of the Iroquois, without any legal rights to the land set aside for them. Lands set aside for both the Shawnees and the Delawares in Pennsylvania were owned by the Iroquois, and migrant tribes resided there at their pleasure.

These far-reaching claims to the interior of the continent, and to the Middle Ohio Valley, might seem irrelevant. But for Algonquians such as the Shawnees, the Delawares, and the Miamis, these intellectual and cartographic imaginings had real consequences. The English supported the Iroquois contention that they had conquered the heart of the continent, and Shawnee territory, in particular. In the Iroquois telling of the story, the

Haudenosaunee were the primary reason why the Shawnees abandoned their homeland. Englishmen's interest in the Iroquois wars was driven mainly by their increasingly continental vision of territorial expansion. As early as 1607, the year in which Jamestown became the first permanent English settlement, Englishmen wondered how they might lawfully divest American Indians of their lands.[9]

In 1763, Sir William Johnson, the British superintendent of Indian Affairs, clearly defined the relationship between Iroquois military history and British land hunger. Johnson was married to Molly Brant, sister of Mohawk sachem Thayendanegea, or Joseph Brant. Familial, diplomatic, and military ties continually reinforced his understanding of the Middle Ohio Valley. According to Johnson, the Iroquois claim to the Ohio "and thence to the [Great] Lakes is not [in] the least disputed by the Shawnees and Delawares."[10] In 1732, the Shawnees themselves described how the Iroquois had ordered them to return "back to the Ohioh, The place from whence you Came." Shawnees then living in Pennsylvania saw the Ohio Valley as their homeland, despite their more than sixty years of exile. One Shawnee diplomat clearly had subversive intentions, including undermining British confidence in the alliance with the Iroquois. According to the Shawnee, the Iroquois had failed to put "pettycoatts" on them. While the Iroquois used feminized portrayals of the Shawnees and Delawares to block them from direct talks with the British, Indian migrants rejected such characterizations. In their telling of the story, the Iroquois had come to the Shawnees and asked them to "fall upon and fight with the English." The Shawnees had rebuffed the Iroquois, citing their own "League" with the British, which they "Canott break." Time and again, Shawnee speakers described themselves as autonomous actors, driven to migrate, and sometimes to fight, as members of independent villages. Nevertheless, the artifice of Iroquois dominion remained inviolate.[11]

By 1811, the Covenant Chain between the Iroquois and the English had become legendary. In that year, the governor of New York, DeWitt Clinton, characterized the Iroquois as "the Romans of this Western World." For the next 175 years, Clinton's characterization informed the widespread belief that the Iroquois were the Native emperors of the lands beyond the mountains. Clinton claimed that the twin merchants of death—the Iroquois and Old World epidemics—combined to depopulate much of the upper country.[12] More recently, scholars have tempered this understanding, and the power of the Iroquois has become more "ambiguous" as a result.[13]

The British certainly overstated Iroquois conquest to enact a very real series of devastating land cessions from the peoples of the upper country.

Yet these legal contrivances hardly amount to historical and legal collusion between the Iroquois and British historians. Indeed, the Iroquois are, perhaps, the greatest literary victims of these misunderstandings. Historians then, and now, have not adequately captured the lived realities of seventeenth- and eighteenth-century Iroquois and Algonquian histories. The Iroquois, as well as the Indians they attacked, struggled against a complex series of colonial forces. Far from being "Roman" conquerors intent on dominating those who stood in their way, the Iroquois cooperated with their Indian neighbors to a greater degree than has been previously understood.[14] These revisions of Iroquois history suggest that complex circumstances drove villagers from the Ohio Valley to abandon their homes and embrace new, colonial worlds.

History, memory, and power combined to disenfranchise the Shawnees of the Ohio Valley during the Seven Years' War. As early as 1732, James Logan learned that Chartier "expects land of us."[15] Again, in 1753, Shawnee leaders complained that "satisfaction had not been made to them by the Proprietaries" for lands that they had lost in Pennsylvania.[16] Chartier and the Shawnees understood themselves to be independent actors, people who migrated to and from Pennsylvania on their own terms. Far from being subjects of the Iroquois or dependents of Pennsylvania, they did not equate generations of movement into violent, colonial borderlands with the loss of sovereignty. Quite the opposite. For the Shawnees, movement became a strategy deployed to preserve what remained of their independence.

The Indian slave trade, Iroquois mourning wars, and disease created ephemeral alliances that necessitated frequent removals. In the 1840s, a Shawnee man named Spybuck knew enough of his history to link himself to the Savannah River Shawnees. His story of survival and adaptation acknowledged the vital role that intertribal alliances have played in Shawnee history. Nevertheless, Spybuck acknowledged the Yuchi creation story, which rejects coalescence, preferring instead a world in which "each tribe goes its own way." In January 1842, amateur historian Thomas Woodward encountered Spybuck somewhere along the Washita River on the southern plains. Woodward had lived among the Creeks in Alabama, and he had subsequently migrated west to Texas, where he found Spybuck traveling along with "a few Cherokees, some Choctaws, one or two Chickasaws, and a Delaware." Spybuck's delegation reflected the wide range of Shawnee migrations and the alliances built across the colonial world. Both Spybuck and Woodward traveled alongside people whose tragic histories had been joined since the dawn of colonialism. Woodward "had some Uchee negroes that spoke the Uchee, Creek, and Hitcheta." And so it was that Spybuck, speaking Uchee with Woodward's multilingual "Uchee negroes," described how the Shawnees had been "forced back from the Savannah and the settlements of the Musqua, in Alabama and Georgia."[17] Spybuck knew *his* version of Shawnee history, and it was a history of migration, conflict, and survival across the centuries.[18]

Notes

Abbreviations

AM   William Hand Browne, ed., *Archives of Maryland*, vols. 1–26 (Baltimore: Maryland Historical Society, 1883–1912)

BT-BPRO   Board of Trade, Maryland, 1696–99, British Public Record Office, Kew, UK

CSP   *Calendar of State Papers: Colonial Series, America and West Indies*, ed. W. Noel Sainsbury (British Public Record Office, London, 1860)

DCNY   E. B. O'Callaghan, ed., *Documents Relative to the Colonial History of the State of New York* (Albany: Weed, Parsons, 1855)

DRIA   William L. McDowell, ed., *Documents Relating to Indian Affairs, May 21, 1750–August 7, 1754* (Columbia: South Carolina Archives Department, 1958)

ETM-DPL   "English Translation of Margry," Detroit Public Library, Detroit, Mich.

EWV-NL   Erminie Wheeler-Voegelin Papers, Newberry Library, Chicago

FRW   Reuben Gold Thwaites, ed., *Collections of the Wisconsin State Historical Society: The French Regime in Wisconsin, 1727–48* (Madison: State Historical Society of Wisconsin, 1906)

HSP   Historical Society of Pennsylvania, Philadelphia

JR   Reuben Gold Thwaites, ed., *The Jesuit Relations and Allied Documents* (Cleveland: Burrows Brothers, 1896–1901)

LFP   Logan Family Papers, Historical Society of Pennsylvania, Philadelphia

LP   Logan Papers, Historical Society of Pennsylvania, Philadelphia

MPA   Dunbar Rowland and A. G. Sanders, eds., *Mississippi Provincial Archives, 1729–1740, French Dominion* (Jackson: Mississippi Department of Archives and History Press, 1927)

MPA-FD   Patricia Galloway, ed., *Mississippi Provincial Archives, 1729–1748, French Dominion* (Baton Rouge: Louisiana State University Press, 1984)

MPCP   Samuel Hazard, ed., *Minutes of the Provincial Council of Pennsylvania* (Harrisburg: Theo. Fenn, 1851–53)

PA   Samuel Hazard, ed., *Pennsylvania Archives, Selected and Arranged from Original Documents in the Office of the Secretary of the Commonwealth*, First Series, vols. 1–12, (Philadelphia: Joseph Severns, 1852–56)

RBPRO-SC   Alexander S. Salley, comp., *Records of the British Public Record Office–South Carolina, 1663–1710* (Columbia: Historical Commission of South Carolina, 1931)

SP-BPRO   Shaftesbury Papers, British Public Record Office, Kew, UK

Chapter 1

1. On allotment, see Hoxie, *A Final Promise*, 44, 70–73; and Atkin, *Appalachian Indian Frontier*, 65. For a description of northeastern Oklahoma and the removed tribes who live there, see Goins and Goble, *Historical Atlas of Oklahoma*, 110–11. Edmond Atkin, a prominent merchant and political figure in South Carolina, went on to become the Southern Superintendent of Indian Affairs. He puzzled over the Shawnees' place in the Southeast, until settling on the notion that they were extraordinary, "the Greatest Travellers in America."

2. Joel Barnes, Ben Barnes, and Greg Pitcher, interview with author, Miami, Okla., February 27, 2012. For the Native American Church, see Stewart, *Peyote Religion*. For Shawnee burial practices, see Wheeler-Voegelin, *Mortuary Customs*, 293, 402. The Shawnees typically lay log slabs in an open-ended "box" over the corpse. The steel pipe was used because this particular grave was ensconced in concrete. George Blanchard, one of the few remaining Shawnees who conducts traditional funerals, notches an opening in the wood to allow for the soul to travel to the west, to the place of the dead. George Blanchard, telephone interview with author, May 11, 2012.

3. Her mother's allotment had been near Alluwe, and she moved to Quapaw with her white husband (Richard Jenks Barnes), who was born in Jenks, Indian Territory, in 1907. The family moved there at the urging of Irvin Wilson, a Quapaw. He let them live there for no rent, and he let Ben's grandfather Richard work for him in trade. Ben Barnes wrote: "If it wasn't for Quapaw generosity, there would have been a great many more folks that never would have had the chance to not only thrive, but even exist." Ben Barnes, email communication with author, May 31, 2012.

4. Warren, "Prairie Tribes," 223–25; Foster, *Being Comanche*.

5. Satz, *American Indian Policy in the Jacksonian Era*. Other examples of the Indian Removal Act and the perpetuation of the vanishing Indian thesis include Remini, *Andrew Jackson and His Indian Wars*; and Richard White, *Middle Ground*. For correctives to the general pattern of ending the history of removed tribes in 1830, see Warren, *The Shawnees and Their Neighbors*; and Bowes, *Exiles and Pioneers*.

6. Atkin, *Appalachian Indian Frontier*, 65.

7. Ben Barnes, interview with author, White Oak, Okla., May 25, 2012.

8. Andy Warrior, interview with author, Little Axe, Okla., August 10, 2005. For more on the War Dance, see Howard, *Shawnee*, 273–85.

9. For the performance of ritual, see Peña, *Performing Piety*, 145–52. For analogous beliefs and practices among the Shawnees' neighbors, see Jackson, *Yuchi Ceremonial Life*, chap. 3.

10. These reflections derive from my attendance at the Bread Dances of both the North and the South Stomp Ground. Author's Ethnographic Field Notes, Little Axe, Okla., October 2009.

11. For more on the War Dance and its intertribal context, see Jackson, "A Yuchi War Dance in 1736," 27–32. On Kickapoo participation in the Shawnee War Dance, see Author's Ethnographic Field Notes, Little Axe, Okla., August 2005. For a contemporary description of the War Dance, see Warren, *The Shawnees and Their Neighbors*, 4–5.

12. For the best descriptions of Shawnee Bread Dances, see Joe Billie, interview with C. F. Voegelin, Shawnee, folders 1–3 (1934), series VI, notebooks, C. F. Voegelin Papers, American Philosophical Society, Philadelphia. See also Alford, *Civilization*, 57–60; and Howard, *Shawnee*, 245–62.

13. Erminie Wheeler-Voegelin to William Fenton, February 20, 1937, box 35, folder 314, EWV-NL; George Blanchard, interview with author, Little Axe, Okla., July 2007. Here I follow William Roseberry, who argues for anthropologies that see "the Other as different but connected, a product of a particular history that is connected but intertwined with a larger set of economic, political, social, and cultural processes to such an extent that analytical separation of 'our' history and 'their' history is impossible." Roseberry, *Anthropologies and Histories*, 13.

14. Author's Ethnographic Field Notes, Little Axe, Okla., June 2005, June 2007.

15. For more on the Loyal Shawnees, see Warren, *The Shawnees and Their Neighbors*, esp. chap. 6. For an overview of Shawnee customs and some of the differences among the three federally recognized tribes, see Howard, *Shawnee*. For an analogous history of the Delawares, see Obermeyer, *Delaware Tribe in a Cherokee Nation*.

16. For Eastern Shawnee and Absentee Shawnee membership numbers, see Oklahoma Indian Affairs Commission, *2011 Oklahoma Indian Nations Pocket Pictorial Directory*, 14, 2. Not much has been written about either the Seneca-Cayugas or the Absentee Shawnees in Oklahoma. For an initial discussion of the Seneca-Cayugas, see Hauptman, *Iroquois in the Civil War*, chap. 7. For an Absentee Shawnee perspective on Shawnee history, albeit from a rare advocate for the allotment of their lands, see Alford, *Civilization*.

17. Foreman, *Indian Removal*; Anthony F. C. Wallace, *Long, Bitter Trail*; Perdue and Green, *Cherokee Removal*.

18. Jackson quoted in Remini, *Andrew Jackson and His Indian Wars*, 231.

19. For examples of scholars who promote the idea that removed tribes have lost their unique tribal identities, see Hamill, *Going Indian*, 61 (who argues that removal, allotment, and education in Oklahoma "contribute to the construction of an Indian ethnic identity"); Howard, "Compleat Stomp Dancer," 5–6; and Howard, "Pan-Indian Culture of Oklahoma," 215–20. For a refutation of these arguments, see Jackson, "Opposite of Powwow."

20. For more on the Yuchis and the practice of "helping out" between tribes in Oklahoma, see Jackson, *Yuchi Ceremonial Life*, chap. 6.

21. Chief Charles Diebold, telephone interview, May 25, 2012. For evidence regarding Shawnee involvement at Cowskin, see Paul Barton, interview with author, Cowskin Ceremonial Ground, June 2004. For Shawnee keepers of False Face masks, see Frank Daugherty, "False Face," IX, 80, C. F. Voegelin Papers, American Philosophical Society, Philadelphia.

22. Warren, *The Shawnees and Their Neighbors*, chap. 2; Chief Charles Diebold, telephone interview, May 25, 2012.

23. Lora Nucholls, interview with author, Eastern Shawnee Tribal Library, June 2004. For more on the position of women in Iroquois society, see Tooker, "Northern Iroquoian Sociopolitical Organization," 93.

24. For a summary of these migrations, see Jennings, *Ambiguous Iroquois Empire*, 186–202. For the Mekoche division, see Warren and Noe, "Greatest Travelers in

America," 169–70. For the Shawnee migration from Fort St. Louis to Maryland, see Hanna, *Wilderness Trail*, 1:137, 152.

25. Fur, *A Nation of Women*, 5–6; Schutt, *Peoples of the River Valleys*, 94–103. For the Delawares and intertribal kinship systems, see Smolenski, *Friends and Strangers*, 200, 203.

26. For more on the alliance between Shawnees and Delawares, see Warren, *The Shawnees and Their Neighbors*, chap. 3; and Obermeyer, *Delaware Tribe in a Cherokee Nation*. Greg Pitcher, interview with author, Miami, Okla., May 2011; Greg Pitcher, interview with author, St. Louis, August 2011. For enrollment figures, see Oklahoma Indian Affairs Commission, *2011 Oklahoma Indian Nations Pocket Pictorial Directory*, 34.

27. Scott Miller and Andy Warrior, interview with author, Brendle Corner, Okla., June 25, 2007.

28. Selstad, "Carrying the World Along," 39. For more on the movement of southeastern villages across space and time, see Jackson, "Opposite of Powwow."

29. Until recently, regional approaches to colonial America have had a tendency to overplay the distinctions between Native peoples from the Northeast and those from the Southeast. For examples of the regional approach to colonial and American Indian histories, see Nellis, *An Empire of Regions*; and Snyder, *Slavery in Indian Country*.

30. This book draws inspiration from Fernand Braudel, whose 1958 essay in *Annales* described the necessity of viewing the past over the *longue dureé*, of taking an interdisciplinary view of history, one that emphasizes continuity as much as change in gaining an understanding of human societies. See Braudel, "Histoire et Science Sociale."

31. For introductions to Fort Ancient archaeology in the precontact and protohistoric periods, see Drooker, "Ohio Valley, 1550–1750," 118–23; Drooker, *View from Madisonville*; and Henderson, "Fort Ancient Period," 839.

32. For the Miami-Potawatomi settlement pattern, see Fitting and Cleland, "Late Prehistoric Settlement Patterns," 297–300. For an argument that corn agriculture became more, not less, important to the Potawatomis during the colonial period, see O'Gorman, "Myth of Moccasin Bluff," 396. For corn agriculture among the Fort Ancient, see Nass, "Fort Ancient Agricultural Systems and Settlement," 327, 344; and Sharp, "Fort Ancient Farmers," 170–76.

33. See Griffin, "Fort Ancient Has No Class," 53–37. On Big Men in tribal societies, see Sahlins, "Poor Man, Rich Man," 289–92. For a more definitive treatment of chiefly authority, see Earle and Johnson, *Evolution of Human Societies*.

34. For an overview of the late and protohistoric Middle Ohio Valley, see Drooker and Cowan, "Transformation of the Fort Ancient Cultures of the Central Ohio Valley," table 8.1; and Merrell, *The Indians' New World*, viii. For the North-South trade axis, see Fox, "North-South Copper Axis," esp. 90–94.

35. Henry Woodward, "A Faithfull Relation," 130–34. For a brief summary of the Shawnees on the Middle Savannah River, see Milling, *Red Carolinians*, 84–91.

36. For the alliance at Starved Rock, see Richard White, *Middle Ground*, 136, 146. For Tonty (French spelling, Tonti), see Murphy, *Henry de Tonty*, chaps. 2, 3. On Shawnee coalescence at Kaskaskia, see La Salle to La Barre, Fort St. Louis, April 2, 1683, ETM-DPL, 2:313.

37. For the Seneca-Susquehannock Wars and the colonization of Maryland, see Menard and Carr, "The Lords Baltimore and the Colonization of Maryland," 171. For a closer look at the Seneca-Susquehannock Wars, see Sempowski, "Early Historic Exchange," 214–16. For the most recent history of the Potomac River and the Susquehannocks and their relationship to colonists in Maryland, see Rice, *Nature and History in the Potomac Country*, 128, 152. For "Naked" and "Inland" Indians in Maryland, see Francis Nicholson to the Council, March 27, 1697, folio a15, CO 5/714, BT-BPRO.

38. Native peoples in the colonial period have been assigned a wide array of sociopolitical identities in recent scholarship. They have ranged from empires to nations to coalescent peoples. In the Northeast, historian Sami Lakomäki has even gone so far as to describe the Shawnees as a "nation" in the colonial period. See Lakomäki, "Building a Shawnee Nation," 199–224; and Lakomäki, "Singing the King's Song." I subscribe to Francis Jennings's argument—he wrote that "political phenomena are too multifarious and fluctuating to encourage a hope that any scheme of nomenclature will achieve universal validity." See Jennings, *Ambiguous Iroquois Empire*, 38.

39. A well-researched book on Tecumseh is Sugden, *Tecumseh*, 22, 31. For other biographical sketches of Tecumseh, see Calloway, *The Shawnees and the War for America*, chap. 7; and Edmunds, *Tecumseh and the Quest for Indian Leadership*.

40. Speech taken from Sugden, *Tecumseh*, 128, 189. For more on Tecumseh's place in reimagining Native polities in the Old Northwest, see Warren, *The Shawnees and Their Neighbors*, chap. 1; and Harrison to Eustis, August 7, 1811, in Clanin, *Papers of William Henry Harrison*, 684–88.

41. Both Brant and Tecumseh dreamed of consolidating tribal and intertribal divisions in the Lower Great Lakes/Ohio Valley region. Both men identified the problem of factionalism but offered very different approaches to its resolution. Brant based his argument on Iroquois mediation of a "dish with one spoon" on an understanding of the Haudenosaunee as an imperial power. As victims of that power, Tecumseh rejected the right of either the British or the Iroquois to act on behalf of the Algonquian peoples of the interior. Tecumseh focused on a history of racial oppression rather than a history of Iroquois dominion to achieve Indian unity. Brant to Simcoe, Miami Rapids, August 4, 1793, John Graves Simcoe Papers, vol. 67, Manuscript Division, William L. Clements Library, University of Michigan, Ann Arbor.

42. For two recent studies of revitalization movements in the *pays d'en haut*, see Dowd, *War under Heaven*; and Brooks, *Common Pot*.

43. Interested readers should consult Sugden, *Blue Jacket*, in addition to Sugden's biography of Tecumseh. See also Dowd, *Spirited Resistance*.

44. See, for example, Silver, *Our Savage Neighbors*.

45. Parkman, *Conspiracy of Pontiac*, 32.

46. Mooney quoted in Blair, *Indian Tribes*, 335n223.

47. Tweed, *Crossing and Dwelling*, 11. Historian Colin Calloway has written of the Shawnees that "no Indian people had moved so often, traveled so widely, or knew better how the invaders had eroded Indian country." See Calloway, *The Shawnees and the War for America*, 20–21. Métis traders such as Peter Chartier certainly contributed to the extraordinary range of Shawnee migrations as well as the perception that somehow Shawnee history is exceptional. For examples of Shawnee exceptionalism, see Merrell,

Into the American Woods, 74–75. For more on the work of Marc Bloch, Fernand Braudel, and Lucien Febvre, principal architects of the Annales school, see Burke, *French Historical Revolution*.

48. Callender, "Shawnee," 634.

49. Wheeler-Voegelin, *Mortuary Customs*, 228–29.

50. Linguistic naysayers overlook the fact that geographic descriptors frequently represent ethnic groups. To cite just two examples, the term "Miami" derives from the Central Algonquian term *myaamia*, or "downstream people," while *meškwahki-haki* means "red earths" in the Algonquian language. For naysayers, see Pearson, "Savannah and Shawnee," 19–22. For linguistic associations between place and identity, see Costa, "Miami-Illinois Tribe Names," 50; and Callender, "Fox," 636.

51. Merrell, *The Indians' New World*, viii. See also Merrell, "The Indians' New World." Perhaps the most obvious example of the rupture of colonialism is Richard White, *Middle Ground*. Other examples of rupture for the Ohio Valley include McConnell, *A Country Between*. Archaeologists have been working for more than a decade to link the archaeological record to the history of the Ohio Valley. See, for example, Drooker, *View from Madisonville*. See also Henderson, "Dispelling the Myth," among many other works by Henderson on the subject.

52. Archaeologists working to close the gap between the prehistoric and colonial periods include Penelope Drooker and Gwynn Henderson. See, for example, Drooker, *View from Madisonville*; and Henderson, "Dispelling the Myth."

53. While important continuities link Shawnee villages to their Fort Ancient ancestors, it is also true that the shifting regional characteristics of their Indian and non-Indian neighbors shaped and maintained Shawnee identities during the colonial period. Shawnee migrations became case studies in what sociologists Michèle Lamont and Virág Molnár describe as "process[es] of differentiation." Following Fredrick Barth, I argue that historians must adopt a "relational approach to ethnicity." See Lamont and Molnár, "Study of Boundaries in the Social Sciences," 170, 174; and Barth, *Ethnic Groups and Boundaries*, 9–38. Important works on ethnogenesis include Roosens, *Creating Ethnicity*.

54. Hickerson, *Jumanos*, 212. On the dyadic nature of identities in the colonial period, see Anderson, *Betrayal of Faith*, 11–69.

55. Sahlins, *Tribesmen*, 15–16; Béteille, "Concept of Tribe," 300. Historians' desire to view Native peoples in the colonial era as members of protean nations has made it more difficult to trace continuities between precontact and postcontact worlds. The anthropologist Marshall Sahlins once attempted to explain the amorphous, seemingly random, nature of tribal societies through the lens of what he called the "segmentary society." Tribal peoples, in Sahlins's view, saw themselves as members of a series of concentric circles, with family first, lineage second, and village, subtribe, and, ultimately, tribe as the outer rings of these concentric circles of importance. The beauty of tribes, Sahlins argued, was their ability to break apart and re-aggregate as the situation warranted. In times of military distress, aggregation as a "tribe" was warranted. But most of the time families and lineages determined daily routines. This was especially true during winter, when wild animals were lean with hunger and difficult to track through heavy winter snows and frozen streams. At these times, it was best to rely on one's

family, or, at most, one's lineage, to survive. For Sahlins, tribal societies are contingent and situational polities that, by their very nature, resist definition. By way of contrast, European colonizers championed nation-states that depended on the use of law and force to compel a fair amount of unity across a geographically widespread population.

56. David D. Hall, *Lived Religion in America*; Foster, *Being Comanche*.

57. Tribal histories, regional studies, and microhistories, when conducted separately, often miss critical components of American Indian identities. But if we integrate these varied perspectives, we can come closer to seeing American Indians as dynamic agents navigating their way through colonial worlds. Religious Studies professor Thomas A. Tweed suggests that we avoid "an omnispective 'view of the whole.'" Based in part on the theories of Michel de Certeau, who rightly criticized scholars for assuming a third-person omniscient voice in the writing of culture and history, Tweed calls for a more "kinetic" description of "homemaking." In his view, "spatial and temporal orientation" requires scholars to examine "individual as well as collective" expressions of identity. Tweed, *Crossing and Dwelling*, 10, 84, 89; de Certeau, *Culture in the Plural*, 123.

58. On contingency in history, see Hackett-Fischer, *Washington's Crossing*, 7–30; and McPherson, *Antietam*, 154. McPherson defines contingency simply as "what might have happened."

59. Miles, *Ties That Bind*, 152, 158. Miles has written that "deriving meaning and tradition from the land is especially important to Indian people." Her assessment of the devastation wrought by the Indian Removal Act is poignant and widely accepted. And yet, for thousands of Indian people including the Shawnees, migration away from their sacred homelands had become a necessary condition of survival by the mid-seventeenth century.

60. Sherman Tiger, interview with author, Shawnee, Okla., June 2006; Burns, transcript of interview with Andy Warrior.

61. Geographer Yi-Fu Tuan writes that "religion could either bind a person to place or free them from it." See Tuan, *Space and Place*, 152.

62. Kinietz and Wheeler-Voegelin, *Shawnese Traditions*, 1–8.

63. Ibid.; Swanton, *Social Organization and Social Usages*, 627. Swanton corroborates the Shawnee Prophet's belief that the alliance was built upon the Creeks' need for the Shawnees' supernatural and medicinal powers.

64. The Prophet's account also suggests that the five divisions of the Shawnees were autonomous political units that shared a common culture. According to the Prophet, "Finding that other nations had sprung up, the Shawanese, Pickaways, and Kishpookoo divisions or tribes of the Shawnee nation began to war upon the Catawba Indians. In their first expedition, they took two female Catawba prisoners who found their way into the possession of one of the Mekoce family."

65. Truman Michelson, collection of legends, etc., received from Joseph Nocktonick, Shawnee, Okla. (1934), manuscript 2719, Smithsonian Institution, National Anthropological Archives, Washington, D.C.

66. George Blanchard, interview with author, Little Axe, Okla., October 27, 2005. Blanchard argued that the survival of the Shawnee divisions depended on movement. Now place-bound in Oklahoma, "a lot of people nowadays don't know" their division.

67. Nabokov, *A Forest of Time*, vi–ix.

68. Historian Colin Calloway writes that for the Shawnees, "tribal homelands were hallowed ground. They drew both physical and spiritual sustenance from it." Historian James Taylor Carson expands his focus, writing that for American Indians from the Southeast, "removal triggered a crisis of cosmology because it upset the spiritual systems of ritual and power that [southeastern] Native Americans had written into the landscape." To the southwest, anthropologist Keith Basso's powerful assessment of Western Apache "place-making" makes clear the "moral significance of geographic locations." In *Where the Lightning Strikes*, anthropologist Peter Nabokov universalizes these ideas. Nabokov contends that American Indian "attitudes and ethics about beings and forces that reside in the natural environment . . . remain a bedrock of American Indian belief systems." Carson sees the Indian Removal Act as the initial act of cultural genocide achieved by attacking tribal homelands through forced relocation. See Basso, *Wisdom Sits in Places*, 61; Calloway, *The Shawnees and the War for America*, 8; Carson, "Ethnogeography and the Native American Past," 769; and Nabokov, *Where the Lightning Strikes*, xiii. For additional examples, see Martin, *The Land Looks After Us*; and Feld and Basso, *Senses of Place*.

69. Richard White prefers villages. But the model of Creek towns makes more sense for the Shawnees because they functioned as political units in which diplomatic, religious, and political leadership are intertwined. For an ethnohistorical description of Creek towns, see Ethridge, *Creek Country*, 94–97; and Richard White, *Middle Ground*, 17.

70. Many anthropologists and historians continue to argue that American Indian identities derive from the land itself. I cannot speak for the communities west of the Mississippi, but my guess is that scholars have failed to grasp the profoundly different notions of place and identity east and west of the Mississippi. Taos Pueblo, for example, is the oldest continuously inhabited village in North America. To cite another example, the recent conflict between the Navajo Nation and the Arizona Snowbowl Ski Resort in Arizona confirms that sacred geography is of fundamental importance to many American Indians, particularly those in the western United States. Native intellectual Vine Deloria argues that space is "determinative of the way that we experience things" and further that "American Indians hold their lands—places—as having the highest possible meaning, and all their statements are made with this reference point in mind." Deloria, *God Is Red*, xvi, 61. Woodland Indian history tells a different story, one in which ritual performance, intertribal alliances, and linguistic diversity enabled small, mobile communities to resist amalgamation into larger southeastern and Iroquoian syntheses.

71. Recognition of these migrations also places the Indian Removal Era in a larger, longer context of geographic mobility.

72. Andy Warrior, interview with author, Little Axe, Okla., June 2005.

Chapter 2

1. A. Gwynn Henderson, telephone communication with author, April 29, 2012. For the best description of the 1937 flood, see Berry, *Jayber Crow*, 75–90.

2. A. Gwynn Henderson, telephone communication with author, April 29, 2012. See also Henderson, "Prehistoric Farmers of Boone County, Kentucky," 23–29.

3. Recodified 1942 Ky. Acts, chap. 208, sec. 1, effective October 1, 1942, from Ky. Stat. sec. 2741p-3, Ky. Act 381.710, "Evidence of Dedication or Use of Land as Burying Ground," October 1, 1942.

4. A. Gwynn Henderson, telephone communication with author, April 29, 2012. See also Henderson, "Prehistoric Farmers of Boone County, Kentucky," 23–29.

5. Henderson, "Lower Shawnee Town on Ohio," 34; Henderson et al., *Indian Occupation and Use in Northern and Eastern Kentucky*, 21–25.

6. David Pollack, email communication with author, February 1, 2013. For more on material connections between the Fort Ancient and Shawnee at the Bentley site, see Henderson and Pollack, "Appendix III: The Bentley Site," A-136. For the larger report, see Henderson and Pollack, "Late Woodland Occupation of the Bentley Site," 140–64.

7. Griffin, *Fort Ancient Aspect*, 28.

8. For "eccentric wanderings," see Parkman, *Conspiracy of Pontiac*, 32. Periodization is the easiest way to discern the disjuncture between archaeological and historical scholarship. Perhaps the most obvious example of the rupture of colonialism in the Great Lakes region is Richard White, *Middle Ground*. Other examples of rupture for the Ohio Valley include McConnell, *A Country Between*. In the last two decades, archaeologists have been working on Late Fort Ancient and protohistoric sites for evidence of linkages to modern tribes. See, for example, Drooker, *View from Madisonville*; and Henderson, "Dispelling the Myth."

9. See Wheeler-Voegelin, *Mortuary Customs*, 373–74. For the Absentee visit to Chillicothe, see Henryetta and Leroy Ellis, interview with author, Little Axe, Okla., June 16, 2007.

10. Hooton and Willoughby, "Indian Village and Cemetery near Madisonville, Ohio," 136. Little Turtle quoted in Black, "Archaeological Survey of Dearborn and Ohio Counties," 180. See also Costa, "Miami-Illinois Tribe Names," 51.

11. Graybill, "The Eastern Periphery of Fort Ancient," 49; Cowan, *First Farmers of the Middle Ohio Valley*, 15. For Shawnee associations with Madisonville, see Griffin, *Fort Ancient Aspect*, 28–35.

12. Hanson, *Hardin Village Site*, 3, 16. Two other sites, Fullerton Field and Lower Shawnee Town, were located within a few miles of Hardin Village. See Henderson, "Lower Shawnee Town on Ohio," 35; and Henderson, "Prehistoric Farmers of Boone County, Kentucky." In their analysis of Lower Shawnee Town, Pollack and Henderson write that "it can be argued that there is a cultural link between the late Fort Ancient Madisonville archaeological culture and the Shawnee." See Pollack and Henderson, "A Mid Eighteenth Century Historic Indian Occupation," 24. For more on the 1990 Native American Graves Protection and Repatriation Act (NAGPRA) law and the "culturally unidentifiable" status of human remains, see National Park Service, Department of Interior, "Recommendations Regarding the Disposition of Culturally Unidentifiable Native American Human Remains," *Federal Register* 65, no. 111 (June 8, 2000).

13. For Ontwaganha, see Clark, "Shawnee Indian Migration," iii.

14. "The Journey of Dollier and Galinée, by Galinée, 1669–1670," in Kellogg, *Early Narratives of the Northwest*, 168.

15. Margry, *Découvertes et Établissements*, 1:141–42.

16. "Message Shawnee Chiefs to Gov. Gordon, 1732," in *PA*, 1:329; Clark, "Shawnee Indian Migration," 21.

17. Pere Joseph Marquette, "An Account of the Discovery of Some New Countries and Nations in North America," in French, *Historical Collections of Louisiana and Florida*, 2:202.

18. There are a number of sites that may be affiliated with Shawnees, from "Chalaque" on the Savannah River, witnessed by de Soto, to "Chawanock," near Roanoke. There are a number of problems with these locations, from faulty synonymy to the absence of archaeological evidence and corroborating primary sources. For these reasons, I have chosen to emphasize post-1670 sites of Shawnee migration, places for which there is archaeological and archival evidence. For a summary of earlier locations, see Clark, "Shawnee Indian Migration," 17–20. For post-1670 sites, see Nicolas Perrot, *Memoir on the Manners, Customs, and Religion of the Savages of North America*, in Blair, *Indian Tribes*, 226–27; and Alvord and Bidgood, *First Explorations*, 198–99.

19. Reuben Gold Thwaites, ed., "A Selection of George Croghan's Letters and Journals Relating to Tours into the Western Country," in Thwaites, *Early Western Travels*, 62.

20. Europeans who knew the Shawnees offered an expansive definition of their pre-contact homeland. To the north, Perrot described the boundary of Shawnee territory as the southern shore of Lake Erie. To the south, in 1772, a Cherokee named Little Corn Planter illustrated his tribe's prowess in war to American revolutionaries by describing how they had expelled Shawnees from the Cumberland River, near modern Nashville, Tenn., a hundred years earlier. Little Corn Planter believed that these Shawnees had moved from the Savannah River to the Cumberland. While nearly all of the sources associate the Shawnees with the land west of the Appalachian Mountains, the far western boundary of their territory is typically associated with a line running south to north, from the falls of the Ohio to northern Indiana. While the bulk of the archival evidence associates the Shawnee with the Middle Ohio Valley, some sources, such as Perrot, indicate that Shawnees may have lived slightly north of the Fort Ancient Tradition. For the Cumberland River Shawnees, see James G. M. Ramsey, *Annals of Tennessee*, 78–79.

21. Wolf, *Europe and the People without History*, 25. For recent examples of historical arguments for Shawnee unity, see Steele, "Shawnee Origins of Their Seven Years' War"; and Lakomäki, "Building a Shawnee Nation," 199–224. Some historians prefer the paradigm of coalescence to characterize Shawnee cultural and political perspectives. See, for example, McConnell, *A Country Between*. For one of many explanations of village-based polities among Fort Ancient peoples, see Griffin, "Fort Ancient Has No Class."

22. For more on Shawnee kin groups, see Wheeler-Voegelin, *Mortuary Customs*, 383–419; Schutz, "Study of Shawnee Myth," 308–456; and Callender, "Shawnee," 623–24.

23. For a detailed discussion of double-barred pendants, see Drooker, *View from Madisonville*, 274. For suggestions that these pendants reflect male authority beyond the level of the village, see Henderson, "Prehistoric Farmers of Boone County, Kentucky." For "Big Man" societies, see Johnson and Earle, *Evolution of Human Societies*, 20–21. See also Anderson, "Evolution of Tribal Social Organization," 246–48.

24. Pauketat, *Ancient Cahokia and the Mississippians*. Like Pauketat, George R. Milner also supports the notion that Cahokia had a fairly limited degree of influence. See Milner, *Cahokia Chiefdom*, 109.

25. Griffin, "Fort Ancient Has No Class," 55; Drooker, *View from Madisonville*, 2, 48, 203. For general population estimates across the Fort Ancient Tradition, in both summer villages and winter hunting camps, see Henderson, "Fort Ancient Period," 746.

26. Drooker, *View from Madisonville*, 108. For 68 percent of diet, see Broida, "An Estimate of the Percent of Maize," 68–82. Nolan and Cook, "An Evolutionary Model," 63; Wagner, "What Seasonal Diet at a Fort Ancient Community Reveals," 266.

27. Nolan and Cook, "An Evolutionary Model," 63; Graybill, "The Eastern Periphery of Fort Ancient," 171; Carskadden and Morton, "Fort Ancient in the Central Muskingum Valley," 172.

28. For a well-researched discussion of Algonquians and seasonal mobility, see Witgen, *An Infinity of Nations*, 42. For the Goolman site, see Henderson, "Fort Ancient Period," 746. See also Turnbow and Jobe, "Goolman Site," 36–37, 39. For additional evidence of summer and winter encampments, see Essenpreis, "Fort Ancient Settlement," 156.

29. Carskadden and Morton, "Fort Ancient in the Central Muskingum Valley," 170.

30. Fitting and Cleland, "Late Prehistoric Settlement Patterns," 289–302. For a critique of their analysis, see O'Gorman, "Myth of Moccasin Bluff," 376–406. For evidence of the Shawnee movement between summer villages and winter hunting camps, see Harvey, *History of the Shawnee Indians*, 146–51.

31. For the size of late Fort Ancient villages, see Henderson, *Kentuckians before Boone*, 7–8. For central plazas, see Johnson and Earle, *Evolution of Human Societies*, 197.

32. Nass, "Fort Ancient Agricultural Systems and Settlement," 328, 331; A. Gwynn Henderson, telephone communication with author, November 12, 2010.

33. Milner, Anderson, and Smith, "The Distribution of Eastern Woodland Peoples," 14; Pollack and Henderson, "Toward a Model of Fort Ancient Society," 287.

34. Cassidy, "Skeletal Evidence for Prehistoric Subsistence Adaptation," 335; Wagner, "Corn and Cultivated Beans of the Fort Ancient Indians," 128, 110.

35. Cronon, *Changes in the Land*; Tankersley, "Bison Exploitation by Late Fort Ancient Peoples," 289–303; Tankersley, "Bison and Subsistence Change." For salt production, see Pollack, Henderson, and Begley, "Fort Ancient/Mississippian Interaction on the Northeastern Periphery," 213.

36. McCullough, "Central Indiana as a Late Prehistoric Borderland"; Munson and Pollack, "Far and Wide"; Cheryl Ann Munson, telephone communication with author, May 3, 2012.

37. On simple chiefdoms, see Blitz, *Ancient Chiefdoms of the Tombigbee*, 9. See also Worth, *Assimilation*, 13–18. On Koasati, see Shuck-Hall, "Alabama and Coushatta Diaspora and Coalescence," 254; and Diron d'Artaguette to Maurepas, October 17, 1729, in *MPA-FD*, 4:29.

38. Shuck-Hall, "Alabama and Coushatta Diaspora and Coalescence," 252–55; Ethridge, *From Chicaza to Chickasaw*, 66–69, 113; Piker, *Okfuskee*, 6.

39. Ethridge, *From Chicaza to Chickasaw*, 24–25; Power, *Early Art of the Southeastern Indians*, 128–29; Ehrhardt, *European Metals in Native Hands*, 136; Marvin T. Smith, *Coosa*, 92.

40. Robert L. Hall, "Calumet Ceremonialism," 29–30; Drooker, "Pipes, Leadership, and Interregional Interaction," 95.

41. Drooker, "Redstone, Shell, and Metal in Late Prehistoric and Protohistoric Fort Ancient Contexts"; Robert L. Hall, "Calumet Ceremonialism," 31. See also Blakeslee, "Origin and Spread of the Calumet Ceremony," 759.

42. Blair, *Indian Tribes*, 325–26.

43. Pease and Werner, *French Foundations*, 389–91; Richard White, *Middle Ground*, 92–93; quoted from Robert L. Hall, "Calumet Ceremonialism," 33.

44. For a description of shell-tempering, see Matson, "Shell-Tempered Pottery and the Fort Ancient Potter," 17, 20, 24; and Cowan, *Excavations and Chronology*, 131.

45. Lankford, "World on a String," 217. Reilly and Garber define the increased interaction across cultures in the Eastern Woodlands as the "Mississippian Ideological Interaction Sphere." Reilly and Garber, "Introduction," 3; Cowan, *Excavations and Chronology*, 137. The rims of Late Fort Ancient pottery tend to be everted without adornos or castellations. For concise definitions of Fort Ancient pottery styles, see Graybill, "The Eastern Periphery of Fort Ancient," 26.

46. For the notion of the "layered cosmos" and conflicts between worlds, see Lankford, "Some Cosmological Motifs in the Southeastern Ceremonial Complex," 8, 17.

47. Penney, "Archaeology of Aesthetics," 47–48; Lankford, "Path of Souls," 211; Power, *Early Art of the Southeastern Indians*, 128–29.

48. For more on diversity within Late Fort Ancient society, see Henderson, *Fort Ancient Cultural Dynamics*, esp. 266–79. See also Cowan, *Excavations and Chronology*, 13.

49. Drooker, "Redstone, Shell, and Metal in Late Prehistoric and Protohistoric Fort Ancient Contexts"; Rice, *Nature and History in the Potomac Country*, 53–61.

50. Drooker, "Pipes, Leadership, and Interregional Interaction," 91.

51. James Morton, email communication with author, February 1, 2013; Graybill, "The Eastern Periphery of Fort Ancient (A.D. 1050–1650)," 23.

52. Drooker, "Exotic Ceramics at Madisonville," 75–76. Archaeologist David S. Brose rejects the contention that the Eries, or proto-Westos, come from northeastern Ohio. See Brose, "Penumbral Protohistory on Lake Erie's South Shore," 61, 64. For historians and historical anthropologists who have argued that there is a connection between the Eries and the Westos in northeastern Ohio, see Bowne, *Westo Indians*, 41–44; and Meyers, "From Refugees to Slave Traders," 82–86. For the archaeology of the Savannah River fall line, see Whitley, "Archaeological Data Recovery," 86–92.

53. Drooker, *View from Madisonville*, 99, 288–92.

54. Ibid., 272–73; Hanson, *Hardin Village Site*, 39, 44; Griffin, "Late Prehistory of the Ohio Valley," 552.

55. Griffin, "Fort Ancient Has No Class," 55.

56. Cassidy, "Skeletal Evidence for Prehistoric Subsistence Adaptation," 329–30; Henderson, "Fort Ancient Period," 784.

57. Scholars interested in the Yuchis have been led astray by John R. Swanton and his numerous works on the Southeast. As an example, Swanton identifies the Yuchi as

Siouan speakers. In fact, their language is a genetic isolate. For examples of Swanton's mistake, see Swanton, "Siouan Tribes and the Ohio Valley," 49–66. For a linguistically and ethnographically informed corrective, see Linn, "Deep Time and Genetic Relationships," 1–32. The archaeologist James B. Griffin erroneously concluded that the Fort Ancient Tradition was an essentially Algonquian one. See, for example, Griffin, *Fort Ancient Aspect*, 35n67; and Griffin, "Fort Ancient Has No Class," 54. More recent scholarship emphasizes both linguistic and ethnic diversity within the Fort Ancient Tradition. See, for example, Carr and Maslowski, "Cordage and Fabrics," 324. For more recent associations between the Yuchi and Siouan speakers, see Spencer, "Evidence of Siouan Occupation," 139.

58. Spencer, "Evidence of Siouan Occupation," 143; Costa, "Miami-Illinois Tribe Names," 31; Graybill, "The Eastern Periphery of Fort Ancient," 37. For evidence of trade between the Massawomecks and Fort Ancient, see Wall, "Late Woodland Ceramics," 15–37.

59. The absence of cultural pluralism at particular Fort Ancient sites, especially between A.D. 1000 and A.D. 1400, once contributed to the belief that Fort Ancient "tradition" must be synonymous with a single, modern tribe such as the Shawnees. Following Griffin, as late as 1970, some archaeologists assumed that the Fort Ancient "tradition" was both ethnically and linguistically coherent. Some case studies of Fort Ancient sites suggested that environmental factors rather than ethnic differentiation accounted for differences across the region. See, for example, Prufer and Shane, *Blain Village*, 239; Gwynn Henderson, telephone communication with author, November 12, 2010; and Cowan, *Excavations and Chronology*, 20.

60. For European trade goods transformed into Native stylistic traditions, see Drooker, *View from Madisonville*, 171. For the movement from burials to trash heaps, I am indebted to Gwynn Henderson. A. Gwynn Henderson, telephone communication with author, November 12, 2010.

61. Kimball-Brown, *Cultural Transformation among the Illinois*, 228; Blair, *Indian Tribes*, 151–57; Emerson and Brown, "The Late Prehistory and Protohistory of Illinois," 79.

62. Associating Danner Phase pottery with specific historic tribes is made all the more difficult, according to Emerson and Brown, by "the mixed content in which it has been found." Emerson and Brown, "The Late Prehistory and Protohistory of Illinois," 84, 89. Griffin quoted in Brown, *The Zimmerman Site: A Report on Excavations at the Grand Village of Kaskaskia*, 74. Archaeologist Penelope Drooker, citing Kenneth Tankersley, argues that "data from Zimmerman and Hotel Plaza [reveals that] a group of Fort Ancient people did move from Madisonville to the vicinity of Fort St. Louis, but that they were actually Illini, unlike other Fort Ancient people, who were probably Shawnee." Here Drooker makes clear that no single historic tribe can lay claim to a pre-Columbian culture. Even Madisonville-phase pottery was shared by a host of Illinois, Miami, and Shawnee Indians. See Drooker, *View from Madisonville*, 104.

63. Emerson and Brown, "The Late Prehistory and Protohistory of Illinois," 105. Following Griffin, in 1975, archaeologist Margaret Kimball-Brown wondered "why, in these locations where the Illinois are known historically to have lived, only 'Shawnee' pottery appears." Kimball-Brown then recognized that archaeologists, like historians,

have been hampered by a consistent vision of American Indian peoples as members of "tightly bound political units." Archival evidence suggests that the entities called tribes by the French and English were, in fact, coalescent peoples adapting, and changing, in response to their new, colonial circumstances. Kimball-Brown concluded that the protohistoric Upper Illinois River Valley was more of a "style zone or tradition" than an ethnically coherent region with relatively stable human societies. See Kimball-Brown, *Zimmerman Site*, 70. Kimball-Brown writes that "only shortly before European contact, the Miami and the Illinois apparently were a single unit." See ibid., 70–71. See also *JR*, 55:201; and Walthall, "Aboriginal Pottery," 156.

64. Writing in 1992, Walthall and Emerson argued that "the current consensus among scholars is that the cord-marked and grooved paddle-finish ceramics of the Danner series [at Starved Rock] were most likely associated with the Illini." See Walthall, "Aboriginal Pottery," 156. In 2001, archaeologist James A. Brown retracted his earlier claim that "the Danner complex, one of the historic period complexes at Zimmerman, is . . . clearly affiliated with the Fort Ancient aspect." For the initial claim, see Brown, *The Zimmerman Site: A Report on Excavations at the Grand Village of Kaskaskia*, 74. For the retraction, see Brown and Sasso, "Prelude to History on the Eastern Plains," 214.

65. Traditional Madisonville traits, including shell-tempered jars, bowls, and pans, probably reflected these long-distance migrations. Fort Ancient bowls typically include wide strap handles and vertical cord-marking, with notched or beaded rims. They were modified as protohistoric potters sat alongside each other in new, multiethnic villages. For the most thorough description of Madisonville ceramic series pottery, see Henderson, *Fort Ancient Cultural Dynamics*, 315–25. Archaeologist Charles Cobb alerted me to the possibility that migratory peoples might have changed their pottery styles. However, Cobb remains unconvinced that there is a Fort Ancient/Shawnee connection along the Middle Savannah River. Charles Cobb to author, email communication, October 10, 2011.

66. Whitley, "Conflict and Confusion"; Tom Whitley to author, email communication, June 28, 2011.

Chapter 3

1. See Goddard, "Central Algonquian Languages," 583; and "The Journey of Dollier and Galinée, by Galinée, 1669–1670," in Kellogg, *Early Narratives of the Northwest*, 167–68.

2. "The Journey of Dollier and Galinée, by Galinée, 1669–1670," in Kellogg, *Early Narratives of the Northwest*, 167–68.

3. Cowan, *Excavations and Chronology*, 155; Drooker and Cowan, "Transformation of the Fort Ancient Cultures of the Central Ohio Valley," 86–87. Twenty-three Late Fort Ancient sites have been radiocarbon dated. Typical radiocarbon dates have a fifty-year range of error. However, when combined with time-sensitive trade goods, our best estimate is that none of these sites were occupied after 1680. The Bentley and Thompson sites, near the confluence of the Scioto and Ohio rivers, have produced contact-period artifacts. However, they cannot be considered Late Fort Ancient sites because they represent artifacts deposited by returning Shawnee migrants, sometime between 1725

and 1740. To date, archaeologists have not found Fort Ancient sites dating to the early historic period, from 1680 to 1725.

4. Colden, *History of the Five Indian Nations of Canada*; Parmenter, *Edge of the Woods*, 178; Everett, "They Shalbe Slaves for Their Lives"; Richard White, *Middle Ground*, 11.

5. For Winslow's understanding of disease, see Jones, *Rationalizing Epidemics*, 58. On children and the first epidemics, see Snow and Lanphear, "European Contact and Indian Depopulation in the Northeast," 20–21, 26.

6. On diffusion, see Ramenofsky, *Vectors of Death*, 170. On the communicability of smallpox, see Kelton, *Epidemics and Enslavement*, 37.

7. Wolfe, Dunavan, and Diamond, "Origins of Major Human Infectious Diseases," 282.

8. Historian Paul Kelton has described the Great Smallpox Epidemic as well as what he terms the "disease ecology" that made American Indians particularly vulnerable to Old World diseases such as smallpox. See Kelton, *Epidemics and Enslavement*, 1, 143–58.

9. Richter, *Ordeal of the Longhouse*, 58–59; Hinderaker, *Elusive Empires*, 3.

10. Drooker and Cowan, "Transformation of the Fort Ancient Cultures of the Central Ohio Valley," 86–87; Drooker, *View from Madisonville*, 44–46.

11. Ramenofsky, *Vectors of Death*, 135–36.

12. Drooker, *View from Madisonville*, 102. Intermediate examples include Witthoft and Hunter, "Seventeenth Century Origins of the Shawnee," 42–57. Recent support for Shawnee affiliation with the Madisonville Focus can be found in Drooker, *View from Madisonville*, 105; and Pollack and Henderson, "Toward a Model of Fort Ancient Society," 287.

13. George, "Gnagey Site," 5–7. For Norris Farm, see Milner, "Warfare in Prehistoric and Early Historic Eastern North America," 115. See also Milner, Anderson, and Smith, "Warfare in Late Prehistoric West-Central Illinois," 589–91.

14. *JR*, 47:146–47, 54:188, 47:144.

15. Wheeler-Voegelin, *Mortuary Customs*, 335.

16. Drooker, "Pipes, Leadership, and Interregional Interaction," 81, 91. For more on Ohio Valley trade pipes, see Penney, "Archaeology of Aesthetics," 43–56; Parmenter, *Edge of the Woods*, 109; and Richter, *Ordeal of the Longhouse*, 121. On Fort Ancient pottery among the Seneca and the Susquehannock, see Drooker, *View from Madisonville*, 104.

17. Baker, "Early Seventeenth Century Trade Beads," 22, 23; Graybill, "The Eastern Periphery of Fort Ancient (A.D. 1050–1650)," 126; Kent, *Susquehanna's Indians*, 211–17.

18. Barbour, *Complete Works of Captain John Smith*, 148–50.

19. Sempowski, "Early Historic Exchange," 214–16; Abler, "Longhouse and Palisade," 20; *JR*, 33:129; Kent, *Susquehanna's Indians*, 45. For a French account of the Iroquois-Susquehannock Wars, see Charlevoix, *History and General Description of New France*, 174; and *JR*, 37:11.

20. For Fort Ancient hunters and down-the-line trade, see Baker, "Early Seventeenth Century Trade Beads," 23. For a parallel example among the Illinois, see Ehrhardt, *European Metals in Native Hands*, chap. 6. For coiled snakes, from Madisonville to Oneota territory, see Drooker, "Redstone, Shell, and Metal in Late Prehistoric and Protohistoric Fort Ancient Contexts."

21. For Fort Ancient hunters as well as the end to the Susquehannock trade, see Drooker, *View from Madisonville*, 73, 75; Graybill, "The Eastern Periphery of Fort Ancient," 126; and Kent, *Susquehanna's Indians*, 211–17.

22. Parmenter, *Edge of the Woods*, 109; Richter, *Ordeal of the Longhouse*, 121.

23. Map reprinted in Griffin, *Fort Ancient Aspect*, 25. Waselkov, "Seventeenth Century Trade in the Colonial Southeast," 117, 119; Fox, "North-South Copper Axis," 85–97.

24. Scholars from John R. Swanton to Steven J. Oatis have used imprecise synonymy to locate the Shawnees in the colonial Southeast. In *A Colonial Complex*, Oatis erroneously claims that both the Shawnees and the Yuchi had relocated to the Apalachicola River by 1640. See Oatis, *A Colonial Complex*, 20. Evidence refuting Oatis's claim includes Warren and Noe, "Greatest Travelers in America," 184n38, 186n46. Vast stretches of the Southeast have not been systematically investigated. With the exception of some from Savannah Town, along the middle Savannah River, pottery indicative of the Middle Ohio Valley peoples remains stubbornly elusive. Gregory A. Waselkov, email communication with author, February 9, 2011.

25. Oatis, *A Colonial Complex*, 20; Henry Woodward, "A Faithfull Relation," 133–34. For the original, see Henry Woodward, "A Faithfull Relation of Henry Woodward's Westoe Voiage," 30/24/48, pt. 3, SP-BPRO. See also Milanich, "The Timucua Indians of Northern Florida and Southern Georgia," 12–13; *JR*, 47:145, 147; and Nicholas Perrot, "Memoir on the Manners, Customs, and Religion of the Savages of North America," in Blair, *Indian Tribes*, 146. For the map of the Florida town, see Clark, "Shawnee Indian Migration," 26.

26. For the best explanation of Indian slavery in Virginia, see Everett, "An Inhuman Practice Once Prevailed in This Country." See also Everett, "They Shalbe Slaves for Their Lives," 77–81.

27. For Gabriel Arthur's journey into the Ohio Valley, see Williams, *Early Travels in the Tennessee Country*, 35–36. See also Henderson, "Early European Contact in Southern Ohio," 231. For a historian's description of the Virginia traders and Gabriel Arthur's captivity, see Briceland, *Westward from Virginia*, 167–68.

28. For the original letter, see Abraham Wood to John Richards, August 22, 1674, 30/24/48, SP-BPRO.

29. Ibid. For more on the Tomahitans, see DeMallie, "Tutelo and Neighboring Groups," 290–91. See also King, *Cherokee Indian Nation*, 39.

30. Williams, *Early Travels in the Tennessee Country*, 36. Another version of Gabriel Arthur's journey appears in "Major-General Abraham Wood to His Honoured Friend John Richards, in London, August 22, 1674," *CSP*, vol. 7. For more on Virginians in the Indian slave trade, see Gallay, *Indian Slave Trade*, 53, 303–8.

31. Olafson, "Gabriel Arthur and the Fort Ancient People," 32–42. In this article, Olafson speculates that the Shawnees were the historic descendants of the Fort Ancient people.

32. Abraham Wood to John Richards, August 22, 1674, 30/24/48, SP-BPRO.

33. Bowne, *Westo Indians*, chap. 4; Mazrim and Esaray, "Rethinking the Dawn of History," 147; Parmenter, *Edge of the Woods*, 77.

34. Anderson, *Betrayal of Faith*, 23; Kinietz, *Indians of the Western Great Lakes*, 200–201.

35. "Narrative of Henri Joutel, 1684–1688," ETM-DPL, 3:493–94.

36. Ibid.

37. Blair, *Indian Tribes*, 335–36.

38. For the number of different groups attacked by the Iroquois, see Brandão, *Your Fyre Shall Burn No More*, 31. For the numbers in Onondaga and Seneca villages, see *JR*, 43:265.

39. Richard White, *Middle Ground*, 2. Teganissorens quoted in Brandão, *Your Fyre Shall Burn No More*, 42.

40. Drooker, "Ohio Valley, 1550–1750," 122–23.

41. Richter, *Ordeal of the Longhouse*, 1; Parmenter, *Edge of the Woods*, 115. For the best comprehensive analysis of Shawnee migrations to date, see Clark, "Shawnee Indian Migration," 21–22. For the three attacks on the Shawnees, see Brandão, *Your Fyre Shall Burn No More*, table D.1. See also Colden, *History of the Five Indian Nations of Canada*; and Charlevoix, *History and General Description of New France*, 74–75.

42. Perrot quoted in Blair, *Indian Tribes*, 226; Charlevoix, *History and General Description of New France*, 174; Greer, *Mohawk Saint*, 27.

43. Richter, *Ordeal of the Longhouse*, 38; Trigger, *Children of Aataentsic*, 87.

44. Seaver, *Life of Mary Jemison*, 56–60. On reincarnation, see Robert L. Hall, *An Archaeology of the Soul*, 40.

45. Calloway, "We Have Always Been the Frontier," 39; Atkin, *Appalachian Indian Frontier*, 65; McDowell, *DRIA*, 363.

46. Callender, "Shawnee," 623–26; Murdock, "Algonkian Social Organization," 29; Hockett, "Proto Central Algonquian Kinship System," 256. Fort Ancient understandings of kinship are difficult to glean from archaeological sources. Shawnee clans are the Turkey, Turtle, Rounded Feet, Horse, Raccoon, and Rabbit name group. See also Voegelin and Wheeler-Voegelin, "Shawnee Name Groups," 617. For the original description of the patrilineal clans, see Kinietz and Wheeler-Voegelin, *Shawnese Traditions*, 16–17.

47. There are some notable instances in which a town was named after the Shawnee people. These include Savannah Town, on what is now the Savannah River. However, Savannah Town was associated with the Thawekila society clan. Shawnee people almost always named their towns after one of these five clans. Callender, "Shawnee," 627; Clark, "Shawnee Indian Migration," 23–51. Contemporary Shawnee spellings of the divisions are: kesepokofi, pekowefi, mekoga, galikifi, and hifiwakela. George Blanchard, telephone communication with author, October 27, 2005.

48. Hanna, *Wilderness Trail*, 1:145. Hanna notes that the Pekowitha, Kispokotha, Chalagawtha, and Mekoche all had towns in colonial Pennsylvania. Towns were frequently named after one of the five society clans. According to my own compilation of these towns, Pekowitha and Mekoche villages predominated. The basis for my own reconstruction of Shawnee villages in Pennsylvania derives from a host of sources, including Clark, "Shawnee Indian Migration," 36–44.

49. Swanton believed that the Shawnees in Carolina were members of the Thawekila division. See Swanton, *Early History of the Creek Indians and Their Neighbors*, 317. Noel Schutz makes the case that the Sawokli and Thawekila are the same division. However, historian John Worth disagrees, arguing instead that Sawokli was a Hichiti village. See Schutz, "Study of Shawnee Myth," 377–81. The strongest documentary evidence for the Thawekila Shawnee–Savannah River connection comes from James Le

Tort, who gave an account of the Indians at Allegheny. Le Tort quoted from "The Examination of James Letort, Indian Trader, Taken before His Honr. Lieut. Governr of Pennsylvania" (1731), in *PA*, 1:302.

50. As early as 1935, both Erminie Wheeler-Voegelin and Carl Voegelin were arguing that the Shawnees were "an Algonkin-speaking tribe composed of five major divisions." See Voegelin and Wheeler-Voegelin, "Shawnee Name Groups," 617. For more on the Shawnees' return to Ohio between 1745 and 1774, at which time cooperation between the various Shawnee towns constituted a tribal polity, see Wheeler-Voegelin, *Indians of Ohio and Indiana prior to 1795*, 2:464–69. Between the 1950s and the 1970s, Wheeler-Voegelin worked exhaustively on behalf of the Indian Claims Commission. Tribal polities were the basic organizing principle of the commission. For example, she organized documents relating to each of the Great Lakes tribes into hundreds of ring binders, arranged chronologically. Thus the intellectual basis for the commission, and the documentary record used to support it, was designed to associate Native identities with tribal polities. Historians tend to follow Wheeler-Voegelin's understanding of the Shawnees as a unified tribe. For examples, see Edmunds, *Shawnee Prophet*, 7–8. See also Calloway, *The Shawnees and the War for America*, 8. John Sugden adopts a more nuanced view of Shawnee identity. He writes that "the Shawnee 'tribe' was really a loose confederation of villages linked by a common language and culture, ties of kinship, and a rudimentary notion of unity." See Sugden, *Blue Jacket*, 7–8. For my own discussion of the relationship between the five divisions and the tribe as a whole, see Warren, *The Shawnees and Their Neighbors*, 13–17.

51. Between 1745 and 1774, most, though not all, Shawnees lived in Ohio, in towns along the Scioto and Ohio rivers. Following their early colonial pattern, their towns were typically named after the division with the largest number of residents in the town. Some Shawnees remained in Alabama, at Tukabatchee and Sawanogi, within the Upper Creek Confederacy. By 1774 and the Battle of Point Pleasant, many Ohio Shawnees voluntarily removed west of the Mississippi River. Thus the evidence for Shawnee political unity rests on their brief, though incomplete, geographic proximity to each other in what is now Ohio. However, the Shawnee return to Ohio must be placed in the much larger context of Shawnee migrations—migrations that did not conclude until the end of the nineteenth century. For one example of that discussion, see Warren, *The Shawnees and Their Neighbors*, 69–70.

52. Trigger, *Children of Aataentsic*, 1. In contrast to my argument, Richard White argues that Central Algonquians such as the Shawnee were so devastated by the events of the seventeenth century that they were "like infants sucking the breasts of their dead mothers." See Richard White, *Middle Ground*, 57; and Drooker, *View from Madisonville*, 4.

Chapter 4

1. "Mr. Carteret's Relation of Their Planting at Ashley River," *CSP*, 7:90. On "Sowee," see Rudes, Blumer, and May, "Catawba and Neighboring Groups," 302. For more on Lords Proprietors, see Gallay, *Indian Slave Trade*, 18.

2. Lawson, *A New Voyage to Carolina*, 173–74; Speck, *Ethnology of the Yuchi Indians*, 143.

3. Merrell, *The Indians' New World*; Calloway, *New Worlds for All*. For ethnogenesis, see Roosens, *Creating Ethnicity*; and Hickerson, *Jumanos*.

4. Alexander Moore, *Nairne's Muskhogean Journals*, 62–63; Meyers, "From Refugees to Slave Traders," 97. On Catawba coalescence, see Merrell, *The Indians' New World*.

5. For two examples of early colonial studies of coalescence and confederation in the Southeast, see Hahn, *Invention of the Creek Nation*; and Ethridge, *From Chicaza to Chickasaw*.

6. Marian E. White, "Erie," 412–16. For a more recent treatment of the Westos and an explanation of their identification with the Eries, see Bowne, *Westo Indians*, 37–53.

7. For the origins of trading American Indian war captives to colonies in the British Caribbean, see Betty Wood, *Origins of Slavery*, chap. 3.

8. Horn, *Adapting to a New World*, 6, 24; Berlin, *Many Thousands Gone*, 369–70.

9. Erminie Wheeler-Voegelin believed that shortly before the historical period, "Shawnee began drifting southward from their northern location. The path they followed probably lay along the eastern Piedmont." See Wheeler-Voegelin, *Mortuary Customs*, 373. Stokes, *The Savannah*, 2; de Vorsey, "Colonial Georgia Backcountry," 8–9.

10. Rountree, *Pocahontas, Powhatan, Opechancanough*, 130; Feest, "Virginia Algonquians," 254–56.

11. Rountree, "Trouble Coming Southward," 69–70. See also Everett, "They Shalbe Slaves for Their Lives," 77–81; Hodge, "Narrative of the Expedition of Hernando de Soto by the Gentleman of Elvas," 171; Beck, "Catawba Coalescence and the Shattering of the Carolina Piedmont," 116–17; and Anderson, *Savannah River Chiefdoms*, 261–63, 283. For a nice definition of the ecology of the Savannah River, see Whitley, "Archaeological Data Recovery," 57–58, 69.

12. De Vorsey, *Georgia–South Carolina Boundary*, 56; Bartram, *Travels and Other Writings*, 260.

13. Whitley, "Archaeological Data Recovery," 372–73; Henry Woodward, "A Faithfull Relation"; Warren and Noe, "Greatest Travelers in America," 169.

14. Crane, "Historical Note on the Westo Indians," 335; Bowne, *Westo Indians*, 76; Joseph M. Hall Jr., "Anxious Alliances," 150–52; Hann, "St. Augustine's Fallout," 182.

15. Quote taken from Joseph M. Hall Jr., "Anxious Alliances," 151. Westo population estimates taken from Gallay, "South Carolina's Entrance into the Indian Slave Trade," 110.

16. "An Act Prohibiting Trade with the Indians for Any Flesh Dead or Alive Except Deer & Wild Foule," June 2, 1692, *AM*, 13:479; Lords Proprietors of Carolina to Governor Joseph West, March 13, 1685, *CSP*, 12:11–13.

17. "An Act Concerning Indians," June 1692, *AM*, 13:525; Governor Nicholson to Council of Trade and Plantations, March 27, 1697, *CSP*, 15:421; William Byrd to His Majesty, September 29, 1683, M237, Virginia Colonial Records Project, p. 149; Joseph M. Hall Jr., *Zamumo's Gifts*, 105, 122.

18. Henry Woodward, "A Faithfull Relation," 134. Figures are taken from Peter H. Wood, "Changing Population of the Colonial South," 38–39. For Woodward's share of the profits, see "Articles of Agreement between the Lords Proprietors of Carolina Concerning the Trade There," April 10, 1677, *CSP*, 10:61.

19. Henry Woodward, "A Faithfull Relation," 134; William Owen to Lord Ashley, September 15, 1670, *CSP*, 7:93; [Maurice Matthews] to Anthony Lord Ashley, August 30, 1671, *CSP*, 7:254.

20. The Lords Proprietors of Carolina to the Governor and Council of Ashley River, February 21, 1681, *CSP*, 11:12; and March 7, 1681, *CSP*, 11:16–17.

21. For the Catawbas, see Merrell, *The Indians' New World*.

22. Instructions from Lord Shaftesbury to Henry Woodward, May 23, 1674, *CSP*, 7:587; Lords Proprietors to the Governor, April 10, 1677, *CSP*, 10:60; Lords Proprietors of Carolina to the Governor and Council of Ashley River, March 7, 1681, *CSP*, 11:16–17.

23. Henry Woodward, "A Faithfull Relation," 134.

24. Le Jau, *Carolina Chronicles*, 68.

25. *RBPRO-SC*, 1:116, 257.

26. Ibid., 1: 257–58; Milling, *Red Carolinians*, 85.

27. Archdale, "New Description of That Fertile and Pleasant Province of Carolina," 277–312. See also Juricek, "Indian Policy in Proprietary South Carolina," 121 24; and Salley, *Narratives of Early Carolina*, 285.

28. *RBPRO-SC*, 1:255, 256.

29. For more on Lamhátty's experience as a slave, see Bossy, "Indian Slavery in Southeastern Indian and British Societies"; and Waselkov, "Indian Maps of the Colonial Southeast," 317. For more on the Timucua, see Milanich, *The Timucua*, 212.

30. Marambaud, *William Byrd of Westover*, 171–78.

31. For the Westo enslavement of Yuchis in 1675, see Worth, *Struggle for the Georgia Coast*, 37–42. For the 1680 attack, see Hann, "St. Augustine's Fallout," 190. For Shawnees, see Oatis, *A Colonial Complex*, 39.

32. Westbrooke quoted in Worth, *Struggle for the Georgia Coast*, 43; Sanders, *History of Beaufort County*, 72.

33. Le Jau, *Carolina Chronicles*, 49.

34. The Illinois word for Yuchi, *taogaria*, was probably adopted from the Shawnee word for Yuchi, *tahokale*. See Jackson, "Yuchi," 428. For Gravier's account, see *JR*, 65:115.

35. CO 700, Carolina 1 (ca. 1695), British Public Record Office, Kew, UK; Gallay, *Indian Slave Trade*, 225, 229–32.

36. *RBPRO-SC*, 1:99, 255. For the Morton letter, see Joseph Morton to the Board of Trade, August 29, 1701, CO 5/1261, BT-BPRO.

37. *RBPRO-SC*, 1:99, 255.

38. Philip M. Brown, "Early Indian Trade in the Development of South Carolina," 121; Crane, "Projects for the Colonization of the South," 26; Covington, "Apalachee Indians," 375–76; Le Jau quoted in Philip M. Brown, "Early Indian Trade in the Development of South Carolina," 121.

39. Bonnie G. McEwan, "Apalachee and Neighboring Groups," 669, 673. See also Worth, "Razing Florida," 302–4; and *RBPRO-SC*, 4:191, 4:194–95, 5:194–95, 5:197.

40. In 1736, the British carefully reconstructed the 1702 and 1704 invasions as part of an effort to extend the southern boundary of South Carolina to include St. Augustine. For these sources, see "Deposition of Matthew Baird," February 12, 1736/7, 30/47/14, SP-BPRO. See also "Copy of Col. Moore's Letter to Sr. Nathaniel Johnson," January

26, 1703/4, 30/47/14, ibid.; "Extract of Col. Moore's Letter to the Lords Proprietors," January 26, 1703/4, 30/47/14, ibid.; and "Report to the Commons House," July 1, 1741, 30/47/14, ibid.

41. On Ochese Creek captive taking, see Nairne, *Muskhogean Journals*, 34; and William Bull to the Lords Commissioners for Trade and Plantations, May 25, 1738, 30/47/14, SP-BPRO.

42. Oatis, *A Colonial Complex*, 62; *RBPRO-SC*, 4:191, 4:194–95, 5:194–95, 5:197.

43. "Thomas Nairne's memorial to Charles Spencer, *Muskhogean Journals*, 79n8; Crane, *Southern Frontier*, 80.

44. Whitley, "Archaeological Data Recovery," 377.

45. Salley, *Journal of the Commons House of Assembly*, February 12, 1707/8, 62, 38; *MPCP*, July 22, 1707, 2:389–90.

46. Salley, *Journal of the Commons House of Assembly*, February 12, 1707/8, 17.

47. Corkran, *Creek Frontier*, 58. Like those of Swanton before him, many of Corkran's conclusions are not based on sound primary source evidence, and for this reason *Creek Frontier* should not be used to substantiate factual claims about the colonial Southeast. Le Jau, *Carolina Chronicles*, 39, 49, 68.

48. Salley, *Journal of the Commons House of Assembly*, 3:27, 145. For "armed posse," see William L. Ramsey, *Yamasee War*, 111; *Nairne's Muskhogean Journals*, 12; and Green, *Search for Altamaha*, 78.

49. Joseph M. Hall Jr., *Zamumo's Gifts*, 105; Ethridge, *From Chicaza to Chickasaw*, 152–53; Gallay, *Indian Slave Trade*, 129–32.

50. For an extended treatment of the Cherokee attack on Chestowe, see Gallay, *Indian Slave Trade*, 319–22; and McDowell, *Journals of the Commissioners of the Indian Trade*, 56.

51. McDowell, *Journals of the Commissioners of the Indian Trade*, 54; Crane, "Tennessee River as the Road to Carolina," 10.

52. Nairne, *Muskhogean Journals*, 37–39.

53. Lawson, *A New Voyage to Carolina*, 48, 35, 31.

54. Paul A. W. Wallace, *Indian Paths of Pennsylvania*, 27–30; Speck, *Catawba Texts*, 6.

55. Salley, *Journal of the Commons House of Assembly*, 62. For 150 men, see *RBPRO-SC*, 5:208.

56. Crane, "Early Indian Trade," 121.

57. Crane, "Historical Note on the Westo Indians," 334. *Tohogoligo* is the Algonquian word for Yuchi (today the Shawnee word for Yuchi is *Tahogaliiki*). References to the *Tohogoligo* confirm that Carolinians used the Shawnee word for Yuchi to identify them. George Blanchard, telephone communication with author, October 27, 2005; Gallay, *Indian Slave Trade*, 211, 267.

58. Francis Moore, *A Voyage to Georgia*, 71–72. For a deeper analysis of this War Dance, see Jackson, "A Yuchi War Dance in 1736," 27–32. For more on the Yuchi defense of English settlements in Georgia and South Carolina, see Hahn, *Invention of the Creek Nation*, 181–82.

59. "Journal of David Taitt's Travels from Pensacola," 516; Hawkins, *Creek Confederacy*, 59.

60. Alexander Moore, *Nairne's Muskhogean Journals*, 39, 21; Le Jau, *Carolina Chronicles*, 175.

61. For Shawnee villages on the Savannah River, see Guillaume Delisle, maps XV, XVII, in Tucker, *Indian Villages of the Illinois Country*. For attacks on Carolina settlements, see Le Jau, *Carolina Chronicles*, 164, 180. On Yuchi inclusion in the "Southern Indian" contingent of the Yamasee War, see William L. Ramsey, *Yamasee War*, 101. On the Yuchi towns on the Savannah River, see Martyn to Pres and Assistants, 1/2/1748–49, in Candler, *Colonial Records of the State of Georgia* 31:115. For Shawnee and Yuchi population figures, see William L. Ramsey, *Yamasee War*, 110.

62. Warren and Noe, "Greatest Travelers in America," 174–76. For the Glover census, see Salley, "Creek Indian Tribes in 1725," 240–41.

63. Piker, *Okfuskee*, 17. A reproduction of the 1737 Chickasaw map can be found in Waselkov, "Indian Maps of the Colonial Southeast," 298.

64. For examples of the mistaken linguistic correlation between the Yuchi and Siouan languages, see Sapir, "A Bird's Eye View of American Indian Languages"; Haas, "The Proto-Gulf Word for Water," 71–79; Thomas S. Woodward, *Reminiscences of the Creek*, 40; and Bartram, *Travels and Other Writings*, 317.

65. McDowell, *DRIA*, 424; Hvidt, *Von Reck's Voyage*, 40; Callender, "Shawnee," 632. For the earliest known painting of a Shawnee warrior, by Marin in 1796, see Houck, *A History of Missouri*, 213. R. Scott Stephenson, interview with author, Philadelphia, September 23, 2011.

66. Waselkov and Braund, *William Bartram on the Southeastern Indians*, 146.

Chapter 5

1. In describing the Shawnee role in the September 1680 attack on the Grand Village of the Kaskaskias, Hanna describes this war party as being composed of 500 Iroquois and 100 Miamis. Margry contends that there were 500 Iroquois and 100 Shawnees. By combining the various primary sources on the 1680 attack, including that of Membré and Tonty, it becomes clear that both Shawnees and Miamis joined the Iroquois in the attack on the Grand Village of Kaskaskias. However, Shawnees were also allied with the Kaskaskias against the Iroquois-led war party. See Hanna, *Wilderness Trail*, 1:158. For Margry, see [Abbé Claude Bernou?], "Official Account of the Enterprise of Cavelier de La Salle from 1679–1681," ETM-DPL, 1:533–43; Father Membré, "Account of the Discoveries and Journies of the Seiur de La Salle," in ibid., 1:547, 570; Henry Tonty, "Memoir on La Salle's Discoveries," in Kellogg, *Early Narratives of the Northwest*, 291; French, *Historical Collections of Louisiana*, 4:151–62; and Weddle, *La Salle, the Mississippi, and the Gulf*, 37–38.

2. Membré writes that Illinois scouts monitoring the Iroquois believed that La Salle was with the Iroquois, because they saw an "Iroquois chief [with] a hat and a kind of vest," and as a result they "talked of tomahawking us." Quoted in French, *Historical Collections of Louisiana*, 4:151–62. For the identities of the Frenchmen in Tonty's party, see [Bernou?], ETM-DPL, 1:550–51. For *engagés*, see Sleeper-Smith, *Indian Women and French Men*, 193n9.

3. Father Membré, "Account of the Discoveries and Journies of the Seiur de La Salle," ETM-DPL, 1:547. Participants in the 1680 attack did not unite around either a

common foe or a common set of rituals. Nevertheless, historian Richard White argues that "creative misunderstandings" between Natives and non-Natives regarding ritual and trade were central characteristics of the upper country. In contrast, James Merrell posits that Native peoples and colonizers compromised in order to forge a shared "new world." These syncretic, coalescent worlds did not result in a common culture shared by Natives and non-Natives. Richard White, *Middle Ground*, xxi; Merrell, *The Indians' New World*, 25. The alliance system at Fort St. Louis blended old and new worlds. Native peoples traveled and traded with peoples they had known in the Indians' old world, and precontact alliances shaped their responses to the challenges of early American life.

4. Historian Keith Thor Carlson, in his description of Coast Salish identities, describes how the "Salish people themselves . . . [had] a host of identity options" that often frustrated Canadian officials who desired "a recognized chief and council" capable of speaking on their behalf. See Carlson, *Power of Place*, 9, 19. For similar arguments regarding the Anishinaabe, see Witgen, *An Infinity of Nations*, 19. For historians and the desire to "make the crooked ways straight," see Maier, *American Scripture*, 216.

5. Blair, *Indian Tribes*, 349.

6. Kellogg, *Early Narratives of the Northwest*, 170, 178, 181.

7. Ibid., 190.

8. Ibid., 170, 165. Robert Weddle writes that La Salle separated from the Dollier-Galinée expedition of 1669 so that he could explore the Allegheny and Ohio rivers as far as present-day Louisville. See Weddle, *La Salle, the Mississippi, and the Gulf*, 31n3. However, Michael McCafferty places La Salle on a route from Lake Erie to the southern shore of Lake Michigan. See McCafferty, *Native American Place Names of Indiana*, 28–29.

9. [Bernou?], ETM-DPL, 1:557–58.

10. Ibid., 1:568.

11. *DCNY*, 9:147; [Bernou?], ETM-DPL, 1:568.

12. For Shawnee population figures, see "Memorial of the Abbé Jean Cavelier," ETM-DPL, 3:570. See also "Robert Cavelier, Sieur de La Salle, Letter Covering Period from August 22, 1680, to the Autumn of 1681," ibid., 2:149. For general population figures, see "La Salle on the Illinois Country, 1680," in Pease and Werner, *French Foundations*, 5.

13. Quoted in "Memoir on La Salle's Discoveries, by Tonty, 1678–1690 (1693)," in Kellogg, *Early Narratives of the Northwest*, 283–84. Murphy, *Henry de Tonty*, 8–9; Pease, *Illinois on the Eve of the Seven Years' War*, 29:xxxix. For the original source of Pease's information, see Margry, *Découvertes et Établissements*, 2:108.

14. Historian James D. Rice writes that in the northern Chesapeake region "fur traders could prosper only in the absence of actual English people." See Rice, *Nature and History in the Potomac Country*, 96. For the French reaction to Chartier following the burning of Crevecoeur, see "La Salle Arrete Ses Déserteurs," in Margry, *Découvertes et Établissements*, 2:104.

15. Pierre Deliette, "Memoir of De Gannes Concerning the Illinois Country," in Pease and Werner, *French Foundations*, 307. For the high figure, see Skinner, *Upper Country*, 56; and Joutel, *Last Voyage Perform'd by de la Sale*, 177.

16. Weddle, *French Thorn*, 16. See also Weddle, "Joutel, Henri"; "Narrative of Henri Joutel, 1684–1688," ETM-DPL, 3:485; and D'Iberville to the Minister of the Navy, February 26, 1700, ibid., 4:443.

17. "Narrative of Henri Joutel, 1684–1688," ETM-DPL, 3:490–91.

18. Ibid., 3:495.

19. Richter, *Ordeal of the Longhouse*, 145; Brandão, *Your Fyre Shall Burn No More*, 75.

20. Hanna, *Wilderness Trail*, 1:124, 158; Engelbrecht, "Iroquoian Ethnicity and Archaeological Taxa," 55–56.

21. *JR*, 59:161; Pere Joseph Marquette, "An Account of the Discovery of Some New Countries and Nations in North America," in French, *Historical Collections of Louisiana*, 2:297.

22. Skinner, *Upper Country*, 52–53. For the tendency to view seventeenth-century Illinois history through the intersection of historical materialism and Iroquois aggression, see Hunt, *Wars of the Iroquois*, 152; and Richard White, *Middle Ground*, 24, 134. Historian Wayne C. Temple acknowledges that "the Illini were probably returning to the Illinois country before the French made contact with them, but the presence of these Europeans seems to have given them courage to face the Iroquois." Temple, *Indian Villages of the Illinois Country*, 19.

23. Shackelford, "Frontier in Pre-Columbian Illinois," 198.

24. Esaray and Conrad, "Bold Counselor Phase of the Central Illinois River Valley," 38–61.

25. Conger, *History of the Illinois River Valley*, 1; Osman, *Starved Rock*, 10–11.

26. Arnold et al., "Environmental Setting of the Upper Illinois River Basin," 23, 43; Hill, *Chicago River*, 28; "Letter from Father Jacques Marquette to the Reverend Father Superior of the Missions" (1668), in *JR*, 54:185–89; Kinietz, *Indians of the Western Great Lakes*, 176–77; "La Salle on the Illinois Country, 1680," in Pease and Werner, *French Foundations*, 8.

27. Parmalee, "Faunal Complex of the Fisher Site, Illinois," 401–2, 405; Turner, "Ecological Studies," 690, 693, 703.

28. *JR*, 55:193–95. The Illinois called buffalo *pisikiou*. See Kimball-Brown, *Zimmerman Site*, 68.

29. Ryan McEwan et al., "Temporal and Spatial Patterns in Fire Occurrence," 655–56.

30. For an eloquent description of the difficulties associated with farming on the prairies of Illinois, see Faragher, *Sugar Creek*, 62–66.

31. De Gannes, "Memoir," in Pease and Werner, *French Foundations*, 346.

32. James A. Brown quoted in Walthall, "Aboriginal Pottery," 155–56. For 1,800 warriors, see "La Salle on the Illinois Country, 1680," in Pease and Werner, *French Foundations*, 5.

33. Emerson and Brown, "The Late Prehistory and Protohistory of Illinois," 112–13.

34. Kimball-Brown, *Zimmerman Site*, 37.

35. Emerson and Brown, "The Late Prehistory and Protohistory of Illinois," 105.

36. Blair, *Indian Tribes*, 300. Marquette quoted in *JR*, 59:125–27. For Illinois-Dakota relations, see ibid., 54:189–90.

37. Hoff, *Dutch Firearms*, 1; Shumway, "English Pattern Trade Rifles," 11; Alan Gutchess, telephone communication with author, November 17, 2010.

38. James Hunter, "Implications of Firearms Remains," 6.

39. Morison, *Of Plymouth Plantation*, 207; *JR*, 68:169–71.

40. The French earthenware faience was particularly popular among the Illinois. The last traces of Illinois ceramics date to 1719, more than fifty years after the Illinois initially traded with the French. See Walthall, "Aboriginal Pottery," 168–69; and Kellogg, *Early Narratives of the Northwest*, 244.

41. Wray, "Firearms among the Seneca," 106; Blair, *Indian Tribes*, 309.

42. *JR*, 55:198–99; Kimball-Brown, *Zimmerman Site*, 10.

43. *JR*, 55:201, 204–5.

44. Emerson and Brown, "The Late Prehistory and Protohistory of Illinois," 79–80; Blair, *Indian Tribes*, 151–57.

45. Temple, *Indian Villages of the Illinois Country*, 11; "Letter from Father Jacques Marquette to the Reverend Father Superior of the Missions" (1668), in *JR*, 54:185–89; Mazrim and Esaray, "Rethinking the Dawn of History," 189.

46. Blair, *Indian Tribes*, 321–22; "M. Du Chesneau's Memoir on the Western Indians," in *DCNY*, 9:160.

47. *JR*, 62:205–13.

48. Ibid.

49. Ibid., 62:207–9.

50. *DCNY*, 9:176; Skinner, *Upper Country*, 49–50.

51. *DCNY*, 9:177.

52. Ibid., 9:179–80.

53. Ibid., 9:182, 181.

54. Ibid., 9:175, 192.

55. Ibid., 9:171, 287. See Brandão, *Your Fyre Shall Burn No More*, fig. 6.1, appendix F.

56. *DCNY*, 9:115, 175.

57. Ibid., 9:115.

58. ETM-DPL, 2:313–14; ibid., 1:162.

59. Ibid., 2:313–14.

60. Ibid., 2:575–86.

61. *DCNY*, 9:194.

62. ETM-DPL, 2:330–31.

63. "Henry de Tonty's Memoir of 1693," 146–47.

64. *DCNY*, 9:276; Skinner, *Upper Country*, 64–65.

65. *DCNY*, 9:284.

66. Blair, *Indian Tribes*, 349.

67. Cox, *Journeys of Rene Robert Cavelier Sieur de La Salle*, 277–83.

68. Pease and Werner, *French Foundations*, 4.

69. *DCNY*, 9:303–5.

70. Green, "Integrative Taxa in Midwestern Archaeology," 34, 27; Essenpreis, "Fort Ancient Settlement," 143; Emerson and Brown, "The Late Prehistory and Protohistory of Illinois," 89. On the Miamis and Illinois, see Kimball-Brown, *Zimmerman Site*, 71.

Chapter 6

1. Sheehan, *Savagism and Civility*, 2–3; *AM*, 8:486. This attack may have been the Candlemas Massacre, an Abenaki-French attack on the town of York, then in Massachusetts Bay and now in Maine. For population figures, see ibid., 19:519–20.

2. "At a Councill in a General Assembly Held the 12th Day of May at Ye Port of Annapolis Anno 1696," folio 62, CO 5/714, BT-BPRO; Herrman, "Journal of the Dutch Embassy to Mary Land, 1659," 311–13; Blumgart, *At the Head of the Bay*, 27.

3. *AM*, 8:524.

4. Ibid., 8:486–87, 517–18.

5. Leder, *Livingston Indian Records*, 83–85. Francis Jennings describes how "these terminal bays witnessed intense international and intertribal competition." See Jennings, *Ambiguous Iroquois Empire*, 77.

6. Nash, "Quest for the Susquehanna Valley," 5; Leder, *Livingston Indian Records*, 116; Jacob Young to John Goode, May 30, 1690, CO 5/713, BT-BPRO; McIlwaine, *Executive Journals of the Council of Virginia*, 125.

7. Paul A. W. Wallace, *Indian Paths of Pennsylvania*, 27, 73; Rountree, "Powhatans and Other Woodland Indians as Travelers," 34.

8. Fur, *A Nation of Women*, 42–50.

9. For Susquehannock "guarantees" of the Shawnees' good behavior and the language of "Mixt Nations," see *AM*, 23:426–31.

10. *DCNY*, 12:436; *AM*, 3:502.

11. *AM*, 5:13, 65.

12. Ibid., 3:530, 421.

13. Malone, *Skulking Way of War*.

14. *AM*, 2:196, 5:245, 8:534.

15. Maryland pursued peace with the Iroquois even though it might "bring warre with the Susquehannoughs." See ibid., 2:378. For further evidence of the diminishing of the Susquehannock, see ibid., 2:428–29.

16. Alsop, "A Character of the Province of Maryland," 366; *AM*, 5:153, 13.

17. *AM*, 2:428–29, 62, 489.

18. Ibid., 5:247. For parallel examples of anglicized Dutch men assuming positions of power in colonial New York, see Richter, *Ordeal of the Longhouse*, 137–39.

19. *AM*, 5:245.

20. Ibid., 5:248. For hostages, see ibid., 2:489. For "friend Indians," see ibid., 2:488.

21. Ibid., 5:65.

22. Ibid., 7:391. For a closer analysis of Lawson and Iroquois wars against the Catawba, see Merrell, *The Indians' New World*, 41–42.

23. For "Sckulking Enemy," see *AM*, 7:271.

24. For Young and his relationship with the Susquehannocks, see ibid., 7:370.

25. For Andros and the growing power of New York, see Webb, *1676*, 340–51; and *AM*, 7:370.

26. For "Cecil County Planter," see *AM*, 7:386. For "unknown Indians," see ibid., 13:560.

27. For Young's threats, see ibid., 7:372. For Young's claims to drunkenness, see ibid., 7:390. For the 1673 Dutch takeover of New York, see Richter, *Ordeal of the Longhouse*, 135.

28. Anderson, *Imagined Communities*; "A Conference Had between His Excellency James Fletcher and the Mahikanders, Lower River Indians, and Shawanoes or Farr Indians," August 28, 1694, Penn Papers, Indian Affairs, vol. 1, folio 32, 1687–1753, HSP; Francis Nicholson to the Council, March 27, 1697, folio a15, CO 5/714, BT-BPRO; "Memorial of Coll. Robert Quarry on the Behalf and by the Order of the Representatives . . . of the Three Lower Countys Adjoyning to Pennsyvania," April 7, 1702, CO 5/1261, ibid.

29. Francis Nicholson to His Majesty's Council, August 20, 1698, CO 5/714, BT-BPRO.

30. To the Right Honorable Lords of the Committee of Trades and Plantations, from Thomas Caurther, Secretary of Maryland, June 25, 1695, folio 304, CO 5/713, ibid.

31. Francis Nicholson to the Council, March 27, 1697, folio a15, CO 5/714, ibid.

32. Treaties between Maryland and Piscataways, Choptanks, and Mattawomans, May 14, 1692, CO 5/713, ibid.; *AM*, 8:518; Sempowski, "Early Historic Exchange," 51–64.

33. Leder, *Livingston Indian Records*, 168–69.

34. Jennings, *Ambiguous Iroquois Empire*, 202; Leder, *Livingston Indian Records*, 217.

35. Hanna, *Wilderness Trail*, 1:142; "Narrative of an Embassy to the Western Indians," 77; Heckewelder, *History, Manners, and Customs of the Indian Nations*, 86. For the relationship between the Iroquois and the Algonquians, see Richter, *Ordeal of the Longhouse*, 239.

36. Keith quoted in Aquila, "Down the Warrior's Path," 218.

37. *MPCP*, July 22, 1707, 2:389–90.

38. Aquila, "Down the Warrior's Path," 215.

Chapter 7

1. For the treaty, see "Articles of Agreement between William Penn and the Susquehannah Indians," April 23, 1701, *MPCP*, 4:338. See also Lemon, *Best Poor Man's Country*. In describing such promises, historian John Smolenski argues that they amounted to a compulsory acceptance of Pennsylvania's laws. Smolenski writes: "If Indians were to be protected, it would have to be under Pennsylvania's laws, not their own." See Smolenski, "Death of Sawantaeny," 113.

2. *MPCP*, 2:600–601.

3. Morgan, "The World and William Penn," 292; Myers, *William Penn's Own Account of the Lenni Lenape*, 62; Nash, "Quest for the Susquehanna Valley," 19.

4. Nash, "Quest for the Susquehanna Valley," 13–14.

5. Merritt, *At the Crossroads*, 46–49; Jennings, *Ambiguous Iroquois Empire*, 365.

6. Historian Francis Jennings argues that the Shawnees arrived as a precondition of the Iroquois and the English and that they were essentially under their control. See Jennings, "Indian Trade of the Susquehanna Valley," 409. More recently, Smolenski has argued that the Shawnees and the Susquehannocks used these treaties to "strengthen

their own relationship to the colonial authorities." See Smolenski, *Friends and Strangers*, 204.

7. *MPCP*, 2:15. For more on the context of French and Indian raids on New England towns, see Haefeli and Sweeney, *Captors and Captives*, 2–6. For more on Le Tort and the French traders, see Merrell, *Into the American Woods*, 112. See also Jennings, *Ambiguous Iroquois Empire*, 233–36; and *MPCP*, 2:131. For further evidence of anxiety regarding French traders, see *MPCP*, 1:436.

8. "Minutes of the Council," April 10, 1694, *MPCP*, 1:454; Dunn and Dunn, *Papers of William Penn*, 2:128; Myers, *William Penn's Own Account of the Lenni Lenape*, 64. See also Smolenski, *Friends and Strangers*, 118–20; and Jennings, *Ambiguous Iroquois Empire*, 215–17.

9. "Memorial of Coll. Robert Quarry on the Behalf and by the Order of the Representatives . . . of the Three Lower Countys Adjoyning to Pennsyvania," April 7, 1702, CO 5/1261, BT-BPRO. For more on the Penn-Quarry dispute, see Nash, *Quakers and Politics*, 218–24.

10. "Mr. Penn's Answer to the Abstract of Several Informants, Relating to Irregular Proceedings & Other Undue Practices in Pennsylvania Sent Him Ye 6 April 1702," December 22, 1703, CO 5/1262, pt. 3, BT-BPRO; "Mr. Penn's Answer to the Abstract of Complaints against Pennsylvania," April 28, 1702, CO 5/1261, ibid.; "In Answer to Col. Quarry's Second Memorial, Presented to the Lords of Trade and Plantations," April 29, 1702, CO 5/1261, ibid.; *MPCP*, 2:131.

11. *MPCP*, 2:182.

12. Smolenski writes that "Pennsylvania was one of only two British colonies that saw vocal cries for the imposition of more royal authority." Smolenski, *Friends and Strangers*, 212; "Mr. Penn's Answer to the Abstract of Several Informants, Relating to Irregular Proceedings & Other Undue Practices in Pennsylvania Sent Him Ye 6 April 1702," December 22, 1703, CO 5/1262, pt. 3, BT-BPRO. Further evidence of the Conestoga sponsorship of Shawnee migrants appears in "Instructions to Smith & Skolehoven," May 21, 1728, in *PA*, 1:223.

13. For more on Logan and dissent toward Penn and his policies, see Anthony F. C. Wallace, *Teedyuscung*, 21. See also Merrell, *Into the American Woods*, 32. For more on immigration in colonial Pennsylvania, see Schwartz, *A Mixed Multitude*, 74, 77–87. For more on Logan and the difficulties of administering Pennsylvania, see Nash, *Quakers and Politics*, 286. For additional evidence of anti-Catholic and anti-French sentiment in British North America, see Demos, *Unredeemed Captive*, 116; and Merritt, *At the Crossroads*, 39–41.

14. Of 580 (ca. 1735), Map Collection, HSP; Survey of Land/Martin Chartiere, folio 2731, 1718, vol. 13, Taylor Papers, HSP. "Shawanah Town" was right beside Chartier's land. See Survey of April 20, 1726, p. 2736, vol. 13, Taylor Papers, HSP. For references to Harry the Interpreter, see *MPCP*, 2:244, 403. See also Merrell, *Into the American Woods*, 57, 111.

15. For more on the Conoys and Conestogas of the lower Susquehanna, see Schutt, *Peoples of the River Valleys*, 64–66; and *MPCP*, 2:244–47.

16. *PA*, 1:133. The original of this document is found in "Deed from Indians on the Susquehannaugh," September 13, 1700, Society Miscellaneous Collection, 1682–1900,

box 11C, folder 1700–49, HSP. See "Articles of Agreement between William Penn & Susquehanna Indians, 1701, in *PA*, 1:145. This treaty was so contested by the Susquehannocks and their neighbors that it had to be redone by James Logan in 1735.

17. Silver, *Our Savage Neighbors*, 8–9. For the Iroquois status on the Susquehanna, see Jennings, *Ambiguous Iroquois Empire*, 289–92. See also Shannon, *Iroquois Diplomacy*, 68–69.

18. *MPCP*, 2:145; Leder, *Livingston Indian Records*, 195.

19. Shannon, *Iroquois Diplomacy*, 70; Leder, *Livingston Indian Records*, 221; Jennings, "Indian Trade of the Susquehanna Valley," 409.

20. *MPCP*, 2:15–17.

21. For more on the Covenant Chain, see Aquila, *Iroquois Restoration*, 55. For the Covenant Chain in Pennsylvania, see Haan, "Covenant and Consensus," 54; and *MPCP*, 2:246–47.

22. *MPCP*, 2:138.

23. For stories of Indian enslavement in Virginia, see McIlwaine, *Executive Journals of the Council of Virginia*, 1:147, 1:157–58, 2:184.

24. *MPCP*, 2:511.

25. Ferguson and Whitehead, *War in the Tribal Zone*, 19; McIlwaine, *Executive Journals of the Council of Virginia*, 4:24–25.

26. *MPCP*, 3:21, 23.

27. Ibid., 3:97, 169, 66.

28. Cutcliffe, "Colonial Indian Policy," 254; *MPCP*, 3:20.

29. *MPCP*, 3:93, 96.

30. Ibid., 2:404.

31. James Logan to William Penn, December 24, 1708, in Armstrong, *Penn and Logan Correspondence*, 2:319; William Penn to James Logan, January 3, 1709, in ibid., 2:323; Eshleman, *Lancaster County Indians*, 199.

32. *MPCP*, 2:489–90.

33. Ibid., 2:247–48. For more on the alcohol trade in the Pennsylvania backcountry, see Mancall, *Deadly Medicine*, 122–23.

34. *MPCP*, 2:389–90. For a description of the Shawnee divisions, see Kinietz and Wheeler-Voegelin, *Shawnese Traditions*, 7; and Wheeler-Voegelin, *Mortuary Customs*. George Blanchard, telephone communication with author, October 27, 2005.

35. *MPCP*, 2:510, 511.

36. Leder, *Livingston Indian Records*, 224.

37. Hanna, *Wilderness Trail*, 1:101, 153. See also *MPCP*, 2:574.

38. *MPCP*, 2:600–601, 3:97. For Sassoonan and Paxtang, see Schutt, *Peoples of the River Valleys*, 64.

39. *MPCP*, 2:604.

40. Ibid., 3:215.

41. Fogleman, *Hopeful Journeys*, 8; Schwartz, *A Mixed Multitude*, 87; "Letter from the Council to the Proprietor against Governor Gookin," folder 74, box 1, LP.

42. James Logan to Isaac Taylor, February 26, 1718, Doc. 2875, Correspondence, 1683–1723, Taylor Papers, HSP; Survey of Land/Martin Chartiere, folio 2731, 1718, vol. 13, ibid.; Survey of April 20, 1726, p. 2736, vol. 13, ibid.

43. For Shickellamy as "viceroy" of the Lower Susquehanna River, see Anthony F. C. Wallace, *Teedyuscung*, 48. For quote, see Shannon, *Iroquois Diplomacy*, 108. See James Logan to A. Hamilton and Edward Shippen, September 7, 1731, box 2, folder 9, LP.

44. James Logan to Edward Shippen, June 20, 1731, box 2, folder 7, letter 1, LP. For evidence of a deed of land given to Edmund Cartlidge by the Delawares, see Merrell, *Into the American Woods*, 199.

45. *PA*, 1:217; James Logan to Edward Shippen, February 2, 1733/4, box 2, folder 49, collection 379, LFP.

46. *MPCP*, 3:169–70. For a brief analysis of Sawantaeny's murder and its repercussions, see Smolenski, *Friends and Strangers*, 271–76, 278. See also Merrell, *Into the American Woods*, 115–16.

47. Edward Shippen to Sally Plumber, August 3, 1725, Balch-Shippen Papers, 1:9, HSP; Assignment of Edward Shippen as Attorney for James Logan, June 24, 1730, box 1, folder 94, collection 379, LFP; *MPCP*, 3:314 15.

48. *PA*, 1:213; Hodge, *Handbook of American Indians North of Mexico*, 1:757. For Wompanosch, see Schutt, *Peoples of the River Valleys*, 100. For Shamokin, see Merritt, *At the Crossroads*, 33–34.

49. Darlington, *Christopher Gist's Journals*, 28; Anthony F. C. Wallace, *Teedyuscung*, inset map. See also Mulkearn, "Why the Treaty of Logstown, 1752," 3–4; James Logan to Edward Shippen, September 3, 1730, box 1, folder 97, collection 379, LFP.

50. James Logan to Harry and John Smith, January 30, 1730, box 1, folder 101, LFP; James Logan to Shekallamy, February 1, 1731, box 1, folder 103, ibid.; James Logan to Edward Shippen, April 18, 1731, box 1, folder 110, ibid.; James Logan to Edward Shippen, April 20, 1731, box 1, folder 118, ibid.

51. James Logan to Conrad Weiser, December 15, 1731, box 2, folder 13, LP.

52. "Lett Intended to ——— of Ye State of America," 1731, box 2, folder 15, LFP; Isaac Norris, William Preston, and James Logan to John, Thomas, and Richard Penn, September 13, 1731, Penn Papers, Indian Affairs, vol. 1, folio 36, HSP.

53. Delawares quoted in Schutt, *Peoples of the River Valleys*, 89. For a brief history of the Walking Purchase, see Dowd, *War under Heaven*, 36–39. For Canasatego, see "Indians' Request to the Government of Pennsylvania," November 19, 1736, Penn Papers, Indian Affairs, vol. 1, folio 39, HSP.

Chapter 8

1. *MPCP*, 3:609.

2. *PA*, 1:302; Schutt, *Peoples of the River Valleys*, 104, 132.

3. "Indians' Request to the Government of Pennsylvania," November 19, 1736, Penn Papers, Indian Affairs, vol. 1, folio 39, HSP; Aquila, *Iroquois Restoration*, 157, 173.

4. Patterson, *Slavery and Social Death*; Breen and Innes, *Myne Owne Ground*, 6.

5. In *Middle Ground*, Richard White describes how "Iroquois attacks had fallen like hammer blows" on the proto-Shawnees and their neighbors, rendering them "shattered peoples." Michael McConnell seconds White's opinion, arguing that "warfare set in motion migrations of people who would later be known as Shawnees and swept the

Ohio region of its other inhabitants." Richard White, *Middle Ground*, 1; McConnell, *A Country Between*, 9. See also Hinderaker, *Elusive Empires*, 9; and Hunt, *Wars of the Iroquois*.

6. Richter, *Ordeal of the Longhouse*, 271–75; Paul A. W. Wallace, *Conrad Weiser*, 44.

7. *PA*, 1:26, 218, 227.

8. "Indians' Request to the Government of Pennsylvania," November 29, 1736, Penn Papers, Indian Affairs, vol. 1, folio 39, HSP.

9. *MPCP*, 4:757–59; Merrell, *Into the American Woods*, 75.

10. James Logan to Edward Shippen, July 2, 1732, box 2, folder 28, LP; James Logan to Shickellamy, February 1, 1731, box 1, folder 103, ibid.; James Logan to Edward Shippen, April 23, 1732, box 2, folder 27, ibid.

11. James Logan to Edward Shippen, October 7, 1732, box 2, folder 31, ibid.; *PA*, 1:299; James Logan to Edward Shippen, June 7, 1733, box 2, folder 36, LP; James Logan to Edward Shippen, April 20, 1731, box 1, folder 118, LFP.

12. *MPCP*, 3:501; James Logan to Edward Shippen, July 2, 1732, box 2, folder 28, LP.

13. James Logan to Edward Shippen, April 23, 1732, box 2, folder 27, LP; James Logan to Edward Shippen, July 3, 1732, box 2, folder 29, ibid.; James Logan to Edward Shippen, October 7, 1732, box 2, folder 31, ibid.; Smolenski, *Friends and Strangers*, 271–79; Merritt, *At the Crossroads*, 69; James Logan to Samuel Preston, August 18, 1736, box 2, folder 55, collection 379, LFP.

14. James Logan to Edward Shippen, February 2, 1733/4, box 2, folder 49, collection 379, LFP; James Logan to Edward Shippen, June 7, 1733, box 2, folder 36, LP. Evidence regarding the dispossession of his traders' lands is abundant. See, for example, "Declaration to James Le Tort Regarding Lands," 1733, box 2, folder 84, collection 379, LFP; and Logan's Power of Attorney to James Martin, July 29, 1735, box 2, Maria Dickinson Logan Papers, HSP.

15. Wainwright, *George Croghan*, 4.

16. *PA*, 1:300.

17. James Logan to Conrad Weiser, December 15, 1731, box 2, folder 13, LP; *FRW*, 17:64.

18. Isaac Norris, William Preston, and James Logan to John, Thomas, and Richard Penn, September 13, 1731, Penn Papers, Indian Affairs, vol. 1, folio 36, HSP; *PA*, 1:243–44.

19. Krech, *Ecological Indian*, 104; *PA*, 1:254, 263, 265.

20. Richard White, *Middle Ground*, 189.

21. Watkins et al., *Michigan Pioneer and Historical Collections: Cadillac Papers*, 34:73–76.

22. Beauharnois, Letter of 1740 Concerning the Shawnee Indians. For further descriptions of the Shawnees as "docile" and as willing to move to Detroit at the request of the French, see *FRW*, 17:331; and "Lett Intended to ——— of Ye State of America," 1731, box 2, folder 15, LP.

23. *MPCP*, 3:459–60, 3:463, 4:341.

24. *DCNY*, 10:206; Richard White, *Middle Ground*, 212–13.

25. *PA*, 1:302; *FRW*, 17:250; [George Miranda], "A True Acct of All the Men of the Shayners in the Three Townes in Alegania," September 27, 2737, IX, 27, LP; "Tostee Affidavit," 1745, Richard Peters Collection, HSP; *DCNY*, 6:99.

26. Conrad Weiser to Col. Lee, July 5, 1746, 1:15, Weiser Papers, HSP; *PA*, 1:302–3; *DCNY*, 6:103.

27. Hodge, *Handbook of American Indians North of Mexico*, 4:757; Watkins et al., *Michigan Pioneer and Historical Collections: Cadillac Papers*, 34:182.

28. *MPA*, 1:265–66; Watkins et al., *Michigan Pioneer and Historical Collections: Cadillac Papers*, 34:109; *FRW*, 17:184.

29. *MPA*, 1:265–66; Anderson, *Imagined Communities*.

30. For the best description of Lower Shawnee Town, see Henderson, "Lower Shawnee Town on Ohio," 34; *FRW*, 18:20.

31. *FRW*, 17:243; Watkins et al., *Michigan Pioneer and Historical Collections: Cadillac Papers*, 34:208.

32. Barron, *Vaudreuil Papers*, 50; "Lett Intended to ———— of Ye State of America," 1731, box 2, folder 15, LP.

33. James Logan to Conrad Weiser, January 22, 1737, box 2, folder 60, collection 379, LFP; Hazard, *Register of Pennsylvania*, 3:212.

34. *MPCP*, 4:234; Dowd, *War under Heaven*, 38.

35. *DCNY*, 6:105–6.

36. James Logan to Conrad Weiser, July 17, 1736, box 2, folder 56, collection 379, LFP.

37. *PA*, 1:549–51.

38. Ibid., 1:261, 394, 3:275–76.

39. *DCNY*, 6:593–94; *MPCP*, 4:342–43.

40. Paul A. W. Wallace, *Conrad Weiser*, 150–51.

41. *MPCP*, 4:649, 633.

42. *FRW*, 18:21, 23; Barron, *Vaudreuil Papers*, 434.

43. *MPCP*, 4:739.

44. For the Lancaster Treaty, see Paul A. W. Wallace, *Conrad Weiser*, 185–86; and Richter, *Ordeal of the Longhouse*, 275. For the Treaty of Fort Stanwix, see Calloway, *Scratch of a Pen*, 100.

45. "Tostee Affidavit," 1745, Richard Peters Collection, HSP; *FRW*, 17:448.

46. John Ellis to Henry Morris, May 10, 1745, in Palmer, *Calendar of Virginia State Papers and Other Manuscripts*, 1:239; "Anonymous Diary of a Trip from Detroit to the Ohio River," May 22–August 24, 1745, Ohio Valley–Great Lakes Ethnohistory Archives; *MPCP*, 5:2, 5.

47. *MPA-FD*, 4:306; *PA*, 4:483.

48. Barron, *Vaudreuil Papers*, 221–22.

49. *FRW*, 17:448; "Anonymous Diary of a Trip from Detroit to the Ohio River," May 22–August 24, 1745, Ohio Valley–Great Lakes Ethnohistory Archives.

50. Trigger, *Children of Aataentsic*, 85–90.

51. *MPCP*, 5:85–87, 137.

52. "Anonymous Diary of a Trip from Detroit to the Ohio River," May 22–August 24, 1745, Ohio Valley–Great Lakes Ethnohistory Archives.

53. Conrad Weiser to Col. Lee, April 15, 1746, 1:14, Weiser Papers, HSP; *MPCP*, 5:139.

54. "Copy of Mr. George Croghan's Account of Indian Affairs, from 1748 to General Braddock's Defeat," n.d., Penn Papers, Indian Affairs, vol. 1, folio 51, HSP.

55. *MPCP*, 5:147, 148–53; Conrad Weiser to Richard Peters, December 8, 1749, 1:19, Weiser Papers, HSP.

56. *FRW*, 18:43.

57. Ibid., 18:45.

58. Edmunds, *American Indian Leaders*, 3; Barron, *Vaudreuil Papers*, 221; Krauskopf, *Ouiatenon Documents*, 141, 141nn3–4.

59. *FRW*, 18:52, 54, 104, 109; Edmunds, *American Indian Leaders*, 16–17.

60. *FRW*, 18:52, 54; Edmunds, *American Indian Leaders*, 16–17.

61. *FRW*, 18:55.

62. Ibid., 18:58; *PA*, 1:742.

63. *FRW*, 18:84, 90–92.

64. Edmunds and Peyser, *Fox Wars*; Rushforth, "Slavery, the Fox Wars, and the Limits of Alliance."

65. An Account of the Proceedings of George Croghan . . . at Ohio, June 29, 2751, Penn Papers, Indian Affairs, vol. 1, folio 72, HSP.

Chapter 9

1. For more on the formation of the Creek Confederacy, see Jenkins, "Tracing the Origins of the Early Creeks," 218. Archaeologist Vernon J. Knight believes that Shawnee migrants settled Tukabatchee between 1675 and 1677. Knight, *Tukabatchee*, 24. For the concept of "deep time," see Nabokov, *A Forest of Time*, 43.

2. Milfort claimed that the Creek town of Tukabatchee, then situated on the Tallapoosa River in present-day Elmore County, Alabama, was founded between 1675 and 1685. See Milfort, *Memoir*, 184; and Clark, "Shawnee Indian Migration," 33. Historian Angie Debo maintains that "a tradition of Creek-Shawnee friendship [goes] . . . back to the dim days of their legendary history." Debo, *Road to Disappearance*, 56.

3. For more on Stiggins, see Thomas S. Woodward, *Reminiscences of the Creek*, 7.

4. Waselkov and Braund, *William Bartram on the Southeastern Indians*, 126; Martin, *Sacred Revolt*, 36, 39. For more on contemporary understandings of the Green Corn Ceremony, see Jackson, *Yuchi Ceremonial Life*, chaps. 7, 8.

5. To this day, members of the Kispokotha division exhibit items that represent the symbolic alliance between the Shawnees and the Creeks during the fast that precedes the Busk, today's War Dance. Today, Shawnees refer to this ceremonial event as "Helenewekawe" (Men's Dance). The use of horses and guns seems to have led to the name "War Dance." According to Absentee Shawnee elder George Blanchard, it is actually intended to promote peace. See Sugden, *Tecumseh*, 14–15.

6. Anthropologist John R. Swanton made the initial scholarly claim that Tukabatchee was settled by Kispokotha Shawnees. Like Swanton, Charles Hanna and Noel Schutz have made similar claims based on the synonymy between "Ispokogi" and "Kispokotha." For these arguments, see Swanton, *Early History of the Creek Indians and Their Neighbors*, 296; Hanna, *Wilderness Trail*, 1:93; and Schutz, "Study

of Shawnee Myth," 423–26. Albert Gatschet contends that in Muskogee, *Tukatachi* means "town of survivors" or, alternately, "town . . . of foreign origin." See Gatschet, *Migration Legend*, 1:147. Both Tecumseh and Tenskwatawa were members of the Kispokotha division. Historian John Sugden argues that kin ties between Tecumseh and the townspeople of Tukabatchee inspired his visit there in 1811. See Sugden, *Tecumseh*, 14, 240–41. Shawnee cosmology, as revealed by Tenskwatawa, a Kispokotha Shawnee, also confirms a link between the Creeks and the Kispokotha Shawnees at Tukabatchee. For more on these plates, see Brannon, "Sacred Creek Relics Found in Alabama"; and Fox, "North-South Copper Axis," 90–91, 94. I thank archaeologist Vernon Knight for these citations and insights into the Tukabatchee plates. The Shawnee Prophet mentions these brass plates in his description of the origins of Shawnee-Creek relations in the Southeast. See Kinietz and Wheeler-Voegelin, *Shawnese Traditions*, 1–8.

7. Hawkins, *Creek Confederacy*, 33. On the relationship between *talwas* and *talofas* in Creek society, see Martin, *Sacred Revolt*, 11; and Walker, "Creek Confederacy before Removal," 383.

8. McDowell, *DRIA*, 128–29.

9. From Bienville and Salmon to Maurepas, June 1736, in *MPA*, 1:315; "Memoir of the King to Serve as Instructions for Sieur de Bienville, the Governor of the Province of Louisiana," in ibid., 3:552.

10. Diron d'Artaguette to Maurepas, October 17, 1729, in *MPA-FD*, 4:29.

11. Vaudreuil to Maurepas, November 5, 1748, in Barron, *Vaudreuil Papers*, 40. For more on the particular towns within the Upper Creek Confederacy, see Ethridge, *Creek Country*, 73, 83–89.

12. Jacobs, *Indians of the Southern Colonial Frontier*, 64–66. See also Steele, "Shawnee Origins of Their Seven Years' War," 658–61; *MPA-FD*, 4:146–47, 222; Diron d'Artaguette to Maurepas, October 24, 1737, in ibid., 4:147; Vaudreuil to Maurepas, July 18, 1743, in Barron, *Vaudreuil Papers*, 169.

13. Vaudreuil to Maurepas, February 6, 1746, and Vaudreuil to Maurepas, May 24, 1747, in Barron, *Vaudreuil Papers*, 216.

14. *MPA-FD*, 4:216.

15. Vaudreuil to La Houssaye, January 15, 1744, in Barron, *Vaudreuil Papers*, 307; Vaudreuil to Le Sueur, November 15, 1745, in ibid., 384; Diron d'Artaguette to Maurepas, October 17, 1729, in *MPA-FD*, 4:29.

16. Vaudreuil to Maurepas, May 24, 1748, in Pease, *Illinois on the Eve of the Seven Years' War*, 70. On Shawnees at Abihka, see Vaudreuil to Maurepas, October 28, 1744, Paris Arch. Nat. Col. C13, A28, pp. 263–66; Vaudreuil to Minister, October 30, 1745, Paris Arch. Nat. Col. C13, A29, pp. 89–92.

17. Vaudreuil to Minister, February 6, 1746, Paris Arch. Nat. Col. C13, A30, pp. 28–33. See Barron, *Vaudreuil Papers*, ix.

18. Vaudreuil to Maurepas, February 6, 1746, and Vaudreuil to Maurepas, May 24, 1747, in Barron, *Vaudreuil Papers*, 216.

19. Vaudreuil to Maurepas, March 15, 1747, in *MPA-FD*, 4:305.

20. "Extract from an Anonymous Letter," March 28, 1747, in ibid., 4:309; Vaudreuil to Hazeur, February 15, 1746, in Barron, *Vaudreuil Papers*, 385; Vaudreuil to Maurepas, April 1, 1746, in *MPA-FD*, 4:267.

21. Vaudreuil to Maurepas, February 12, 1744, in *MPA-FD*, 4:216; Vaudreuil to Rouillé, September 22, 1749, in ibid., 5:36.

22. Vaudreuil to Maurepas, April 12, 1746, and November 20, 1746, in Barron, *Vaudreuil Papers*, 222–25.

23. McConnell, *A Country Between*, 52; Richard White, *Middle Ground*, 212–13; Eccles, *Canadian Frontier*, 128; Ross, "Fur Trade of the Ohio Valley," 419.

24. Vaudreuil to Maurepas, July 12, 1746, in Barron, *Vaudreuil Papers*, 221; Krauskopf, *Ouiatenon Documents*, 141, 141nn3–4; Vaudreuil to Maurepas, April 1, 1746, in *MPA-FD*, 4:266–67; Jacobs, *Diplomacy and Indian Gifts*, 29.

25. "Journal of the Journey of M. de Beauchamp," August 1746, in *MPA-FD*, 4:276.

26. Ibid., 4:289.

27. Bienville to Maurepas, October 4, 1734, in *MPA*, 3:672–73.

28. Vaudreuil to Maurepas, March 15, 1747, in *MPA-FD*, 4:305.

29. "Extract from an Anonymous Letter," March 28, 1747, in ibid., 4:308; "Memoir for the King on the Choctaws," September 6, 1748, in ibid., 4:324. For a brief biography of Red Shoe, see Carson, *Searching for the Bright Path*, 30–33.

30. Vaudreuil to Maurepas, March 20, 1748, in *MPA-FD*, 4:316; Vaudreuil to Maurepas, June 15, 1748, in ibid., 4:323.

31. Vaudreuil to Maurepas, May 24, 1748, in Pease, *Illinois on the Eve of the Seven Years' War*, 68–69. On Lower Shawnee Town, see Caldwell, "Shawneetown," 200–203; and Vaudreuil to Benoist, July 25, 1750, and Vaudreuil to Maurepas, May 24, 1747, in Barron, *Vaudreuil Papers*, 69.

32. Vaudreuil to Maurepas, May 24, 1748, in Barron, *Vaudreuil Papers*, 35.

33. Vaudreuil to Rouillé, May 10, 1751, in *MPA-FD*, 5:75; Kerlérec to De Machault d'Arnouville, December 18, 1754, in ibid., 5:144.

34. Vaudreuil to Maurepas, May 24, 1747, in Barron, *Vaudreuil Papers*, 33. For the number of men along with Chartier, see William A. Hunter, "Peter Chartier," 9; and Vaudreuil to Rouillé, June 24, 1750, in *MPA-FD*, 5:48.

35. For the original site of Wakatomica, see Hurt, *Ohio Frontier*, 58. For the second, western Ohio site of Wakatomica, see Richard White, *Middle Ground*, 393; and McDowell, *DRIA*, 427, 215.

36. Excerpts from the interrogations come from McDowell, *DRIA*, 421, 424, 432. These same Shawnees changed their story and tried to explain that they were in South Carolina to attack their traditional enemies, the Catawbas. However, they were captured on the Lower Salkehatchie River, very near Laurel Bay, far south of Catawba territory. For these reasons, King Tom's story about being captured by Shawnees makes sense. Historian Ian Steele takes the Shawnees at their word and argues that they wanted to capture Catawbas. See Steele, "Shawnee Origins of Their Seven Years' War," 661.

37. McDowell, *DRIA*, 463. For the Seneca attack on the Yuchis, see ibid., 47. For a full explanation of the role of settlement Indians in slavery, see Gallay, *Indian Slave Trade*, 348–49; and Jacobs, *Indians of the Southern Colonial Frontier*, 44–45.

38. McDowell, *DRIA*, 246–47, 465; Mandell, *Behind the Frontier*. For Shawnees "capable of any Villany," see Merrell, *Into the American Woods*, 75.

39. McDowell, *DRIA*, 246–47, 465.

40. Ibid., 246–47, 465; Mandell, *Behind the Frontier*. Historian Ian Steele has argued that this episode was the principal cause of the Shawnees' alliance with France during the Seven Years' War. But, as this history suggests, the Shawnees' relationship to the Covenant Chain alliance and their long history with New France provided more than enough reasons for fighting the British. See Steele, "Shawnee Origins of Their Seven Years' War."

41. Dwight L. Smith, "Shawnee Captivity Ethnography."

42. Dowd, *War under Heaven*, 264.

Epilogue

1. Guha, *Dominance without Hegemony*, 3.

2. Ferguson and Whitehead, *War in the Tribal Zone*, 28.

3. Adas, *Machines as the Measure of Men*, 199.

4. Canny, "Ideology of English Colonization," 587; Davies, *Discovery of the True Causes*, 742.

5. Lepore, *Name of War*, xxi.

6. Mitchell, "A Map of British and French Dominions"; McConnell, *A Country Between*, 20–21, 69–73. Francis Jennings wrote: "Britain would have the Iroquois rights of conquest because Iroquois dependency meant that what belonged to the Iroquois belonged to Britain." See Jennings, *Ambiguous Iroquois Empire*, 11.

7. *DCNY*, 5:577.

8. "To the Honourable Robert Hunter Morris," November 22, 1755, *MPCP*, 6:726. For Logan's version of this same history, see "At a Council Held at Philadelphia," July 27, 1739, *MPCP*, 4:337.

9. Townsend, *Pocahontas and the Powhatan Dilemma*, 35.

10. For the Johnson quote, see McConnell, "Peoples 'In Between,'" 93.

11. "Message Shawnee Chiefs to Gov. Gordon, 1732," in *PA*, 1:329. Also quoted in Richard White, *Middle Ground*, 190.

12. Clinton quoted in Richter and Merrell, *Beyond the Covenant Chain*, 5. For the most prominent example of the Iroquois empire, see Hunt, *Wars of the Iroquois*.

13. Jennings, *Ambiguous Iroquois Empire*, 10–13.

14. For newer scholarship that challenges the paradigm of the Iroquois empire, see Richter, *Ordeal of the Longhouse*; and Aquila, *Iroquois Restoration*. The pendulum seems to have swung back toward the Iroquois empire in one recent study. See Parmenter, *Edge of the Woods*, esp. xxxiii–xxxv.

15. James Logan to Edward Shippen, October 7, 1832, box 2, folder 31, LP.

16. "To the Honourable Robert Hunter Morris," November 22, 1755, *MPCP*, 6:725.

17. Thomas S. Woodward, *Reminiscences of the Creek*, 41. The Spybuck name is famous among the Bird Creek Shawnees in and around Sperry, Okla.

18. Ethnologist Frank Speck certainly believed that the Yuchi-Shawnee alliance was quite old. One of his interlocutors was Charley Wilson, "a Shawnee of the band affiliated loosely with the Yuchi and Creeks since very early times and now with them in the northwestern part of Creek Nation." See Speck, "Ceremonial Songs of the Creek and Yuchi Indians," 241.

Bibliography

Primary Sources

Alvord, Clarence Walworth, and Lee Bidgood. *The First Explorations of the Trans-Allegheny Region by the Virginians, 1650–1674.* Cleveland: Arthur H. Clark, 1912.

Alsop, George. "A Character of the Province of Maryland" (1666). In *Original Narratives of Early American History: Narratives of Early Maryland, 1633–1684,* edited by Clayton Colman Hall. New York: Scribner's, 1910.

Archdale, John. "A New Description of That Fertile and Pleasant Province of Carolina, by John Archdale, 1707." In *Narratives of Early Carolina, 1650–1700,* edited by Alexander S. Salley Jr. New York: Scribner's, 1911.

Armstrong, Edward, ed. *The Penn and Logan Correspondence.* Philadelphia: Lippincott, 1872.

Atkin, Edmond. *The Appalachian Indian Frontier: The Edmond Atkin Report and Plan of 1755.* Edited by Wilbur R. Jacobs. Columbia: University of South Carolina, 1954.

Barbour, Philip L., ed. *The Complete Works of Captain John Smith.* Chapel Hill: University of North Carolina Press, 1986.

Barron, Bill, ed. *The Vaudreuil Papers: A Calendar and Index of the Personal and Private Records of Pierre de Rigaud de Vaudreuil, Royal Governor of the French Province of Louisiana, 1743–1753.* New Orleans: Polyanthos, 1975.

Bartram, William. *Travels and Other Writings: Travels through North and South Carolina, Georgia, East and West Florida* (1791). Cambridge: Cambridge University Press, 2011.

Beauharnois, Marquise de. Letter of 1740 Concerning the Shawnee Indians. French Archives and Depositories, Archives Nationale, Colonies, box 7, folder C 11 A-74, F.236, Illinois Historical Survey, University of Illinois Library, Urbana.

Blair, Emma Helen. *The Indian Tribes of the Upper Mississippi Valley and the Region of the Great Lakes.* 2 vols. in 1. 1911. Reprint, Lincoln: University of Nebraska Press, 1996.

Board of Trade, Maryland, 1696–99. British Public Record Office, Kew, UK.

Browne, William Hand, ed. *Archives of Maryland.* Vols. 1–8 and 13–26. Baltimore: Maryland Historical Society, 1883–1912.

Calendar of State Papers: Colonial Series, America and West Indies. Edited by W. Noel Sainsbury. British Public Record Office. London, 1860.

Candler, Allen D., ed. *Colonial Records of the State of Georgia.* Atlanta: Franklin and Turner, 1914.

Clanin, Douglas E., ed. *The Papers of William Henry Harrison, 1800–1811*.
  Indianapolis: Indiana Historical Society, 1999.
Cox, Isaac Joslin, ed. *The Journeys of Rene Robert Cavelier Sieur de La Salle*. New
  York: Allerton Books, 1905.
Darlington, William M., ed. *Christopher Gist's Journals, with Historical,
  Geographical, and Ethnological Notes*. Pittsburgh: J. R. Weldin, 1893.
Davies, John. *A Discovery of the True Causes Why Ireland Was Never Entirely
  Subdued, nor Brought under Obedience of the Crowne of England until the
  Beginning of the Happy Reign of King James*. In *The Carisbrooke Library*, vol. 10,
  edited by Henry Morley. London, 1890.
Department of the Interior. National Park Service. "Recommendations Regarding
  the Disposition of Culturally Unidentifiable Native American Human Remains."
  Federal Register 65 (June 8, 2000): 111.
Dunn, Richard S., and Mary Maples Dunn, eds. *The Papers of William Penn*, vol. 2.
  Philadelphia: University of Pennsylvania Press, 1982.
"English Translation of Margry." Detroit Public Library, Detroit, Mich.
French, B. F., ed. *Historical Collections of Louisiana and Florida*. 4 vols. New York:
  Albert Mason, 1875.
Galloway, Patricia, ed. *Mississippi Provincial Archives, 1729–1748, French Dominion*.
  Baton Rouge: Louisiana State University Press, 1984.
Gatschet, Albert S. *A Migration Legend of the Creek Indians with a Linguistic, Historic,
  and Ethnographic Introduction*. 4 vols. Philadelphia: D. G. Brinton, 1884–88.
Harvey, Henry. *History of the Shawnee Indians*. Cincinnati: Ephraim Morgan, 1855.
Hawkins, Benjamin. *Creek Confederacy, and a Sketch of the Creek Country*. Savannah:
  Georgia Historical Society, 1848.
Hazard, Samuel, ed. *Minutes of the Provincial Council of Pennsylvania*. Harrisburg:
  Theo. Fenn, 1851–53.
———. *Pennsylvania Archives, Selected and Arranged from Original Documents
  in the Office of the Secretary of the Commonwealth*. First Series, vols. 1–12.
  Philadelphia: Joseph Severns, 1852–56.
———. *The Register of Pennsylvania*. Philadelphia, 1829.
Heckewelder, John. *History, Manners, and Customs of the Indian Nations*.
  Philadelphia: Historical Society of Pennsylvania, 1876.
"Henry de Tonty's Memoir of 1693." In *Collections of the Illinois State Historical
  Library*, vol. 1. Springfield, Ill., 1903.
Herrman, Augustine. "Journal of the Dutch Embassy to Mary Land, 1659." In
  *Original Narratives of Early American History: Narratives of Early Maryland,
  1633–1684*, edited by Clayton Colman Hall. New York: Scribner's, 1910.
Hodge, Frederick W., ed. "The Narrative of the Expedition of Hernando de Soto by
  the Gentleman of Elvas." In *Spanish Explorers in the United States, 1528–1543*,
  edited by Frederick W. Hodge. New York: Scribner's, 1907.
Hvidt, Kristian, ed. *Von Reck's Voyage: Drawings and Journal of Philip Georg
  Friedrich von Reck*. Savannah: Beehive Press, 1980.
Jacobs, Wilbur R. *Indians of the Southern Colonial Frontier: The Edmond Atkin Plan
  of 1755*. Columbia: University of South Carolina Press, 1954.

"Journal of David Taitt's Travels from Pensacola, West Florida, to and through the Country of the Upper and the Lower Creeks, 1772." In *Travels in the American Colonies*, edited by Newton D. Mereness. New York: Macmillan, 1916.

Joutel, Henri. *The Last Voyage Perform'd by de la Sale* (1714). Ann Arbor: University Microfilms.

Kellogg, Louise Phelps, ed. *Early Narratives of the Northwest, 1634–1699.* New York: Scribner's, 1917.

Kinietz, Vernon W., and Erminie Wheeler-Voegelin, eds. *Shawnese Traditions: C. C. Trowbridge's Account.* Ann Arbor: University of Michigan Press, 1939.

Krauskopf, Frances, trans. and ed. *Ouiatenon Documents.* Indianapolis: Indiana Historical Society, 1955.

Lawson, John. *A New Voyage to Carolina.* Edited by Hugh Talmage Lefler. Chapel Hill: University of North Carolina Press, 1984.

Leder, Lawrence H., ed. *The Livingston Indian Records, 1666–1723.* Gettysburg: Pennsylvania Historical Association, 1956.

Le Jau, Francis. *The Carolina Chronicles of Dr. Francis Le Jau, 1706–1717.* Edited by Frank J. Klingberg. Berkeley: University of California Press, 1956.

Logan Family Papers. Historical Society of Pennsylvania, Philadelphia.

Logan Papers. Historical Society of Pennsylvania, Philadelphia.

Logan, Maria Dickinson, Papers. Historical Society of Pennsylvania, Philadelphia.

Margry, Pierre, ed. *Découvertes et Établissements des Français dans l'Ouest et dans le Sud de L'Amérique Septentrionale* (1614–1754). *Mémoires et Documents Originaux.* Paris, 1876.

McDowell, William L., Jr., ed. *Documents Relating to Indian Affairs, May 21, 1750–August 7, 1754.* Columbia: South Carolina Archives Department, 1958.

———. *Journals of the Commissioners of the Indian Trade, September 20, 1710–August 29, 1718.* Columbia: South Carolina Archives Department, 1955.

Merrens, Roy H., ed. *The Colonial South Carolina Scene: Contemporary Views, 1697–1774.* Columbia: University of South Carolina Press, 1977.

MicIlwaine, H. R., ed. *Executive Journals of the Council of Virginia.* Richmond: Virginia State Library, 1925.

Milfort, Louis LeClerc. *Memoir, or a Cursory Glance at My Different Travels and My Sojourning the Creek Nation.* Edited by John Francis McDermott and translated by Geraldine de Courcy. Chicago: R. R. Donnelley, 1956. Mitchell, John. "A Map of British and French Dominions." London, 1757.

Moore, Alexander, ed. *Nairne's Muskhogean Journals: The 1708 Expedition to the Mississippi River.* Jackson: University Press of Mississippi, 1988.

Moore, Francis. *A Voyage to Georgia, Begun in the Year 1736.* London: Jacob Robinson, 1744.

Myers, Albert Cook, ed. *William Penn's Own Account of the Lenni Lenape or Delaware Indians.* Somerset, N.J.: Middle Atlantic Press, 1970.

"A Narrative of an Embassy to the Western Indians from the Original Manuscript of Hendrick Aupaumut, with Prefatory Remarks by Dr. B. H. Coates." *Historical Society of Pennsylvania Memoirs* 2, pt. 1 (1827): 61–131.

O'Callaghan, E. B., ed. *Documents Relative to the Colonial History of the State of New York*. Albany: Weed, Parsons, 1855.

Ohio Valley–Great Lakes Ethnohistory Archives. Glenn A. Black Laboratory of Archaeology, Miami Collection, Bloomington, Ind.

Oklahoma Indian Affairs Commission. *2011 Oklahoma Indian Nations Pocket Pictorial Directory*. Oklahoma City: Indian Affairs Commission, 2011.

Palmer, William P., ed. *Calendar of Virginia State Papers and Other Manuscripts, 1652–1781*. Richmond: R. F. Walker, 1875.

Pease, Theodore Calvin, ed. *Illinois on the Eve of the Seven Years' War, 1747–1755*. Springfield: Illinois State Historical Library, 1940.

Pease, Theodore Calvin, and Raymond C. Werner, eds. *The French Foundations, 1680–1693*, vol. 23 of *Collections of the Illinois State Historical Library*. Springfield: Illinois State Historical Library, 1934.

Penn Papers. Indian Affairs. Historical Society of Pennsylvania.

Richard Peters Collection. Historical Society of Pennsylvania.

Rowland, Dunbar, and A. G. Sanders, eds. *Mississippi Provincial Archives, 1729–1740, French Dominion*. Jackson: Mississippi Department of Archives and History Press, 1927.

Salley, Alexander S. "The Creek Indian Tribes in 1725." *South Carolina Historical and Genealogical Magazine* 32, no. 3 (July 1931): 241–42.

———, comp. *Records of the British Public Record Office–South Carolina, 1663–1710*. Columbia: Historical Commission of South Carolina, 1931.

———, ed. *Journal of the Commons House of Assembly*. 21 vols. Columbia: Historical Commission of South Carolina, 1951–.

———, ed. *Narratives of Early Carolina, 1650–1708*. New York: Scribner's, 1911.

Shaftesbury Papers. British Public Record Office, Kew, UK.

Simcoe, John Graves, Papers. Manuscript Division, William L. Clemnts Library, Univesity of Michigan, Ann Arbor.

Smithsonian Institution, National Anthropological Archives.

Thwaites, Reuben Gold. *Early Western Travels, 1748–1846*. Cleveland: Arthur H. Clark, 1904.

———. *The Jesuit Relations and Allied Documents*. Cleveland: Burrows Brothers, 1896–1901.

———, ed. *Collections of the Wisconsin State Historical Society: The French Regime in Wisconsin, 1727–1748*. Madison: State Historical Society of Wisconsin, 1906.

Tucker, Sarah Jones, comp. *Indian Villages of the Illinois Country, 1670–1830: Atlas and Supplement*. Springfield: Illinois State Museum, 1975.

Virginia Colonial Records Project. John D. Rockefeller Library. Colonial Williamsburg Foundation.

Voegelin, C. F., Papers. Manuscript Collection 68, American Philosophical Society, Philadelphia.

Waselkov, Gregory A., and Kathryn E. Holland Braund. *William Bartram on the Southeastern Indians*. Lincoln: University of Nebraska Press, 1995.

Watkins, L. D., et al., eds. *Michigan Pioneer and Historical Collections: Cadillac Papers*. Lansing: Wynkoop, Hallenbeck, Crawford, 1904.

Weddle, Robert S. *La Salle, the Mississippi, and the Gulf: Three Primary Documents.*
College Station: Texas A&M University Press, 1987.
Weiser Papers. Historical Society of Pennsylvania.
Wheeler-Voegelin, Erminie, Papers, 1934–85. Newberry Library, Chicago.
Williams, Samuel Cole, ed. *Early Travels in the Tennessee Country, 1540–1800.*
Johnson City, Tenn.: Watauga Press, 1928.
Woodward, Henry. "A Faithfull Relation of My Westoe Voiage." In *Narratives of Early
Carolina, 1650–1708*, edited by Alexander S. Salley Jr. New York: Scribner's, 1911.
Woodward, Thomas S. *Reminiscences of the Creek, or Muscogee Indians Contained
in Letters to Friends in Georgia and Alabama* (1859). Tuscaloosa: Alabama Book
Store and Birmingham Book Exchange, 1939.

Secondary Sources

Abler, Thomas S. "Longhouse and Palisade: Northeastern Iroquoian Villages of the
Seventeenth Century," *Ontario History* 62 (1970): 17–40.
Adas, Michael. *Machines as the Measure of Men.* Ithaca: Cornell University Press,
1989.
Alford, Thomas Wildcat. *Civilization and the Story of the Absentee Shawnees.*
Norman: University of Oklahoma Press, 1936.
Anderson, Benedict. *Imagined Communities: Reflections on the Origin and Spread of
Nationalism.* New York: Verso, 1991.
Anderson, David G. "The Evolution of Tribal Social Organization in the Southeastern
United States." In *The Archaeology of Tribal Societies*, edited by William A.
Parkinson, 246–77. Archaeological Series 15, International Monographs in
Prehistory (March 2003).
———. *The Savannah River Chiefdoms: Political Change in the Prehistoric Southeast.*
Tuscaloosa: University of Alabama Press, 1994.
Anderson, Emma. *The Betrayal of Faith: The Tragic Journey of a Colonial Native
Convert.* Cambridge: Harvard University Press, 2007.
Aquila, Richard. "Down the Warrior's Path: The Causes of the Southern Wars of the
Iroquois." *American Indian Quarterly* 4, no. 3 (August 1978): 211–21.
———. *The Iroquois Restoration: Iroquois Diplomacy on the Colonial Frontier,
1701–1754.* Detroit: Wayne State University Press, 1983.
Arnold, Terri L., et al. "Environmental Setting of the Upper Illinois River Basin and
Implications for Water Quality." *Water Resources Investigation Report* 98-4268.
Washington, D.C.: U.S. Geological Survey, 1999.
Baker, Stanley W. "Early Seventeenth Century Trade Beads from the Upper Ohio
Valley." *Ohio Archaeologist* 36, no. 4 (1986): 21–24.
Barth, Fredrick. *Ethnic Groups and Boundaries: The Social Organization of Culture
Difference.* London: Allen and Unwin, 1969.
Basso, Keith H. *Wisdom Sits in Places: Landscape and Language among the Western
Apache.* Albuquerque: University of New Mexico Press, 1996.
Beck, Robin A., Jr. "Catawba Coalescence and the Shattering of the Carolina
Piedmont, 1540–1675." In *Mapping the Mississippian Shatter Zone: The Colonial*

Indian Slave Trade and Regional Instability in the American South, edited by
Robbie Ethridge and Sheri Shuck-Hall, 115–41. Lincoln: University of Nebraska
Press, 2009.

Berlin, Ira. *Many Thousands Gone: The First Two Centuries of Slavery in North
America*. Cambridge: Harvard University Press, 1998.

Berry, Wendell. *Jayber Crow: A Novel*. New York: Counterpoint, 2000.

Béteille, André. "The Concept of Tribe with Special Reference to India." *European
Journal of Sociology* 27, no. 2 (1986): 297–318.

Black, Glenn A. "Archaeological Survey of Dearborn and Ohio Counties." *Indiana
History Bulletin* 11, no. 7 (1934): 173–260.

Blakeslee, Donald J. "The Origin and Spread of the Calumet Ceremony." *American
Antiquity* 46, no. 4 (October 1981): 759–68.

Blitz, John H. *Ancient Chiefdoms of the Tombigbee*. Tuscaloosa: University of
Alabama Press, 1993.

Blumgart, Pamela James. *At the Head of the Bay: A Cultural and Architectural
History of Cecil County, Maryland*. Elkton: Maryland Historic Trust Press, 1996.

Bossy, Denise I. "Indian Slavery in Southeastern Indian and British Societies, 1670–
1730." In *Indian Slavery in Colonial America*, edited by Alan Gallay, 207–50.
Lincoln: University of Nebraska Press, 2009.

Bowes, John. *Exiles and Pioneers: Eastern Indians in the Trans-Mississippi West*.
New York: Cambridge University Press, 2007.

Bowne, Eric E. *The Westo Indians: Slave Traders of the Early Colonial South*.
Tuscaloosa: University of Alabama Press, 2005.

Brandão, José António. *"Your Fyre Shall Burn No More": Iroquois Policy toward New
France and Its Native Allies to 1701*. Lincoln: University of Nebraska Press, 2000.

Brannon, Peter A. "Sacred Creek Relics Found in Alabama." *Arrow Points* 19, nos. 1–2
(1930): 3.

Braudel, Fernand. "Histoire et Science Sociale: La Longue Durée." *Annales* 13, no. 4
(1958): 725–53.

Breen, T. H., and Stephen Innes. *"Myne Owne Ground": Race and Freedom on
Virginia's Eastern Shore, 1640–1676*. New York: Oxford University Press, 2005.

Briceland, Alan Vance. *Westward from Virginia: The Exploration of the Virginia-
Carolina Frontier*. Charlottesville: University Press of Virginia, 1987.

Broida, M. "An Estimate of the Percent of Maize in the Diets of Two Kentucky Fort
Ancient Villages." In *Late Prehistoric Research in Kentucky*, edited by D. Pollack,
C. Hockensmith, and T. Sanders, 68–82. Frankfort: Kentucky Heritage Council,
1984.

Brooks, Lisa. *The Common Pot: The Recovery of Native Space in the Northeast*.
Minneapolis: University of Minnesota Press, 2008.

Brose, David S. "Penumbral Protohistory on Lake Erie's South Shore." In *Societies in
Eclipse: Archaeology of the Eastern Woodlands*, A.D. *1400–1700*, edited by David
S. Brose, C. Wesley Cowan, and Robert C. Mainfort Jr., 49–65. Washington, D.C.:
Smithsonian Institution Press, 2001.

Brown, James A. *The Zimmerman Site: A Report on Excavations at the Grand Village
of Kaskaskia*. Springfield: Illinois State Museum, 1961.

Brown, James A., and Robert F. Sasso. "Prelude to History on the Eastern Plains." In *Societies in Eclipse: Archaeology of the Eastern Woodlands Indians, A.D. 1400–1700*, edited by David S. Brose, C. Wesley Cowan, and Robert C. Mainfort Jr., 205–28. Washington, D.C.: Smithsonian Institution Press, 2001.

Brown, Philip M. "Early Indian Trade in the Development of South Carolina: Politics, Economics, and Social Mobility during the Proprietary Period, 1670–1719." *South Carolina Historical Magazine* 76, no. 3 (July 1975): 118–28.

Burke, Peter. *The French Historical Revolution: The Annales School, 1929–1989*. Palo Alto: Stanford University Press, 1990.

Burns, Ric. Transcript of interview with Andy Warrior, Norman, Okla., December 2006, for *Tecumseh's Vision*, pt. 2 of *We Shall Remain: A Native History of America*, directed by Ric Burns and Chris Eyre. Boston: WGBH/American Experience, 2009.

Caldwell, Norman W. "Shawneetown: A Chapter in the History of Illinois." *Journal of the Illinois State Historical Society* 32, no. 2 (June 1939): 193–205.

Callender, Charles. "Fox." In *Northeast*, vol. 15 of *Handbook of North American Indians*, edited by William C. Sturtevant and Bruce Trigger, 636–67. Washington, D.C.: Smithsonian Institution, 1978.

———. "Shawnee." In *Northeast*, vol. 15 of *Handbook of North American Indians*, edited by William C. Sturtevant and Bruce Trigger, 622–35. Washington, D.C.: Smithsonian Institution, 1978.

Calloway, Colin G. *New Worlds for All: Indians, Europeans, and the Remaking of Early America*. Baltimore: Johns Hopkins University Press, 1998.

———. *The Scratch of a Pen: 1763 and the Transformation of North America*. New York: Oxford University Press, 2006.

———. *The Shawnees and the War for America*. New York: Viking, 2008.

———. "'We Have Always Been the Frontier': The American Revolution in Shawnee Country." *American Indian Quarterly* 16, no. 1 (1992): 39–52.

Canny, Nicholas P. "The Ideology of English Colonization: From Ireland to America." *William and Mary Quarterly* 30, no. 4 (October 1973): 575–98.

Carlson, Keith Thor. *The Power of Place, the Problem of Time: Aboriginal Identity and Historical Consciousness in the Cauldron of Colonialism*. Toronto: University of Toronto Press, 2010.

Carr, Christopher, and Robert F. Maslowski. "Cordage and Fabrics: Relating Form, Technology, and Social Processes." In *Style, Society, and Person: Archaeological and Ethnological Perspectives*, edited by Christopher Carr and Jill E. Neitzel, 297–344. New York: Plenum Press, 1995.

Carskadden, Jeff, and James Morton. "Fort Ancient in the Central Muskingum Valley of Eastern Ohio: A View from the Philo II Site." In *Cultures before Contact: The Late Prehistory of Ohio and Surrounding Regions*, edited by Robert A. Genheimer, 158–93. Columbus: Ohio Archaeological Council, 2000.

Carson, James Taylor. "Ethnogeography and the Native American Past." *Ethnohistory* 49, no. 4 (2002): 765–84.

———. *Searching for the Bright Path: The Mississippi Choctaws from Prehistory to Removal*. Lincoln: University of Nebraska Press, 1999.

Cassidy, Claire Monod. "Skeletal Evidence for Prehistoric Subsistence Adaptation in the Central Ohio River Valley." In *Paleopathology at the Origins of Agriculture*, edited by Mark N. Cohen and George J. Armelagos, 307–46. New York: Academic Press, 1984.

Charlevoix, Pierre François-Xavier, de. *History and General Description of New France* (1866–72), translated by John Gilmary Shea. Vol. 3. Reprint, Chicago, 1962.

Clark, Jerry Eugene. "Shawnee Indian Migration: A System Analysis." Ph.D. diss., University of Kentucky, 1974.

Colden, Cadwallader. *History of the Five Indian Nations of Canada*. New York: Allerton Books, 1747.

Conger, John Leonard. *History of the Illinois River Valley*. Vol. 1. Chicago: S. J. Clarke, 1932.

Corkran, David H. *The Creek Frontier, 1540–1793*. Norman: University of Oklahoma Press, 1967.

Costa, David J. "Miami-Illinois Tribe Names." In *Papers of the Thirty-first Algonquian Conference*, edited by John Nichols, 30–53. Winnipeg: University of Manitoba, 2000.

Covington, James W. "Apalachee Indians, 1704–1763." *Florida Historical Quarterly* 50, no. 4 (April 1972): 366–84.

Cowan, C. Wesley. *Excavations and Chronology*. Vol. 2 of *Fort Ancient Chronology and Settlement Evaluation in the Great Miami Valley*. Cincinnati: Ohio Historic Preservation Office Survey, 1986.

———. *First Farmers of the Middle Ohio Valley: Fort Ancient Societies, A.D. 1000–1670*. Cincinnati: Cincinnati Museum of Natural History, 1987.

Crane, Verner W. "An Historical Note on the Westo Indians." *American Anthropologist* 20, no. 3 (July–September 1919): 331–37.

———. "Projects for the Colonization of the South." *Mississippi Valley Historical Review* 12, no. 1 (June 1925): 23–35.

———. *The Southern Frontier, 1670–1732*. Durham: Duke University Press, 1928.

———. "The Tennessee River as the Road to Carolina: The Beginnings of Exploration and Trade." *Mississippi Valley Historical Review* 3, no. 1 (June 1916): 3–18.

Cronon, William. *Changes in the Land: Indians, Colonists, and the Ecology of New England*. New York: Hill and Wang, 1983.

Cutcliffe, Stephen H. "Colonial Indian Policy as a Measure of Rising Imperialism: New York and Pennsylvania, 1700–1755." *Western Pennsylvania Historical Magazine* 64, no. 3 (July 1981): 237–68.

Debo, Angie. *The Road to Disappearance: A History of the Creek Indians*. Norman: University of Oklahoma Press, 1979.

de Certeau, Michel. *Culture in the Plural* (1974). Minneapolis: University of Minnesota Press, 1997.

Deloria, Vine. *God Is Red: A Native View of Religion* (1973). Golden, Colo.: North American Press, 2003.

DeMallie, Raymond J. "Tutelo and Neighboring Groups." In *Southeast*, vol. 14 of *Handbook of North American Indians*, edited by Raymond Fogelson and William C Sturtevant, 286–300. Washington, D.C.: Smithsonian Institution, 2004.

Demos, John. *The Unredeemed Captive: A Family Story from Early America*. New York: Vintage, 1994.

de Vorsey, Louis, Jr. "The Colonial Georgia Backcountry." In *Colonial Augusta: "Key of the Indian Countrey,"* edited by Edward J. Cashin, 3–26. Macon: Mercer University Press, 1986.

———. *The Georgia–South Carolina Boundary: A Problem in Historical Geography*. Athens: University of Georgia Press, 1982.

Dowd, Gregory Evans. *A Spirited Resistance: The North American Indian Struggle for Unity, 1745–1815*. Baltimore: Johns Hopkins University Press, 1993.

———. *War under Heaven: Pontiac, the Indian Nations, and the British Empire*. Baltimore: Johns Hopkins University Press, 2004.

Drooker, Penelope. "Exotic Ceramics at Madisonville: Implications for Interaction." In *Taming the Taxonomy: Toward a New Understanding of Great Lakes Archaeology*, edited by R. F. Williamson and Christopher M. Watts, 71–81. Toronto: Eastend Press, 1998.

———. "The Ohio Valley, 1550–1750: Patterns of Sociopolitical Coalescence and Dispersal." In *The Transformation of the Southeastern Indians, 1540–1760*, edited by Robbie Ethridge and Charles Hudson, 115–33. Jackson: University of Mississippi Press, 2002.

———. "Pipes, Leadership, and Interregional Interaction in Protohistoric Midwestern and Northeastern North America." In *Smoking and Culture: The Archaeology of Tobacco Pipes in Eastern North America*, edited by Sean M. Rafferty and Rob Mann, 73–123. Knoxville University of Tennessee Press, 2004.

———. "Redstone, Shell, and Metal in Late Prehistoric and Protohistoric Fort Ancient Contexts." Paper given at Midwest Archaeological Conference, LaCrosse, Wisc., 2011.

———. *The View from Madisonville: Protohistoric Western Fort Ancient Interaction Patterns*. Memoirs of the Museum of Anthropology, no. 31. Ann Arbor: University of Michigan Press, 1997.

Drooker, Penelope B., and C. Wesley Cowan. "Transformation of the Fort Ancient Cultures of the Central Ohio Valley." In *Societies in Eclipse: Archaeology of the Eastern Woodland Indians, A.D. 1400–1700*, edited by David S. Brose, C. Wesley Cowan, and Robert C. Mainfort Jr., 83–106. Washington, D.C.: Smithsonian Institution, 2006.

Earle, Timothy, and A. Johnson. *The Evolution of Human Societies* (1987). Stanford Stanford University Press, 2000.

Eccles, W. J. *The Canadian Frontier, 1534–1760*. Albuquerque University of New Mexico Press, 1983.

Edmunds, R. David. *American Indian Leaders: Studies in Diversity*. Lincoln University of Nebraska Press, 1980.

———. *The Shawnee Prophet*. Lincoln University of Nebraska Press, 1983.

———. *Tecumseh and the Quest for Indian Leadership*. New York Longman, 2006.

Edmunds, R. David, and Joseph L. Peyser. *The Fox Wars: The Mesquakie Challenge to New France*. Norman University of Oklahoma Press, 1993.

Ehrhardt, Kathleen L. *European Metals in Native Hands: Rethinking the Dynamics of Technological Change, 1640–1683*. Tuscaloosa University of Alabama Press, 2005.

Emerson, Thomas E., and James A. Brown. "The Late Prehistory and Protohistory of Illinois." In *Calumet and Fleur-de-lys: Archaeology of Indian and French Contact in the Mid-Continent*, edited by John A. Walthall and Thomas E. Emerson, 77–128. Washington, D.C.: Smithsonian Institution Press, 1992.

Engelbrecht, William. *Iroquoia: The Development of a Native World*. Syracuse Syracuse University Press, 2003.

———. "Iroquoian Ethnicity and Archaeological Taxa." In *Taming the Taxonomy: Toward a New Understanding of Great Lakes Archaeology*, edited by R. F. Williamson and Christopher M. Watts, 51–59. Toronto Eastend Books, 1999.

Esaray, Duane, and L. A. Conrad. "The Bold Counselor Phase of the Central Illinois River Valley: Oneota's Middle Mississippian Margin." *Wisconsin Archaeologist* 79, no. 2 (1998): 38–61.

Eshleman, H. Frank. *Lancaster County Indians*. Lancaster, Pa.: Express Printing, 1909.

Essenpreis, Patricia S. "Fort Ancient Settlement: Differential Response at a Mississippian–Late Woodland Interface." In *Mississippian Settlement Patterns*, edited by Bruce D. Smith, 141–67. New York Academic Press, 1978.

Ethridge, Robbie. *From Chicaza to Chickasaw: The European Invasion and the Transformation of the Mississippian World, 1540–1715*. Chapel Hill University of North Carolina Press, 2010.

———. *Creek Country: The Creek Indians and Their World*. Chapel Hill University of North Carolina Press, 2003.

Everett, C. S. "'An Inhuman Practice Once Prevailed in This Country': Indian Slavery in Virginia." Ph.D. diss., Vanderbilt University, 2009.

———. "'They Shalbe Slaves for Their Lives': Indian Slavery in Colonial Virginia." In *Indian Slavery in Colonial America*, edited by Alan Gallay, 67–108. Lincoln University of Nebraska Press, 2009.

Faragher, John Mack. *Sugar Creek: Life on the Illinois Prairie*. New Haven Yale University Press, 1986.

Feest, Christian F. "Virginia Algonquians." In *Northeast*, vol. 15 of *Handbook of North American Indians*, edited by Bruce G. Trigger, 253–70. Washington, D.C.: Smithsonian Institution, 1978.

Feld, Steven, and Keith H. Basso. *Senses of Place*. Santa Fe School of American Research Press, 1996.

Ferguson, R. Brian, and Neil L. Whitehead. *War in the Tribal Zone: Expanding States and Indigenous Warfare*. Santa Fe SAR Press, 2000.

Fitting, James E., and Charles E. Cleland. "Late Prehistoric Settlement Patterns in the Upper Great Lakes." *Ethnohistory* 16, no. 4 (Autumn 1969): 289–302.

Fogleman, Aaron Spencer. *Hopeful Journeys: German Immigration, Settlement, and Political Culture in Colonial America, 1717–1775*. Philadelphia University of Pennsylvania Press, 1996.

Foreman, Grant. *Indian Removal: The Emigration of the Five Civilized Tribes of Indians*. Norman University of Oklahoma Press, 1974.

Foster, Morris W. *Being Comanche: A Social History of an American Indian Community*. Tucson: University of Arizona Press, 1992.

Fox, William A. "The North-South Copper Axis." *Southeastern Archaeology* 23, no. 1 (Summer 2004): 85–97.

Fur, Gunlög. *A Nation of Women: Gender and Colonial Encounters among the Delaware Indians*. Philadelphia: University of Pennsylvania Press, 2011.

Gallay, Alan. *The Indian Slave Trade: The Rise of the English Empire in the American South, 1670–1717*. New Haven: Yale University Press, 2002.

———. "South Carolina's Entrance into the Indian Slave Trade." *Indian Slavery in Colonial America*, edited by Alan Gallay, 109–45. Lincoln: University of Nebraska Press, 2009.

Ganson, Barbara. *The Guaraní under Spanish Rule in the Rio de la Plata*. Palo Alto: Stanford University Press, 2005.

George, Richard L. "The Gnagey Site and the Monongahela Occupation of the Somerset Plateau." *Pennsylvania Archaeologist* 53, no. 4 (1983): 1–79.

Goddard, Ives. "Central Algonquian Languages." In *Northeast*, vol. 15 of *Handbook of North American Indians*, edited by William C. Sturtevant and Bruce G. Trigger, 583–87. Washington, D.C.: Smithsonian Institution, 1978.

Goins, Charles Robert, and Danny Goble, eds. *Historical Atlas of Oklahoma*. Norman: University of Oklahoma Press, 2006.

Graybill, Jeffrey R. "The Eastern Periphery of Fort Ancient." *Pennsylvania Archaeologist* 54, nos. 1–2 (1984): 40–50.

———. "The Eastern Periphery of Fort Ancient (A.D. 1050–1650): A Diachronic Approach to Settlement Variability." Ph.D. diss., University of Washington, 1981.

Green, William. "Integrative Taxa in Midwestern Archaeology." In *Taming the Taxonomy: Toward a New Understanding of Great Lakes Archaeology*, edited by R. F. Williamson and Christopher M. Watts, 25–36. Toronto: Eastend Press, 1998.

———. *The Search for Altamaha: The Archaeology and Ethnohistory of an Early 18th Century Yamasee Indian Town*. Columbia: South Carolina Institute of Archaeology and Anthropology, University of South Carolina, 1992.

Greer, Allan. *The Jesuit Relations: Natives and Missionaries in Seventeenth-Century North America*. Boston: Bedford/St. Martin's, 2000.

———. *Mohawk Saint: Catherine Tekakwitha and the Jesuits*. New York: Oxford University Press, 2005.

Griffin, James B. *The Fort Ancient Aspect: Its Cultural and Chronological Position in Mississippi Valley Archaeology*. Ann Arbor: University of Michigan, Museum of Anthropology, Anthropological Papers no. 28, 1943.

———. "Fort Ancient Has No Class: The Absence of an Elite Group in Mississippian Societies in the Central Ohio Valley." Archaeological Papers of the American Anthropological Association 3, no. 1 (January 1992): 53–59.

———. "Late Prehistory of the Ohio Valley." In *Northeast*, vol. 15 of *Handbook of North American Indians*, edited by William C. Sturtevant and Bruce G. Trigger, 547–59. Washington, D.C.: Smithsonian Institution, 1978.

Guha, Ranajit. *Dominance without Hegemony: History and Power in Colonial India*. Cambridge: Harvard University Press, 1997.

Haan, Richard L. "Covenant and Consensus: Iroquois and English, 1676–1760." In *Beyond the Covenant Chain: The Iroquois and Their Neighbors in Indian North*

America, 1600–1800, edited by Daniel K. Richter and James H. Merrell, 41–57. Syracuse: Syracuse University Press, 1987.

Haas, Mary. "The Proto-Gulf Word for Water (with Notes on Siouan-Yuchi)." *International Journal of American Linguistics* 17, no. 2 (1951): 71–79.

Hackett-Fischer, David. *Champlain's Dream: The European Founding of North America*. New York: Simon and Schuster, 2009.

———. *Washington's Crossing*. New York: Oxford University Press, 2006.

Haefeli, Evan, and Kevin Sweeney. *Captors and Captives: The 1704 French and Indian Raid on Deerfield*. Amherst: University of Massachusetts Press, 2003.

Hahn, Steven C. *The Invention of the Creek Nation, 1670–1763*. Lincoln: University of Nebraska Press, 2004.

Hall, David D. *Lived Religion in America: Toward a History of Practice*. Princeton: Princeton University Press, 1992.

Hall, Joseph M., Jr. "Anxious Alliances: Apalachicola Efforts to Survive the Slave Trade, 1638–1705." In *Indian Slavery in Colonial America*, edited by Alan Gallay, 147–84. Lincoln: University of Nebraska Press, 2009.

———. *Zamumo's Gifts: Indian-European Exchange in the Colonial Southeast*. Philadelphia: University of Pennsylvania Press, 2009.

Hall, Robert L. *An Archaeology of the Soul: North American Indian Belief and Ritual*. Urbana: University of Illinois Press, 1997.

———. "Calumet Ceremonialism, Mourning Ritual, and Mechanisms of Inter-tribal Trade." In *Mirror and Metaphor: Material and Social Constructions of Reality*, edited by Daniel W. Ingersoll Jr. and Gordon Bronitsky, 29–43. Lanham, Md.: University Press of America, 1987.

Hamill, James. *Going Indian*. Urbana: University of Illinois Press, 2006.

Hann, John H. "St. Augustine's Fallout from the Yamasee War." *Florida Historical Quarterly* 68, no. 2 (October 1989): 180–200.

Hanna, Charles A. *The Wilderness Trail or the Ventures and Adventures of the Pennsylvania Traders on the Allegheny Path with Some New Annals of the Old West, and the Records of Some Strong Men and Some Bad Ones* (1911). 2 vols. Reprint, New York: AMS Press, 1971.

Hanson, Lee H., Jr. *The Hardin Village Site*. Lexington: University of Kentucky Press, 1966.

Hauptman, Laurence M. *The Iroquois in the Civil War: From Battlefield to Reservation*. Syracuse: Syracuse University Press, 1993.

Henderson, A. Gwynn. "Dispelling the Myth: Seventeenth and Eighteenth Century Indian Life in Kentucky." *Register of the Kentucky Historical Society* 90 (1992): 1–25.

———. "Early European Contact in Southern Ohio." In *Ohio Archaeology: An Illustrated Chronicle of Ohio's Ancient American Indian Cultures*, edited by Bradley T. Lepper, 231. Wilmington: Orange Frazer Press, 2005.

———. *Fort Ancient Cultural Dynamics in the Middle Ohio Valley*. Madison: Prehistoric Press, 1992.

———. "Fort Ancient Period." In *The Archaeology of Kentucky: An Update*, edited by David Pollack, 739–902. Frankfort: Kentucky Heritage Council, State Historic Preservation Comprehensive Plan 2, no. 3 (2010).

———. *Kentuckians before Boone*. Lexington: University Press of Kentucky, 1992.

———. "The Lower Shawnee Town on Ohio: Sustaining Native Autonomy in an Indian "Republic."" In *"The Buzzel bout Kentuck": Settling the Promised Land*, edited by Craig Thompson Friend, 24–55. Lexington: University Press of Kentucky, 1999.

———. "The Prehistoric Farmers of Boone County, Kentucky." *Education Series No. 8*. Lexington: Kentucky Archaeological Survey, 2006.

Henderson, A. Gwynn, and David Pollack. "The Late Woodland Occupation of the Bentley Site." In *Woodland Period Research in Kentucky*, edited by David Pollack, Thomas N. Sanders, and Charles D. Hockensmith, 140–64. Frankfort: Kentucky Heritage Council, 1985.

———. "Appendix III: The Bentley Site." In *Continuity and Change: Fort Ancient Cultural Dynamics in Northeastern Kentucky*, edited by A. Gwynn Henderson, A-136. Frankfort: Kentucky Heritage Council, 1990.

Henderson, A. Gwynn, David Pollack, Cynthia E. Jobe, and Christopher A. Turnbow. *Indian Occupation and Use in Northern and Eastern Kentucky during the Contact Period (1540–1795): An Initial Investigation*. Frankfort: Kentucky Heritage Council, 1986.

Hickerson, Nancy P. *The Jumanos: Hunters and Traders of the Southern Plains*. Austin: University of Texas Press, 1994.

Hill, Libby. *The Chicago River: A Natural and Unnatural History*. Chicago: Lake Claremont Press, 2000.

Hinderaker, Eric. *Elusive Empires: Constructing Colonialism in the Ohio Valley, 1673–1800*. New York: Cambridge University Press, 1997.

Hockett, Charles F. "The Proto Central Algonquian Kinship System." In *Explorations in Cultural Anthropology*, edited by Ward H. Goodenough, 239–57. New York: McGraw Hill, 1964.

Hodge, Frederick Webb. *Handbook of American Indians North of Mexico*. Washington, D.C.: Smithsonian, 1912.

Hoff, Arne. *Dutch Firearms*. London: Sotheby Parke Bernet Publications, 1978.

Hooten, Earnest Albert, and Charles Clark Willoughby. "Indian Village and Cemetery near Madisonville, Ohio." *Papers of the Peabody Museum of American Archaeology and Ethnology* 3, no. 1 (1920): 1–137.

Horn, James. *Adapting to a New World: English Society in the Seventeenth-Century Chesapeake*. Chapel Hill: University of North Carolina Press, 1994.

Houck, Louis. *A History of Missouri: From the Earliest Explorations and Settlements until the Admission of the State into the Union*. Chicago: R. R. Donnelley, 1908.

Howard, James H. "The Compleat Stomp Dancer." *Museum News: South Dakota Museum* 26, nos. 5–6 (May–June 1965).

———. "Pan-Indian Culture of Oklahoma." *Scientific Monthly* 18, no. 5 (November 1955): 215–20.

———. *Shawnee! The Ceremonialism of a Native American Tribe and Its Cultural Background*. Athens: Ohio University Press, 1981.

Hoxie, Frederick E. *A Final Promise: The Campaign to Assimilate the Indians*. Lincoln: University of Nebraska Press, 2001.

Hunt, George T. *The Wars of the Iroquois: A Study in Intertribal Trade Relations.* Madison: University of Wisconsin Press, 1940.

Hunter, James. "The Implications of Firearms Remains from Saint Marie among the Hurons, A.D. 1639–1649." In *Proceedings of the 1984 Trade Gun Conference*, edited by Charles F. Hayes III. Rochester: Rochester Museum and Science Center, 1985.

Hunter, William A. "Peter Chartier: Knave of the Wild Frontier." *Historical Papers: Cumberland County Historical Society* 9, no. 4 (1973).

Hurt, Douglas. *The Ohio Frontier: Crucible of the Old Northwest, 1720–1830.* Bloomington: Indiana University Press, 1998.

Jackson, Jason Baird. "The Opposite of Powwow: Ignoring and Incorporating the Intertribal War Dance in the Oklahoma Stomp Dance Community." *Plains Anthropologist* 48 (2003): 237–53.

———. "Yuchi." In *Southeast*, vol. 14 of *Handbook of North American Indians*, edited by Raymond D. Fogelson, 415–28. Washington, D.C.: Smithsonian Institution, 2004.

———. *Yuchi Ceremonial Life: Performance, Meaning, and Tradition in a Contemporary American Indian Community.* Lincoln: University of Nebraska Press, 2003.

———. "A Yuchi War Dance in 1736." *European Review of Native American Studies* 16, no. 1 (2002): 27–32.

Jacobs, Wilbur R. *Diplomacy and Indian Gifts: Anglo-French Rivalry along the Ohio and Northwest Frontiers, 1748–1763.* Stanford: Stanford University Press, 1950.

Jenkins, Ned J. "Tracing the Origins of the Early Creeks, 1050–1700 CE." In *Mapping the Mississippian Shatter Zone: The Colonial Indian Slave Trade and Regional Instability in the American South*, edited by Robbie Ethridge and Sheri M. Shuck-Hall, 188–249. Lincoln: University of Nebraska Press, 2009.

Jennings, Francis. *The Ambiguous Iroquois Empire: The Covenant Chain Confederation of Indian Tribes with English Colonies.* New York: Norton, 1990.

———. "Indians and Frontiers in Seventeenth Century Maryland." In *Early Maryland in a Wider World*, edited by David B. Quinn, 216–39. Detroit: Wayne State University Press, 1982.

———. "The Indian Trade of the Susquehanna Valley." *Proceedings of the American Philosophical Society* 110, no. 6 (December 1966): 406–24.

———. "Jacob Young: Indian Trader and Interpreter." In *Struggle and Survival in Colonial America*, edited by David G. Sweet and Gary B. Nash, 347–61. Berkeley: University of California Press, 1981.

Johnson, Allen W., and Timothy Earle. *The Evolution of Human Societies: From Foraging Group to American State.* Stanford: Stanford University Press, 1987.

Jones, David S. *Rationalizing Epidemics: Meanings and Uses of American Indian Mortality since 1600.* Cambridge: Harvard University Press, 2004.

Juricek, John T. "Indian Policy in Proprietary South Carolina, 1670–1693." Master's thesis, University of Chicago, 1962.

Kelton, Paul. *Epidemics and Enslavement: Biological Catastrophe in the Native Southeast, 1492–1715.* Lincoln: University of Nebraska Press, 2007.

Kent, Barry C. *Susquehanna's Indians.* Harrisburg: Pennsylvania Historical and Museum Commission, 1989.

Kimball-Brown, Margaret. *Cultural Transformation among the Illinois: An Application of a Systems Model.* East Lansing: Michigan State University Press, 1979.

———. *The Zimmerman Site: Further Excavations at the Grand Village of Kaskaskia.* Springfield: Illinois State Museum, 1975.

King, Duane H. *The Cherokee Indian Nation: A Troubled History.* Knoxville: University of Tennessee Press, 2005.

Kinietz, W. Vernon. *Indians of the Western Great Lakes, 1615–1760.* Ann Arbor: University of Michigan Press, 1965.

Knight, Vernon J., Jr. *Tukabatchee: Archaeological Investigations at an Historic Creek Town, Elmore County, Alabama, 1984,* no. 45. Tuscaloosa: University of Alabama, Office of Archaeological Research, Report of Investigations, 1985.

Krech, Shepard, III. *The Ecological Indian: Myth and History.* New York: Norton, 1999.

Lakomäki, Sami. "Building a Shawnee Nation: Indigenous Identity, Tribal Structure, and Socio-Political Organization, 1400–1770." In *Reconfigurations of Native North America: An Anthology of New Perspectives,* edited by John R. Wunder and Kurt E. Kinbacher, 199–224. Lubbock: Texas Tech University Press, 2009.

———. "Singing the King's Song: Constructing and Resisting Power in Shawnee Communities, 1600–1860." Ph.D. diss., Oulu University Press, 2009.

Lamont, Michèle, and Virág Molnár. "The Study of Boundaries in the Social Sciences." *Annual Review of Sociology* 28 (2002): 167–95.

Lankford, George E. "The 'Path of Souls': Some Death Imagery in the Southeastern Ceremonial Complex." In *Ancient Objects and Sacred Realms: Interpretations of Mississippian Iconography,* edited by Kent Reilly III and James F. Garber, 174–212. Austin: University of Texas Press, 2007.

———. "Some Cosmological Motifs in the Southeastern Ceremonial Complex." In *Ancient Objects and Sacred Realms: Interpretations of Mississippian Iconography,* edited by Kent Reilly III and James F. Garber, 8–38. Austin: University of Texas Press, 2007.

———. "World on a String: Some Cosmological Components of the Southeastern Ceremonial Complex." In *Hero, Hawk, and Open Hand: American Indian Art of the Ancient Midwest and South,* edited by Richard F. Townsend, 206–17. New Haven: Yale University Press, 2004.

Lemon, James T. *The Best Poor Man's Country: Early Southeastern Pennsylvania.* Baltimore: Johns Hopkins University Press, 2002.

Lepore, Jill. *The Name of War: King Philip's War and the Origins of American Identity.* New York: Knopf, 1998.

Linn, Mary S. "Deep Time and Genetic Relationships: Yuchi Linguistic History Revisited." In *Yuchi Indian Histories before the Removal Era,* edited by Jason Baird Jackson, 1–32. Lincoln: University of Nebraska Press, 2012.

Maier, Pauline. *American Scripture: Making the Declaration of Independence.* New York: Vintage, 1998.

Malone, Patrick M. *The Skulking Way of War: Technology and Tactics among the New England Indians.* Toronto: Madison Books, 2000.

Mancall, Peter C. *Deadly Medicine: Indians and Alcohol in Early America.* Ithaca: Cornell University Press, 1995.

Mandell, Daniel R. *Behind the Frontier: Indians in Eighteenth Century Massachusetts.* Lincoln: University of Nebraska Press, 1996.

Marambaud, Pierre. *William Byrd of Westover, 1674–1744.* Charlottesville: University Press of Virginia, 1971.

Martin, Joel W. *The Land Looks After Us: A History of Native American Religions.* New York: Oxford University Press, 1999.

———. *Sacred Revolt: The Muskogees' Struggle for a New World.* Boston: Beacon, 1991.

Mason, Carol I. *The Archaeology of Ocmulgee, Old Fields, Macon, Georgia.* Tuscaloosa: University of Alabama Press, 2005.

Matson, Frederick R. "Shell-Tempered Pottery and the Fort Ancient Potter." In *Pottery Technology: Ideas and Approaches*, edited by Gordon Bronitsky, 15–31. Boulder: Westview Press, 1989.

Mazrim, Robert, and Duane Esaray. "Rethinking the Dawn of History: The Schedule, Signature, and Agency of European Goods in Protohistoric Illinois." *Midcontinental Journal of Archaeology* 32, no. 2 (Fall 2007): 145–200.

McCafferty, Michael. *Native American Place Names of Indiana.* Urbana: University of Illinois Press, 2007.

McConnell, Michael N. *A Country Between: The Upper Ohio Valley and Its Peoples, 1724–1774.* Lincoln: University of Nebraska Press, 1997.

———. "Peoples 'In Between': The Iroquois and the Ohio Indians, 1720–1768." In *Beyond the Covenant Chain: The Iroquois and Their Neighbors in Indian North America, 1600–1800*, edited by Daniel K. Richter and James H. Merrell, 93–112. Syracuse: Syracuse University Press, 1987.

McCullough, Robert G. "Central Indiana as a Late Prehistoric Borderland: Western Basin, Fort Ancient, and Oneota Interactions on the Periphery." *Midcontinental Journal of Archaeology* (forthcoming).

McEwan, Bonnie G. "Apalachee and Neighboring Groups." In *Southeast*, vol. 14 of *Handbook of North American Indians*, edited by Raymond D. Fogelson, 669–76. Washington, D.C.: Smithsonian Institution, 2004.

McEwan, Ryan, et al. "Temporal and Spatial Patterns in Fire Occurrence during the Establishment of Mixed-Oak Forests in Eastern North America." *Journal of Vegetation Science* 18 (2007): 655–64.

McPherson, James M. *Antietam: Crossroads of Freedom.* New York: Oxford University Press, 2002.

Menard, Russell R., and Lois Green Carr. "The Lords Baltimore and the Colonization of Maryland." In *Early Maryland in a Wider World*, edited by David B. Quinn, 168–203. Detroit: Wayne State University Press, 1982.

Merrell, James H. *The Indians' New World: Catawbas and Their Neighbors from European Contact through the Era of Indian Removal.* New York: Norton, 1991.

———. "The Indians' New World: The Catawba Experience." *William and Mary Quarterly*, 3rd ser., 41 (1984): 537–65.

———. *Into the American Woods: Negotiators on the Pennsylvania Frontier.* New York: Norton, 1999.

Merritt, Jane T. *At the Crossroads: Indians and Empires on a Mid-Atlantic Frontier, 1700–1763*. Chapel Hill: University of North Carolina Press, 2003.

Meyers, Maureen. "From Refugees to Slave Traders: The Transformation of the Westo Indians." In *Mapping the Mississippian Shatter Zone: The Colonial Indian Slave Trade and Regional Instability in the American South*, edited by Robbie Ethridge and Sheri Shuck-Hall, 81–103. Lincoln: University of Nebraska Press, 2009.

Milanich, Jerald T. *The Timucua*. Oxford: Blackwell, 1996.

———. "The Timucua Indians of Northern Florida and Southern Georgia." In *Indians of the Greater Southeast: Historical Archaeology and Ethnohistory*, edited by Bonnie G. McEwan, 1–25. Gainesville: University of Florida Press, 2000.

Miles, Tiya. *Ties That Bind: The Story of an Afro-Cherokee Family in Slavery and Freedom*. Berkeley: University of California Press, 2005.

Milling, Chapman J. *Red Carolinians*. Chapel Hill: University of North Carolina Press, 1940.

Milner, George R. *The Cahokia Chiefdom: The Archaeology of a Mississippian Society*. Gainesville: University Press of Florida, 2006.

———. "Warfare in Prehistoric and Early Historic Eastern North America." *Journal of Archaeological Research* 7, no. 2 (1999): 105–51.

Milner, George R., David G. Anderson, and Marvin T. Smith. "The Distribution of Eastern Woodland Peoples at the Prehistoric and Historic Interface." In *Societies in Eclipse: Archaeology of the Eastern Woodlands Indians, A.D. 1400–1700*, edited by David S. Brose, C. Wesley Cowan, and Robert C. Mainfort, 9–18. Washington, D.C.: Smithsonian Institution, 2001.

———. "Warfare in Prehistoric and Early Historic Eastern North America." *Journal of Archaeological Research* 7, no. 2 (1999): 105–51.

Milner, George R., Eve Anderson, and Virginia G. Smith. "Warfare in Late Prehistoric West-Central Illinois." *American Antiquity* 56, no. 4 (October 1991): 581–603.

Morgan, Edmund S. "The World and William Penn." *Proceedings of the American Philosophical Society* 127, no. 5 (October 1983): 291–315.

Morison, Samuel Eliot. *Of Plymouth Plantation*. New York: Modern Library, 1967.

Mulkearn, Lois. "Why the Treaty of Logstown, 1752." *Virginia Magazine of History and Biography* 59, no. 1 (January 1951): 3–20.

Munson, Cheryl Ann, and David Pollack. "Far and Wide: Late Mississippian/Protohistoric Extraregional Interactions at the Mouth of the Wabash." Paper given at Society of American Archaeology, 77th Annual Meeting, Memphis, Tenn., April 2012.

Murdock, George Peter. "Algonkian Social Organization." In *Context and Meaning in Cultural Anthropology*, edited by Melford E. Spiro, 24–35. New York: Free Press, 1965.

Murphy, Edmund Robert. *Henry de Tonty: Fur Trader of the Mississippi*. Baltimore: Johns Hopkins University Press, 1941.

Nabokov, Peter. *A Forest of Time: American Indian Ways of History*. Cambridge: Cambridge University Press, 2002.

———. *Where the Lightning Strikes: The Lives of American Indian Sacred Places*. New York: Viking, 2006.

Nash, Gary B. *Quakers and Politics: Pennsylvania, 1681–1726*. Princeton: Princeton University Press, 1968.

―――. "The Quest for the Susquehanna Valley: New York, Pennsylvania, and the Seventeenth Century Fur Trade." *New York History* 48, no. 1 (1967): 3–40.

Nass, John, Jr. "Fort Ancient Agricultural Systems and Settlement: A View from Southwestern Ohio." *North American Archaeologist* 9, no. 4 (1988): 319–47.

Nellis, Eric Guest. *An Empire of Regions: A Brief History of Colonial British America*. North Toronto: University of Toronto Press, 2010.

Nolan, Kevin C., and Robert A. Cook. "An Evolutionary Model of Social Change in the Middle Ohio Valley: Was Social Complexity Impossible during the Late Woodland but Mandatory during the Late Prehistoric?" *Journal of Anthropological Archaeology* 29 (2010): 62–79.

Oatis, Steven J. *A Colonial Complex: South Carolina's Frontiers in the Era of the Yamasee War, 1680–1730*. Lincoln: University of Nebraska Press, 2004.

Obermeyer, Brice. *Delaware Tribe in a Cherokee Nation*. Lincoln: University of Nebraska Press, 2009.

O'Gorman, Jodie. "The Myth of Moccasin Bluff: Rethinking the Potawatomi Pattern." *Ethnohistory* 54, no. 3 (Summer 2007): 373–406.

Olafson, Sigfus. "Gabriel Arthur and the Fort Ancient People." *West Virginia Archaeologist* 12 (December 1960): 32–42.

Osman, Eaton G. *Starved Rock: A Chapter of Colonial History*. Chicago: A. Flanagan, 1895.

Parkman, Francis. *The Conspiracy of Pontiac and the Indian War after the Conquest of Canada*. Boston: Little, Brown, 1884.

Parmalee, Paul W. "The Faunal Complex of the Fisher Site, Illinois." *American Midland Naturalist* 68, no. 2 (October 1962): 399–408.

Parmenter, Jon. *The Edge of the Woods: Iroquoia, 1534–1701*. East Lansing: Michigan State University Press, 2010.

Patterson, Orlando. *Slavery and Social Death: A Comparative Study*. Cambridge: Harvard University Press, 1982.

Pauketat, Timothy R. *Ancient Cahokia and the Mississippians*. Cambridge: Cambridge University Press, 2004.

Pearson, Bruce L. "Savannah and Shawnee: Same or Different?" *Names in South Carolina* 21 (Winter 1974): 19–22.

Peña, Elaine A. *Performing Piety: Making Sacred Space with the Virgin of Guadalupe*. Berkeley: University of California Press, 2011.

Penney, David. "The Archaeology of Aesthetics." In *Hero, Hawk, and Open Hand: American Indian Art of the Ancient Midwest and South*, edited by Richard F. Townsend, 43–55. New Haven: Yale University Press, 2004.

Perdue, Theda, and Michael D. Green. *The Cherokee Removal: A Brief History with Documents*. Boston: Bedford/St. Martin's, 2005.

Piker, Joshua. *Okfuskee: A Creek Indian Town in Colonial America*. Cambridge: Harvard University Press, 2004.

Pollack, David, and A. Gwynn Henderson. "A Mid Eighteenth Century Historic Indian Occupation in Greenup County, Kentucky." In *Late Prehistoric Research in*

Kentucky, edited by David Pollack, Charles Hockensmith, and Thomas Sanders, 1–24. Lexington: Kentucky Heritage Council, 1984.

———. "Toward a Model of Fort Ancient Society." In *Fort Ancient Cultural Dynamics in the Middle Ohio Valley*, edited by A. Gwynn Henderson, 281–94. Madison: Prehistory Press, 1992.

Pollack, David, A. Gwynn Henderson, and Christopher Begley. "Fort Ancient/ Mississippian Interaction on the Northeastern Periphery." *Southeastern Archaeology* 21, no. 2 (2002): 206–20.

Power, Susan C. *Early Art of the Southeastern Indians: Feathered Serpents and Winged Beings*. Tuscaloosa: University of Alabama Press, 2004.

Prufer, O. H., and O. C. Shane III. *Blain Village and the Fort Ancient Tradition in Ohio*. Kent, Ohio: Kent State University Press, 1970.

Ramenofsky, Ann F. *Vectors of Death: The Archaeology of European Contact*. Albuquerque: University of New Mexico Press, 1987.

Ramsey, James G. M. *The Annals of Tennessee to the End of the Eighteenth Century* (1853). Kingsport: Kingsport Press, 1926.

Ramsey, William L. *The Yamasee War: A Study of Culture, Economy, and Conflict in the Colonial South*. Lincoln: University of Nebraska Press, 2008.

Reilly, Kent, III, and James F. Garber. "Introduction." In *Ancient Objects and Sacred Realms: Interpretations of Mississippian Iconography*, edited by Kent Reilly III and James F. Garber, 1–7. Austin: University of Texas Press, 2007.

Remini, Robert V. *Andrew Jackson and His Indian Wars*. New York: Viking, 2001.

Rice, James D. *Nature and History in the Potomac Country: From Hunter-Gatherers to the Age of Jefferson*. Baltimore: Johns Hopkins University Press, 2009.

Richter, Daniel K. *The Ordeal of the Longhouse: The Peoples of the Iroquois League in the Era of European Colonization*. Chapel Hill: University of North Carolina Press, 1992.

Richter, Daniel K., and James H. Merrell. *Beyond the Covenant Chain: The Iroquois and Their Neighbors in Indian North America, 1600–1800*. Syracuse: Syracuse University Press, 1987.

Roosens, Eugene. *Creating Ethnicity: The Process of Ethnogenesis*. London: Sage, 1989.

Roseberry, William. *Anthropologies and Histories: Essays in Culture, History, and Political Economy*. New Brunswick: Rutgers University Press, 1989.

Ross, Frank E. "The Fur Trade of the Ohio Valley." *Indiana Magazine of History* 34, no. 4 (December 1938): 417–42.

Rountree, Helen C. *Pocahontas, Powhatan, Opechancanough: Three Indian Lives Changed by Jamestown*. Charlottesville: University Press of Virginia, 2005.

———. "The Powhatans and Other Woodland Indians as Travelers." In *Powhatan Foreign Relations, 1500–1722*, edited by Helen C. Rountree, 20–52. Charlottesville: University Press of Virginia, 1993.

———. "Trouble Coming Southward: Emanations through and from Virginia, 1607–1675." In *The Transformation of the Southeastern Indians, 1540–1760*, edited by Robbie Ethridge and Charles Hudson, 65–78. Jackson: University Press of Mississippi, 2002.

Rudes, Blair A., Thomas J. Blumer, and J. Alan May. "Catawba and Neighboring Groups." In *Southeast*, vol. 14 of *Handbook of North American Indians*, edited by Raymond D. Fogelson, 301–18. Washington, D.C.: Smithsonian Institution, 2004.

Rushforth, Brett. *Bonds of Alliance: Indigenous and Atlantic Slaveries in New France*. Chapel Hill: University of North Carolina Press, 2012.

———. "'A Little Flesh We Offer You': The Origins of Indian Slavery in New France." *William and Mary Quarterly* 60, no. 4 (October 2003): 777–803.

———. "Slavery, the Fox Wars, and the Limits of Alliance." *William and Mary Quarterly* 63 (January 2005): 53–80.

Sahlins, Marshall D. "Poor Man, Rich Man, Big-Man, Chief: Political Types in Melanesia and Polynesia." *Comparative Studies in Society and History* 5, no. 3 (April 1963): 285–303.

———. *Tribesmen*. Englewood Cliffs: Prentice-Hall, 1968.

Sanders, Lawrence Rowland. *The History of Beaufort County, South Carolina*. Columbia: University of South Carolina Press, 1996.

Sapir, Edward. "A Bird's Eye View of American Indian Languages North of Mexico." *Science* 54 (1921): 408.

Satz, Ronald N. *American Indian Policy in the Jacksonian Era*. Norman: University of Oklahoma Press, 2002.

Schutt, Amy C. *Peoples of the River Valleys: The Odyssey of the Delaware Indians*. Philadelphia: University of Pennsylvania Press, 2007.

Schutz, Noel William. "The Study of Shawnee Myth in an Ethnographic and Ethnohistorical Perspective." Ph.D. diss., Indiana University, 1975.

Schwartz, Sally. *A Mixed Multitude: The Struggle for Toleration in Pennsylvania*. New York: New York University Press, 1987.

Seaver, James Everett. *Life of Mary Jemison* (1856). Edited by Lewis Henry Morgan. Reprint, New York: Garland, 1977.

Selstad, Leif. "Carrying the World Along: Minority Fields and Identity Management in a Shawnee Indian Community in Oklahoma." Master's thesis, Sosialantropologisk Institutt, 1986.

Sempowski, Martha L. "Early Historic Exchange between the Seneca and the Susquehannock." In *Archaeology of the Iroquois: Selected Readings and Research Sources*, edited by Jordan E. Kerber, 194–218. Syracuse: Syracuse University Press, 2007.

Shackelford, Alan G. "The Frontier in Pre-Columbian Illinois." *Journal of the Illinois State Historical Society* 100, no. 3 (Fall 2007): 186–206.

Shannon, Timothy J. *Iroquois Diplomacy on the Early American Frontier*. New York: Viking, 2008.

Sharp, William E. "Fort Ancient Farmers." In *Kentucky Archaeology*, edited by R. Barry Lewis, 161–82. Lexington: University Press of Kentucky, 1996.

Sheehan, Bernard W. *Savagism and Civility: Indians and Englishmen in Colonial Virginia*. Cambridge: Cambridge University Press, 1980.

Shuck-Hall, Sheri M. "Alabama and Coushatta Diaspora and Coalescence in the Mississippian Shatter Zone." In *Mapping the Mississippian Shatter Zone: The Colonial Indian Slave Trade and Regional Instability in the American South*, edited by Robbie Ethridge and Sheri M. Shuck-Hall, 250–71. Lincoln: University of Nebraska Press, 2009.

Shumway, George. "English Pattern Trade Rifles." In *Proceedings of the 1984 Trade Gun Conference*, edited by Charles F. Hayes III, 11–49. Rochester: Rochester Museum and Science Center, 1985.

Silver, Peter. *Our Savage Neighbors: How Indian War Transformed Early America.* New York: W. W. Norton, 2008.

Skinner, Claiborne A. *The Upper Country: French Enterprise in the Colonial Great Lakes.* Baltimore: Johns Hopkins University Press, 2008.

Sleeper-Smith, Susan. *Indian Women and French Men: Rethinking Cultural Encounter in the Western Great Lakes.* Amherst: University of Massachusetts Press, 2001.

Smith, Dwight L. "Shawnee Captivity Ethnography." *Ethnohistory* 2 (1955): 29–41.

Smith, Marvin T. *Coosa: The Rise and Fall of a Southeastern Mississippian Chiefdom.* Gainesville: University Press of Florida, 2000.

Smolenski, John. "The Death of Sawantaeny and the Problem of Justice on the Frontier." In *Friends and Enemies in Penn's Woods: Indians, Colonists, and the Racial Construction of Pennsylvania*, edited by William A. Pencak and Daniel K. Richter, 104–28. University Park: Pennsylvania State University Press, 2004.

———. *Friends and Strangers: The Making of a Creole Culture in Colonial Pennsylvania.* Philadelphia: University of Pennsylvania Press, 2011.

Snow, Dean R., and Kim M. Lanphear. "European Contact and Indian Depopulation in the Northeast: The Timing of the First Epidemics." *Ethnohistory* 35, no. 1 (Winter 1988): 15–28.

Snyder, Christina. *Slavery in Indian Country: The Changing Face of Captivity in Early America.* Cambridge: Harvard University Press, 2010.

Speck, Frank G. *Catawba Texts.* New York: Columbia University Press, 1934.

———. "Ceremonial Songs of the Creek and Yuchi Indians." Philadelphia: Museum Anthropological Publications 1, no. 2 (1911): 159–245.

———. *Ethnology of the Yuchi Indians.* Edited by Jason Baird Jackson. Lincoln: University of Nebraska Press, 2004.

Spencer, Darla. "Evidence of Siouan Occupation." *Quarterly Bulletin: Archaeological Society of Virginia* 64, no. 3 (September 2009): 139–54.

Steele, Ian. "Shawnee Origins of Their Seven Years' War." *Ethnohistory* 53, no. 4 (Fall 2006): 657–87.

Stewart, Omer C. *Peyote Religion: A History.* Norman: University of Oklahoma Press, 1987.

Stokes, Thomas L. *The Savannah.* Athens: University of Georgia Press, 1951.

Sugden, John. *Blue Jacket: Warrior of the Shawnees.* Lincoln: University of Nebraska Press, 2000.

———. *Tecumseh: A Life.* New York: Holt, 1997.

Swanton, John. *Early History of the Creek Indians and Their Neighbors.* Washington, D.C.: Smithsonian Institution, 1922.

———. "Siouan Tribes and the Ohio Valley." *American Anthropologist* 45 (1943): 49–66.

———. *Social Organization and Social Usages of the Creek Confederacy*. Washington, D.C.: Government Printing Office, 1928.

Tankersley, Kenneth B. "Bison and Subsistence Change: The Protohistoric Ohio River Valley and Illinois Valley Connection." In *Research in Economic Anthropology*, Supplement 6, edited by Barry Isaac, 103–30. Greenwich: JAI Press, 1992.

———. "Bison Exploitation by Late Fort Ancient Peoples in the Central Ohio River Valley." *North American Archaeologist* 7, no. 4 (1986): 289–303.

Temple, Wayne C. *Indian Villages of the Illinois Country: Historic Tribes*. Springfield: Illinois State Museum, 1958.

Tooker, Elisabeth. "Northern Iroquoian Sociopolitical Organization." *American Anthropologist* 72, no. 1 (February 1970): 90–97.

Townsend, Camilla. *Pocahontas and the Powhatan Dilemma*. New York: Hill and Wang, 2004.

Trigger, Bruce G. *The Children of Aataentsic*, vol. 1 of *A History of the Huron People to 1660*. Montreal: McGill-Queen's University Press, 1976.

———. "Maintaining Economic Equality in Opposition to Complexity: An Iroquoian Case Study." In *The Evolution of Political Systems: Sociopolitics in Small-Scale Sedentary Societies*, edited by Steadman Upham, 119–45. Cambridge: Cambridge University Press, 1990.

Tuan, Yi-Fu. *Space and Place: The Perspective of Experience*. Minneapolis: University of Minnesota Press, 1977.

Turnbow, Christopher A., and Cynthia E. Jobe. "The Goolman Site: A Late Fort Ancient Winter Encampment in Clark County, Kentucky." In *Late Prehistoric Research in Kentucky*, edited by David Pollack, Charles D. Hockensmith, and Thomas N. Sanders, 25–48. Frankfort: Kentucky Heritage Council, 1984.

Turner, Lewis M. "Ecological Studies in the Lower Illinois River Valley." *Botanical Gazette* 97, no. 4 (June 1936): 689–727.

Tweed, Thomas A. *Crossing and Dwelling: A Theory of Religion*. Cambridge: Harvard University Press, 2006.

Voegelin, Carl F., and Erminie Wheeler-Voegelin. "Shawnee Name Groups." *American Anthropologist* 37 (1935): 617–35.

Wagner, Gail E. "The Corn and Cultivated Beans of the Fort Ancient Indians." *Missouri Archaeologist* 47 (1986): 107–35.

———. "What Seasonal Diet at a Fort Ancient Community Reveals about Coping Mechanisms." In *Case Studies in Environmental Archaeology*, edited by Elizabeth J. Reitz, Lee A. Newsom, and Sylvia J. Scudder, 277–97. New York: Plenum Press, 1996.

Wainwright, Nicholas B. *George Croghan: Wilderness Diplomat*. Chapel Hill: University of North Carolina Press, 1959.

Walker, Willard B. "Creek Confederacy before Removal." In *Southeast*, vol. 14 of *Handbook of North American Indians*, edited by Raymond D. Fogelson, 373–92. Washington, D.C.: Smithsonian Institution, 2004.

Wall, Robert D. "Late Woodland Ceramics and Native Populations of the Upper Potomac Valley." *Journal of Middle Atlantic Archaeology* 17 (2001): 15–36.

Wallace, Anthony F. C. *The Long, Bitter Trail: Andrew Jackson and the Indians*. New York: Hill and Wang, 1993.

———. *Teedyuscung, 1700–1763: King of the Delawares* (1949). Syracuse: Syracuse University Press, 1990.

Wallace, Paul A. W. *Conrad Weiser, 1696–1760: Friend of Colonist and Mohawk*. Philadelphia: University of Pennsylvania Press, 1945.

———. *Indian Paths of Pennsylvania* (1965). Harrisburg: Pennsylvania Historical Commission, 1993.

Walthall, John A. "Aboriginal Pottery and the Eighteenth-Century Illini." In *Calumet and Fleur-de-Lys: Archaeology of Indian and French Contact in the Midcontinent*, edited by John A. Walthall and Thomas E. Emerson, 155–76. Washington, D.C.: Smithsonian Institution Press, 1992.

Warren, Stephen. "Prairie Tribes." In *Dictionary of American History*, edited by Frederick Hoxie. New York: Scribner's, 2003.

———. *The Shawnees and Their Neighbors, 1795–1870*. Urbana: University of Illinois Press, 2005.

Warren, Stephen, and Randolph Noe. "'The Greatest Travelers in America': Shawnee Survival in the Shatter Zone." In *Mapping the Shatter Zone: The Colonial Indian Slave Trade and Regional Instability in the American South*, edited by Robbie Ethridge and Sheri Shuck-Hall, 163–87. Lincoln: University of Nebraska Press, 2009.

Waselkov, Gregory A. "Indian Maps of the Colonial Southeast." In *Powhatan's Mantle: Indians in the Colonial Southeast*, edited by Peter H. Wood, Gregory A. Waselkov, and M. Thomas Hatley, 292–343. Lincoln: University of Nebraska Press, 1989.

———. "Seventeenth Century Trade in the Colonial Southeast." *Southeastern Archaeology* 8, no. 2 (Winter 1989): 117–33.

Webb, Stephen Saunders. *1676: The End of American Independence*. Syracuse: Syracuse University Press, 1995.

Weddle, Robert S. *The French Thorn: Rival Explorers in the Spanish Sea, 1682–1762*. College Station: Texas A&M Press, 1991.

———. "Joutel, Henri." In *Texas State Historical Association: A Digital Gateway to Texas History*, accessed 9/1/2012, http://www.tshaonline.org/handbook/online/articles/fjo77.

Wheeler-Voegelin, Erminie. *Indians of Ohio and Indiana prior to 1795: Ethnohistory of Indian Use and Occupancy in Ohio and Indiana prior to 1795*. New York: Garland, 1974.

———. *Mortuary Customs of the Shawnee and Other Eastern Tribes*. Indianapolis: Indiana Historical Society, Prehistoric Research Series 2, no. 4 (1944).

White, Marian E. "Erie." In *Northeast*, vol. 15 of *Handbook of North American Indians*, edited by William C. Sturtevant and Bruce G. Trigger, 412–17. Washington, D.C.: Smithsonian Institution, 1978.

White, Richard. *The Middle Ground: Indians, Empires, and Republics in the Great Lakes Region, 1650–1815*. New York: Cambridge University Press, 1991.

Whitley, Thomas G. *Archaeological Data Recovery at Riverfront Village (38AK933): A Mississippian/Contact Period Occupation in Aiken County, South Carolina*, vol. 1. Atlanta: Brockington and Associates, 2013.

———. *Conflict and Confusion on the Middle Savannah River: The 17th to 18th Century Occupation of Riverfront Village (38AK933) Aiken County, South Carolina.* Atlanta: Brockington and Associates, 2009.

Witgen, Michael. *An Infinity of Nations: How the Native New World Shaped Early North America.* Philadelphia: University of Pennsylvania Press, 2012.

Witthoft, John, and William A. Hunter. "The Seventeenth Century Origins of the Shawnee." *Ethnohistory* 2, no. 1 (1955): 42–57.

Wolf, Eric. *Europe and the People without History.* Berkeley: University of California Press, 1982.

Wolfe, Nathan D., Claire Ponasian Dunavan, and Jared Diamond. "Origins of Major Human Infectious Diseases." *Nature* (May 2007): 279–83.

Wood, Betty. *The Origins of Slavery: Freedom and Bondage in the English Colonies.* New York: Hill and Wang, 1998.

Wood, Peter H. "The Changing Population of the Colonial South: An Overview by Race and Region, 1685–1790." In *Powhatan's Mantle: Indians in the Colonial Southeast,* edited by Peter H. Wood, Gregory A. Waselkov, and M. Thomas Hatley, 35–103. Lincoln: University of Nebraska Press, 1989.

Worth, John E. *Assimilation,* vol. 1 of *Timucuan Chiefdoms of Spanish Florida.* Gainesville: University of Florida Press, 1998.

———. "Razing Florida: The Indian Slave Trade and the Devastation of Spanish Florida, 1659–1715." In *Mapping the Shatter Zone: The Colonial Indian Slave Trade and Regional Instability in the American South,* edited by Robbie Ethridge and Sheri Shuck-Hall, 295–311. Lincoln: University of Nebraska Press, 2009.

———. *The Struggle for the Georgia Coast: An Eighteenth Century Retrospective on Guale and Mocama.* Tuscaloosa: University of Alabama Press, 1995.

Wray, Charles F. "Firearms among the Seneca: The Archaeological Evidence." In *Proceedings of the 1984 Trade Gun Conference,* edited by Charles F. Hayes III, 106–7. Rochester: Rochester Museum and Science Center, 1985.

Index

Barth, Fredrick, 236 (n. 53)
Bartram, William, 87, 105–6, 209
Basso, Keith, 238 (n. 68)
Batts, Thomas, 67–68
Beauharnois, Charles de la Boische, Marquis de, 186, 187, 190, 191, 192–93, 198, 199, 200
Beneath World, 46
Bentley site, 32, 244 (n. 3)
Berkeley, Robert, 94
Berkeley, William, 161
Bermuda, 83, 86, 89
Bernou, Claude, 111, 112
Beschefer, Thierry, 125
Big Jim (chief), 11, 12
Big Men, and Fort Ancient Tradition, 13
Billy, Joe, 22
Bizaillon, Peter, 159, 160, 161, 162, 164, 169–70
Blanchard, George, 22–23, 78, 232 (n. 2), 237 (n. 66), 263 (n. 5)
Blue Jacket, 17–18
Boisrondet, Sieur de, 107–8
Bradford, William, 122
Brant, Joseph (Thayendanegea), 17, 18, 227, 235 (n. 41)
Braudel, Fernand, 234 (n. 30)
Brose, David S., 242 (n. 52)
Brown, James A., 243 (n. 62), 244 (n. 64)
Bull, William, 97
Burnet, William, 226
Bussell Island, 42
Byrd, William, 88–89

Cabeza de Vaca, Álvar Núñez, 61
Caborn-Welborn peoples, 42
Caddoans, 117
Cahokia, 36, 63, 120–21, 241 (n. 24)
Cakundawanna (Shawnee diplomat), 172, 173
Calloway, Colin, 235 (n. 47), 238 (n. 68)
Calumet Ceremony, 44–45, 107, 116, 121, 172
Canada, 202, 212
Canasatego (Onandaga speaker), 179

Candlemas Massacre on York, 256 (n. 1)
Carlson, Keith Thor, 253 (n. 4)
Carristauga, 137, 142, 144, 150, 151
Carson, James Taylor, 238 (n. 68)
Carteret, John, 83, 88
Cartlidge, Edmund, 175, 177–78, 184, 196
Cartlidge, John, 163, 169, 174–75, 184, 196
Cartography, 225–26
Catawbas: and Shawnees, 15, 22, 99, 101–2, 219–20, 265 (n. 36); and Iroquois Confederacy, 15, 137, 139, 140, 150, 164, 165, 167, 168, 169, 198; and English colonizers, 83; and Creeks, 84; and Westos, 89; confederacy of, 90; and Santee Fort, 95
Cayugas, 164, 165, 188, 191, 202. *See also* Seneca-Cayugas
Céleron de Blainville, Pierre Joseph, 203–5
Central Algonquians: Shawnees as, 10, 18, 19, 218; and Grand Village of the Kaskaskias, 14, 53–54, 116–17; and Iroquois Confederacy, 17; and English colonizers, 31, 225; settlement patterns of, 39; and Fort Ancient Tradition, 51; oral histories of, 53; and colonialism, 54, 248 (n. 52); Dollier's study of, 57; and concept of souls, 72; and parochial cosmopolitanism, 109; French alliance with, 116; religious practices of, 125
Chabert de Joncaire, Phillipe-Thomas, 204
Chalagawtha division, 22, 35, 77, 78, 108, 180, 208, 220, 222, 247 (n. 48)
Charles Town: and Indian slave trade, 50, 84, 87, 95–96; founding of, 61; and trade networks, 68, 83, 87, 108, 215; Indian towns allied with, 101, 102; and Shawnees, 101, 102, 220, 222
Chartier, Martin: and Fort Crevecoeur, 112–13; and Shawnees, 113, 135–36, 137, 146, 147–48, 169, 171, 179, 206;

and English colonizers, 147–48; and trade networks, 159, 160, 161, 162, 169–70, 174, 183, 184; and Lower Susquehanna River, 163; death of, 174, 175, 179, 188

Chartier, Peter: and Shawnee migration, 155, 178, 179, 183, 187, 191, 193, 199, 200, 206, 211, 217–19, 220, 221, 228, 235 (n. 47); and Martin Chartier's land, 174, 183; and trade networks, 178, 183–85, 188, 195, 215, 218; and Covenant Chain, 183–85; and Lower Shawnee Town, 188; and French colonizers, 191, 206; robbery of English traders, 199, 213; and Shawnee identity, 217, 219

Chequamegon Bay, 123, 124

Cherokees: alliance with Confederacy, 7; and Hickauhaugau, 91; and Shawnees, 94, 212, 216, 218, 222; as coalescent population, 100; and Yamasee War, 104; and Indian slave trade, 213; and French colonizers, 214–15, 218; and settlement Indians, 220

Chesapeake Bay: and Shawnee migration, 79, 82, 98–99, 135–37, 139–40, 142, 149–50; and colonial borderlands, 81, 140–43; and Susquehannocks, 136; and trade networks, 137, 143, 145; violence in, 139, 140; and Iroquois Confederacy, 153

Chestowe, 100, 105

Chickasaws: Illinois peoples, 19, 101, 121, 199; and Hickauhaugau, 91; and Moore, 96; and trade networks, 98; and Indian slave trade, 99, 101, 213; as coalescent population, 100; and Shawnees, 211, 214, 218–19; and French colonizers, 213–15, 218

Chillicothe, Ohio, 31, 76

Chiwere Siouans, 117

Choctaws, 99, 213–14, 216–17, 218

Choptanks, 137, 142, 147, 152

Chota, 219–20

Christianity: and indigenous spirituality, 2; and concept of souls, 71

Cincinnati, Ohio, 28

Civil War, 2, 7

Clinton, DeWitt, 227

Cobb, Charles, 244 (n. 65)

Cofitachiqui, 87

Colbert, Jean-Baptiste, 128, 129

Colden, Cadwallader, 58, 182, 225

Colonial America: and Shawnee migration, 12, 20; regional approaches to, 19, 234 (n. 29); and archaeological study of prehistoric and protohistoric sites, 19–20, 29–30, 236 (n. 52); and continuities between precontact and postcontact worlds, 25, 77, 82, 236 (n. 55); Native peoples' sociopolitical identities in, 235 (n. 38)

Colonial borderlands: and Shawnee migration, 12, 76, 81–82, 83, 91, 98–99, 155, 206, 224; violence of, 14, 76, 81–82, 90, 140–43, 193, 218; and multiethnic towns, 15

Colonialism: and Fort Ancient Tradition, 13–14, 25, 55, 58, 62; expansion of, 15; and Shawnee identity, 16, 24, 79; rupture of, 19, 29, 58, 82, 236 (n. 51), 239 (n. 8); and multiethnic nature of Indian communities, 20; and migration, 42, 224–25; and Siouan speakers, 54, 83; and Central Algonquians, 54, 248 (n. 52); psychological trauma caused by, 75; and Westos, 106; settler colonialism, 164, 213; and literary advantage, 225

Comanches, 2

Conestoga Manor, Pa., 15, 158, 162–71, 172, 173, 175, 176, 179, 182

Confederacy (Civil War), Cherokees' alliance with, 7

Conoys, 159, 162–63, 164, 169, 177, 179, 202

Cooper, Anthony Ashley, 90–91

Coosa (Creek town), 211

Coosa peoples, 42–43, 50, 53, 211

Corkran, David H., 251 (n. 47)

Costeen, Michel, 134–35

Coste village, 42

Coursey, Henry, 143–44

Coushattas, 211, 214

Coweta, 94, 212

Cowskin Stomp Ground, 9, 10–11

Coxe, Daniel, 136

Creek Indians: and Tecumseh, 16; and Shawnees, 22, 99, 105, 208–10, 212, 213, 237 (n. 63), 263 (nn. 2, 5); towns of, 42–43, 208, 209, 210–11, 213, 217, 238 (n. 69); as coalescent communities, 84, 90, 100; and Lower Creek Confederacy, 90–91; and Indian slave trade, 93, 99–100, 213; and Moore, 96–97; war rituals of, 103; and Yamasee War, 104; influence of, 106; and French colonizers, 206; and trade networks, 210–11

Croghan, George, 185, 187, 192, 199, 200, 202, 205, 206

Cundy (Indian woman), 99

Cunningham, James, 183

Cussita, 94

Dablon, Claude, 119, 123

Dakota Sioux, 121

Dallas-Phase peoples, 42, 53

Danner Phase pottery, 243 (n. 62), 244 (n. 64)

D'Artaguette, Diron, 211, 213

Davenport, Jonah, 185, 196

Davies, John, 224–25

De Bertet, M., 217

Debo, Angie, 263 (n. 2)

De Certeau, Michel, 237 (n. 57)

Deganawidah (Great Peacemaker), 167

Dekanoagah, 162–63, 176

De la Jonquière, Jacques-Pierre de Taffanel, 33

De la Ribourde, Gabriel, 107–8

De la Tore, Francis, 172, 173

Delawares: and Spring River Baptist Church, 1; and Native American Church, 2; removal from Kansas lands, 7; alliances of, 10, 15, 143, 176, 190, 199, 200; towns of, 15, 23; Shawnees' connections with, 18, 98, 140, 150, 198; war rituals of, 103; and Chesapeake Bay, 137, 140; and Iroquois Confederacy, 159, 195, 225, 226, 227; and Lower Susquehanna River, 162, 172–73; and hunting, 168; and trade networks, 171, 186, 201; migration of, 178, 179, 181–82, 190, 194; and land fraud, 178–79; and French colonizers, 186, 191, 200, 201, 203, 205; and Ohio River Valley, 203

Delaware Tribe of Oklahoma, 10

Delaware Water Gap, 148–49

Deliette, Pierre, 45, 118, 120

De l'Isle, Guillaume, 226

Deloria, Vine, 238 (n. 70)

Denonville, Jacques-René Brisay de, 131

De Soto, Hernando, 23, 41, 42, 43, 50, 61, 87, 240 (n. 18)

Dhegiha Siouan-speaking tribes, 2, 51, 53

Díaz Vara Calderon, Gabriel, 88

Diebold, Charles (chief), 9

Dinnen, James, 199, 213

Diplomacy: and Lower Shawnee Town, 32, 192–93; and Fort Ancient Tradition, 42, 58; and pipes, 43–45; and English colonizers, 101, 141–42, 145–46, 150–52, 161–62; and Chesapeake Bay, 140, 144; and Lower Susquehanna River, 162–63, 164, 165–66, 174, 175–76; and Logstown, 177; and Logan, 184; and Shawnee migration, 207, 211, 212, 213, 214–19, 223, 227

Disease: and Fort Ancient Tradition, 13, 25, 29, 42, 58; and colonialism, 19, 59, 117; Native people fleeing, 34; and Shawnee migration, 35; and archaeological record, 53; and epidemics, 59–61, 63, 75, 115, 188, 191, 227, 245 (n. 8); smallpox epidemics, 59–61, 63, 115, 188, 191, 245 (n. 8); crowd infections, 60; and disease ecology, 61, 245 (n. 8); adoption and captive taking, 72, 115; and alliances, 228

Dollier de Casson, François, 57, 110, 253 (n. 8)

Dongan, Thomas, 148, 158–59, 182

Douglas, James, 100

Dowd, Gregory Evans, 179

Drooker, Penelope, 236 (n. 52), 243 (n. 62)

Duchesneau, Jacques, 124, 128

Dushane, Viola, 1–3, 9, 11

Dutch colonizers: and trade networks, 64, 122, 134–35, 137, 142; and Chesapeake Bay, 137, 139; reclaiming of New York, 145

Eastern Algonquians, 10, 18, 137, 190

Eastern Shawnees, 8, 9, 10, 11

Eastern Woodland Indians: and Shawnee migration, 2–3, 19, 224; identities of, 16; as parochial cosmopolitans, 21; and forced removals, 23; towns of, 23, 238 (n. 70); and Calumet Ceremony, 44, 45; and overarching religious system, 46–47; and concept of souls, 71; and war rituals, 103–4

Ecotones, 40, 121

Ecunhutke, 210

Edict of Nantes, 160

Edistos, 89

Emerson, Thomas E., 243 (n. 62), 244 (n. 64)

English colonizers: and Shawnees, 15, 20, 34, 35, 81, 83, 125–26, 146–47, 155–56, 185, 188, 190, 192, 198–200, 213, 216, 217, 220, 227; and Middle Ohio Valley, 29, 31, 33; and Iroquois Confederacy, 31, 141–43, 144, 158, 202–3, 225–28, 256 (n. 15), 266 (n. 6); and trade networks, 50, 64, 66, 68, 98, 132–33, 135, 136, 142, 201, 203, 204, 211, 213, 215, 216, 217; Puritans, 60; and Indian slave trade, 67, 84, 88–89,

95–97, 99, 100, 102, 104, 153; and Occaneechees, 70; and cash-crop agriculture, 86; and warfare, 96–97, 250 (n. 40); and diplomacy, 101, 141–42, 145–46, 150–52, 161–62; and Susquehannocks, 140, 141, 142, 143, 144, 145, 147, 256 (n. 15); and Chesapeake Bay, 143–44; and Delawares, 195; civilizing mission of, 224–25

Eries, 48, 49, 50, 71, 85–86, 242 (n. 52)

Ethnicity: geographic descriptors representing, 236 (n. 50); relational approach to, 236 (n. 53)

Ethnogenesis, Shawnees as example of, 20

Ethnography, history understood through, 2

European colonizers: and Middle Ohio Valley, 29, 59; and nation-states, 133, 236–37 (n. 55); and Shawnees' homeland, 240 (n. 20). *See also* Dutch colonizers; English colonizers; French colonizers; Spanish colonizers; Swedish colonizers

Eustis, William, 17

Evans, John, 151, 163, 169, 170

Eycott, John, 210–11

Fallam, William, 67–68

Five Nations. *See* Iroquois Confederacy

Fletcher, Benjamin, 160

Fort Amstel, 137

Fort Ancient Tradition: and ancestors of Shawnees, 12, 13, 14, 19–20, 29, 31–35, 51, 53, 54, 55, 58, 239 (n. 12), 246 (n. 31); and trade networks, 12, 13, 25, 29, 41–51, 53, 56, 58, 64, 65–66, 77, 211; and Little Ice Age, 12, 37–39, 40, 41; and village-based egalitarian social systems, 12–13, 25, 32, 34, 35, 36, 37, 41, 42, 48, 49, 50, 53, 56, 58, 61, 62, 66, 77, 79, 236 (n. 53); and colonialism, 13–14, 25, 55, 58, 62; colonial descendants of, 23, 239 (n. 8); and burial practices, 28, 49, 51,

53, 62, 65; residence patterns, 29, 38, 40; decline of, 29, 61; archaeological legacy of, 29–30, 32, 55, 74; ritual life of, 35, 39–40, 44, 49; and multiethnic settlements, 35, 45–46, 48, 50, 77, 117, 243 (n. 57); and supralocal symbols of chiefly authority, 36; and migrations, 38, 53, 55, 58, 66, 67, 77; and coalescence of summer villages, 38–40; and ecotones, 40; and Eastern Eight Row corn, 41; and religious ideas and iconography, 42, 43–44, 46, 47–48, 49, 50, 53, 56; and north-south trade axis, 42, 48; and disk pipes, 43–44; cooking pots of, 45–46, 50, 242 (n. 45); and parochial cosmopolitanism, 48, 56, 58; and ceramic evidence, 49; and intermarriage, 49–50, 58; and protohistoric period, 51, 53–56, 62, 63; pottery of, 54–55, 64; as ethnically coherent, 243 (n. 59); radiocarbon dating of sites, 244–45 (n. 3)

Fort Christiana, 137
Fort Duquesne, 76, 177
Fort Frontenac, 109
Fort Henry (Virginia), 67
Fort Michilimackinac, 109, 124, 126, 128
Fort Ouiatenon, 192, 200
Fort St. Louis (Illinois): and Loyal Shawnees, 10; and Tonty, 14, 112, 113, 116, 118, 124, 131; and Shawnees, 114, 115, 129; alliance system at, 115, 117, 253 (n. 3); Iroquois assaults on, 125, 130–31
Fort Toulouse, 200, 206, 211, 212–13
Fort Vincennes, 200
Fox, William A., 210
Franquelin, Jean-Baptiste Louis, 66
Franscians, 128
French and Indian War. *See* Seven Years' War
French Calvinists, 160
French colonizers: and Shawnees, 15, 20, 33–34, 81, 109–11, 113, 114, 125–26, 132, 135–36, 147, 155–56, 178,

185–88, 191–93, 196, 197–98, 199, 200, 201, 203, 204, 205–6, 212–15, 219, 220, 226, 266 (n. 40); and Lower Great Lakes/Ohio Valley region, 17; and Middle Ohio Valley, 29, 33; and Indian slave trade, 33; and Iroquois Confederacy, 33, 128, 202, 203, 204, 205; census of Shawnee warriors, 54; and Nitarikyk's slave, 57–58; and trade networks, 64, 66, 71, 98, 109, 113, 114, 122–24, 129, 130, 146–47, 159–60, 201, 203–4, 211, 212–18; and Shawnee mourning rituals, 72; and exploration, 109–11; and Grand Village of the Kaskaskias, 127–28; and intercolonial competition, 128–31, 215–17; and Chesapeake Bay, 139
French Huguenots, 160
Frontenac, Louis de Baude, Comte de, 126–28, 129, 130
Fullerton Field site, 239 (n. 12)

Gabriel, Abbé de Queylus, 58
Galinée, René de Bréhant de, 58, 253 (n. 8)
Garber, James F., 242 (n. 45)
Gathering, and Fort Ancient Tradition, 41
Gatschet, Albert, 264 (n. 6)
Gender roles: and Shawnee Bread Dances, 6–7, 9–10; and Fort Ancient Tradition, 25, 26, 38, 39, 40, 41; and Yuchis, 104; and Illinois Confederacy, 124
Gibson, Richard (chief), 5, 7
Gitchi-manitou (master of the sky), 46–47
Glen, James, 220–22
Glorious Revolution (1688–89), 160
Glover, Charlesworth, 105
Gnagey site, 63
Godfroy, Gabriel, 32
Godin, David, 220
Gookin, Charles, 173
Goolman site (Clark County, Ky.), 38

settlement Indians, 220; characterizations of, 227, 266 (n. 14); synthesis
of, 238 (n. 70)
Iroquois-Susquehannock Wars, 64, 65,
67, 139
Itawachcomequa (Shawnee chief), 220,
222

Jackson, Andrew, 2, 8, 31
Jamaica, 86
James River, 85, 86, 139
Jemison, Mary, 75–76
Jennings, Francis, 235 (n. 38), 257 (n. 6),
266 (n. 6)
Jesuits: and Iroquois Confederacy,
32–34, 62, 65, 67, 74, 130, 141; and
Shawnees, 63; and Yuchis, 95; Sault
Sainte Marie mission, 110; and Il-
linois peoples, 123, 125; on warfare,
124–25; and Algonquians, 128
Johnson, Molly Brant, 227
Johnson, William, 227
Joliet, Louis, 73, 109, 110, 116
Joutel, Henri, 73, 114–15, 129

Kahnawake, 141
Kakowatchy (Shawnee leader), 148, 149,
188
Kansas people, and Fort Ancient Tradi-
tion, 51
Kasihtas, 216
Kaskaskias: and Shawnees, 10, 14,
108, 109, 117, 129, 132; and Illinois
Confederacy, 107, 108, 116; and Iro-
quois Confederacy, 116; foodways of,
119–20; burial practices of, 121. *See
also* Grand Village of the Kaskaskias
Kawitas, 216
Keith, William, 150, 168, 175, 177
Kelton, Paul, 245 (n. 8)
Kentucky Archaeological Survey, 27–28
Kerlérec, M. de, 218–19
Kickapoos: and Shawnee War Dance,
5; as linguistic relative of Shawnees,
19; towns of, 23; and Fort Ancient

Tradition, 49; war rituals of, 103;
and alliances, 124, 200; and French
colonizers, 215
Kimball-Brown, Margaret, 243–44
(n. 63)
King George's War, 197–202, 212, 214,
215, 219
King Philip's War of 1675, 95, 130, 139
King Tom (Yuchi), 220, 265 (n. 36)
Kiskanon Ottawas, 126–27
Kispokotha division, 5, 16, 22, 35, 77–78,
108, 208–9, 247 (n. 48), 263 (n. 5),
263–64 (n. 6)
Kispokotha Shawnee War Bundle, 5
Kittanning, 15
Knight, Vernon J., 263 (n. 1), 264 (n. 6)
Koasati peoples, 42, 55, 66, 211
Kokumthena (Our Grandmother), 22

La Barre, Joseph-Antoine le Fèbvre de,
115, 130, 131
La Demoiselle (Old Briton), 204–5, 217
Lake Erie, 85, 213
Lakomäki, Sami, 235 (n. 38)
Lalemant, Jérôme, 63
Lamberville, Jean de, 127, 130
Lamhátty, 92–94
Lamont, Michèle, 236 (n. 53)
Langlade, Charles, 204
La Point, Wisconsin, 34
La Potherie, Bacqueville de, 73
La Salle, René-Robert Cavelier, Sieur de:
and Shawnee guides, 33, 113–14, 132,
211; and Senecas, 63–64, 110; and
Franquelin, 66; and Tonty, 107; and
French exploration, 109–11, 112, 253
(n. 8); and attack on Grand Village
of the Kaskaskias, 111–12, 252 (n. 2);
and Illinois Confederacy, 116, 120,
127; on Upper Illinois River, 118; and
consolidation of Indian people, 128,
129, 130; and trade networks, 159, 161
Lawson, John, 83, 101
Laypareawah, 195
Le Jau, Francis, 91, 94–95, 96, 99, 104

Le Moyne, Jean-Baptiste, Sieur de Bien-
ville, 211, 217
Le Moyne, Pierre, Sieur d'Iberville, 114
Lenapes. *See* Delawares
Le Pied Froid (Miami leader), 205
Lepore, Jill, 225
Le Tort, James, 78, 160–62, 166, 169–70,
174, 178, 185, 247–48 (n. 49)
Little Carpenter, 222
Little Corn Planter, 240 (n. 20)
Little Ice Age, and Fort Ancient Tradi-
tion, 12, 37–39, 40, 41
Little Turtle (Miami chief), 32
Livingston, Robert, 165
Llewellin, John, 143
Logan, James: and trade networks, 136,
162, 163, 170, 174–75, 177–78, 183–85,
190, 194–95, 215; and Penn's policies,
162, 259 (n. 16); and Shawnees, 169,
178, 187, 193–96, 213, 217, 226, 228;
land confiscated by, 174, 175, 176, 177,
179, 183, 194–95, 261 (n. 14); and Iroquois conquest, 182; as historian, 226
Logstown: as multiethnic town, 15,
176–77, 203; and Shawnee migration,
177, 178, 182, 185, 188, 190, 193, 206,
212; and trade networks, 183, 192,
204, 205; and neutrality, 188
Long, Alexander, 100
Louis XIV (king of France), 128, 129
Lower Creek Confederacy, 90–91
Lower Great Lakes/Ohio Valley region:
and Shawnees, 14; and narrative
of American Indian identity and
politics, 17, 235 (n. 41); autonomous
villages of, 23, 142; and Tecumseh,
31; and Iroquois Confederacy, 225–26
Lower Shawnee Town: as multiethnic
town, 15; and trade networks, 28–29,
32, 204, 205; and Shawnee migration, 32, 192–93, 200, 201, 206–7,
212, 213; and Fort Ancient Tradition,
32, 239 (n. 12); Shawnee leaders
of, 188; and French colonizers, 198,
205–6

Lower Susquehanna River: and Seven
Years' War, 15; and trade networks,
64, 136, 157–58, 161, 162, 175, 177;
and Shawnee migration, 113, 146,
147, 148, 149, 150, 152, 162, 213; and
"Mixt Nations," 150–53; and Penn's
treaties, 158–59; and diplomacy,
162–63, 164, 165–66, 174, 175–76
Loyal Shawnees, 7, 8–9, 10, 11
Loyal Shawnee Tribe of Oklahoma, 10

Madisonville site: as Fort Ancient Tradition site, 28, 53, 54; material artifacts
of, 29, 43, 49, 50, 54, 64, 239 (n. 12),
244 (n. 65); cemeteries of, 30; ar-
chaeological study of, 32; and barred
copper pendants, 36; and hunting, 41
Mahicans, 81, 130, 148
Margry, Pierre, 252 (n. 1)
Marquette, Jacques: and Shawnees,
34–35, 63, 110; and Illinois peoples,
63, 121, 122, 123, 124; and Kas-
kaskias, 109, 116
Mascoutins, 44–45, 49, 123, 200, 215
Massachusetts people, 60
Massawomecks, 48, 64–65
Matasit (Munsee Delaware chief), 148
Matchi-manitou (master of the under-
world), 47
Mattawomans, 142, 144, 147, 152
Matthews, Maurice, 95
McCafferty, Michael, 253 (n. 8)
McConnell, Michael, 239 (n. 8), 260–61
(n. 5)
McDowell, William L., Jr., 265 (n. 36)
McPherson, James M., 237 (n. 58)
Mekoche division, 22, 35, 77, 78, 108,
171, 176, 180, 208, 247 (n. 48)
Membré, Zénobe, 107–8, 252 (nn. 1, 2)
Merrell, James H., 13, 253 (n. 3)
Meskwakis, 19, 124, 205–6
Miamis: and Shawnees, 18, 129, 135,
191–92, 199, 218, 219; as linguistic
relative of Shawnees, 19; towns of,
23; and Indian removal, 31; and Fort

Oatis, Steven J., 246 (n. 24)

Occaneechees, 58–59, 67, 68–69, 70, 71, 85

Odawas, 33, 57

Oglethorpe, James, 87

Ohio River Valley: scorched-earth campaigns of American Revolution, 8; and Fort Ancient Tradition, 12, 41–42; Algonquians finding autonomy in, 15; and trade networks, 15, 28, 34, 186–87, 215; and Tecumseh, 16; and Iroquois Confederacy's claims, 33, 202, 203; and brass snakes, 43; and Shawnee migration, 155, 168–69, 177, 178–79, 181–82, 188, 190–93, 200, 206; and hunting, 168; and multiethnic towns, 177, 196, 203. *See also* Middle Ohio Valley

Ojibwes, 46–47, 57, 73

Oklahoma: and Indian Removal Act, 2; federally recognized tribes in, 8

Okowelah (Shawnee chief), 190

Olafson, Sigfus, 246 (n. 31)

Old Hop (Chota headman), 222

Omahas, 51

Oneidas, 165, 202

Oneotas, 42–44, 45, 49, 117

Oneota Tradition, 43, 53–54

Onondagas, 74, 107, 202

Ontwaganha, as name for Shawnee captives of Iroquois, 32–33

Opakethwa (Shawnee leader), 188

Opakhassit (Delaware leader), 176

Opessa (Shawnee chief), 150, 151–52, 163–66, 168, 170, 171–73, 177, 188, 195

Osages, 121

Otos, 117

Ottawas: as Shawnee neighbors, 18, 205; as guides, 110; and trade networks, 123, 124, 201, 204; and Iroquois Confederacy, 123, 126, 127

Oumiamis, 127

Outreouate (Onondaga chief), 115

Palmer's Island, 143

Pamunkeys, 137, 142, 144

Pan-Indian racial unity: and tribal identities, 8; and Tecumseh, 16–17, 235 (n. 41); and Shawnee migration, 155, 223; and shared history, 196, 197

Panquash (Nanticoke "emperor"), 153

Pauketat, Timothy R., 241 (n. 24)

Pawnees, 121

Pekowitha division, 22, 35, 77–78, 108, 150, 171, 176, 180, 190, 208, 247 (n. 48)

Penn, Thomas, 194, 195

Penn, William: and trade networks, 136, 157–58, 160, 161, 164, 166–67, 170, 173, 174, 176, 186; and Susquehannocks, 157, 158–59, 161, 162, 163–64, 257–58 (n. 6), 259 (n. 16); and Shawnees, 158–59, 162, 163–64, 190–91, 194, 257–58 (n. 6); manorial system of, 162; myth of, 195

Pequehan, 162–63, 166, 171, 172, 176

Pequot War of 1637, 95

Perrot, Nicolas, 34, 44–45, 73, 74–75, 240 (n. 20)

Petersburg, Kentucky, 27–28, 29, 30, 31, 54, 55

Phélypeaux, Jean-Frédéric, Comte de Maurepas, 214

Philippe (chief), 130

Piankashaws, 192, 200, 204, 205, 216–17, 218

Pickawillany, 31, 204

Pilette, Richard, 131

Piscataways, 136, 137, 140–43, 144, 147, 152–53

Pitcher, Greg, 10

Plymouth Plantation, 122

Point Pleasant, Battle of, 248 (n. 51)

Pollack, David, 27–28, 239 (n. 12)

Poncas, 51

Portsmouth, Ohio, 28, 29, 30

Potawatomis: as Shawnee neighbors, 18; as linguistic relative of Shawnees, 19; as guides, 33, 110; settlement patterns of, 39; and Fort Ancient Tradition, 49; and Tonty, 108; and trade networks, 124, 201

Potomac River, 136, 150

Power, and cosmology, 47–48, 51, 53, 123

Proto-Westos, 242 (n. 52)

Pugh, Daniel, 153

Quakers. *See* Society of Friends

Quapaw Agency, 1

Quapaws: and Spring River Baptist Church, 1; burial practices of, 2; and Seneca-Cayugas, 9; and Fort Ancient Tradition, 51; and trade networks, 98; and Chickasaws, 99; and Grand Village of the Kaskaskias, 120; generosity of, 232 (n. 3)

Quarry, Robert, 160–62

Quassenung (Shawnee leader), 188

Queen Anne's War (1702–13), 96, 97, 161

Race: pan-Indian racial unity, 8, 16–17, 155, 196, 197, 223, 235 (n. 41); and planter-oligarchs' racial caste system, 146; racial consciousness for Indian peoples, 155, 156, 197, 222

Rale, Sébastien, 122

Red Shoe (Choctaw chief), 216–17

Reilly, Kent, III, 242 (n. 45)

Revitalization movements: in upper country, 17–18; and Shawnee migration, 207, 223; and Tecumseh, 209, 223

Rice, James D., 253 (n. 14)

Rickahockan Town, 86

Riverfront Village, 53, 54–55

Roseberry, William, 233 (n. 13)

Sabb, Morgan, 220

Sacred places, 21, 23, 237 (n. 59), 238 (n. 70)

Sacred space, sharing of, 9, 10–11

Sagohandechty (Iroquois diplomat), 180–81, 210

Sahlins, Marshall, 236–37 (n. 55)

St. Kitts, 81, 86

St. Lawrence River Valley, 201

Sandusky Tradition, 49

Santee Fort, 95

Saponis, 53

Sassoonan (Delaware leader), 157, 172–73, 177, 178

Sauks, as linguistic relative of Shawnees, 19

Savannah River: and Indian slave trade, 50; and Shawnees, 50, 79, 240 (nn. 18, 20); fall line of, 84, 87, 92, 94, 96, 98. *See also* Middle Savannah River

Savannah Town: and Shawnees, 20, 54, 104, 105, 211, 247 (n. 47); and trade networks, 87, 94, 98; and Indian slave trade, 92, 94, 96; and English colonizers, 98, 99; Catawbas' attack on, 99; Cherokees' attack on, 100; and pottery of Middle Ohio Valley people, 246 (n. 24)

Sawanogi, 206, 210, 211–12, 213, 214, 216, 219–20

Sawantaeny, 175–76, 184

Schutz, Noel, 247 (n. 49), 263 (n. 6)

Schuyler, Arent, 148, 165

Seneca-Cayugas: removal to Oklahoma, 8; Green Corn Ceremony held by, 8–9; alliances of, 9, 10, 15; matrilineal kinship system of, 10; towns of, 23

Senecas: and Jesuits, 32–33; and La Salle, 63–64, 110; and Shawnees, 63–64, 140, 147, 148, 151–52, 165, 169, 191; captives of, 74, 126, 127; and Illinois peoples, 130; and Chesapeake Bay, 134, 144; and Lower Susquehanna River, 136–37; and colonial borderlands, 140, 143; and English colonizers, 142, 144, 202; and Conestoga Manor, 164; and Tuscaroras, 167; and trade networks, 171; and Logstown, 177; and settlement Indians, 220

Settlement Indians, 220–21, 222

Seven Years' War: and Shawnee migration, 2, 32, 76, 156, 218, 223, 228,
266 (n. 40); and Lower Susquehanna
River, 15; and Iroquois Confederacy,
33; violence in years leading up to,
220

Shamokin, 176, 177, 182, 190, 201

Shawnee Bread Dances: tribal values
conveyed by, 3, 232 (n. 10); and
Shawnee identity, 6–7; and White
Oak Stomp Ground, 9–10, 11; and
Fort Ancient Tradition, 35

Shawnee exceptionalism, 18

Shawnee identity: and Indian removal,
2; and Stomp Grounds, 3, 7; re-
creation of, 3–5, 24; and Shawnee
Bread Dances, 6–7; and migration,
10, 11, 16, 20, 23, 24, 26, 35, 91; and
Shawnee rituals, 11, 24; and colonialism, 16, 24, 79; historical philosophy
of, 23; and villages, 56, 197, 219, 248
(n. 50); and Iroquois Confederacy, 76;
and society clans, 78; and hairstyles,
106; differences in, 155; race-based
understandings of, 156, 222; voluntary nature of, 190; and Indian slave
trade, 222–23; and shifting regional
characteristics, 236 (n. 53)

Shawnee language, as trade language,
94–95, 223

Shawnee migration: as Shawnee signature, 1, 3, 76–77, 222, 232 (n. 1); as
survival strategy, 2, 12, 19, 20, 21, 237
(n. 59); and Seven Years' War, 2, 32,
76, 156, 218, 223, 228, 266 (n. 40);
and Eastern Woodland Indians, 2–3,
19, 224; and federally recognized
Shawnee tribes, 7; Jackson on, 8;
and identity, 10, 11, 16, 20, 23, 24,
26, 35, 91; and rituals, 11, 210; and
colonial borderlands, 12, 76, 81–82,
83, 91, 98–99, 155, 206, 224; and
trade networks, 14, 21, 35, 79, 81, 179,
210, 212–13; and colonialism, 14–16,
79; and adaptation, 15–16, 24, 35,

155–56, 176, 205–7; Tecumseh on,
16; and Shawnee exceptionalism, 18;
consequences of, 18–19; motivations
for, 21–22, 31, 85, 188, 195, 224; and
villages, 25–26, 55, 76, 78, 206–7,
212, 214–19; and Middle Ohio Valley,
29; and Lower Shawnee Town, 32,
192–93, 200, 201, 206–7, 212, 213;
and divisions, 78; and archaeological record, 79; and Chesapeake Bay,
79, 82, 98–99, 135–37, 139–40, 142,
149–50; contexts of, 79, 248 (n. 51);
independence of, 84; and English
colonizers, 91, 92; range of, 95; and
Lower Susquehanna River, 113, 146,
147, 148, 149, 150, 152, 162, 213; and
Ohio River Valley, 155, 168–69, 177,
178–79, 181–82, 188, 190–93, 200,
206; and neutrality, 155, 188, 195,
198, 213–14, 216, 217; and refugee
status, 181–82, 183, 206; and sovereignty, 195, 206–7, 225, 228; and
Death Feast, 200–201; and diplomacy, 207, 211, 212, 213, 214–19,
223, 227; and revitalization movements, 207, 223; conceptions of,
224–25, 229; as processes of differentiation, 236 (n. 53); post-1670 sites
of, 240 (n. 18); and eastern Piedmont,
249 (n. 9)

Shawnee Prophet. *See* Tenskwatawa

Shawnee rituals: challenges associated
with, 3; as physical expressions of
culture, 3–5, 7, 11, 24; as mark of
differences, 7; and bonds with other
tribes, 10, 264 (n. 6); and migration,
11, 210; and Fort Ancient Tradition,
35; and Death Feast, 200–201; Busk
or Green Corn Ceremony, 208

Shawnees: and Spring River Baptist
Church, 1; burial practices of, 2,
232 (n. 2); alliances of, 3, 9, 11, 15,
21–22, 23, 79, 81–82, 84, 91, 92, 135,
228–29, 237 (n. 63); Absentee, 4, 8,
9–10, 11, 21, 22–23, 31; Loyal, 7, 8–9,

10, 11; federally recognized tribes, 7–11, 13; Eastern, 8, 9, 10, 11; songs of, 8, 72; and Fort Ancient Tradition, 12, 13, 14, 19–20, 29, 31–35, 51, 53, 54, 55, 58, 239 (n. 12), 246 (n. 31); echoes of precontact civilizations in, 12, 29; war with Westos, 13–14, 91–92, 99; parochial cosmopolitanism of, 18, 24, 25, 78, 79, 109, 155, 212, 221, 223; origin of name, 19; as coalescent community, 19, 20, 40, 78, 240 (n. 21); lack of archaeological signature for, 19–20; sacred stories of, 21–23; society clans of, 22–23, 77–78, 208, 237 (n. 66), 247 (n. 47), 248 (n. 50); warfare of, 23, 96–97, 101–2, 167–68; and trade networks, 63–64, 66–67, 91, 94, 101, 114–15, 132, 170, 171–72, 185, 201, 210–11; and rituals of adoption and mourning, 72; and concept of souls, 72–73; mourning rituals of, 72–73, 75; as captives of Iroquois, 73, 75; ceremonial calendar of, 78; war rituals of, 103; and attack on Grand Village of Kaskaskias, 107, 108–9, 252 (n. 1); Penn's treaties with, 158–59, 162, 163–64, 190–91, 194, 257–58 (n. 6); temperance pledges, 195, 196; territory of, 240 (n. 20)

Shawnee villages: autonomy of, 16, 24, 36, 76, 79, 84, 106, 156, 192; localism based in, 18, 219; distinctions maintained in, 20, 24, 79, 219; and alliances, 23; as parochial cosmopolitans, 24, 25; and migration, 25–26, 55, 76, 78, 206-7, 211, 214–19; and Fort Ancient Tradition, 35, 54, 236 (n. 53); and kin groups, 35–36; and Shawnee divisions, 35–36, 77, 78, 108, 247 (n. 48), 247–48 (n. 49), 248 (n. 51); and identity, 56, 219, 248 (n. 50); as target of war parties, 72; and egalitarianism, 115; fragmentation of, 190; and sacred brass plates,

209, 264 (n. 6); and Creek towns, 210; and Indian slave trade, 213; diversity of, 215; and violence, 224

Shawnee War Dance (Men's Dance), 3–6, 7, 263 (n. 5)

Shawydoohungh (Harry the Interpreter), 163, 169–70

Shickellamy (Oneida leader), 174, 177, 182, 183–84, 193, 197

Shippen, Edward, 169, 175, 176, 183–84

Siouan speakers: and Fort Ancient Tradition, 12, 48, 51; and Shawnees, 23; and colonialism, 54, 83; and Grand Village of the Kaskaskias, 117; and burial practices, 121

Skiagunsta, 222

Slavery: in colonial period, 19; African slaves, 86, 89, 104; African American slaves, 141. *See also* Indian slave trade

Smallpox epidemics, 59–61, 63, 115, 188, 191, 245 (n. 8)

Smith, John, 64, 142

Smolenski, John, 257 (n. 1), 257–58 (n. 6), 258 (n. 12)

Society of Friends, 158, 160

South Bend, Ind., 32

South Stomp Ground, 8, 11, 232 (n. 10)

Sowee Indians, 84, 88, 89

Spanish colonizers: missions of, 13, 66, 67, 69, 88, 90, 94, 96; and Shawnees, 15, 125–26; *entradas* of, 61; and trade networks, 63–64, 66–67, 98; and Middle Savannah River, 84

Speck, Frank, 266 (n. 18)

Spencer, John, 210

Spotswood, Alexander, 153

Spring River Baptist Church, 1

Spybuck (Shawnee man), 228–29, 266 (n. 17)

Steele, Ian, 265 (n. 36), 266 (n. 40)

Steelman, John Hans, 143

Stiggins, George, 208–9

Stomp Grounds: definition of, 3; and Shawnee identity, 3, 7; White Oak Stomp Ground, 3, 9–10, 11; North

Dutch colonizers, 64, 122, 134–35, 137, 142; and guns, 121–24, 133; and Penn, 136, 157–58, 160, 161, 164, 166–67, 170, 173, 174, 176, 186; and rum trade, 170–71, 172, 173, 184, 195, 196; and alcohol, 175, 184, 196, 197. *See also* Indian slave trade

Treaty of Fort Stanwix (1768), 198

Treaty of Greenville (1795), 32

Treaty of Lancaster (1744), 159, 178, 198, 199, 220

Treaty of 1701, 150, 159, 163–64, 259 (n. 16)

Tribes: shifting ethnic boundaries around, 2; federal recognition, 7–11, 13; coalescence resisted by, 8–9, 11, 24, 224, 228; tribal identities, 8–9, 20, 21, 24, 56, 237 (n. 57), 238 (n. 70), 243–44 (n. 63); alliances of, 9; and local expressions of identity, 17; coalescent reinvention in colonial period, 19, 20, 244 (n. 63); multiethnic nature of, 20; American Indian histories emphasizing tribal identity, 20–21; Sahlins on, 236–37 (n. 55). *See also specific peoples*

Tuan, Yi-Fu, 237 (n. 61)

Tukabatchee, 92, 208, 209–10, 263 (nn. 1, 2), 263–64 (n. 6)

Tuscaroras, 93, 102, 104, 164, 166–67, 202

Tuscarora War of 1711–12, 102

Tutelos, 53, 164

Tweed, Thomas A., 237 (n. 57)

Tyler, Thomas, 153

Umpeachy (Yuchi chief), 102

Union (Ciivl War), Loyal Shawnees' alliance with, 7

U.S. Army Corps of Engineers, 54

Upper Creek Confederacy, 206, 208, 209, 210, 211–12, 248 (n. 51)

Upper Illinois River Valley: and Shawnees, 11, 113, 114, 116, 118, 131–32, 218; and Kaskaskias, 14; and Fort

Ancient Tradition, 53, 54; and colonial borderlands, 81, 82; and alliances, 117; abundant resources of, 117–20, 121; and warfare, 124–28; lack of ethnic coherence in, 133, 244 (n. 63)

Upper Mississippi Valley, 19, 43, 49, 50, 203

Vaudreuil, Pierre de Riguad, Marquis de, 198, 199, 200, 204, 206, 212–19

Viele, Arnout, 148–49

Village-based egalitarian social systems: and Fort Ancient Tradition, 12–13, 25, 32, 34, 35, 36, 37, 41, 42, 48, 49, 50, 53, 56, 58, 61, 62, 66, 77, 79, 236 (n. 53); histories of, 21, 56; and disease, 61. *See also* Shawnee villages; *and specific villages*

Violence: of colonial borderlands, 14, 76, 81–82, 90, 140–43, 193, 218; de Soto's expedition, 42; and Calumet Ceremony, 45; archaeological evidence of, 63; and trade in guns, 122; interregional violence, 166–67; and Indian slave trade, 213; and Shawnee migration, 219–23, 224. *See also* Warfare

Voegelin, Carl, 248 (n. 50)

Von Reck, Philip Georg Friedrich, 106

Wakatomica, 20, 206, 219–20, 221, 222

Walker, John, 93, 94

Walking Purchase (1737), 159, 178, 182, 194, 195

Walthall, John A., 244 (n. 64)

Wampanoags, 60, 130

Wanniahs, 89

Warfare: of Shawnees, 23, 96–97, 101–2, 167–68; and Fort Ancient Tradition, 29, 53, 58; and Shawnee migration, 35; and Iroquois Confederacy, 50, 58–59, 73–74, 85, 115, 167, 223; and archaeological record, 53; Iroquois mourning wars, 59, 62, 67, 71, 72; and Susquehannocks, 64, 65, 67, 74, 75,